AQA English Language

A LEVEL AND AS

Dan Clayton
Angela Goddard
Beth Kemp
Felicity Titjen

SERIES EDITOR:
Angela Goddard

OXFORD
UNIVERSITY PRESS

OXFORD
UNIVERSITY PRESS

Great Clarendon Street, Oxford, OX2 6DP, United Kingdom

Oxford University Press is a department of the University of Oxford. It furthers the University's objective of excellence in research, scholarship, and education by publishing worldwide. Oxford is a registered trade mark of Oxford University Press in the UK and in certain other countries

British Library Cataloguing in Publication Data

Data available

ISBN 978-019-833400-2
Kindle edition ISBN 978-019-837457-2

10 9 8 7 6 5

Printed in India by Multivista Global Pvt. Ltd

Acknowledgements

The authors wish to thank the following for their help on this project:

Adrian Beard, Francesca Beswick, Shahnaz Biggs, Alfie Brennan, Stanley, Liam and Ruby Clayton, Jo Eggleton, Joel Hawkins, Paul Kerswill, Mattie and Mandy Shannon, Imogen and Oliver Titjen.

The authors and publisher are grateful for copyright permission to reprint extracts from the following material:

Extracts from the *Authorized Version of the Bible (The King James Bible)*, the rights in which are vested in the Crown, are reproduced by permission of the Crown's Patentee, Cambridge University Press.

Jean Aitchison: 'Is our language in Decay?', 1996 Reith Lecture, from *The Language Web: The Power and Problems of Words* (CUP, 1997), reprinted by permission of Cambridge University Press and the author.

Catherine Bennett: 'Dangerous Dogs: oh, don't worry, he doesn't really mean you any harm', *The Observer*, 10 November 2013, copyright © Guardian News and Media Ltd 2013, reprinted by permission of GNM Ltd.

Doreen du Boulay: *Study Skills For Dummies* (Wiley 2009), reprinted by permission of John Wiley & Sons via Copyright Clearance Center.

Bill Bryson: *The Life and Times of The Thunderbolt Kid* (Doubleday, 2006), copyright © Bill Bryson 2006, reprinted by permission of The Random House Group Ltd.

Anthony Burgess: *Language Made Plain* (Collins, 1975), reprinted by permission of David Higham Associates Ltd.

Simon Calder: '48 hours in: York', Travel Essentials, *Independent*, 24 January 2014, copyright © The Independent 2014, http://www.independent.co.uk/ reprinted by permission of ESI Syndication.

Frances Christie: 'Genres and genre theory: a response to Michael Rosen', 31 July 2013 at www.interstrataltension.org, reprinted by permission of the author.

Devon and Cornwall Police Force dog training information from ACPO *Police Dog Manual of Guidance* on www.devon-cornwall.police.uk, reprinted by permission of the Force Dog Training Manager.

J A Darby: 'Tom and the Chickens', reprinted by permission of Jess Darby.

G Deutscher: *The Unfolding of Language* (Arrow, 2006), reprinted by permission of The Random House Group Ltd.

Matthew Engel: 'Say no to the get-go: Americanisms swamping English, so wake up and smell the coffee', *Mail online*

Michael Erard: 'English as she will be spoke', *New Scientist*, 29 March 2008, copyright © Reed Business Information UK 2008, reprinted by permission of Tribune Content Agency. All rights reserved.

Penelope Friday: 'More than words' published on the blog at www.disabiltynow.org.uk, reprinted by permission of Disability Now.

Ruth Gledhill: 'Voice coaches hired to rub the polish off posh accents', *The Times*, 7 April 2014, copyright © Ruth Gledhill/News UK and Ireland Ltd 2014, reprinted by permission of News Syndication.

Afua Hirsch: 'Ghana calls an end to tyrannical reign of the Queen's English', *The Guardian*, 10 April 2012, copyright © Guardian News and Media Ltd 2012, reprinted by permission of GNM Ltd.

Eva Hoffman: *Lost in Translation: A life in a New Language* (Heinemann, 1989), copyright © Eva Hoffman 1989, reprinted by permission of The Random House Group Ltd.

Richard Hogg and **David Denison** (Eds): *A History of the English Language* (CUP, 2006), reprinted by permission of Cambridge University Press.

John Humphrys: 'I h8 txt msgs: How texting is wrecking our language', *Daily Mail*, 24 September 2007, copyright © 2007, reprinted by permission of Solo Syndication.

Paul Ibbotson: 'Child Language Acquisition' in *Language: a student handbook on key topics and theories* (English & Media Centre, 2012), reprinted by permission of the English and Media Centre.

Lindsay Johns: 'Ghetto grammar robs the young of a proper voice', *The Evening Standard*, 16 August 2011, copyright © The Evening Standard 2011, reprinted by permission of ESI Syndication.

Daniel Jones: *The Pronunciation of English: phonetics and phonetic transcriptions* (CUP, 1909/1956), reprinted by permission of Cambridge University Press.

Jon King: 'We need to love kids...not fear them', Daily Mirror, 3 June 2008, copyright Trinity Mirror Group © 2008, reprinted by permission of Mirror Syndication International.

Dr Martin Luther King Jr: 'I Have a Dream', spoken at a Civil Rights rally in Washington DC, 28 August 1963, copyright © 1963 Dr Martin Luther King Jr, © renewed 1991 by Coretta Scott King, reprinted by arrangement with the Heirs to the Estate of Martin Luther King Jr., c/o Writers House as agent for the proprietor, New York, NY, USA.

E V Knox: 'Cinema English', *Living Age* 338 (April 1930), copyright © 2015 the Estate of E V Knox, reprinted by permission of Maria Lake for the Estate.

Elaine Lemm: 'Lemon Possett Recipe' reprinted from www.britishfood.about.com by permission of Elaine Lemm.

Francesco Marciuliano: 'I Lose My Mind When You Leave the House' from *I Could Chew On This and Other Poems by Dogs* (Chronicle Books, 2013), copyright © Francesco Marciuliano 2013, reprinted by permission of Chronicle Books LLC, San Francisco, www.ChronicleBooks.com.

Stefanie Marsh: 'The rise of the interrogatory statement' *The Times*, 28 March 2006, copyright © Stefanie Marsh/News UK and Ireland Ltd 2006, reprinted by permission of News Syndication.

Brandon Robshaw: 'Hold on to your arse', *The Times*, 31 July 2004, copyright © Brandon Robshaw 2004, reprinted by permission of The Joanna Devereux Literary Agency for the author.

Matthew Saxton: *Child Language: Acquisition and Development* (Sage, 2010), reprinted by permission of Sage Publications Ltd.

John Simon: 'The Corruption of English' in L Michaels and C Ricks (Eds): The State of the Language (University of California Press, 1980), reprinted by permission of the author.

Hilary Spurling: 'To Make a Possett', recipe from *Elinor Fettiplace's Receipt Book: Elizabethan Country House Cooking* (Penguin, 1986), reprinted by permission of David Higham Associates.

Lynne Truss: 'Lynne Truss has a grammatical axe to grind', *Daily Telegraph*, 5 January 2014, copyright © Telegraph Media Group Ltd 2014, reprinted by permission of TMG Ltd.

Matt Vicker: 'Language of Football Fans' from 'Lingo: Linguistics and English Language news and views at UWE', 14 February 2014, reprinted by permission of the author.

Janet Wall: extract from Getting Started on Obedience Training at www.loveyourdog.com, reprinted by permission of the author.

Georgia Webster: 'Sluts are reappropriating language', *Superlinguo* 5 June 2011, reprinted by permission of the author.

Ed West: '"Jafaican" may be cool, but it sounds ridiculous', *Daily Telegraph*, 7 June 2011, copyright © Telegraph Media Group Ltd 2011, reprinted by permission of TMG Ltd.

Alex White, Philip Mann and **Richard Rieser:** *Speaking for Ourselves: A teacher's guide to disability and oral history*, reprinted by permission of Scope, www.scope.org.uk.

Cover: esolla/iStock; **p1:** esolla/iStock; **p17:** With kind permission from www.guidedogs.co.uk; **p24:** With kind permission from Premier Inn, via Frank PR; **p28:** With kind permission from www.guidedogs.co.uk; **p29:** (l) With kind permission from Premier Inn, via Frank PR, (m) With kind permission from Toad & Co. International, Inc. (formerly Horny Toad Activewear, Inc.), (r) With kind permission from Virgin Trains East Coast; **p31:** Angela Goddard; **p33:** With kind permission from East Devon Council; **p39:** Danny Alvarez/Shutterstock; **p40:** (tl) Phillip Holland/Shutterstock, (tr) Angela Goddard, (bl) Beth Kemp; **p41:** (tl) Dmitry Kalinovsky/Shutterstock, (tr) Russ Beinder/Shutterstock, (b) Beth Kemp; **p91:** With kind permission from Manflu Ltd, via Mancfrank; **p101:** Adrian Murrell/Allsport/Getty Images; **p128-148:** Felicity Titjen; **p162:** Christos Georghiou/Shutterstock; **p202:** Angela Goddard; **p203:** With kind permission from www.helpineedhelp.com; **p238:** With kind permission from Virgin Trains East Coast

Page layout by Phoenix Photosetting.

Any third party use of this material, outside of this publication, is prohibited. Interested parties should apply to the copyright holders indicated in each case.

Although we have made every effort to trace and contact all copyright holders before publication this has not been possible in all cases. If notified, the publisher will rectify any errors or omissions at the earliest opportunity.

Contents

Key

AS level and A level

A level only

Introduction to the Student Book

This book is divided into chapters, which each cover a distinctive topic area or skill that is developed and assessed in the AQA specifications. Key features of the book include the following:

- **Chapter aims:** Each chapter has a clear statement of aims at the start.
- **Key term:** This label indicates that a term is important, because it will recur throughout the course. The first time that such a term is used in the book, it appears in bold and is defined briefly in the margin. Many subsequent appearances of each key term throughout the rest of the book have also been emboldened, to emphasize that they are key terms.
- **Glossary:** A glossary at the back of the book lists all of the key terms, with their definitions, for easy reference.
- **Activity:** This book explains and teaches concepts and ideas, and the topics to be covered in each chapter should be clear from the aims listed at the start. But in order to learn thoroughly, you need to try things out for yourself and have hands-on experience. Activities are included that will allow you to develop transferable skills.
- **Feedback:** For most of the activities, feedback is available at the back of the book. Feedback will indicate the main points that would be likely to arise, but is not provided for more open-ended activities.
- **Extension activity:** These activities are designed to take you further into a particular area of learning.
- **Research idea:** This is a larger-scale piece of work, such as is required for the coursework component. A research idea cannot be completed immediately: it takes time to plan and develop.
- **Link:** This feature indicates the ways in which your work on a topic may link to other chapters in the book, to ideas for further reading, or to information online.
- **Remember:** This prompt will give you advice on developing good study skills.
- **Did you know?:** This feature introduces interesting facts that will be helpful to your studies.
- **Looking ahead:** This feature explains the ways in which the skills you are developing will be relevant to the whole course, and to any future career plans.
- **Review your learning:** A few short questions at the end of each chapter will remind you of what you have learned, and help you to summarize it.
- **References and Further reading:** Some of the ideas referred to are related to past research work. Where this is the case, the name of the researcher is given in the text. You can read the full reference at the end of the respective chapter. The 'Further reading' section includes a list of texts that you will find useful when pursuing the subject further.
- **Index:** An alphabetical list of topics is provided at the back of the book. It enables you to find material you want to look at again.
- **Weblinks** are included throughout this book. Please note that Oxford University Press is not responsible for third-party content and although all links were correct at the time of publication, the content and location of this material may change over time.

A note on spelling

Certain words, for example 'specialized' and 'organized' have been spelt with 'ize' throughout this book. It is equally acceptable to spell these words and others with 'ise'.

Introduction to the English Language AS level and A level specifications

Key features of the AQA English Language AS level and A level specifications

The following list describes the key features of the AQA AS level and A level specifications, and the ways in which this book supports them.

- *AQA's AS and A level specifications have been designed so that they can be taught together.* This book follows the AQA structure and therefore can be used by both AS and A level students. Each chapter will map which AS and A level papers are covered.

- *AQA's study of English Language combines creative work with critical analysis.* This means that you will develop your own writing skills as well as your ability to evaluate the language choices made by others. Both of these areas are developed by the activities in this book.

- *AQA's approach to assessment prioritizes texts and data as starting points.* Stimulating examples of language are used in this book to give you something tangible to relate to and explore.

- *AQA's specifications include a wide range of topic areas.* These support progression to higher education and help you to identify your own areas of research interest. This book covers all of the relevant topics.

- *AQA's A level specification requires a coursework folder consisting of both creative and investigative work,* so both elements are brought together to maximize opportunities for you to be successful. Two chapters of this book are devoted to coursework requirements and ideas.

This chapter covers the:
- key features of the AQA English Language specifications
- Assessment Objectives that apply to this subject
- different writing skills that you need to develop
- language levels that underpin analytical methods.

The specifications at a glance

The A level specification

The A level specification has three components:

- Paper 1: Language, the Individual and Society – 2½ hour exam; 40% of A level
- Paper 2: Language Diversity and Change – 2½ hour exam; 40% of A level
- Non-exam assessment: Language in Action – coursework folder; 20% of A level.

Paper 1: Language, the Individual and Society

This paper is divided into the following sections:

Section A: Textual Variations and Representations

This section requires you to analyse two texts on a common theme, one of which will be an older text. The focus of the analysis will be, first, on meanings and representations, then on the contexts from which the texts come. First you say what each text means and how it conveys ideas about its subject matter, then you explore the similarities and differences between the texts.

Section B: Children's Language Development

This requires an essay, and there will always be a choice of two options. Each of the questions will have some data attached, in order to give you an active start. The data will vary between the questions – it could be children's speech, their writing, or their multimodal communication (where modes are mixed and blended). The essay question will ask you to evaluate an idea about children's language. Evaluation means weighing up and setting out the different aspects of an argument. Language is never cut and dried, so there are always different ideas to be discussed.

Paper 2: Language Diversity and Change

This paper is divided into the following sections:

Section A: Diversity and Change

This requires an essay, and there will be a choice of two options. The essay will require you to evaluate a question about diversity or change. Evaluation means, as mentioned above, weighing up different ideas.

Section B: Language Discourses

This section involves two tasks: the first is analytical and the second is creative.

You will be provided with two texts on the topic of language diversity and change. First, you will be asked to analyse the texts, showing how their choice of language conveys certain ideas and attitudes to language. Then you will be given a writing task, where you will be directed to write on the topic covered by the texts. The directions will be specific about how to approach the writing.

Non-exam assessment: Language in Action

This is a coursework folder. It consists of two equally weighted elements:

- A language investigation (2,000 words excluding data).
- A piece of original writing and commentary (1,500 words in total, 750 words for each).

The AS Level specification

The AS level specification has two papers:

- Paper 1: Language and the Individual – 1 ½ hour exam; 50% of AS level
- Paper 2: Language Varieties –1 ½ hour exam; 50% of AS level.

Paper 1: Language and the Individual

This paper has just one section, called Textual Variations and Representations. It consists of an analysis of two texts on a common theme. There will be no older text on this paper. The focus of the analysis will be, first, on meanings and representations, then on the contexts from which the texts come. First you say what each text means and how it conveys ideas about its subject matter, then you explore the similarities and differences between the texts.

Paper 2: Language Varieties

This paper is divided into the following sections:

Section A: Language Diversity

This requires a discursive essay about language diversity. There will be two options to choose from.

Section B: Language Discourses

This is a directed writing task about attitudes towards language.

The English Language Assessment Objectives

Assessment Objectives describe the different skills, knowledge and understanding on which you will be assessed, in any subject. Each task you carry out, either on an exam paper or in your coursework folder, will be assessed through more than one of the Assessment Objectives listed below. Nowhere in either the A level or the AS level specification will you be assessed through only one of the objectives. This is because work in English requires a number of different elements in order to be successful. You should be able to see this as you read through the descriptions of the Assessment Objectives below.

Assessment Objective 1 (AO1)

Apply appropriate methods of language analysis, using associated terminology and coherent written expression.

This Assessment Objective rewards you for three things:

1. Being able to apply the approaches that are part of the subject area – for example, applying some aspects of the language levels that are set out later in this chapter.

2. Being able to use the key terms that are relevant for the subject area. The key terms that are highlighted throughout the book are exactly that.

3. Being able to write coherently. This means that your writing makes sense and the points you make link together in a logical way.

Assessment Objective 2 (AO2)

Demonstrate critical understanding of concepts and issues relevant to language use.

A concept is an idea or thought, so concepts are the ideas that language experts have about language. An issue is a factor or problem that arises from language use. For example, a concept about language is that it varies; an issue is that people have strong attitudes towards the idea of difference. This Assessment Objective rewards you for understanding both of those aspects.

Assessment Objective 3 (AO3)

Analyse and evaluate how contextual factors and language features are associated with the construction of meaning.

Meanings are not fixed, so this Assessment Objective rewards you for understanding that, and for showing how meanings are made. Meanings are negotiated – people make language choices and others interpret them, but many different aspects of context help to shape what something 'means'. It is important to be able to identify language features (even if you can't label them to get AO1 credit), but also you need to say how context – for example, the historical period, the setting, the topic, the participants, the mode, and so on – affects the meaning of the word, expression, or utterance. Think of a swear word: does it always have the same effect, regardless of where and when someone says it, who the speaker is, and who is within earshot?

Key terms

Discourse. A stretch of language (spoken, written or multimodal) considered in its context of use. The plural use of the term – **discourses** – refers to repeated ways of talking or writing about a topic.

Genre. In language study, a type of text in any mode which is defined by its purpose, its features, or both. In literary fields, genre tends to refer primarily to the literary genres of prose, poetry and drama, but it can also refer to types of content (for example, crime or romance).

Intertextuality. The way in which one text echoes or refers to another.

Assessment Objective 4 (AO4)

Explore connections across texts, informed by linguistic concepts and methods.

No text exists in isolation. Sometimes, texts make explicit reference to other texts, and this relationship is termed **intertextuality**. This language strategy is often employed by writers or speakers who want to draw attention to their message by harnessing the meaning and power of a previous text. Intertextuality can also form the basis of humour and language play, which in themselves create memorability. For example, a café called *Bill's* in Sussex sells its own leaf tea called 'Brewhaha' (playing on the word *brouhaha*, which in itself is a startling word, French for 'hubbub'); Starbucks sells salad boxes called 'Thai and Mighty', 'Hail Caesar', and 'Feta Compli'. If you 'get' the reference, then the strategy has done its work; if you don't, it may still have been successful if it puzzles you and therefore stays in your mind. You may even ask someone else what it means, so it becomes a topic of conversation.

Connections between texts are not just about words and expressions. As a student of English Language, you are expected to explore the idea of **genres**, or types of text that exist in a society for particular functions. You are also expected to think about the way texts group together to form **discourses** – repeated ways of talking and writing about a topic or idea, influencing our thinking and behaviour. For example, texts that are food recipes exist in a genre relationship with each other, and contribute to our social discourses about food.

Assessment Objective 5 (AO5)

Demonstrate expertise and creativity in the use of English to communicate in different ways.

This is about your own writing skills. It involves some basic aspects such as technical accuracy, but it is also about being able to choose and control a style of writing for a particular audience and purpose, and to suit a specified format. The term 'creativity' means being able to show some flair and originality by thinking about how to do things in new ways rather than simply following familiar routines.

Writing skills develop over time, and you should be prepared to draft and re-draft your writing, and make use of constructive criticism from readers of your work. This Assessment Objective stresses the idea of writing in different ways. The next section provides a summary of the different types of writing that you are expected to demonstrate across both AS level and A level specifications.

Writing skills you need to develop

Assessment Objective 5 specifically rewards writing tasks, such as the directed writing task in Paper 2 of both the A level and the AS level. However, writing skills are important throughout both specifications, because – if your writing is not clear – you won't be able to demonstrate the other Assessment Objectives: you won't be able to show that you can use specialist terminology, or debate meaning, or discuss context, or explore textual connections.

You therefore need general writing skills of clarity and accuracy. However, you do not need a special type of academic voice in your writing. Being academic is not about using as many long words as possible, or about writing very long sentences. It is about expressing yourself clearly – with each sentence you write making one main point. Specialist terms can be useful, because they are a kind of shorthand used by experts in a field, so they can save time and space. But don't use terms you don't understand. It is better to show that you understand something in a non-technical way than to use technical terms without understanding.

Sometimes, students worry about how personal or objective to be – saying that they are unsure about whether to use the first-person pronoun 'I', or a passive style. This is a false choice, and somewhat over-simplified. There's nothing wrong with using 'I' now and then, but if a piece of writing repeatedly uses the phrase 'I think', this can sound like a lack of confidence. At the same time, it is odd to express your own ideas in a style that implies you had nothing to do with the interpretation, such as 'the view was taken that…'.

The best, neutral-sounding style is a kind of statement style, and you will see this exemplified throughout this book. A statement style makes statements about a text or an idea, for example:

'this part of the text suggests that…'

'this idea is only partly true because…'

Statements can also be phrased tentatively, which is important, given that many different readings of a text, and different views about a language topic, are possible:

'this may mean that…'

'it could be the case that…'

Writing a text analysis

Writing a text analysis is all about organizing your points in a logical way. Going line-by-line through a text is not helpful, because the same language feature might occur in lines 3, 8, and 14 of a text, so you would be repeating yourself. It is much better to find all the examples of a certain language feature or strategy and group them together in one paragraph, then move on to the next group of features. This will read as a much more thoughtful and thorough analysis.

To group features takes time, so writing a text analysis can mean that you spend almost as much time preparing to write as doing the writing itself. But the reward for this preparation will be writing that is concise and succinct. Writing more is not necessarily a good thing: it's quality that counts, not quantity.

A text analysis is your interpretation of its meanings. The language features in the text act as a form of evidence for your reading, so the more examples you can give, the better. However, remember that any text adds up to something holistic: it's not simply a collection of parts, but a complete entity. Make sure that you don't lose sight of the bigger picture – what the whole text is trying to say (including ideas about any contradictions in its messages), its context, its genre, and so on.

Pay attention to any structures that are given to you at the outset, on an exam paper or in coursework guidance. For example, in Paper 1 of both the A level and the AS level, you are asked to analyse the first text, analyse the second text, then compare the two. The mark scheme follows this format, so if you depart from this structure, it will be more difficult for markers to reward you for what you've done.

Writing a discussion

A text analysis differs from a discussion in that discussions are responses to ideas or views, while a text analysis is a response to an extract or some data. A discussion essay is an opportunity to take an idea and tease it out in as much detail as you can. This might well mean setting out different arguments, or at least showing that you are aware of different views while in the process of setting out your own.

Writing a discussion is not about splitting yourself in half and arguing all in one direction to start with, then arguing a different point of view. It is more about arguing a case, but with concessions to the fact that there are different views about a topic or text.

Directed writing

Directed writing is writing to a specific brief. Directed writing tasks occur in exam conditions and, for that reason, you need to get right to the point about what is needed. Your directed writing will always be on a topic, and there will always be some stimulus material to spur you on and get you thinking.

Original writing

This writing is very different from directed, exam-based writing, because it is up to you what you write about and how. It is also different because, as coursework, it is produced over a considerable period of time. You select the topic, the purpose, the audience, and the genre. But first, you do some research about the type of writing you are thinking of doing, and collect some style models that will help you to think about what others have done. Assessment Objective 5 emphasizes creativity as well as expertise. Part of the reason for collecting some style models is to help you think – not about how to imitate what has gone before, but about how to plan a fresh approach.

Writing a commentary

A commentary is a piece of reflective work where you explain the choices you made in your original writing. You need to be selective in the things you focus on – describing some of the major features of your writing and explaining what effects you were trying to achieve. Your original writing and your commentary have a word limit of 750 words each: see Chapter 8 for more details about both of these.

Writing a report

A report is an account of an activity. It looks back over time and describes a set of procedures that were followed in order to investigate an area. It offers findings and draws conclusions. The investigation element of the coursework component is written up as a report of no more than 2,000 words: see Chapter 7 for more details.

Referencing

Referencing is a way of showing the source of ideas and facts, and it is used to indicate where a writer or academic field has contributed to our knowledge of a subject. It is also used, more specifically, to show where quotations are from. Referencing is an important skill to acquire, especially if you are thinking about going on to university and further study. If you quote from an academic's work and don't acknowledge it correctly, you can be accused of plagiarism, which is a serious issue.

Many subjects in the arts and social sciences use the Harvard referencing system, and several reliable referencing guides are available online, often on university library websites.

References could be used in any of the work across the specifications, but they will most likely be needed when you are discussing a language topic or doing an investigation. You will see references in the different chapters of this book, and the sources suggested for further reading are to be found in a reference list at the end of each chapter. If you are quoting from an academic book or article, use the correct procedure for referring to this in the body of your writing, and for listing full details at the end of your work. This system enables anyone to follow up your reference and find it in a library or online.

Language levels

Both the A level and the AS level specifications for English Language require you to understand 'language levels'. This refers to the way in which language study has traditionally categorized language in order to make analysis easier.

When we use language we don't separate it into parts, but in order to study language we need to do so. The difference between using something and analysing it is similar in many other areas. For example, riding a bicycle certainly requires skill. But analysing how a bicycle works is a different kind of activity, involving looking in some detail at the mechanics of its parts.

Think of language levels, then, as a way to help you focus in on particular aspects of language. However, you still need to be able to keep a wider perspective. Language is for doing things, and for being someone. It is part of our thinking and our behaviour, as well as our individual and group identity. So the bicycle still needs to be something you can appreciate for its ability to get you around and give you pleasure, as well as being uniquely yours to display with pride. Language is a fascinating phenomenon that can tell us a lot about cultural history and diversity, and about power and influence.

The English Language AS level and A level specifications are about analysing language and debating the issues surrounding it. They are also, crucially, about your own language use. Language is a creative tool which can be honed and sharpened so that you develop more control over your own language use, and more insights into why others use language in the way they do.

AQA's AS level and A level specifications require understanding of the following language levels:

- **Phonetics, phonology** and **prosodics**: how speech sounds and effects are articulated and analysed
- **Lexis** and **semantics**: the vocabulary of English, including social and historical variation

> **! REMEMBER**
>
> When you have done some reading, keep a detailed record of what you have read, including the author's name, the date of the publication, the exact title of the book or article, the place of publication and the name of the publisher. If you write down a quotation, you will need the page number. If you are accessing websites, keep an accurate record of each URL and date you accessed it. It is a good idea to keep a notebook in order to assemble your references; or use a digital tool such as delicious.com

> **Key terms**
>
> **Lexis.** The vocabulary of a language.
>
> **Phonetics / Phonology.** The study of the sound system. Phonetics refers to the physical production and reception of sound, while phonology is a more abstract idea about all the sounds of a particular language.
>
> **Prosodics / Prosody.** Prosody is the melody that our voices create via prosodic aspects such as rhythm and intonation.
>
> **Semantics.** Semantics refers to the meanings of words and expressions. Semantics can also refer to meaning in a broader sense, i.e. the overall meaning of something.

Key terms

Grammar. The structural aspects of language that tie items together. Grammar includes **syntax**, or word order; and **morphology**, or the elements added to words to show their grammatical role (such as 'ed' to indicate the past tense of a verb).

Graphology. All the visual aspects of textual design, including colour, typeface, layout, images and logos.

Morphology. The aspect of grammar that refers to grammatical markings. For example, the 's' ending on nouns can indicate a plural form (one book, two books).

Phonemic alphabet. An alphabet for transcribing general sounds, suitable for a specific language. An individual sound is called a **phoneme**.

Pragmatics. Assumptions made about what is meant, or the inferences drawn from what is said or written.

Looking ahead

At university level and in professional work such as speech and language therapy, forensic linguistics, accent coaching (such as for actors), and teaching English to speakers of other languages (TESOL), phonetics can involve some very scientific work – looking at how individual sounds are pronounced in specific contexts.

- **Grammar**, including **morphology**: the structural patterns and shapes of English at sentence, clause, phrase, and word level
- **Pragmatics**: the contextual aspects of language use
- **Discourse**: extended stretches of communication occurring in different genres, modes and contexts
- **Graphology**: the visual aspects of textual design and appearance.

The levels identified above have to be understood, but not simply for their own sake. They have to be applied to language data and to language issues, as well as to your own writing. They form the basis for your study of how users of English vary their language according to a range of social factors, and how language varies according to context.

Phonetics, phonology and prosodics

This level is all about sound. **Phonetics** refers to the study of sounds on an individual basis.

This can be studied at a very detailed level. For example, we might think that we recognize a /t/ sound as an unchanging, single sound. But, in fact, it changes considerably – depending on where it occurs. In the examples below, when /t/ is at the beginning of the word, as in 'top' and 'tin', it is typically pronounced with more explosive force than it is when at the ends of words, as in 'hot' and 'pot'.

top   tin
hot   pot

You will not need this level of detail in your A level work: what is known as a phonemic level is enough. This means a more general look at the individual sounds that underlie spoken English. A **phoneme** is an individual sound, studied without all its complex possible variations.

The phonemes or sounds that a speaker makes can be transcribed by using a special alphabet designed for that purpose. It is called a **phonemic alphabet** and a commonly used version is set out below. Don't be confused by the fact that some common alphabetic letters are used for some sounds. These relate to the sound made when the underlined part of the word is said.

single vowels				diphthongs	
iː sheep	ɪ ship	ʊ book	uː shoot	ɪə here	eɪ wait
e left	ə teacher	ɜː her	ɔː door	ʊə tourist	ɔɪ coin	əʊ show
æ hat	ʌ up	ɑː far	ɒ on	eə hair	aɪ like	aʊ mouth

consonants

p pea	b boat	t tree	d dog	tʃ cheese	dʒ joke	k coin	g go
f free	v video	θ thing	ð this	s see	z zoo	ʃ sheep	ʒ television
m mouse	n now	ŋ thing	h hope	l love	r run	w we	j you

A phonemic alphabet chart

The chart opposite can be found online at http://www.phonemicchart.com. Explore the links on the site to get a clickable chart, with sound.

It is important to understand why a special alphabet for sound is required, and this can be simply illustrated by showing the mismatch between the symbols we use for writing and the sounds we make. There is no straightforward like-for-like relationship between sounds and written letters in English, as we have 26 written symbols and roughly 44 sounds (depending on your accent). So the same written symbols can produce some very different sounds.

Activity

Transcribe the following words by saying them aloud and then writing down their pronunciation, using the phonemic chart opposite. When you have finished, look at how 'ough' has been pronounced in each case. How does it vary?

- through
- thorough
- cough
- thought
- bough
- dough

Answers are at the back of the book.

Phonology differs from **phonetics** in looking at the sound system of a whole language, and comparing it with others. Although English Language A level focuses centrally on English, there are some important applications of phonological knowledge. For example, the study of children's language involves looking at how a child learns the **phonological system** of the language around him or her (see Chapter 4). Different languages, including different Englishes, will have different phonological systems, and so speakers have to adapt when they move from one language or variety to another (see Chapter 6 for more information on **World Englishes**). There are also differences in the phonological **repertoires** of UK-based English regional speakers. For example, many northern speakers have no phoneme /ʌ/. This is the sound that **Received Pronunciation** (**RP**) speakers will use when they say the word 'up'. You will notice that the English phonemic alphabet is based on RP, rather than on any regional accent – already showing you that not all language varieties are treated equally. You will look at this in more detail in Chapter 3.

Prosodics is about sound, but not individual sounds. Prosodic features make up what you might call the soundtrack behind the words we speak: areas such as rhythm, pitch, volume, and intonation are all included. These are hard to mark in transcriptions, but sometimes even being able to mark and understand one or two features can be useful, because they can be important contributors to meaning.

There are also aspects of **paralanguage** that can be very significant, such as voice quality and other vocal effects (for example, whispering and laughter) and **non-verbal behaviour**, such as eye contact and facial expression.

There is no better way to learn about **prosody** and **paralanguage** than to record and transcribe some speech. Although during the course of your

Key terms

Non-verbal behaviour. Communication that takes place via the body (such as gesture and facial expression).

Paralanguage. Aspects of an individual's vocal expression, such as whispering, laughter, breathiness.

Phonological system. The system of sounds within any language variety.

Received pronunciation (RP). An accent traditionally associated with high social status. 'Received' refers to the idea of social acceptance in official circles.

Repertoire. The range of language forms or styles used by a speaker.

World Englishes. Varieties of English that are used in different countries around the world, mainly in areas that were formerly colonised, such as India and Singapore. These countries have their own version of Standard English.

studies you will be able to work from original speech recordings, in exams you will be working from transcripts alone. Paying attention to those things that a transcriber chooses to mark is therefore important; and the more you have experienced the process of making your own recordings, the more you will be able to 'hear' the transcript from some of its markings.

Activity

The following is a transcript of a brief conversation held between four strangers on a bus. The conversation starts as the bus is parked on a riverside quay, then continues as the bus starts up and moves off. A, B and C are local residents; D is an American visitor.

Read the transcript and focus on the following aspects of prosody:

- How do you explain the emphasis given to some of the words?
- Why do you think there are points where there are significant pauses?
- Why does laughter occur at a particular point?

Now think more broadly about speech in general:

- How characteristic is this of speech between strangers?
- How do you explain the simultaneous speech?
- How much of this would you have been able to understand without being given some contextual detail about the speakers and their environment?
- How much of the conversation involves speakers using sentences?
- How important do you think non-verbal aspects would have been?

There is some feedback on this activity at the back of the book.

Transcription key

(.) normal pause

(1.0) numbers in brackets indicate length of pauses in seconds

bold indicates a stressed syllable

| vertical lines show simultaneous speech

heh heh indicates laughter

? indicates a questioning intonation

[ ] square brackets indicate contextual information

A: it was thundering this morning (.) here
B: sorry?
A: thundering and lightning |here
B: |yeah it woke me up
A: [*bus starts up*] here we go
C: nobody on the quay today
A: no (.) a few boats out
C: there were kayaks out yesterday
D: is there usually a lot of river traffic?
A: oh yes |a lot of families with children
B: |leisure stuff you can hire boats
A: you can go up to the double locks by river boat
D: you can go through the |locks?
A: |yes yes you can go through
D: so what does **quay** mean?
B: |waterfront
A: |by **boat** (.) by **quay**
D: I associate that word with water (.) but I didn't know why

B: I think it means a dock a **dock**

B: what do you say in the States then?

D: we say a **dock** or a **port** (.) something like that

B: well this was the port for Exeter it was a big wool trade area

D: oh yes there's the Custom House

B: they had to weigh the wool and big ships came in here (2.0) in the tourist office there's a big board with a register of all the stuff that came in and went out (1.0) some strange things (1.0) **bones** and **hooves** *heh heh* stuff like that (.) really **odd** things

D: oh *heh heh* was that was that for the factories for glue?

B: could have been (.) yeah

How is phonetic knowledge useful?

Knowing about sounds and spoken language helps you to understand some of the differences between speech and writing, which are important insights for any work on **mode**. You will also have a better understanding of **language acquisition**, because you will appreciate what is required both in learning to make sounds and in learning how to read and write. You will be able to describe some important aspects of language variation, particularly **accent variation**.

Understanding phonology will also give you some insights into public attitudes towards language differences, especially the way people **stereotype** others. Picking on a distinctive sound as used by groups of speakers – such as people from a particular region, or those speaking **English as an additional language** – has long been a staple of stereotyping, both with humorous and more sinister intent. Language is an important aspect of identity, and language differences can be used both to include and to exclude.

Sounds can act as a **Shibboleth**, a term that dates back to the Bible but describes something which still continues today. 'Shibboleth' was a Hebrew word for an ear of corn, but different cultural groups pronounced the 'sh' differently: the Ephraimites as /s/ and the Gileadites as /ʃ/. During a battle, this acted as a way to discover people's allegiances, with tragic results for some:

> …the men of Gilead said unto him, Art thou an Ephraimite? If he said, Nay; then said they unto him, Say now Shibboleth: and he said Sibboleth: for he could not frame to pronounce it right. Then they took him, and slew him at the passages of Jordan: and there fell at that time of the Ephraimites forty and two thousand.
>
> Judges 12: 5-6

Nowadays, we still use the term 'Shibboleth' to mean a 'marker' or a 'test' word. 'Framing it right' in language terms for the people whose group you hope to join is still significant thousands of years later. In your English Language course you will have opportunities to debate issues about attitudes to language and you will be asked to produce your own articles and opinion pieces. Understanding how language can act both as a badge of allegiance and as a way to assert power over others, is a key aspect of this study.

Not everyone who tries to represent speech or suggest sound will use a phonemic alphabet. Sometimes writers such as literary authors, writers of comics, and users of new communication tools – which includes most of us – will try to suggest sounds by manipulating the conventional written alphabet.

■ Key terms

Accent variation. The way that pronunciations vary between different speakers, or the variations a single speaker might produce in different contexts.

English as an additional language. The use of English where it is not the person's first language learned.

Language acquisition. The development of language within an individual.

Mode. Speech and writing are called different modes. Digital communication can draw on both of these modes, so is often called a hybrid form of communication.

Shibboleth. A language item used as a marker or test of group membership.

Stereotype. A stereotype is based on the idea that whole groups of people conform to the same, limited, range of characteristics.

Key terms

Arbitrary. Having no real connection beyond that of social convention.

Constructed dialogue. Dialogue that is artificially created rather than occurring naturally. For example, in novels or playscripts.

Onomatopoeia. The way in which some words appear to echo the sounds they describe, such as 'crash' and 'thud'.

Referent. The thing or person being referred to.

Sound symbolism. The way in which sounds are used to represent ideas – for example, in onomatopoeia, where sounds represent noises. There is no logical connection between the sounds and the ideas they represent.

Linguists claim that there is no relationship between the sounds we make or the written symbols we produce and the thing being described. Language is said to be **arbitrary** – the relationship between any word and its **referent** is only created by social convention.

Yet we have a whole array of terms that we seem to believe echo the noises they describe. These words are called **onomatopoeic**, and examples are 'crash', 'thud', 'bang', 'tinkle'. Terms such as these, and the deliberate grouping together of sounds to suggest certain ideas, show the operation of **sound symbolism**. This area – the suggestive power of certain sounds – will certainly be something to consider in your text analysis work, as will the idea of **constructed dialogue**. You would be unlikely to see the real bus conversation you studied earlier appearing in a piece of fiction in transcript form.

Activity

Writers of fiction are seen as having particular expertise in manipulating language, but we all do this in our own way most days in our digital communications. Below are some examples of students using an online 'chat' tool. They are all altering language in order to achieve particular effects. None of them are using the phonemic alphabet but they are all trying to suggest aspects of spoken language. Can you identify what they are trying to do? Some context is given, to help you.

There is some feedback on this activity at the back of the book.

These exchanges occurred after another participant said she had to leave the chat site early:

> NO NO NO NO NO!!!!
> don't go pleaseeeeeeeeeee

This occurred when many people were trying to communicate all at once:

> ssslllllllooooowww

This person was asked if he wanted to go out for dinner:

> ooh… erm… flibble… maybe… don't know… aahhh…

Below are examples of laughter from different participants in a variety of contexts. Which would you use, if any, and for what intended meaning?

> ha ha ha
> he he he
> heh heh
> tee hee
> oh har har
> a-hah-hah-hah
> hee hee hee ha ha ha hooooo hoo

Source: Goddard (2005)

Lexis and semantics

This level of language is all about vocabulary (**lexis**) and the different phrases and expressions (**semantics**) that help to shape meanings.

The English Language specification refers to social and historical variation within lexis and semantics. **Social variation** refers to the different social groups that people identify with. For example, people can have strong regional affiliations, or close ties to people in their own occupation or of a similar age. They might have a close-knit social group of same-sex friends or people with the same interests, and those interests might include staying in touch with others who share an **ethnic identity**. New communication technologies have given everyone new ways to connect with others, so that physical proximity is no longer an overriding factor. But however people connect, an important part of all social group identities involves an idea of 'speaking the same language'. This can be literally true of course, but it can also refer to having the same mindset or a similar outlook on life, which in itself both constructs and reflects language use.

Social variations of language are bound to involve **representation**, which is all about how people are described and defined. The relationship between variation and representation is a complex one, because how people identify themselves isn't always how others identify them. For example, deafness could be seen as a disability within mainstream society, but people who are deaf might not view themselves as disabled. Attitudes to social variation also change over time, so this topic cannot be considered in isolation from that of language change, or from the changes in attitude that go with new thinking. For example, attitudes to accent, ideas about male and female language, and the way we label different groups have all undergone considerable change. See Chapter 3 (Language and people), for more on social variation; see also Chapter 5 for more on historical variation. Chapter 2 will help you to understand how representation works.

The study of lexis is about far more than just what words are said to mean in a dictionary. For a start, words have different functions. Some words have a grammatical function, which means that they help with the structure of a sentence or utterance. Other words have more content and direct meaning in the sense that they refer to something in the world. For example, in the text below, the words 'dogs', 'Santa', 'puppy' and 'Christmas' refer to specific people or things, whereas many of the other words have a function to tie the text together.

Lexical items are much more subject to change than grammatical items, which tend to be more fixed and slower to vary over time. The specification does not require you to know about the history of English as such, but understanding something about how aspects of English came to be the way they are – particularly vocabulary – is useful for a number of reasons, including an awareness of **formality** in modern English.

Many of the lexical items we use in everyday English still reflect the Germanic and Scandinavian varieties that were brought to Britain with the invasion of Anglo-Saxon and Viking groups from about AD 400 onwards. Regional place names show the distribution of those early colonizers, with terms such as 'gate', 'thwaite', 'thorpe' and 'by' indicating Scandinavian settlements and 'ton', 'stead', 'stow' and 'ham' Anglo-Saxon ones.

Key terms

Ethnic identity / ethnicity. Feeling connected with people who have similar cultural backgrounds, heritage, or family ties.

Formal / Formality. Designed for use on serious or public occasions where people pay attention to behaviour and appearance.

Representation. Something that stands in place of something else. Representation is how something *appears* to be, not how it really *is*.

Social variation. The variation that occurs as a result of the social groups that people connect with. For example, groups based on common interests such as sport or cookery.

Key terms

Connotation. The associations that we have for a word or phrase.

Etymology / Etymological. The study of word origins.

Style. In language study, a distinctive way of speaking or writing for different contexts (akin to styles of dress in studies of fashion).

Synonym. Synonyms are words that have a similar meaning, such as 'help' and 'assist'.

Thesaurus. A type of dictionary that groups words together on the basis of similar meaning.

From 1066 on, however, French became prominent after the Norman invasion, with most official functions, such as court cases, conducted in French rather than English, and with the country's powerful positions occupied by French lords. And, of course, since those early days English has absorbed terms from many different languages, as a result of hundreds of years of cultural contacts and conquests. In addition, Latin-based terms have been promoted at different points in history by privileged elites as signifiers of power and status.

The early waves of Germanic languages and French, plus the adoption of Latin terms, have resulted in groups of **synonyms** in English – terms which are supposedly equivalents but where we perceive one term to be more formal or to have higher status than another. For example, if someone talks about 'cuisine', in theory this is a synonym for 'cookery', but the **connotations**, or associations, we have for the two terms are very different. Cookery could involve sausages and mash; cuisine is more likely to be steak tartare or foie gras. A 'cook' sounds more basic than a 'chef', and perhaps even a different gender. The TV programme *Masterchef* would have a different profile if called *Mastercook*, let alone *Mistresscook*.

Activity

Below are pairs of terms that have been absorbed into English from different origins. In theory they are synonyms, in that they refer to the same thing. But in practice the selection of one term over another produces a more or less formal **style**. To see the practical effects of these choices, write a short passage using words based on the Germanic/Scandinavian lists. Then write a parallel version using the French/Latin choices.

Germanic or Scandinavian origin	French or Latin origin	Germanic or Scandinavian origin	French or Latin origin
snag	impediment	make	manufacture
house	residence	task	assignment
work	employment	help	assistance
meet	encounter	meeting	rendezvous
rude	offensive	date	appointment
sweat	perspire	graveyard	cemetery
die	expire	drunk	intoxicated
breathe	respire	underwear	lingerie
talk	converse	driver	chauffeur
friendly	amicable	tired	fatigued
loving	amorous	brew	concoct
keep	preserve	scold	chastize

REMEMBER

Awareness of formality is a powerful tool for text analysis and it can sometimes help you to understand the effects of word choice if you substitute a synonym that is more or less formal, and consider the results. You then have a way of talking about the choices that writers or speakers have made.

There are ways to extend your awareness of this aspect of English lexis. Collections of synonyms are housed in a **thesaurus** and can be found in both book form and online. **Etymological** dictionaries are very useful and interesting sources of information about word origins. There are phone apps for both these sorts of collections.

An awareness of the diversity of the origins of English vocabulary can help you to engage with arguments about so-called language 'purity'. Sometimes, commentators about language issues want to resist change on the basis that English is a 'pure' language and should not be 'corrupted' by foreign words; and yet English contains words from many different languages.

 Activity

Find out the origins of these common English words:

bungalow	chocolate	banana
nosh	arsenal	skipper
cafeteria	jockey	bureau
boss	rap	ouch
ravioli	teenager	bangle
berserk	tea	coffee

Answers are at the back of the book.

Word origins are also sometimes connected with **register**, which refers to language use involving **semantic fields**. Semantic fields are areas of language that are used by particular groups and in specific contexts. The easiest way to demonstrate the idea of semantic fields is to think about occupations. The terms used by different groups of workers can be unique: for example, a 'corbel' in architecture, a 'velouté' in cooking, 'allegro' in musical notation, and 'habeus corpus' in law all have a unique reference for workers in those areas. But terms that are in general use can also have a specific meaning in some occupations. For example, the term 'poor' in general use can mean either 'lacking money' or 'not very good'. On teachers' reports, however, a statement such as 'Robert has been poor this term' would not be referring to Robert's poverty.

The examples in the activity above are all from specific languages. French terms proliferate in cooking and Italian terms in musical notation, because those cultural groups have been credited with particular expertise in those activities. The classical languages of Latin and Greek underlie the terms from architecture and law, because Western cultures have based many of their architectural styles and rules of government on those ancient civilizations.

There has been a further role for terms with Latin and Greek roots, more specifically to do with language change. When a new item or concept is invented, a new term needs to be created. Latin and Greek terms have been very useful in this process, and continue to be, because they often contain **morphemes** – elements of meaning smaller than a word – that can be used again and again. For example, the morpheme 'micro' – 'small' in Greek – has helped to name many new inventions and ideas. In addition, 'phone', meaning 'sound', and 'scope', meaning 'focusing on a target', have been found useful:

microphone

microscope

microwave

microdot

microfilm

microbe

microbrewery

Key terms

Morpheme. A morpheme is an element of meaning smaller than a word. Morphemes often mark grammatical features. For example, 'talked' has two morphemes – 'talk' and 'ed', which indicates that the talk occurred in the past. Morphemes can also occur as bigger elements, such as the suffixes 'ship' and 'hood' in the nouns 'partnership' and 'neighbourhood'.

Register. A form of specialist language. For example, the language of sport or science.

Semantic field. A group of terms from the same domain. For example, names for food or aspects of computer communication.

Similarly, Latin morphemes often feature in new names for inventions, and both Greek and Latin proliferate within medicine and the sciences more generally.

Activity

Find out the word origins of the following terms:

post mortem	video	television	telegraph
automobile	telephone	periscope	psychology
subterranean	sub-aqua	submarine	photography
megaphone	phobia	graph	biology

Answers are at the back of the book.

Key terms

Dysphemistic / Dysphemism. A direct form of language that doesn't attempt to disguise sensitive or difficult topics.

Euphemistic / Euphemism. An indirect form of language that enables speakers to avoid mentioning something unpleasant or offensive.

Lingua franca. Where speakers don't share the same first language, a lingua franca acts as a kind of bridging language enabling them to communicate. In modern times, English acts as a lingua franca in many parts of the world.

Taboo. Something that is off limits or forbidden.

Classical languages had high status in former times, and even up to the late 20th century familiarity with Latin was a requirement for studying history at university. This was because many older texts were written in Latin, which was a **lingua franca** – a common language – within educated groups across Europe. Because of this status, it can still attract people who want to draw on its reputation. For example, August Horch, who founded the German car company Audi, reputedly chose 'Audi' because it was a Latin equivalent of his German name. And the name of the Swedish car company Volvo is Latin for 'I roll'.

Latin and Greek terms, especially within science, can suggest something very abstract, and there are different ways of looking at this. For example, 'diarrhoea' is a Greek term, and this can be seen as usefully removing us from the difficulty of facing something unpleasant that is happening to our body. So it can be seen as **euphemistic**, protecting us from a **taboo** topic. But the German for this same bodily ill is 'Durchfall', which means 'falling through'. Is this **dysphemistic** (disagreeable or unpleasant) or just plain speaking?

For all its high status and useful formality in some contexts, Latin-based and abstract-sounding vocabulary can be off-putting and seem remote from ordinary people and their language.

Activity

The following two extracts are from political speeches. Compare them – focusing on the level of formality and the nature of the vocabulary in each one. How would you describe the approach taken by each of the speakers?

- The first extract is from 1982, and was given by a US president, Ronald Reagan, to the House of Commons in the UK. In it he set out his view of the former Soviet Union as an 'evil empire'.

- The second extract is from 1963, given at the Lincoln Memorial in Washington, D.C. by Dr. Martin Luther King, a civil rights activist who campaigned against racism in the USA.

There is some feedback on this activity at the back of the book.

We're approaching the end of a bloody century plagued by a terrible political invention – totalitarianism. Optimism comes less easily today, not because democracy is less vigorous, but because democracy's enemies have refined their instruments of repression. Yet optimism is in order because day by day democracy is proving itself to be a not at all fragile flower. From Stettin on the Baltic to Varna on the Black Sea, the regimes planted by totalitarianism have had more than thirty years to establish their legitimacy. But none – not one regime – has yet been able to risk free elections. Regimes planted by bayonets do not take root.

I have a dream that one day on the red hills of Georgia, the sons of former slaves and the sons of former slave owners will be able to sit down together at the table of brotherhood […]

I have a dream that my four little children will one day live in a nation where they will not be judged by the color of their skin but by the content of their character.

I have a dream today!

Many speeches are available online, where you can hear speakers as well as read transcripts of their speeches. For example, explore this site:

http://www.americanrhetoric.com

Both of the speakers quoted above used **metaphor**, which is an important area of **idiomatic** English. Idiomatic language in general is language the meaning of which cannot be derived just from adding its parts together: idioms work as whole, fixed texts. For example, a phrase such as 'giving someone the brush-off' is invariable, so 'giving someone the brush' doesn't mean the same type of thing. Similarly, 'getting hold of the wrong end of the stick' can't be changed to 'getting hold of the wrong end of the twig' – unless a speaker is being playful and deliberately changing the expression for humorous reasons. There is a fine line between calling something a mistake and labelling it creativity.

Metaphor is a specific kind of idiomatic language where two elements that are not normally associated with each other are brought together, in order to create a new perspective. Ronald Reagan says:

Regimes planted by bayonets do not take root.

This expression regards governments as plants, and guns as gardeners. The idea links back to his earlier reference to democracy as 'a not at all fragile flower'.

Martin Luther King uses the phrase:

at the table of brotherhood

Equality of rights and citizenship are seen as a table, which suggests ideas of participation, the sharing of food and sociable company.

Metaphors and other types of idiomatic language are not confined to speeches or other highly fashioned language practices, such as poetry. We use idioms frequently and draw on different semantic fields for our sources.

Key terms

Idiom / Idiomatic. An expression whose meaning is not dependent on the meanings of the words it contains. For example, saying that someone 'has a chip on their shoulder' or that something costs 'an arm and a leg'.

Metaphor. A language strategy for bringing two unrelated ideas together in order to suggest a new way of looking at something. Metaphors are common where something is difficult to understand because it is complex or abstract, so it is compared with something simpler or more concrete.

Activity

Guess which fields of activity the following idioms come from:

He's top dog.	I'm supporting the underdog.
She hit the ground running.	I just boiled over.
That hit the nail on the head.	Let's kick that idea into touch.
They got the sack.	We need to work to a deadline.
Let's go back to square one.	He gave me the cold shoulder.
Put a sock in it!	They went for it lock, stock and barrel.
She's got a chip on her shoulder.	He needs to step up to the plate.

There is some feedback on this activity at the back of the book.

In many cases, the connection between an idiom and its source field has been lost, so it's unlikely that when you use a phrase, you think of its basis. However, the fact that we use expressions from certain fields can mean that we build up a sense that a particular way of thinking about something is the right one. For example, the fact that we have so many expressions comparing time to money can mean that we don't even see the idea as metaphorical: we waste time, spend time, invest time in things; time is valuable; time is gained and lost; time is squandered and frittered away; time is saved; people are said to be 'time rich' or 'time poor'. Analysing groups of expressions in this way can reveal the values of a society: in capitalist cultures, the time of the workforce is bought and sold, like a product. Different cultures will have different metaphors to express their realities.

Activity

To explore the idea of the relationship between metaphor and thinking, look at the different ways of talking about learning and teaching that are listed below. Identify the basis of the metaphor (underlined) in each case, and say how you think the use of the metaphor might structure a certain way of thinking and acting.

- Teaching is all about packaging a course and then delivering it.
- Teaching needs to lay foundations and learners need to build on them.
- Students really blossom in the right environment.
- Students need to be challenged to achieve new heights.
- Assessment is all about getting a snapshot of achievement.
- Teachers need to diagnose how their students' learning is progressing.
- Good record-keeping as evidence of learning is essential.
- The course needs to be bite-sized, making it easier to digest.
- Learning is all about navigating the subject and getting to the right point.
- To be a good teacher you need faith in yourself and then your students will believe in themselves.

There is some feedback on this activity at the back of the book.

Grammar

Two important aspects of **grammar** have already been covered: **morphology**, and the idea of some words having a grammatical, rather than a lexical, function. Morphology, the study of the meaningful parts of words, is exemplified in the second sentence listed in the previous activity, where the 's' on the word 'foundations' is meaningful – it tells us that the word it belongs to is plural.

Grammar is also about word order, or **syntax**, and this is often language-specific, but is not fixed – particularly in English. For example, in the text 'Dear Santa' (page 17), there are six uses of the word 'please' at the start of the letter. These wouldn't have given the same message if they'd come at the end, as below. This might have suggested the child was having a bit of a tantrum (instead of, in the original, imploring in a heartfelt way):

> Dear Santa,
> Can I have a puppy for Christmas please please please please please please?

Grammar is also about **cohesion**, or the way texts connect across sentences or utterances. Look again at the second sentence from the metaphor activity:

> Teaching needs to lay foundations and learners need to build on them.

Here, 'and' is a **connective** which links together the two **clauses**, 'Teaching needs to lay foundations' and 'learners need to build on them'. But the **pronoun** 'them' also has a linking function, in this case, to refer back to 'foundations'.

Cohesion is a key aspect of literacy skill for beginning readers and writers because, without it, stretches of text can appear as a random series of sentences. It is also a key aspect of analysis for advanced students, because it is at the heart of how texts of all kinds achieve dynamism.

Cohesion is just as important in spoken language but can work differently. Below is an example of spoken cohesion in action, from the 'Bus conversation' that was transcribed earlier (pages 14–15). The cohesion here is both lexical (the quay, boats, kayaks, river traffic, leisure stuff, boats; nobody, families, children), grammatical (the **adverbs** 'today' and 'yesterday') and **pragmatic**, which relates to the unspoken rules that people follow and the assumptions that they make about how others understand them. In the extract below, A agrees with C's observation about not much happening; D uses C's statement in order to ask a question about what happens normally. Both A and B reply to D's question. Back-and-forth exchanges in spoken language, where one statement mirrors or agrees with another, or a question gets an answer, are termed **adjacency** relationships.

> C: nobody on the quay today
> A: no (.) a few boats out
> C: there were kayaks out yesterday
> D: is there usually a lot of river traffic?
> A: oh yes |a lot of families with children
> B: |leisure stuff you can hire boats

One area where both spoken and written texts can be analysed in similar ways is **modification**. This is where more information is given by **adjectival** or **adverbial** elements, telling us more about nouns and verbs. In the speech extract above, you have already seen how adverbs can express time ('today', 'yesterday'), telling us more about when activity occurred (or not, in this case).

Key terms

Adjacency. The positioning of elements in an interaction, so that one follows on from another, although they don't have to occur immediately afterwards. Elements in an **adjacency relationship** often occur in **adjacency pairs**. For example, greetings are usually reciprocal, questions are followed by answers, etc.

Adjective / Adjectival. Adjectives give more information about nouns, describing the qualities of people and things.

Adverb / Adverbial. Adverbs give more information about verbs – typically, where, when and in what manner the action of the verb takes place. Adverbial elements can be phrases, so aren't necessarily single words.

Clause. Clauses are grammatical units and can be main clauses, which stand on their own, or subordinate clauses, which cannot stand alone but have to accompany main clauses. A main clause gives information about people or things (nouns and pronouns) and their states or actions (verbs).

Cohesion. The way sentences or utterances join together to form a whole text.

Connective. A word that joins elements together, such as 'and' and 'or'. These are also called **conjunctions**.

Adverbial and adjectival elements can also appear as whole phrases: for example, 'on the quay' is adverbial, as well as the word 'out', telling us about placement and whereabouts. Adjectivally, the word 'river' tells us more about 'traffic'; and 'with children' gives us more information about 'families'.

Adjectives and adverbs can also exist as comparatives and superlatives, for example: good, better, best; cheap, cheaper, cheapest; early, earlier, earliest; near, nearer, nearest. You can probably see why comparatives (the '-er', or 'more x' versions) and superlatives (the '-est', or 'most x' versions) are favoured by advertisers.

Activity

Explore as many different aspects of cohesion as you can find in the text on the left. It is from a hotel and is asking guests to make decisions about whether they want to re-use their towels.

Think about grammar, but also think about the other levels of language you have studied so far. Any aspect of language – including images and colour – can have a function in constructing cohesion.

There is some feedback on this activity at the back of the book.

Knowing a little about how grammar works will be useful in many areas of study beyond text analysis. It has an obvious relevance in language acquisition. Children don't necessarily learn how to label language, but they learn its rules at an early age, or they wouldn't be able to communicate. You may not have looked at grammar before in an analytical way, but you must be a skilful communicator or you would not be studying at advanced level.

Grammar is also an area that causes much debate and controversy. There are regional variations in grammar – just as there are in dialect vocabulary. **Standard English**, which is the form of the written language that is taught in UK schools as a common language for official purposes, has different grammatical structures from some English regional dialects (see Chapter 3), and also from the many different Englishes that are used worldwide (see Chapter 6). Standard English was once itself a dialect – from the south-east Midlands area – and had its own patterns.

Different grammatical structures that are used by large populations cannot be simply dismissed as 'bad' or 'wrong' in themselves. However, they can be used as a Shibboleth by those who want to deny the claims of others to power. For example, John Simon, writing in 1980 (see opposite) is objecting to the use of 'was', instead of 'were' by speakers of Afro-Caribbean English. While Standard English uses a mixture of 'was' and 'were' for the past tense of the verb 'to be', several English regional dialects, as well as Afro-Caribbean English, use 'was' throughout. Some regional dialects also use 'were' throughout.

Activity

How is John Simon using the idea of grammar as a Shibboleth in the following text? Look particularly at his use of the pronoun 'we'/'us': who does it refer to? What metaphors does he use and why? How would you counter his argument?

There is some feedback on this activity at the back of the book.

Key terms

Modifier / Modification. Modifiers add information. For example, adverbs add information to verbs (run *quickly*), and adjectives add information to nouns (a *lovely* day).

Pronoun. Pronouns can stand in place of nouns, hence the term 'pro-noun'. Standard English personal pronouns are: I, you, he, she, it, and one (singular); we, you and they (plural).

Standard English (SE). A language system that acts as an agreed common language, especially for formal uses. This primarily refers to the writing system of English.

Syntax. Syntax is about how words are arranged, or the word order that is typical of a language.

Why should we consider some, usually poorly educated, subculture's notion of the relationship between sound and meaning? There is more to it, though. Maintaining the niceties of 'was' and 'were' links our language to that of the giants of the English tongue who preceded us, one of those great writers and speakers who were – not *was* – in the ball game that counts: the great struggle to use English as clearly and beautifully as possible [...] should we destroy a beautiful old building because it has decorative elements on its façade and replace it with a square box because it has a simpler structure? Of course, there are people who tear down architectural masterpieces for just such reasons; but whatever they call themselves, *we* should call them barbarians [...] there is, I believe, a morality of language: an obligation to preserve and nurture the niceties, the fine distinctions, that have been handed down to us.

Simon (1980)

Pragmatics

Pragmatics are all about assumptions in language use – unspoken rules, meanings that have to be inferred because they are not spelled out, and practices that are shared because they are learned as part of growing up in a particular community, but not known beyond that group.

Looking back at the texts in this chapter is a useful starting point for thinking about pragmatics. The question to ask is: What social knowledge does someone need in order to understand this text? Understanding pragmatics is difficult because everything around us feels natural, just 'the ways things are'. So you have to step out of your own shoes and imagine explaining everything to someone who knows nothing about the society in which you live.

For example, to understand the 'Dear Santa' text (page 17) you need to know who Santa is, what Christmas is, the fact that children write letters to this mythical figure, and the fact that receiving a puppy as a present is something that many children long for – and pester their parents about. At a more detailed level, you might also explain that the image isn't of just any puppy, but the kind of adorable puppy that has featured on UK TV screens in product advertising for many years. Finally, you need to know that the word 'please' is an important politeness marker in English.

The 'Bus conversation' (pages 14–15) also demonstrates some interesting pragmatic features. The earlier work on cohesion covered pragmatic areas in discussing turn-taking and adjacency. Politeness issues are certainly involved there, as they are in rules around overlaps and interruptions. But politeness also connects with choice of topic. The transcript shows the very beginning of the conversation: before that, all the participants were sitting in silence, and they were all complete strangers. To understand this dialogue – and learn how to participate in future dialogues of this kind in the UK – you need to know that if you want to strike up a conversation with strangers in this kind of context, you are not free to choose any topic: you need to find something 'safe', such as the weather, as is the case here.

Rules of talk and silence vary considerably between cultures. Berry et al (2004) show how Finnish communities place a high value on silence – seeing it not as problematic but as an important opportunity to reflect peacefully on life. They call this quality 'quietude', but show how, in dialogue with their American peers, Finnish university students were labelled as shy and withdrawn. The researchers claim that, for many Americans, talk is an important defining quality of sociability, and to be silent is problematic.

Different cultural groups also have different rules about directness and indirectness in speech. Eva Hoffman, who emigrated to the USA from Poland as a child during World War II, talks below about the fact that she had to learn to be more indirect:

> I learn also that certain kinds of truth are impolite. One shouldn't criticize the person one is with, at least not directly. You shouldn't say, 'You are wrong about that' – though you may say, 'On the other hand, there is that to consider.' You shouldn't say, 'This doesn't look good on you,' though you may say, 'I like you better in that other outfit.' I learn to tone down my sharpness, to do a more careful conversational minuet.

Hoffman (2008: 146)

In the following additional extract, Hoffman goes on to describe how she learnt the rules of 'dating' in the American culture of the 1960s:

> I know several of the rules: First, you should never let the boy honk for you from the outside; he should come in from his car, so you can introduce him to your parents, with whom he can make small talk for a few minutes. This is the first serious stumble in my imagination. It is very unlikely that I could get my parents to behave with the mixture of white-toothed cheerfulness and offhand casualness that I've seen in American parents on TV, or that they could produce small talk of the 'Nice to see you, young man', or 'Now be sure to bring my daughter back on time', variety. Then there are the tense moments of getting into the car and negotiating the evening's activity – followed by what is presented as the extremely tricky challenge of making conversation. By this, what is apparently meant is that the girl is supposed to make the boy comfortable enough to get something out of him – an article in *Seventeen* goes so far as to suggest that you bone up on an athletic event, since all of Them are bound to be interested in sports. If there's an uncomfortable silence, you can always break it by reverting to the one unfailing subject – himself.

Hoffman (2008: 149)

Activity

Think about some of the cultural rules that you have to follow in some of the situations you know. Consider the language use but also all of the other aspects of behaviour too, in the way Hoffman does. Imagine that you are explaining the rules to someone who knows nothing about your community at all.

For example, what are the rules for managing the following successfully?

- Ordering and consuming food and drink in your school or college café
- Being a successful user of a social media site
- Participating in a family event or celebration
- Dating
- Texting, when communicating with same-sex friends
- Texting, when communicating with the opposite sex
- Talk and silence in your community
- Mobile phone use when you are out with friends
- If you do any part-time jobs, language use (such as terms of address) to customers and other work colleagues

If you know more than one language, are there variations in how the different groups manage their language and behaviour?

You will return to the topic of pragmatics in looking at language and **gender**, because one school of thought is that the sexes are trained to follow different rules for conversations – resulting in miscommunication. Issues of pragmatics are involved in workplace communication, as well as in ethnic variation. Children have to learn pragmatic skills and, if they have certain disabilities, such as autism, this might prove very difficult for them. There may be subtle differences between speakers on a regional basis, for example in the informal terms of address that are part of regional dialect: does being called 'love' or 'm'duck' by strangers make you warm to the interaction or evoke a hostile stare from you?

Finally, as with all other aspects of language use, pragmatics can change with time. There are now 'Quiet' coaches on trains, because we are having more conversations in public spaces as a result of mobile communications. People now often tend to say 'I'm good' rather than 'I'm well' in response to the greeting 'How are you?' And we have had to evolve whole new ways of negotiating openings and closings in emails and other environments that didn't exist until relatively recently.

Discourse and graphology

You may find that in older books and articles on language, the term 'discourse' refers just to spoken language. But nowadays, 'discourse' and 'text' can refer to speech, writing, or any of the newer hybrids that are part of our digital communication repertoires. A discourse is a whole text and, in a sense, this level is the most large-scale language level of all, because it is what all the others add up to.

The term 'discourse' has a plural form – 'discourses'. In the plural, this refers to repeated ways of representing people, things, and ideas in the same way, so that this comes to seem natural. It is thought that discourses shape the way we think and behave, so language doesn't have just a describing function, but a much more powerful role in shaping our cognition and actions. The discussion about metaphor and time earlier (page 22) relates to this society-wide idea of discourse: you could say that in the UK, we have discourses about time that portray time as money.

The discourse level also includes ideas about **genres**, or different text types, as well as aspects of textual design and layout – an area referred to as **graphology**. Graphology is considered here alongside discourse, because it, too, is a whole-text dimension. Graphological features are wide ranging and encompass all the things to do with the look of a text, including images, typeface and font, the use of colour, and all the physical aspects to do with how we interact with a text. Sometimes, you will also see these areas described as **semiotics** – the study of how 'signs' of different kinds are interpreted, and how they relate to each other. At the most basic level, the idea of a sign can be a logo or an image; but it can achieve a meaning larger than itself by pointing outwards from a text and linking with other, similar references within a culture.

When discussing the pragmatics of the 'Dear Santa' text, the idea of the type of dog featured in the text was mentioned. A semiotic approach to that image would consider how dogs are represented in UK culture – what they are associated with, whether different breeds are connected with different ideas, and so on. For example, currently there is an O2 communications advertisement with the slogan 'be more dog', where the idea of the dog is associated with being bold and adventurous.

Did you know?

An influential figure in the field of pragmatics was the philosopher H. P. Grice, who was interested in the difference between what people said and what they meant. He suggested a **co-operative principle** for language use, whereby speakers assume that others try to speak the truth, try to be relevant, and try to give the right amount of information. These ideas have come to be called Grice's 'maxims'. Read about Grice in *Babel* magazine's free digital copy at http://www. babelzine.com/docs/2013/ issue1/index.html

Key terms

Co-operative principle. An idea from the philosopher H. P. Grice that in conversations, speakers expect others to share certain basic rules of co-operation, such as telling the truth.

Gender. The social expectations that arise as a result of being one sex or another.

Semiotics. The study of how signs and symbols work within human communication.

Did you know?

The idea of discourses as shaping the way we think and creating a sense of reality is associated with the French philosopher Michel Foucault (1926–1984).

! REMEMBER

Linking between texts is called intertextuality: this was discussed earlier in this chapter, in relation to Assessment Objective 4 (see page 8).

Intertextuality is hard at work in 'Dear Santa', but this doesn't become clear until you open the pamphlet and recognize it fully as a charity advertisement, not simply as a child's pleading letter to Father Christmas. The back of the pamphlet, reproduced below, suggests that instead of buying your child a puppy, you could use the money to sponsor a puppy for guide dog training on behalf of your child – to support blind and partially sighted people. The type of puppy is of course a breed that is regularly used for guiding. But the breed has also featured on TV advertisements for different products for many years (representing a cuddly playmate for children). Another relevant piece of cultural knowledge is that puppies bought as Christmas presents are sometimes rapidly abandoned afterwards. An animal charity campaign was set up with the slogan 'A dog is for life, not just for Christmas'. Adults who read this charity appeal will at some level be aware of all these intertextual echoes.

As with all the other language levels that have been described, discourses can and do change over time. Although genres work because we recognize that they fit into a system of texts, producers of texts try new ways to refresh their message.

The group of three texts opposite shows writers using well-known genres but taking new approaches to the communication. The first text is a notice that guests hang on the door of their hotel room when they don't want cleaners to come in; the second is a guarantee label that was attached to a dress bought in Vancouver, Canada; the third is the front of a card that a railway company places on tables and in seat pockets throughout train carriages.

 Activity

Read the three texts opposite and, referring to the language levels as appropriate, comment on the ways in which they are adopting new approaches to traditional genres. Also consider, for each text, how much pragmatic knowledge about cultural practices is required to understand it.

There is some feedback on this activity at the back of the book.

pleaz^{zzz}
don't
disturb

A Great Night's Sleep Guaranteed — **Premier Inn**
premierinn.com

OUR GUARANTEE

If you don't get a compliment within three wearings, send it back. Or if you find something wrong with it we'll take it back for refund or replacement, no questions asked. Easy, huh?

Vous n'avez pas reçu de compliments après que vous ayez porté le vêtement trois fois? Retournez-le. Pour toutes insatisfactions, nous le remplacerons ou nous vous rembourserons sans poser de questions. Facile, n'est-ce pas?

Feel at home with our
House Rules

So that all our customers can enjoy their journey with us.

For more information please visit eastcoast.co.uk/houserules

FEEL AT HOME
EAST COAST

REVIEW YOUR LEARNING

- Have you understood the key features of the AQA English Language AS level and A level specifications?
- Do you understand the different Assessment Objectives?
- Are you aware of the different writing skills that you need to develop?
- Do you understand the language levels that underpin the study of English Language?

If you have understood the aspects above, then you are ready to learn about how to apply the analytical methods that underpin the specifications. The first area you will learn more about is textual variation and representation.

Further reading

Do some further exploration of the online sites that you have been pointed towards in this introductory chapter (for example, the referencing site, the phonemic chart, the collection of speeches). Search for some more online resources yourself, such as good dictionary sites that include etymological information and thesaurus options. Set up a way to organize the links you find – for example, you could use delicious.com to create your own database.

There are many further online resources, particularly on university sites. For example, University College London has a grammar page at the following address: http://www.ucl.ac.uk/internet-grammar/home.htm

References

Berry, M., Carbaugh, D. and Nurmikari-Berry, M. (2004). 'Communicating Finnish Quietude: A Pedagogical Process for Discovering Implicit Cultural Meanings in Languages', *Language and Intercultural Communication*. Vol. 4, Issue 4. Taylor and Francis.

Goddard, A. (2005). *Being Online*. University of Nottingham PhD thesis.

Hoffman, E. (2008) *Lost in Translation: A Life in a New Language*. Vintage Books.

Simon, J. (1980) 'The Corruption of English', in Michaels, L., and Ricks, C. (eds) *The State of the Language*. Berkeley and Los Angeles: University of California Press.

This chapter will:

- help you understand the nature of textual variation
- give you some frameworks for analysing texts of different kinds
- show you how and why representation is a key concept in the specification.

AS Level and A Level assessment

Paper 1 of both the AS level and the A level requires you to show that you can analyse texts of different kinds. The texts that will be presented to you can come from any source, but they will have a theme in common. The theme won't necessarily be language – it can be any topic. The topic itself is irrelevant, because what is being tested is not your knowledge of different subjects, but your ability to say how texts convey their messages.

Having a common topic is helpful to you because it allows you to see the issue of **representation** more clearly than if the texts had been on different topics. If texts on a common theme express their ideas differently about that theme, then it is easier for you to think about why those differences and variations exist.

The texts presented to you for analysis on both the AS level Paper 1 (Language and the Individual) and the A level Paper 1 (Language, the Individual and Society) will also display significant differences. For example, they may be different in **genre**, or text type. They may differ in their **mode**: one may originally have been spoken, while the other was written; or one written text may be from a digital and interactive site, while the other is from a paper-based source. The texts may differ in their purposes and they may have been aimed originally at very different audiences. All of these dimensions are important aspects of variation, and they give you points to discuss.

One distinctive difference between the AS level task and the A level task is that the A level paper will include a text from an earlier historical period. The factor of time is always relevant in text analysis work in general, because texts can date very quickly. Writers can also deliberately create a 'retro' feel in their texts by using **intertextual** techniques – linking their text with those of former times. However, the A level English Language qualification specifically includes the topic of language change, and this is not covered at AS level; therefore it is appropriate to emphasize changes over time more at A level than at AS.

The older text on the A level paper could come from any period from 1600 onwards. This date was chosen because it represents the beginning of what is known as 'modern English'; that is English which is recognizably connected with the language we use today. The idea of connection is important, because there will still be a common theme to explore. Don't think of the A level text analysis as asking you about the history of English. Think about the older text in the same way as you think about modern texts – ask yourself what the text is (and was) trying to communicate, how it does this, and why it is using language in this way.

Text analysis skills are fundamental to the A level qualification more generally. Paper 2 of the A level includes a text analysis task that focuses on how people express their attitudes to language change and diversity. You may also choose to use text analysis as your methodology for your investigation coursework. See Chapter 7 for information about the investigation.

Relevant Assessment Objectives

Both AS level Paper 1 and A level Paper 1 help you to structure your text analysis work by splitting your task into three parts: an analysis of the first text; an analysis of the second text; and, finally, an analysis of the similarities and differences between the two texts. All three parts carry a similar weighting.

Did you know?

The term 'text' originally meant 'something woven'. You can still see this meaning in the related word 'textile'. Other terms also liken the weaving of words to other kinds of material creations: for example, 'spinning a yarn', and 'a tissue of lies', as well as the word 'material' itself. A story can be 'fabricated', which originally meant 'made with skill', like 'fabric'.

The question on each of the texts asks you to analyse how they use language to create **meanings** and **representations**. Your answer is credited for AO1 (your use of relevant aspects of the language levels and the terms associated with them, plus the coherence of your writing) and for AO3 (how language features build into patterns of meaning and are shaped by context – including genre, audience, purpose, and mode). A level answers will also be expected to consider the factor of the time period, for the older text.

The third question asks you about connections, through the instruction to compare and contrast the texts; and this aspect is rewarded through AO4.

A level Paper 2 Section B (Language Discourses) includes a compulsory text analysis task on two extracts where writers express their attitudes towards language use. The analysis is also credited through AO1, AO3, and AO4.

What is a text?

One of the most interesting things about studying language in the way required for the English Language A Level is that any piece of language can be studied. Unlike literary study, where there is often debate about which texts are worthy of study, linguistic study does not make any assumptions about value or merit in the texts studied. You will not be studying texts to see 'good' (in the sense of valuable, skilful or impressive) examples of language use. Rather, we study texts to see *how* language is used – warts and all.

Activity

1. Look through your pockets and/or bag and bring out as many examples of texts as you are happy to share. Don't dismiss anything by saying it's not big enough or doesn't have enough writing to be called a text – anything that communicates a message can be called a text. If you have digital devices, give one or two examples of communication from those sources. In addition to what you carry in your pockets or bag, you could also think about what you are wearing: our bodies can be seen as walking texts, expressing meanings through the logos and statements (or even just the colours) that adorn our carrier bags, badges, hats and T-shirts. The T-shirt worn by the young man in the photograph recycles an old sexist joke by using the language of new technologies: it says CTRL+ALT+DEL MY MOTHER IN LAW PLEASE

2. When you have gathered all your texts together, classify them by inventing headings and grouping the texts under each heading.

3. Choose three of the found texts from one of your categories and then make notes about how this commonality affects the language used.

4. So far, you have been thinking about the meanings conveyed by the texts and how an analyst might go about classifying different examples. But texts do more than communicate a message from A to B; they also represent people and ideas. This is more than just what something 'means', which is why in your exam you are asked about 'meanings and representations'.

Key term

Meanings. Messages that are communicated. Meanings are never fixed, but are negotiated between speakers (or writers) and listeners (or readers), and vary considerably according to context.

Old joke, new technology

▶

In the photograph overleaf, the young man's T-shirt communicates a message. But it also represents him, as the wearer; and it requires us to take up a position in response. It expresses ideas about him – about his sense of humour, about his attitude to technology, about his idea of masculinity. It recycles a familiar **discourse** about women, and that discourse goes beyond a single individual to represent wider cultural attitudes and values. But the T-shirt also represents a foreign language, because the wearer is Turkish. So does he understand the message himself? Do we always understand the messages that we use to decorate our bodies?

How does your collection of texts represent you? What do they say about you and about the culture you live in? If you are working in a group, a good way to answer this question would be to pass your texts to another member of the group and ask him or her to describe how the texts represent their 'owner'.

How are texts studied?

You have already been introduced to the language levels used for analysis in Chapter 1. Chapter 2 will explore these in more detail. From the outset, it is important to think about the language levels in an interconnected way, and not as isolated areas. Similarly, the different aspects of context are inter-related.

Think about the language used in this textbook. It is **multimodal** because it has pictures and diagrams as well as words, so this is an aspect of mode. Its multimodal nature is connected with its purpose to inform, and information is key because of the target audience. The language tries not to be overly formal, because its aim is to be accessible to a wide range of students; but, at the same time, slang terms are avoided, because these could be read as patronizing. A feature of the book's information structure is its division into chapters, with headings, key terms, an index, and other aspects of design which allow readers to spot **salient** features and locate information more easily. This type of design is typical of a reference text, and other examples of the genre would include recipe books and car manuals, where reading is not cover-to-cover, but focused on specific areas as needs arise.

You should already have grasped the essential point that, in terms of both language levels and contextual aspects, nothing exists in isolation. But precisely because texts are complex entities where all the aspects are connected, a good analysis has to be well structured in order to move logically from one point to the next.

Getting started: texts as material

The way in which a text appears and has been produced is relevant when assessing the meanings it creates or supports. For example, if a class of small children were asked to draw 'a bank', they might need to be told whether a riverbank or a high-street bank was the intended subject. However, on a street plan, it is sufficient to write 'bank', as the word's location allows us to understand the word in its context.

Key terms

Multimodal. A multimodal text employs more than one mode of communication – for example, by using images as well as words, or by drawing on an aspect of speech as well as writing.

Salient. Most important, prominent, or noteworthy.

! REMEMBER

Text analysis at this level means linking any text's language features with its context in as detailed and precise a way as possible. But don't lose sight of the 'big picture' – how the text represents its subject matter.

Words work alongside pictures to create meanings, and you need to discuss both. As soon as you do this, you are using the language level of **graphology** and you are talking about **mode.**

Where and when a text was produced can be an important factor in contributing to its meanings. You need to consider these aspects of context when analysing all texts, not just those that have a historical text as part of the A level pairing. Later in this chapter you will be able to explore a pair of texts on a common theme, one of which is from 1604. However, there are historical changes between texts that are much closer together in time, and you would need to discuss this aspect regardless of the qualification you are studying for. Don't ignore the idea of 'history' just because you are working at AS level: think about the radical changes to our textual **repertoires** over the past 20 years, as a result of new technologies. In textual history, a few years can make a massive difference, so explore anything that seems relevant.

As well as aspects of time, aspects of place and space are also very important. Any exam paper will always give you some indication of where a text is from, so that you can think about its original appearance in spatial as well as temporal terms.

Activity

The text below was mounted on the wall of a public toilet at a busy bus station in a Devon town. Why do you think East Devon District Council decided to put the notice there?

Analyse the language of the text, including all of its graphological aspects. What meanings and representations are created by the language choices?

A sign displayed by East Devon District Council

Link

See Chapter 7 for information about analysing images in the investigation part of your coursework.

! REMEMBER

Producers of texts sometimes go for a 'retro' feel, particularly if they want to create nostalgia for past times. A classic example is the Hovis bread TV advertisements that represented an idyllic Yorkshire village of cobbled streets and cottages, with a baker's delivery boy pushing an old-fashioned bicycle.

Link

To research advertisements from the past – and, if the product is still current, to compare them with present day advertising – visit the Museum of Advertising Brands, either online at http://www.museumofbrands.com or in person, in London.

Research idea

Explore the spatial aspect of context by collecting some examples of language that take important aspects of their meaning from their physical placement. You could collect the data by taking pictures of the texts, and if you wanted to test out how important physical placement is, you could ask different people how they understand the messages, and where they think the messages were originally placed. For more ideas see Scollon (2003) in the Further reading section. ●

Who are they talking to? Ideas about audience

When writing about audience, it is important to think as specifically as possible. Obviously, the location of a text will provide some information about audience, but this is not the whole story. For example, a newspaper column about Twitter etiquette is likely to be read by people from all of the following groups:

- regular readers of the particular newspaper
- fans of the specific columnist
- people interested in Twitter and the ways in which people behave on social media.

It is usually possible to make some assumptions about audience from a text's location, genre and topic, but this does not always tell you everything about the type of audience that the writer/speaker had in mind when producing the text. For example, a piece about Twitter etiquette may well be written for those new to the site, but it could also be intended as entertainment for those 'in the know'. Either of these choices would influence the way in which the piece has been written, and would be clear when reading it.

Activity

Imagine that you are writing a piece about social-media etiquette, focusing on a platform you know well (such as Twitter, Facebook, or Tumblr). List five features or ideas that you could include:

a) for an inexperienced audience

b) for an audience familiar with the platform.

Key terms

Audience construction. In language study, texts are seen as constructing audiences, not just addressing them. This means that texts create an idea of who the audience is, by 'speaking' to them in a certain way.

Narratee. A fictional receiver; the person that the text appears to be aimed at.

Narrator. A fictional 'teller'; the apparent voice behind the text as created by the author.

A further level of awareness is needed when thinking about audience. **Audience construction** refers to how audiences are constructed through the language chosen by the writer or speaker. When you completed the activity above, you had an idea in your mind about what the audience was like in each case. Assumptions about what others know, and the ways in which those assumptions shape our language use, are part of the language level of **pragmatics**. To explore this, you need to forget about writers and readers as real people and think more about the idea of **narrators** and **narratees**. The narrator of any text is the persona or fictionalized figure that is chosen by the writer. However conscious or unconscious you were of the process, the language choices you made in your writing created the idea of a person behind the text. You will have changed your persona or narrative voice when you wrote for a different audience in the activity above.

Activity

Go back to the East Devon District Council notice on page 33.

What kind of narrative voice is created by the language used in the text? What kind of person do you imagine addressing you? We don't know who the real writer was, but the language choices in the text give a strong impression of a kind of character. This is what is meant by a narrator.

There is some feedback on this activity at the back of the book.

Earlier in this explanation of audience construction the term 'narratee' was used. Just as the language choices in a text create a sense of a certain kind of person addressing us, those same language choices create an idea of who the audience is. This might, of course, be very different from who we really are. This fictionalized idea of an audience is a text's narratee.

For example, the assumed or implied audience of the East Devon District Council notice are not the 'irresponsible dog owners' referred to in the text, but people who are being encouraged to take action against them. In reality, all sorts of people would read a notice like this, so the real audience is bound to include some 'irresponsible dog owners'. So, as you can see, it is useful to separate the real people who exist at either ends of a text from the fictionalized figures constructed by the language used in the text. This can perhaps be more easily understood diagrammatically, as shown below.

Real writer or speaker → Narrator → **TEXT** → Narratee → Real reader or listener

What is it and what's it for? Ideas about genre and purpose

You will have seen, when analysing the texts that you carry around with you, that texts rarely have a single purpose. For example, a magazine article about the latest music or fashion trend may give you information, but is that really why people pick up a magazine? Many texts that we encounter have multiple purposes: such a magazine article could be said to have a primary purpose of entertaining (since that is probably why someone would be reading a magazine in the first place) and a secondary purpose of informing. It is more sensible, therefore, to think in terms of multiple purposes for texts, while recognizing that there may be a primary purpose that you can identify for particular attention.

Purpose and genre are closely connected, because central to the concept of genre is the idea of family resemblances between texts, and this can be on the basis of a text's purposes or social functions. Hodge & Kress define a genre as: 'a kind of text that derives its form from the structure of a (frequently repeated) social occasion, with its characteristic participants and their purposes' (Hodge & Kress 1988: 183).

Part of the distinctiveness of different genres is also, of course, reflected in the features of language use that recur. We expect a shopping list, or a joke, or a phone call, or an email to have some recognizable and distinctive language features and routines. But genres are not fixed: they are very fluid, and open to dispute and interpretation. They also vary culturally, with differences in how groups expect genres to work: for example, phone call routines vary a lot between different groups. Examiners are aware of the complexities of genre, so you should not feel that you have to come up with definitive answers: the important quality to show is that of active thinking.

! **REMEMBER**

Narrators and narratees don't just exist in the world of novels and advertising. You become a narrator when you write an essay, or even a diary that only you will read. Speakers also adopt different narrative voices: think about the different representations of yourself that you construct when you speak to different people.

Research idea

Collect a range of texts that construct their audiences in very particular ways. You could focus just on written texts, or on spoken texts – for example, by collecting a range of speeches. Or you could study multimodal texts, by collecting examples from TV or online sources. Analyse your data by identifying the aspects of language that contribute to the narrative constructions. ●

Did you know?

Etymologically, genre simply means 'type', and you can see in the word that it is related to other kinds of categories – for example, 'gender', 'genealogy', 'genus' (ideas about people or things having characteristics in common).

Activity

Go back to your own collection of texts, taken from your bag or pockets, and look at them again from the perspectives of purpose and genre.

● What are the purposes of the different texts you had in your possession?
● How many different genres of text can you identify in your collection?

Compare your findings with those of your classmates, if possible. Are there any texts that are difficult to categorize? If so, why?

Key terms

Affordances. Things that are made possible. For example, a website can be read by many people simultaneously.

Computer-mediated communication (CMC). Human communication that takes place via the medium of computers.

Hybrid. Hybrids are blends of two or more elements. For example, new forms of communication are often seen as having some of the characteristics of both spoken and written language.

Interlocutors. People engaged in a spoken interaction.

Limitations. Things that are prevented or restricted. For example, an SMS has no way to convey the subtleties of non-verbal communication (hence the need for emoticons).

Literacy. Literacy refers primarily to reading and writing, including the new types of reading and writing that occur in digital contexts. ▶

Traditionally, a text's mode was seen as a simple question of whether it was written or spoken, with various aspects of texts ascribed to their 'writtenness' or 'spokenness'. If you compare something like a paper-based encyclopaedia with a casual face-to-face conversation, you can clearly see that the writing and speech in these particular genres would have different characteristics. The writing would have been composed at the keyboard, using visual symbols, while the speech would have been communicated through sound, using oral and aural systems. The speech would have been produced in real time, while the written text could have been read, or not, at any time after its production. Unless the speech had been recorded, it would have probably been forgotten by the **interlocutors**, while the book could be revisited many times. The language used in the two genres would have been very different, with informal and perhaps non-standard styles of speech featuring in the spoken interaction and being supported by prosodic, paralinguistic and non-verbal aspects of spontaneous communication rooted in a shared physical space. The written text would have been highly planned and edited, formal in style, using Standard English and having to make sense without the ability to re-run any elements of ambiguity or non-comprehension.

This all sounds very neat and tidy, but unfortunately attempts to draw up checklists of features that characterize speech and writing are doomed to failure. The differences above only work because the two genres chosen represent extremes of difference. Note that even the encyclopaedia had to be specified as a paper-based text – because times have moved on, and encyclopaedias can now be highly interactive and include sound and video as part of a digital presence. But even thinking about as simple and everyday a tool as a messaging system on a computer or phone, shows you that traditional ideas about speech and writing cannot be applied: our communication in these contexts is interactive, like speech, but also editable at a keyboard, like writing.

You can perhaps see why our constantly evolving new communication genres are often described as **hybrids**, because they have features of both speech and writing as they were formerly understood. Modern thinking about mode cannot rely on what went before, so it has to take a different approach and consider the **affordances** and **limitations** of any particular format – in other words, what any communication tool allows us to do, and what it prevents us from doing or limits our ability to do.

Ideas about mode are not just about new technologies, however. Older texts can combine different modes in order to convey meaning, and some linguists – for example Gunther Kress (2003) – argue that this has been overlooked in an over-simplification of how texts work. For example, any text that uses images alongside written text is using different modes of communication and is therefore **multimodal** in its operation. If you look back at the East Devon District Council notice and several others in this book, you will see that all of them could be described as multimodal, because they use combinations of images and written text to convey their meanings.

Similarly, some linguists have argued that older ideas about speech and writing as different systems have been unhelpful, because they have obscured the important connections between the two. While writing is certainly not just speech written down, speech and writing are interconnected, as you saw in the examples of students representing speech in their online writing in Chapter 1. You will return to the connections between **oracy** and **literacy** when you look at children's language in Chapter 4.

Activity

In order to test out the approaches to mode described above, do the following:

1. Focusing on any of the texts in your collection, or on any of the texts that have appeared in this book up to this point, explore the idea of multimodality: does the text communicate by using more than one symbolic system? If so, explain how this works.

2. Focus on any 'new communication' genre. Include SMS and email, although these are older than more recent tools such as Twitter. You can also include published texts, such as online newspapers and magazines. Explain the affordances and limitations of this type of communication. What are the texts able to do, and what are you able to do in response to them? What is more difficult or problematic in using or responding to your chosen genre?

3. Having established your ideas, identify examples of the language choices that are associated with the affordances or limitations you've identified.

Key term

Oracy. Speaking and listening, the skills required to communicate in spoken language.

Bringing aspects of context together

So far, you have been introduced to:

- the language levels that are relevant to English Language study (in Chapter 1) and that are assessed through AO1

- aspects of context (in this chapter) that are assessed through AO3.

As has already been outlined, these two AOs form the basis for the assessment of your text analysis work. In addition, AO4 rewards you for being able to compare and contrast texts.

Now it is time for you to get some more hands-on experience of working with texts of different kinds. On the following pages are ten texts that share the common theme of dogs.

Activity

Carefully read all of the following texts (A–J). Each text has been taken from a very different context. Identify the key contextual factors for each text, and then select some language features to comment on for each one. You should also refer back to the Guide Dogs for the Blind charity advertisement in Chapter 1 (pages 17 and 28) and the East Devon District Council public notice in this chapter (page 33) and add those texts to the collection below.

When you have done some preparatory work for all of the texts, choose two to analyse formally and write about in more detail. Follow the sequence of the exam question format in your analysis:

1 Analyse how your first text uses language to create meanings and representations.

2 Analyse how your second text uses language to create meanings and representations.

3 Explore similarities and differences in the ways in which your two texts use language.

At the end of texts A–J is a set of prompts, which will help you to identify some language features in your chosen pairing.

Text A: Dog show announcement

This transcript is from a village dog show, where the judge is announcing the names of the dogs that have won.

> Judge: in third position (1.0) is **Bu**ttons [*sound of cheering and clapping*]
>
> Judge: in second position is (1.0) **Lot**tie [*sound of louder cheering and clapping*]
>
> Member of audience: [*to his dog, in response to its bark*] **oh** was that a comment?
>
> Judge: and in first position (1.0) and this was a unanimous choice by the panel as a very worthy winner (2.0) is **Fer**gie [*sound of very loud cheering and lengthy clapping*]

Transcription key

(.) normal pause

(1.0) numbers in brackets indicate length of pauses in seconds

bold indicates a stressed syllable

[ ] square brackets indicate contextual information

Text B: Dog training school

This extract is from a document published online, explaining the work done by the Devon and Cornwall Police to train their police dogs.

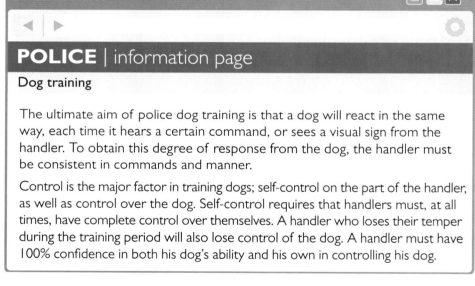

Web Browser

POLICE | information page

Dog training

The ultimate aim of police dog training is that a dog will react in the same way, each time it hears a certain command, or sees a visual sign from the handler. To obtain this degree of response from the dog, the handler must be consistent in commands and manner.

Control is the major factor in training dogs; self-control on the part of the handler, as well as control over the dog. Self-control requires that handlers must, at all times, have complete control over themselves. A handler who loses their temper during the training period will also lose control of the dog. A handler must have 100% confidence in both his dog's ability and his own in controlling his dog.

Text C: Love Your Dog website

This extract is part of a website called 'How To Love Your Dog... A Kid's Guide to Dog Care'.

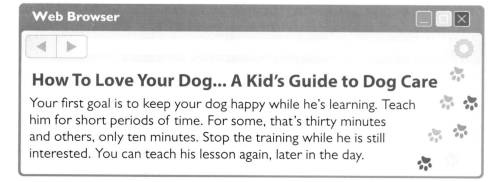

Web Browser

How To Love Your Dog... A Kid's Guide to Dog Care

Your first goal is to keep your dog happy while he's learning. Teach him for short periods of time. For some, that's thirty minutes and others, only ten minutes. Stop the training while he is still interested. You can teach his lesson again, later in the day.

Text D: Poem

This is from *I Could Chew On This and Other Poems by Dogs*, by Francesco Marciuliano – a collection written as if by dogs.

I Lose My Mind When You Leave the House
The plants are torn
The garbage strewn
The wires chewed
The couch and I had a fight
Your bed is soaked
Your liquor spilled
Your TV smashed
Your laptop no longer has any vowels
There's a smartphone in the toaster
There's a toaster in the toilet
There's a toilet in the hallway
There's underwear in my mouth
I went places I should never go
I saw a side of myself I should never see
I said things to the cat I can never take back
So please don't ever leave again

Text E: Newspaper article

This is an extract from an article featured in the *Observer*, 10 November 2013.

Dangerous dogs: oh don't worry, he really doesn't mean you any harm

by Catherine Bennett

Since, statistically, a small dog may bite as often, if not more, than a large one, defenders of scary-looking animals rally behind the slogan 'the deed, not the breed'. This would have been a soothing thought a few weeks ago when, trotting apathetically around Hampstead Heath, in north London, I heard a woman shouting in panic, turned, and saw a mastiff-like creature, around the size of a small pony or wild pig, charging towards me in what looked, to a non-dog-expert, to be a mood of murderous ferocity. At a minimum, its behaviour was not compliant with byelaw 21 – control.

The deed, not the breed, I could have thought cheerfully to myself as I waited to be mauled; the deed, not the breed, trust the massive-dog enthusiasts, physical measurements count for nothing. In the event, the only comfort came from the sight, as the animal got close, of a muzzle over its jaws: at least it could only stamp, scratch or butt me to a pulp.

Anticlimactically – I apologise – to relate, the spirited pet had only managed some circling and lunging and rearing its paws down my back before its supposed walker caught up. She shouted, made the thing retreat, whacked it, failed to get a lead on it, said sorry, then, hearing the word 'police', made for the woods, accompanied, at some distance, by a sullen Fido.

Text F: A pavement sign in Vancouver, Canada

The sign on the right is advertising a pub by picturing a dog using a particular form of language called 'Doge' – a made-up language, like Lolspeak, supposedly used by dogs to express their identities. Read about Doge in the following *Guardian* article. Make sure that you also read the responses to the journalist's article:

http://www.theguardian.com/technology/2014/feb/18/doge-such-questions-very-answered

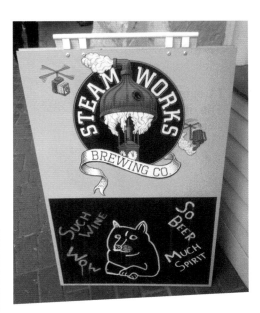

A sign advertising a pub in Vancouver, Canada

Text G: Novel extract

This extract is from *Hero* by Sarah Lean, a novel aimed at young readers.

I didn't know if dogs had imaginations or if they thought like us at all, but this little dog looked me right in the eye and turned his head to the side as if he was asking the same question that I was: How can you lose when you're the hero of your own story? Which was a bit strange seeing as nobody can see what's in your imagination.

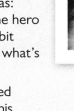

I leaned up on my elbows and stared back. The dog had ginger fur over his ears and eyes, like his own kind of helmet hiding who he really was, and circles like ginger biscuits on his white back.

Text H: A vaccination record for a pet dog

Text I: Game fair brochure

This extract describes a competitive activity at a country fair where dogs are set challenges to perform.

GUNDOG SCURRY

Blind Retrieve

50 yard (approx) launch of single seen dummy. Dog to retrieve this before launch of second seen dummy. Time recorded is total time to retrieve both.

Text J: A tweet by an individual about the behaviour of her two dogs

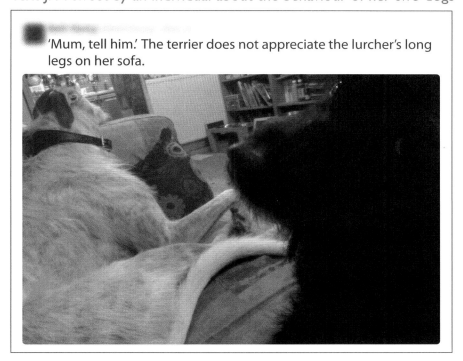

'Mum, tell him.' The terrier does not appreciate the lurcher's long legs on her sofa.

Below are some prompts to help you think about the language levels you studied in Chapter 1 and in this chapter. The identification and labelling of features is an important first stage of analysis. But you will see, as you work, that the areas do not work in isolation, but are connected. A good analysis will therefore use the identified features as a basis from which to build a picture of how the texts work overall. There are some examples of features given for each area, to get you started.

● **Graphological** aspects – all aspects of textual appearance, design and arrangement, such as: colour, typeface, layout, logos and other symbols, images, punctuation, links and other aspects of digital text, multimodality. Examples above: the different images of dogs and how they relate to the written texts they accompany; different layouts and their connections with genres.

- **Phonological** aspects – the use of sounds and prosodics (volume, pitch, stress and intonation patterns), paralinguistic effects, aspects of connected speech, the physical environment in which face-to-face speech is embedded; how sounds are symbolized and manipulated in writing to achieve particular effects. Examples above: phonology of 'announcements' and audience behaviour in A; the manipulation of sound patterning in the public notice (page 33) phrase 'scooping the poop'; in E 'the deed, not the breed'; the construction of a dog 'voice' in some of the texts.

- **Lexical and semantic** aspects – formality and informality, taboo and euphemism, connotation, collocation, semantic fields (registers), idiomatic language, changes in meaning, social variations, metaphor and simile, naming and terms of address. Examples above: the dog names in A and E; formality in B; American English in D; taboo in the public notice; simile in G – 'circles like ginger biscuits'; register in B, H and I.

- **Grammatical** aspects – pronouns, modifiers, verbs, sentence types and functions, word order. Examples: repeated structures in D and E; gendered pronouns in B and C; rule-breaking in F; ellipsis in I; modal verbs in B; instructions via imperatives in C; point of view and pronoun use in the texts.

- **Pragmatic** aspects – inference, assumed shared meanings, politeness, routines and rituals, cultural variations, narrators, audience construction. Examples: ritual and routine in A; politeness in the public notice; audience construction in B, C and D; variation in who narrates the texts; language play; assumed knowledge of aspects of human–canine relationships.

- **Discourse** – cohesion, genre, context, different discourses. Examples: different genres of text, each with their own internal structure and distinctive features; mode; different purposes and audiences; what the texts reveal as a collection about our society's attitudes towards dogs (different ways of talking and writing about dogs).

Discourses

Working on a range of texts with a common theme should have helped you to see how analysis benefits from a shared topic. You can immediately see some different ways in which people in a community or across a whole society talk and write about a topic, including ways in which they play with and break rules as well as follow familiar formats. Rule-breaking in genres is important – otherwise we would be trapped within pieces of formulaic communication and be unable to show any creativity.

The text analysis tasks in Paper 1 of both the AS level and the A level use a shared topic, because they aim to help you do the kind of work you have just done, which is to see beyond individual texts and think more generally about how we use language to represent ideas about 'how things are'. There is limited scope in a timed assessment to explore this fully, but the whole of the AQA English Language specification is underpinned by this idea. How does language use create a sense of reality for the users? How does it define who we think we are? How does the way in which messages are framed construct particular attitudes and values? In attempting to answer these questions, the concept of discourses (in the plural) is key.

As explained in Chapter 1, the concept of discourses constructing our realities owes much to the work of the French philosopher Michel Foucault. Foucault regarded the role of language as crucial in establishing norms in our thinking and behaviour that seem so natural to us that we don't question them. Foucault saw that unpicking the way in which discourses work and achieve this air of naturalness, can reveal power structures within society, and give people the ability to resist and fight back. In modern language study, this idea of analysing texts in order to reveal and question the powerful vested interests behind them is referred to as **critical discourse analysis**.

You may be wondering what connection there is between a batch of texts about dogs and the idea of constructing realities. In fact, the collection you have just been studying reveals a lot about how people in our society view these animals. They are clearly a great source of play, pleasure and pride to humans, and we value the emotional connections we have with them, but we also feel the need to regulate them in different ways – training, dealing with their health needs and bodily functions – and we are aware of their potential ferocity as wild animals that we have domesticated. All of the attitudes expressed are culture-specific, and you would find a different set of discourses in a different culture. For example, in the UK we don't think of dogs as edible animals, as in some other cultures – so there are no recipes here.

The ability to stand back and take a text apart to reveal how writers and speakers construct their views of the world is particularly important for the text analysis task on A level Paper 2, which concerns discourses about language. Unlike Paper 1 text analysis tasks, where the topic is irrelevant, the text analysis task on A level Paper 2 is always about language itself. Language is a topic as well as a skill, and people have as many attitudes towards language as they have towards any other topic. Paper 2 of the A level is entitled 'Language Diversity and Change', so the texts for you to analyse in Section B of that paper, which also form a stimulus for a directed writing task, are focused on the idea of language change and language variety.

Language variety is covered in the next chapter, Language and People; and Language Change is the topic of Chapter 5. When you come to your Paper 2 text analysis task, you will therefore have many ideas about how language varies and changes. But in analysing the texts you are presented with, you will need to apply all the same skills you develop in analysing texts in general, in order to show that you understand how texts work.

Critical discourse approaches

Critical discourse analysis tries to show how people make claims to power in the texts that they produce. Taking these claims apart requires an understanding of how they are put together in the first place. To help you in this work, there are some aspects of language that are worth exploring in more detail from the list of language levels you worked with earlier.

As a starting point, it is useful to recognize that the same word or phrase, particularly an abstract one such as 'language', can be coloured in different ways, depending on what surrounds it in a sentence or utterance.

> **Key term**
>
> **Critical discourse analysis.** A type of text analysis that tries to reveal the power structures that are maintained in society through the discourses used.

Did you know?

Erving Goffman was the originator of **Face Theory**, the idea that we all present a 'face' in each conversation we have. This may be a clear role, like 'customer', or it may be related to our purpose in that conversation, like 'listening friend'. The ways in which speakers protect, support or challenge each other's faces is described as **facework**. Face theory has been developed further to include the idea that we all have two basic face needs that are constantly in tension. Our **positive face need** is to be accepted and liked, while our **negative face need** is to be independent, and not to be imposed upon. A **face-threatening act** (FTA) directly challenges someone's face needs.

Key terms

Face Theory. The idea that we all have a public self-image that we need to project and protect.

Face-threatening act. In Face Theory, something that threatens a person's self-image.

Facework. The effort that we put in to manage our public image.

Framing. The idea that speakers mark their understanding of the context they are in. For example, by smiling or laughing to show that they are being playful.

Negative face need. In face theory, the need not to be imposed on by another person. ▶

Activity

Look at the following sentences, which were all found in an online search for the phrase 'English language'. How does each one seem to view English? What attitudes towards English do you think the producers of these sentences hold? In answering these questions, you are exploring the pragmatics of language use: each of these writers has a set of assumptions about what English language 'means', both to them and to you as a reader supposedly sharing their perspective.

1. The English language belongs to the Anglo-Frisian sub-group of the West Germanic branch of the Germanic languages.
2. Are 'grammar Nazis' ruining our English language?
3. English is being mangled by new technologies and it is being destroyed before our very eyes. Fight back!
4. GCSE English Language allows students to show their ability to analyse language and to use language creatively.
5. You might need to prove your knowledge of the English language if you're over 18 and applying for citizenship or to settle in the UK.
6. The English language is a vast flea market of words, handed down, borrowed or created over more than 2000 years.

- The various representations here include the idea of English language as one of many languages within a category (sentence 1). This representation takes a very scholarly and structural approach to English – viewing it as something to be classified.

- Sentences 2 and 3 both see language as something under attack. In these representations of English, it seems to need protection from the control of destructive people and machines. 'Nazis' in particular has extremely strong connotations, implying that these people are committing a terrible crime against English.

- Sentence 4 presents English as an academic school subject, a skill and a form of communication.

- Sentence 5 represents English as a badge of membership, which has to be shown in order to join a group. English is seen as a skill to be demonstrated or perhaps a hurdle to be jumped in order to achieve your goals.

- Sentence 6 suggests that English has a lively and interesting history, but one that has resulted in a messy situation. The flea-market idea perhaps implies a lack of organization or something ungoverned – quite a contrast to the 'grammar Nazis' or the academic tool suggested in some of the other sentences.

One way of thinking about how the descriptions above work is to draw on the idea of **framing** in discourse. This idea, from Erving Goffman, uses the image of a picture frame in thinking about language use. Picture frames function to make the space inside them something distinctively different from whatever surrounds them. In the same way, we signal through our language choices how we intend our communication to be understood. This idea has taken a modern twist in our use of emoticons to ensure that those on the receiving end of our digital texts don't misunderstand our meanings. We can, for example, use emoticons to signal that we are being playful and don't expect to be taken seriously.

The idea of framing can be useful in pointing out different registers of language – the field-specific styles of language that indicate speakers or writers are in a particular context. For example, doctor–patient dialogues and the language used in a courtroom are examples of different registers, and therefore different frames are in action in these situations.

Looking back at the six sentences in the activity opposite can help you to explore this further. It doesn't take long to identify the larger frames from which these opinions have been taken. Sentences 1 and 6 are in an explanatory frame, suggesting some kind of academic information source. Sentences 2 and 3 are in a 'complaint' frame, expressing the kinds of views that feature in conservative newspapers. Sentences 4 and 5 suggest an official, institutional frame – of education and immigration, respectively.

Whatever the frame, all of the examples offer representations of the world as the writer sees it. This really takes us inside the picture frame, to think about how the picture has been painted – who is in the picture, what they are doing, who is in the foreground, and so on. This picture shows 'reality' according to the writer, encoding his or her own perspectives. These perspectives may be unique to an individual, but they are more likely to conform to a pattern of thinking that is prevalent in the social group of the writer (or speaker). You will learn more about social groups in Chapter 3, and more about attitudes to language change and diversity in Chapters 5 and 6.

The idea of perspective on a topic can also be explored by using the concept of **subject positions.** One event or issue can be viewed from a number of different subject positions, which means that a writer can choose to foreground or highlight some ideas and leave others out of the picture. Looking at the representations of the English language in the six sentences opposite, you can see that different subject positions are apparent, with each of these different 'voices' coming to the fore to the exclusion of others. They include:

- an academic and analytical voice
- an official, regulatory voice
- an emotional voice expressing anger and fear.

Looking closely at language enables us to see what is being displayed and what is concealed – which, in turn, helps us to analyse how particular ideas, items, events and people are represented. Language choices clearly have a powerful role in shaping our thinking and therefore our behaviour towards different groups of people or individuals, which you will explore in more detail in Chapter 3.

Critical discourse tools

Analysing critically means paying close attention to how meanings are built from language, so all of the work you did on text analysis earlier in this chapter is very relevant. However, there are certain areas of language that are worth paying particular attention to, because they are instrumental in creating perspectives.

Sentence and clause functions

Different types of sentences have different functions. You will have noticed that all but one of the six sentences in the activity opposite are statements. Statements suggest how things are, and can use the verb 'to be' to suggest

---

Key terms

Positive face need. In face theory, the need for positive reinforcement, a feeling that we are appreciated and liked by others.

Subject position. The perspective taken on a topic, where some aspects are foregrounded and emphasized while others are downplayed.

The sociologist Harvey Sacks founded a field of study called **Conversation Analysis**, which looks at how people organize routines in their spoken interactions. For example, he identified paired structures such as mutual greetings, conversational openings and closings, questions and answers, requests and acceptances or refusals, and commands and compliance or resistance. Some of these structures can also be seen in writing: for example, Hoey (2000) has shown that many advertisements use 'problem–solution' structures. Question-and-answer routines are sometimes used to structure information texts, in order to break up factual information and not appear **monostylistic** or hectoring.

Key terms

Conversation Analysis. A field of analysis devised by the sociologist Harvey Sacks focusing on the routines that occur in spoken language.

Declarative. A clause or sentence that has a statement function.

Modal verbs. Modal verbs accompany main verbs and are often used to express degrees of certainty, desirability or obligation.

Monostylistic. Having only one style of communication.

Rhetorical question. A question that is posed for its persuasive effect and not because the speaker really expects an answer. ▶

factual accuracy. Stating that 'The English language is a vast flea market', or 'English is being mangled' appears to leave no room for debate. These statement sentences tell us that this is how things are, which is why you will see them described as **declaratives**. In these examples, there is no attribution to particular individuals, which would have been the case if 'I think that' had been at the front of the sentences. Look for unattributed statement sentences when writers are offering propositions about 'the truth'.

One of the statements above is a question, however: 'Are "grammar Nazis" ruining our English language?' In conversations, questions are normally seen as part of a language routine that is called an **adjacency pair**.

Why insert a question into paper-based writing when it is obvious that there will be no answer? The answer is that no answer is expected, because the question is not a genuine, open-ended one, but something we call a **rhetorical question**. Rhetorical questions are part of a group of persuasive techniques that are studied in the field called **rhetoric**. Other rhetorical techniques include repetition, the use of parallel patterns, paired contrasts, and lists – particularly lists of three items. The most commonly studied data in this field consist of speeches, and you could look back to Chapter 1 to see some of these techniques in action in the speeches included there (page 21).

The writer who asks whether 'grammar Nazis' are at work, doesn't expect you to say 'no'. As a reader (or listener) you are expected to mentally review the question and agree with the proposition.

Below is another example of a rhetorical question, taken from the complaint about English that featured in Chapter 1. John Simon is attacking the use of non-standard forms of the verb 'to be', such as 'we was' instead of Standard English 'we were'. You can see here that what he really means is 'We should not consider…':

> Why should we consider some, usually poorly educated, subculture's notion of the relationship between sound and meaning?

Simon (1980)

Two further sentence types – exclamatory sentences and command, or imperative, sentences, are also illustrated in the six sentences. The exclamation is easy to spot because of its punctuation mark, and this mark accompanies a command to fight back.

Modality

Sentence 5 seems to be a sort of command, but one that is indirect: 'You might need to prove…'. 'Might' is an example of a **modal verb**, expressing possibility. Modals accompany main verbs, in order to express a range of meanings: for example, 'may', and 'could' express possibility, while 'must', 'shall' and 'will' express certainty. 'May' can also express permission ('you may do that'), and 'should' can express obligation ('you should do that'). Some adverbs, such as 'possibly' and 'definitely', can also express modality.

Pronouns

As with modal verbs, pronouns are small words that can pack a big punch, but are often overlooked. Pronouns, as their name suggests, stand in place of nouns and have a major role in creating cohesion and stylistic variation in texts.

Personal pronouns are a limited group of terms: 'I', 'he', 'she', 'it', 'we', 'you', 'they', and 'one' (the latter is used rarely). There are some regional variations – for example, the use of 'yous' as a plural form of 'you' in Liverpool (see Chapter 3). There are also **possessive determiners** that are derived from the pronouns, such as 'my', 'his', 'her', and so on.

Did you notice the possessive determiner in the following sentence?

● *Are 'grammar Nazis' ruining our English language?*

The writer's use of 'our' establishes a strong subject position. He or she constructs the audience as sharing the language, and therefore being on the same side as the writer.

The use of 'we' can also be seen at work in the John Simon extract (opposite) and in Chapter 1. Note how Simon's use of 'we' not only assumes that the audience shares his values but also that they are different from the 'poorly educated subculture' that he looks down on.

Pronouns can also shift their point of reference as a text proceeds. For example, the extract below is from a news article, 'We need to love kids … not fear them', about the attitudes of different generations to each other. In the first three sentences, the writer uses 'we' to position himself as part of an older group, and 'their' to refer to young people. But in the final two sentences, the writer uses 'our' to refer to himself as part of a younger group, and 'they' refers to the older generation:

> The old hate the young. We don't like their styles or their music. We can't speak their language or understand their problems.
>
> It was the same with our own parents. They hated our hair, complained about our clothes and tutted at our noisy naïveté.

Activity

Look at the repeated use of pronouns and possessive determiners in the text below.

1. How does Fogle use them to construct the idea of a relationship with his readers?
2. What assumptions are made about the audience?

Your New Dog
by Bruce Fogle

Believe me, if you start by giving your new dog a personal den and playroom … and at first introduce it to other areas only under vigilant supervision, the behaviour of your kids and spouse will give you more problems than your dog ever will. It's amazingly easy to introduce a pup into your home if you do it properly; it's jaw-clenchingly frustrating if you start wrong. The rules are really simple. You want your dog to feel relaxed in its own space, to play there without wreaking havoc, to chew, and to empty both tanks where both of you are happy for it to do so.

Key terms

Rhetoric / Rhetorical. Rhetoric is the study of persuasive language, an area of study dating back to ancient Greece.

Possessive determiners. Determiners, as the name suggests, help to determine what a noun refers to – in this case, ownership ('my', 'our').

■ **Key terms**

Active voice. This is when the person or thing doing the action specified by the verb is the subject of the sentence. For example, in the sentence 'I ate a good dinner', 'I' is the subject, doing the eating. 'A good dinner' is the object (person or thing affected by the action of the verb).

Disjunct. An adverb that expresses a writer's or speaker's attitude, such as 'frankly', 'fortunately'.

Noun phrase. A phrase that has a noun or pronoun as its main word (called the head word).

Passive voice. Use of the passive voice turns elements around, so that the thing or person being acted upon goes at the front. So, when changing the active sentence 'I ate a good dinner' to a passive, it becomes 'A good dinner was eaten (by me)'. The last part is in brackets because it can be left out and the sentence still makes sense.

Metaphor

You have already looked at metaphor in Chapter 1, but it is worth returning to this aspect of language because it can be a very powerful meaning-making strategy. Because metaphor is all about redefining the way we think – by describing something as if it were something else – it can often have a central role in establishing representations. Metaphors can be more noticeable, or less. For example, in the list of six sentences on page 44, you probably noticed the metaphor in sentence 6 ('The English language is a vast flea market') but perhaps you didn't notice the metaphor in sentence 1, where English was said to belong to a 'branch' of languages, representing languages as if they were a 'family tree'.

Metaphor can be closely connected with taboo, because if something is difficult to mention then defining it as something else can be useful. This is exemplified by Fogle's reference to a dog's bladder and bowels as 'both tanks', overleaf. You will look at some of the common metaphors used about language change in Chapter 5.

Modification

The ways in which nouns and **noun phrases** are modified by adjectives is another important area within representation. We often expect to see evaluative adjectives attached to nouns – pre-modifying them – in order to express opinions: 'an excellent idea'; 'a brilliant book'; 'a terrible song'. But certain adjectives do their work more subtly, evoking an attitude and covertly constructing a perspective. Noun phrases, such as 'suspected terrorist', 'discredited education policies', or 'stifling red tape', often signal an ideological position through the pre-modifying adjective.

Adverbs can also be **modifiers**. Particular interpretations can be foregrounded with the use of adverbs such as 'obviously', 'clearly', 'evidently' and 'of course'. These often work by making it appear that any other interpretation of the evidence runs contrary to popular opinion or common sense. These adverbs of comment, or **disjuncts**, act differently from many adverbs in that, instead of telling us how, why, where or when something happened, they give a writer's particular stance or opinion on it.

If you look again at the extract from *Your New Dog* on page 47, you will see that the modification contributes to a representation of the writer's views as correct and worth following. For example:

> It's amazingly easy to introduce a pup into your home if you do it properly; it's jaw-clenchingly frustrating if you start wrong.

The use of the adverbs 'amazingly' and 'jaw-clenchingly' serve to represent the author's method as simple, and to contrast it with the terrible time that readers will have if they get it wrong and fail to follow his advice. This representation is further supported by the intensifying adverb 'really' in 'The rules are really simple'.

Active and passive voices

The **active** and **passive voices** are different ways of expressing who is doing what in a sentence. The terms 'active' and 'passive' relate to the verb. In an active sentence, the person or thing carrying out the action of the verb occurs at the front, while in a passive sentence the person or thing on the receiving end of the verb's action goes at the front.

One of the six sentences you studied on page 44 was in a passive form: 'English is being mangled by new technologies and it is being destroyed before our very eyes.'

You can see that this is a passive sentence because it is not the English language that is doing the action – it is suffering from the action of 'mangling' and 'destroying'.

You can also see that the doer of the action (sometimes called the agent) is at the end of the first clause, introduced using 'by'. But the agent can be left out, in which case readers would be given no information whatsoever about who or what is behind the action. This would read: 'English is being mangled and it is being destroyed'.

If the whole passive sentence had been written in an active voice, it would have read: 'New technologies are mangling and destroying English'.

As you can see, passive structures can be particularly useful if writers want to hide ideas about who or what is responsible for actions.

Nominalization

Nominalization means changing the word class of language items by turning them into nouns. This process has been a common source of new language, particularly from American English. For example:

 Let's have some <u>eats</u> (verb changed to noun)
 He's a <u>natural</u> (adjective changed to noun)
 Don't be a <u>kill-joy</u> (verb + noun changed to noun)
 She has the <u>know-how</u> (verb + adverb changed to noun)

But nominalizations can also work, like passive structures, to obscure agency in sentences. Look at the different versions of the same event, below. Can you see how the representation is different at each stage?

 Troops shoot rioters (active sentence)
 Rioters are shot by troops (passive sentence including agent)
 Rioters are shot (passive sentence without agent)
 Rioters shot (passive sentence without agent and without part of verb structure)
 Rioters die in shooting (verb 'shoot' is nominalized – 'shooting')
 The shooting of rioters (nominalization – 'the shooting' is foregrounded rather than the rioters)

Sentence and clause linking

The ways in which clauses and sentences are linked, can affect the ways in which representations are created and understood. For example, look at this **complex sentence** from a charity ad: 'If you donate £5 a month, we can save the sight of up to one hundred children'. The first clause – a subordinate clause of condition – sets up a grammatically dependent relationship between the two clauses, where the latter effect (saving the sight of up to one hundred children) seems to be possible only if the first clause is fulfilled (you donate £5 a month). This relationship implies that 'you' – the narratee – are the only person who can create this situation. In this way, the grammar works to mirror the charity's dependent relationship with the target audience.

Key terms

Complex sentence. A sentence involving at least one main or independent clause (one that can stand alone and make sense) and a subordinate clause (one that cannot stand alone and make sense). For example, in the sentence 'When I came into the house, I saw the flood damage', the first clause is subordinate and the second is a main clause.

Nominalization. The process of turning different grammatical elements into nouns or noun phrases. For example, in the title of the TV comedy show *Feed My Funny*, the adjective 'funny' has been nominalized, or turned into a noun.

There was a dependent clause in one of the six sentences on page 44, where the first part of the sentence is modified by the dependent clause that follows it:

> You might need to prove your knowledge of the English language if you're over 18 and applying for citizenship or to settle in the UK.

The type of structure above is very different from that in another of the group sentences:

> English is being mangled by new technologies and it is being destroyed before our very eyes.

This is a **compound sentence**, because it has two main clauses: 'English is being mangled' and 'it is being destroyed'.

Register, style and lexical choices

Lexical choices can play an important part in how a narrator appears, and therefore in the relationship between narrator and narratee. Sophisticated or technical Latinate lexis can create the impression that the writer is well educated and knowledgeable, but at the same time this could seem alienating. On the other hand, more Anglo-Saxon-based lexis might create the impression of less expertise but greater equality between narrator and narratee.

It is important to realize that **colloquial** styles can be a deliberate, persuasive strategy: there is nothing necessarily 'natural' about them. Naturalized (natural-seeming) colloquial language can resonate strongly with its target audience to a degree that might not be achieved by writing in a more abstract style: you saw this in Chapter 1 when two different political speeches were compared (page 21). But the idea of 'common sense' that is sometimes associated with everyday language use needs to be critiqued. As linguists such as Fairclough (2010) and Hyatt (2008) show, common-sense ideas are in fact ideologies or ways of thinking about the world, which themselves have been naturalized. In other words, a 'common-sense' idea such as 'making money is good' is only common sense because the ideology that has given rise to it – capitalism – has prevailed up to now in Western societies.

Key terms

Colloquial. Colloquial expressions are items of everyday language used in informal contexts.

Compound sentence. Two main clauses joined by a connective. For example 'I came into the house and I saw the flood damage'.

Link

See Chapter 1 for a discussion of word origins, and Chapter 3 for occupational registers.

REVIEW YOUR LEARNING

The best way to consolidate your learning for this chapter is to put it to use in some text analysis activities.

Activity

AS level activity

As was outlined at the start of the chapter, AS students are required to analyse two texts on a common theme. The activity below simulates this idea by providing two texts about York. Your task is to analyse how language is used in these two texts to create different representations. Follow the instructions below in analysing the texts.

- Text A is taken from '48 Hours in York', one of a travel series on the *Independent* website.
- Text B is adapted from the Chavtowns website.

1. Analyse how Text A uses language to create meanings and representations.
2. Analyse how Text B uses language to create meanings and representations.
3. Compare and contrast Text A and Text B, showing ways in which they are similar and different in their language use.

Text A: 48 Hours in York

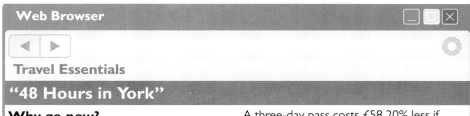

Web Browser

◄ ►

Travel Essentials

"48 Hours in York"

Why go now?

Resolve to make 2014 the year to visit the northern bastion of Roman Britain. It's a tribute to York's spirituality, history and sheer good looks that it was chosen as the starting point for the second stage of the 2014 Tour de France on 6 July. So, before the crowds converge, explore the historic streets then shop and feast splendidly.

Touch down

All rail lines lead to York station, the halfway point on the East Coast mainline between London and Edinburgh. Trains from the English capital take two hours or less. The lowest East Coast fares are available at eastcoast.co.uk; one-way tickets start at £13 from London, £15 from Edinburgh. Fast trains run to York from across Britain with other operators (08457 48 49 50 or nationalrail.co.uk for fares and times).

Get your bearings

York Minster dominates the city, providing a universal reference point. York has more intact walls than any other city in England. They wrap around the core, but are at their most complete close to the Minster, Bootham Bar gatehouse providing easy access.

The Visit York Information Centre is at 1 Museum Street (01904 550099; visityork. org); sells the York Pass, which provides free entry to more than 30 attractions and a range of discounts. A two-day pass costs £48; 10 per cent less if you book your accommodation through visityork.org.

A three-day pass costs £58 20% less if you book your accommodation through visityork.org.

Beyond the city's walls there is a fascinating mix of tranquil parkland and industrial heritage. The Tour de France stage will begin at the racecourse at Knavesmire, two miles south of the city walls.

Check in

On the south-east edge of the racecourse, amid beautifully landscaped grounds, is Middlethorpe Hall (01904 641241; www.middlethorpe.com). This 300-year-old manor house has been a boarding school and nightclub (though not at the same time). It is now a luxury hotel and spa, and won VisitYork's Hotel of the Year in 2013. Double rooms begin at £199, including breakfast and use of the spa, with specials available on some nights before Easter. All profits go to the National Trust.

Si vales valeo – 'if you're well, I'm well' – is the Roman saying painted on an interior wall of a serviced apartment in the Old Brewery, on Ogleforth close to the Minster grounds (07771 966 895; yorkoldbrewery.co.uk). The property sleeps four; a two-night stay costs £350.

To sample some of York's history on a budget, the 1752 Micklegate House is now the Ace Boutique Hostel, close to the station at 88 Micklegate (01904 627720; acehotelyork.co.uk). A night in a dorm can cost as little as £16, with twin rooms from £60.

Text B: Chavtowns – York

Chavtowns – York

Ahh – York. Arrive at the wonderful Victorian train station, walk up towards the Minster through the beautiful streets and many snug little pubs, and you feel as though you're in heaven… but wait! The place is teeming with evil gangs of rat-faced charvers! You wonder if it's only you who can see them, spitting and snarling and destroying everything that they cannot steal, lurking in the back alleys and parks to pounce on or torment the tourists and students, tease old and disabled people, and when they feel brave, rob them in broad daylight. They are all Burberry-clad with tracksuits and prison white trainers, and a large cross-bred fighting dog is de rigueur.

York is surrounded by a ring of shite – huge post-war council estates which are true no-go areas for the buses and the police, and real shit-ridden ghettos. Small, sunken-eyed undernourished feral little charver boys with cracked-cornered mouths hunch over spliffs and drink lager in every green space. With often less than 50 words in their vocabulary, they speak out of one nostril and have permanently knitted brows. Heroin and crack cocaine are rife. Car crime, burglary, drug dealing and mindless violence are the norm. A feeling of menace pervades these chav estates, and like in many other English towns, that menace has moved into the city where hooded rat boys move in gangs robbing, destroying and committing acts of random violence against ordinary people going about their business.

Activity

A level activity

As was outlined at the start of the chapter, A level students are also required to analyse two texts on a common theme, but including an older text. The following activity simulates this idea by providing two recipes. Your task is to analyse how language is used in the two texts to create different representations. Follow the instructions below in analysing the texts.

- Text A is a recipe from 1604, explaining how to make a posset.
- Text B is an online recipe for making a posset.

1. Analyse how Text A uses language to create meanings and representations.
2. Analyse how Text B uses language to create meanings and representations.
3. Explore the similarities and differences in the ways that Text A and Text B use language.

Did you know?

'Secke' was similar to sherry and Crudde (or curd) may be the origin of the 'head' on beer.

Source: Spurling, H. 1986. *Elinor Fettiplace's Receipt Book*. London: Penguin (a book of Elizabethan recipes from 1604)

Text A: Elizabethan posset recipe

To Make A Possett

Take the heade of yr milcke, boyle it then take the yelkes of 4 egges and beate them mingleinge them wth some cowld milcke, then put grated bred, Nutmeggs, and sugger, into yr milcke, when yr milcke boyles on the ffire putt it all in, stirring it once Rownde then powre it into A Bason, sett it on the fire till it boyle, then put in yr Secke and ale, and stirr it once aboute to the botome, and soe lett it stand untill the Crudde Riseth

Text B: Online posset recipe

Web Browser

◀ ▶

Lemon Posset

Lemon Posset is making a comeback. There's nothing easier than a Lemon Posset recipe for a quick, and deliciously tangy pudding – perfect for summer days. Originally a posset was a drink made from hot milk and honey, spiced and laced with ale or wine. It was popular in the Middle Ages as a remedy for colds and minor ailments and a sleep-aid. A posset appeared in Shakespeare's *Macbeth*, when Lady Macbeth used a poisoned posset to knock out the guards outside Duncan's quarters.

INGREDIENTS

- 2¼ cups/500ml heavy/double cream
- 3 lemons, juiced, zest removed and cut into strips
- 1 tbsp honey

Prep time: 20 minutes

Total time: 20 minutes

PREPARATION

Note: At no time should you vigorously boil the posset as this will inevitably curdle the mixture.

- Place the cream, lemon zest and juice into a saucepan and bring to a **gentle** boil. Remove from the heat and leave to infuse for 30 minutes.
- Strain the cream through a fine sieve into a jug then return to the pan and bring back to a gentle boil. Add the honey and stir. Simmer gently for 5 minutes until the cream starts to thicken.
- Leave the cream to cool slightly then pour into 6 ramekin dishes

filling two-thirds full. Leave to cool then chill in the refrigerator until set (about 2 hours).

Serve with summer berries and Scottish Shortbread

USER REVIEWS

Maryelley   User Rating: ★★★★★

Success at last

I have tried several recipes for posset and have never been able to get that thick, sweet cream right until now. This is so simple if you follow the instructions carefully and is a taste sensation. Lovely.

Activity

Further A level activity

As was outlined at the start of the chapter, A level students are required on Paper 2 to analyse texts that take language as the topic. The task is to show how writers use language to construct their arguments, show their attitudes and values, and set up their perspectives.

To practise this, read Text A and Text B, below.

● Text A is from a commentator writing in 1930 about the effects of the growing film industry on language use.

● Text B is from the writer Anthony Burgess, writing in 1964 about the language of the media more generally.

  I. Analyse how the writers use language to present their views.

  2. Examine any similarities and differences you find between the two texts, and explore how effectively the texts present their views.

Text A

The wave of animated photography which has swept over Europe from the West has made every girl and boy of fourteen in this country innocent accomplices in the matricide of their mother tongue. Cinemaese is a lingua franca, or a lingua californica. It has devastated Europe. The subtitlers have created a wilderness and called it prose.

Text B

Propaganda always lies, because it overstates a case, and the lies tend more and more to reside in the words used. A 'colossal' film can only be bettered by a 'super-colossal' one; soon the hyperbolic forces ruin all meaning. If moderately tuneful pop songs are described as 'fabulous', what terms can be used to evaluate Beethoven's Ninth Symphony? The impressionable young – on both sides of the Atlantic – are being corrupted by the salesmen; they are being equipped with a battery of inflated words, being forced to evaluate alley-cat copulation in terms appropriate to the raptures of Tristan and Isolde. For the real defilers of language – the cynical inflators – a deep and dark hell is reserved.

Paper 2 will also require you to do a piece of writing of your own in response to the texts you are given. As a simulation of this, try the task below.

Activity

Write an opinion article about the language of the media in which you assess the ideas and issues raised in Text A and Text B and argue your own views.

References

Bennett, C. (2013) 'Dangerous dogs: oh don't worry, he really doesn't mean you any harm', *Observer*, 10 November

Burgess, A. (1975) *Language Made Plain*. London: Fontana/Collins,

Calder, S. (2014) '48 hours in York', *Independent,* 24 January

Fairclough, N. (2010). *Critical Discourse Analysis*. London: Routledge.

Fogle, B. (2008) *Your New Dog*, Richmond Hill, ON: Firefly Books

Goddard, A. (2009) (3rd edn) 'Language and new technologies', in Malmkjaer, K. (ed.), *The Routledge Linguistics Encyclopedia*. London: Routledge

Goddard, A. and Geesin, B. (2011) *Language and Technology*. London: Routledge.

Goffman, E. (1974). *Frame Analysis*. Harmondsworth: Penguin.

Hodge, R. and Kress, G. (1988). *Social Semiotics*. Cornell University Press.

Hoey, M. (2000). *Textual Interaction: An Introduction to Written Discourse Analysis*. London: Routledge.

King, J. (2008) 'We need to love kids… not fear them', *Daily Mirror*, 3 June

Knox, E. V. (1930) 'Cinema English', *Living Age* 338 (April 1): 187–89

Kress, G. (2003). *Literacy in the New Media Age*. London: Routledge.

Lean, S. (2014) *Hero*. London: HarperCollins

Marciuliano, F. (2013) 'I Lose My Mind When You Leave the House' in *I Could Chew On This and Other Poems by Dogs*. San Francisco: Chronicle Books

Sacks, H. (1995). (Vols I & II, ed. G. Jefferson) *Lectures on Conversation*. Oxford: Blackwell.

Spurling, H. (1986) *Elinor Fettiplace's Receipt Book*. London: Penguin.

http://britishfood.about.com/od/dessert/r/lemonposset.htm

http://www.loveyourdog.com/training.html © Janet Wall and Rick Wall

'York – Chavarama' (with corrections) http://www.ilivehere.co.uk/york-chavarama.html

Further reading

Carter, R. and Goddard, A. (2015) *How to Analyse Texts: A Toolkit for Students of English*. London: Routledge

Clayton, D. (2008) 'Language matters: investigating representation', in *emagazine*, 42, December Issue. London: English and Media Centre

Fairclough, N. (2010). See above.

Goddard, A. (2014) 'Looking beyond the label: mode and new forms of communication', in *emagazine*, 64, April Issue. London: English and Media Centre.

Hall, S. 'Representation and the Media', Open University lecture series: https://www.youtube.com/watch?v=aTzMsPqssOY

Hyatt, D. (2008) 'Beneath the surface of language – the critical analysis of discourse', in *emagazine*, 42, December Issue. London: English and Media Centre

Key terms

Directed writing. A writing activity where you are asked to write to a specific brief, rather than inventing your own.

Sociolinguistics. The study of the relationship between language use and social factors.

REMEMBER

You can show some creativity in your directed writing task right at the outset by giving your writing an interesting title or heading.

REMEMBER

The more you read widely across different styles of journalism and different academic books and articles, the more you will understand how writers vary their styles when they write about language.

AS level assessment

AS level (Paper 2: Language Varieties) covers the following areas: social and occupational groups, gender, and dialects (to include regional and national varieties of English within the British Isles).

In Section A of AS Paper 2, you are required to answer one essay question from a choice of two options. The two questions will ask about different areas of sociolinguistics. You will be given some data to help you to get started by seeing an example from the topic area. You will be asked to 'discuss' the question and you will be expected to talk about the data but not confine yourself to it. The data is really a kind of springboard to give your essay some momentum.

Section B of AS Paper 2 will also include a stimulus text. This could be of any type but it will not cover the same areas of sociolinguistics as the questions in Section A. As you can probably already see, there are no shortcuts in covering sociolinguistics, so don't hedge your bets and leave out any aspects. You will also see throughout this chapter that the different areas of sociolinguistics don't exist in isolation, so that is another reason to range as widely as possible.

In Section B, you are required to do a **directed writing** task, where you write about a specified topic but you don't write in an essay format. You will be given a writing brief with clear instructions about the task. This offers you an alternative type of assessment, where your writing skill is assessed as well as your subject knowledge.

Relevant Assessment Objectives

AS level essay questions are credited through AO1: your understanding of linguistic methods, such as the areas included in the language levels; your use of relevant terminology from the subject area; and the coherence of your writing.

They are also credited through AO2, which rewards you for your critical understanding of concepts and issues relevant to language use.

The AS level directed writing task is credited through AO2, as above, which represents the content of your writing in terms of how you understand the topic; and AO5, which rewards you for the style of your writing – your creativity, which means its liveliness and the ability to sustain a style that is appropriate for your audience.

A level assessment

A level (Paper 2: Language Diversity and Change) covers the following areas: social and occupational groups, gender, ethnicity, and dialects (to include regional, national and international varieties of English).

As you can see, A level assessment adds ethnicity and international varieties of English to the AS level list. Ethnicity is covered in this chapter; international English has a chapter of its own (Chapter 6), because there is a lot to say about it and it is a relatively new area in A level language study.

A level Paper 2, Section A mirrors that of AS above: you are required to answer one essay question from a choice of two options. Because at A level, language change is added to the specification, only one of those essays will be on social varieties, since the other option will be on language change.

At A level, you will not necessarily be given data, as you are at AS. The essay question will ask you to 'evaluate' an idea, which goes further than simply discussion: it requires weighing up arguments about the view being expressed.

In Section B, Language Discourses, you will be asked to analyse two texts and then complete a directed writing task. This task could be on an aspect of language variety or an aspect of language change. Chapter 5 will explain more about this A level paper and about the connections between variety and change.

Relevant Assessment Objectives

The A level essays on Paper 2 Section A are assessed in exactly the same way as at AS level, through AO1 and AO2 (see above).

In Section B, the text analysis task is assessed again through AO1, but also AO3, which rewards your ability to connect language features with contextual factors; and in addition AO4, which credits you for your ability to make connections between the two texts.

The directed writing task is assessed in exactly the same way as the AS level equivalent (see opposite).

Beyond the lists of sociolinguistic topics above, there are further areas that you may be interested in exploring for your coursework folder – either by carrying out an investigation or by producing some original writing: for example, on aspects of language and age, disability, sexuality, or religious beliefs. See Chapters 7 and 8 for more information about the coursework folder.

Introduction

As the name suggests, the area of sociolinguistics explores the relationship between the **social groups** that people belong to, and their language use. It covers the language used by different groups, but also the language that is used to them, and about them.

The elements above – the language used by people, and the language used to and about them – can be different. People can feel that they are part of a group; for example, you might include yourself within an age group or student group. You might be aware that, as part of your social group identity, you use language in a particular way. But you may well feel that the language used to describe your age group or your student group doesn't really match with reality as you experience it. This mismatch connects back to the work you did in the previous chapter, on representation and on discourses.

However, the language that is used to and about people does have connections with the ways in which those people use language themselves, because it helps to shape social attitudes and behaviour. Below is an example of how that can work.

Many academic studies on language and gender have looked at questions about how men and women use language, and particularly whether they use language differently from each other. At the same time, there are representations all

Link

To explore an interesting aspect of language and sexuality, read Baker, P. (2002) *Polari – The Lost Language of Gay Men*. London: Routledge.

Did you know?

The study of language and religion has its own subject name – **theolinguistics**.

Key terms

Social group. Individuals who share interests and connections with others, or who are classified as having something in common.

Theolinguistics. The study of the relationship between language use and religious faith.

Did you know?

Modern approaches to sociolinguistics connect the language we use with the language that's used around us. For example, in *Delusions of Gender*, Cordelia Fine says: 'the social context influences who you are, how you think and what you do. And these thoughts, attitudes and behaviours of yours, in turn, become part of the social context'.

around us every day about how men and women are supposed to be: we are given stories in advertising, novels, films and TV, song lyrics, and by people at home and in school, about what's 'natural' for men and women, including what's appropriate in terms of their language use. If we take the topic of swearing, it's possible to see that the strong social messages about how men and women should behave can explain why men and women might use language differently, for example in using different swear words, or in swearing more or less often, or in swearing in different contexts.

Speakers will be sensitive to the social norms that define the ways in which they should use language, and also shape how they are supposed to behave more generally. It's not enough, therefore, just to look at what social groups do with language; it is also important to think about the language that describes and defines them. What people do is only half the story: why they do it is equally important.

This chapter will cover both areas – the language that people use, and also the language that's used to and about them. Having as broad a picture as possible of the areas of social variation that are set for study will give you a head start in any of your assessments.

The remainder of this chapter has been divided into five numbered sections to cover each of the sociolinguistic areas. Each section will outline its aims at the start, and provide a learning review, references and further reading at the end.

What is a social group?

The term 'social group' refers to the fact that any society is not simply a collection of isolated individuals. People connect with others and those connections can be made on many different bases. We may identify ourselves very consciously as members of a particular group, for example when we vote or when we join a club. But we tend to be unaware of the extent of our social connections until we are made to think about them for a particular reason. When we do, it can lead us to see that our social networks are part of a complex structure, often with language at its heart.

Activity

Read the account below, which was written by Colette, a 19-year-old psychology student at Sheffield University. Colette lives in a shared flat with six others (including three other students on her course). Her school friend, Emily, also goes to Sheffield. Colette and Emily are both on the university cheerleading committee and are in the cheerleading squad, which competes in national competitions. Other ex-schoolfriends are also at the same university and she sees them occasionally, mainly when she's home. Colette works part-time in a children's centre near her family home. One of her co-workers, Beth, is Emily's cousin.

As you read the account, note how Colette's language varies according to her group connections and the contexts she describes.

My conversations change depending on who I'm with. For example, topics of conversations with my housemates differ from those with cheerleading friends because my housemates consist of more boys whereas cheerleading does not. Also, because my housemates are all close friends and we are a tight group, the language used is more colloquial and relaxed than if I was at work with my colleagues who I'm not as close to. My accent also slightly changes in the company I'm in and it's been noted that my northern accent becomes stronger when I'm in the presence of Emily, my friend from home, in comparison to when I'm with my university friends who come from southern areas of the country. I also notice this change of accent in my flatmate Tilly, from Somerset, as hers gets suddenly much stronger as soon as she speaks to a family member or when she has been at home for some time. Being at university and mixing with a wide range of people from different areas, I have also picked up different phrases. For example, Tilly uses the word 'lush' to describe something nice and this is a word I've started to use myself. Olivia and Chloe (cheerleading friends) also use 'man' and 'mate' quite often but I only ever use these words when talking to them. Megan (my flatmate from North London) also has started using 'tea' instead of 'dinner' as a result of being around four northerners who all call it 'tea'.

This section of Chapter 3 will:

- help you to understand the meaning of the term 'social groups'
- explore the relationship between social group membership and language use
- show you how approaches to researching this area have changed over time
- give you some frameworks and concepts for analysing data and answering essay questions on this topic.

Key:

student group

interest group

gender group

friendship group

occupational group

regional group

The activity above should have helped you to see that in everyday life we manage to move between social groups with little difficulty, even though our language might vary considerably between those different contexts. But there is a difference between using language and studying it. What early sociolinguists tried to do was to isolate different social factors and study them one by one in order to understand the effects they had on language use.

Macro-level and micro-level approaches

Early sociolinguists approached the study of social groups at a **macro-level**, or as large categories – for example, social class, or age or gender. At the same time other researchers, interested in language but influenced more by psychology, took a **micro-level** approach, studying individuals and how their language varied in small-scale interactions.

For example, the social psychologist Howard Giles developed Communication Accommodation Theory (CAT), which showed how individuals adapt aspects of their own language to signal their feelings about the person they are talking to. Colette describes this process in her account of how both she and her flatmate Tilly change their accents. In Giles's theory, Colette is describing **convergence**, trying to match the style of other speakers. Sometimes we choose **divergence**, exaggerating the differences between our speech style and that of others in order to distance ourselves, or as a sign of disapproval.

Early studies of language and social class

One of the earliest studies of the effects of social class on language was William Labov's *The Social Stratification of English in New York City* in 1966. Labov concluded that differences in the pronunciation of certain sounds could be attributed to social class.

He conducted an experiment in New York department stores and his results showed that speakers in the more prestigious stores who were aspiring to use a prestige accent used a particular feature, the **post-vocalic /r/**. This refers to pronouncing an /r/ sound where it follows a vowel in a word – for example, in the words 'cart' or 'park'. In repeating his request for the whereabouts of an item he knew to be on the fourth floor of each shop, Labov made speakers carefully demonstrate their usage of the /r/. It was striking that those he identified as middle class strove most to use the prestige form.

Sociolinguists in the UK were also researching the effects of social class on language use. For example, Peter Trudgill's 1974 study of Norwich speech explored the differences between people of working- and middle-class backgrounds in their pronunciation of certain sounds, including the velar nasal

---

Key terms

Convergence. In language study, changing one's language in order to move towards that of another individual.

Divergence. In language study, changing one's language in order to move away from that of another individual.

Macro-level. Operating on a large scale.

Micro-level. Operating on a small scale.

Post-vocalic /r/. Pronouncing an /r/ after a vowel where there is an r in the spelling. For example, 'farm', 'sir', 'horse'.

Did you know?

Labov's results showed how culture-specific ideas about language and status are. Pronouncing the /r/ in American English in words like 'cart' and 'park' is seen as high-status, whereas in the UK post-vocalic /r/ is an aspect of rural speech and is often stereotyped. Speakers of **Received Pronunciation (RP)**, the traditional prestige accent in the UK, do not pronounce /r/ in those words, which would be spoken as /kɑːt/ and /pɑːk/.

/ŋ/ at the ends of words like 'running'. He concluded that changing the velar nasal /ŋ/ to an alveolar /n/ – saying 'runnin' instead of 'running'– was more likely to feature in working-class speech than in middle-class speech, although he also found differences between men's and women's use of the non-standard forms.

These early studies used the type of categorizing system shown in the table below, which was based on the occupation of the 'head' of each household. So, as you can see, this was a fairly crude measurement. For example, for a married couple where the woman did not work, her category was based on that of her husband; for a single woman, it was based on that of her father. Trying to identify **gender** variations using this system was therefore problematic.

A	Higher managerial, administrative or professional
B	Intermediate managerial, administrative or professional
C1	Supervisory or clerical and junior managerial, administrative or professional
C2	Skilled manual workers
D	Semi-skilled and unskilled manual workers
E	Casual or lowest grade workers, pensioners and others who depend on the state for their income

Social network theory

A different way of looking at the idea of social connections is embodied in the theory of **social networks**. You may feel familiar with the term 'social network', because of its connection with online activities on social media where you 'network', albeit remotely from your computer, with many different people. However, the concept of a social network has a long history and has been a popular research tool for sociologists since the 1970s. One of the most significant sociolinguistic studies using this method was Lesley Milroy's work on Belfast speech in 1987.

Milroy described the idea of a social network as a 'web of ties'. The concept focuses on the relationships between individuals and the contact patterns between group members. Another important factor is the strength of the ties between people – from the close ties of family members to the weak ties of acquaintances. Also significant is the nature of the connections within a group, which can be measured according to both their **density** and their **multiplexity**. Social networks can be represented graphically, as a web.

Milroy studied three inner-city working-class communities in Northern Ireland and found that variations in language use could be explained by the residents' social networks. She found that where people had a high network density score – through factors such as working together, living close to family members and socializing with each other – their accents were reinforced and stayed strong. On the other hand, people who were more isolated – perhaps through being unemployed or looking after children at home – had less strong accents. Where men were the ones who were isolated (one community had a lot of male unemployment) their accents were weaker than those of the women, who had high-density scores through working together in local factories.

Did you know?
Social network analysis has many applications, from its use by advertisers to target their products, to counter-intelligence work analysing terrorist networks.

Key terms
Density. In studies of social networks, density refers to the number of connections that people have.

Multiplexity. In studies of social networks, multiplexity refers to the number of ways in which two individuals might relate to each other, for example, as friends, workmates and family members.

Social network. A network of relations between people in their membership of different groups.

For the speakers in these social networks, the strong ties within communities were powerfully associated with their identity, and maintaining a strong accent was a way of demonstrating and affirming this sense of themselves. Milroy's study showed that this was as true for women as for men, showing that there was nothing necessarily gender-based about accent strength. If women used more standard speech forms than men, it could be to do with how they lived, rather than simply because they were female.

If you look again at Colette's account of her social connections, you can see that it would be possible to draw a web of her network. You can begin to identify the multiplexity in the networks, as three of her flatmates are also known to her from her psychology course. The highest number of separate connections she has is with Emily, showing a greater multiplexity than her relationships with others. Not only is Emily in Colette's home-friend network, she is also part of her university-friend network. In addition, they are both members of the cheerleading squad and committee.

Research idea

1. See how far you can apply ideas about social network density to online connections, either your own or those of someone who is prepared to be your **informant** in a **case study**. Social media sites allow users some control over access to their personal information, so you could start by looking at who belongs to an individual's inner circle of friends and who is more peripheral.

2. Research distinctive uses of language by online groups. This could range from the specific registers used by interest groups, to the elaborate language used on playful sites such as Lolcats (http://icanhas.cheezburger.com/lolcats) or Doge (http://www.theguardian.com/technology/2014/feb/18/doge-such-questions-very-answered). ●

Activity

Return to the list of groups that you belong to (from page 60). Now try to divide them into separate social networks. Identify the people who are in more than one group. See if you can represent the networks visually by drawing a diagram showing the connections between groups. How dense are your networks – does everyone know everyone else? Is there a multiplex social network – do you work with your neighbours, or friends, or people you go to school with?

Key terms

Case study. An in-depth study of a single context that can be used to offer insights for further studies or other cases.

Informant. Someone who offers information to a researcher.

What is social class now?

Although there is endless discussion about 'the British class system', there are more stereotypes, myths and humorous anecdotes than watertight definitions. However, in 2013, the BBC collaborated with academics from the London School of Economics, and York and Manchester Universities, to come up with a potentially new system of categories – basing their work on a survey of 161,000 people. In this new system, the following aspects are key factors:

● Household income.

● Whether you own a property or rent it.

● Savings.

● The kinds of people you mix with and know socially.

● The cultural activities you engage in.

Activity

Go to the Great British Class Calculator weblink below and take the test – perhaps with your family in mind, rather than yourself. Calculate how your family is categorized, and you will also be able to see how the different groups are named and described:
http://www.bbc.co.uk/news/magazine-22000973

The jocks and the burnouts

Approaches towards language and social groups aren't always about class, or about accent alone. Building on a social network approach, Penelope Eckert (2000) focused her observational research on the **social practices** of American high-school students. She identified two distinctive types of group. One group were the 'jocks', a group who participated in school life enthusiastically. Their behaviour contrasted markedly with that of the 'burnouts', who were actively rebellious and refused to take part in school activities. She found that people tended to speak more like those with whom they shared social practices and values. In this case, the 'burnouts' more often used the exaggerated pronunciations associated with the urban accent of their Detroit neighbourhood, while the 'jocks' were more concerned with speaking in a socially prestigious way – sometimes reflecting their more middle-class backgrounds. However, even within the 'burnouts', there were sub-groups who spoke slightly differently from the more-established group members.

Eckert also asked them to talk about each other's use of language. The jocks were critical of the burnouts for their ungrammatical language, their frequent swearing and for not being articulate. Unsurprisingly, the jocks were seen as talking just like their parents.

Teenagers and their **sociolects** have also been a rich source of study in UK contexts. Jenny Cheshire (1982) recorded the speech of groups of teenagers in an adventure playground in Reading – to look at the effects of peer-group culture. Although many of her findings were connected with gender, she also found that the 'toughest' girls and boys conformed to the group use of non-standard grammatical forms, such as 'ain't'.

Lexical items have also been found to be strong indicators of social group membership in studies and commentaries of different kinds. For example, Harriet Powney refers to the notion of the **familect**, where people in a family invent their own private lexis to refer to shared meanings, perhaps calling up events in the family's history or the language of different group members. This same phenomenon can, of course, feature within intimate relationships of all kinds, perhaps involving pet names for loved ones.

Activity

Do the studies of Eckert and Cheshire have any relevance to your own school or college context? Are there different social groups whose language use and behaviour is distinctive? Can you identify different 'profiles' for groups and examples of their typical language use?

Research idea

1. Research examples of familects by interviewing fellow students about any terms that are used within their families to refer to particular things or people. For example, what do they call their TV remote control?

2. Research examples of teenage slang. A 2013 Mumsnet thread included the following examples of teenspeak that puzzled adults: beast, peak, hench, bare, swag, bredrin, butters, ting, fam, don, blad and banter. ●

Did you know?

The suffix 'lect' (from 'lexis') is added onto many words to describe a common language. You've seen it here with 'familect', but some people also talk about **genderlect**, **ethnolect** and **dialect**. You'll be exploring these aspects of language variation later in this chapter.

Key terms

Dialect. A style of language used within a particular geographical region.

Ethnolect. A style of language thought to be characteristic of a particular ethnic group.

Familect. A style of language used within a family.

Genderlect. A style of language thought to be distinctive of either men or women.

Social practices. The ways in which people in groups habitually behave.

Sociolect. A style of language used within a particular social group.

Link

Read Powney's article at http://www.theguardian.com/media/mind-your-language/2013/jul/19/mind-your-language-family-slang

Key terms

Community of practice. A group of people who share understandings, perspectives and forms of language use as a result of meeting regularly over time.

Deficit model. An assumption that something is lacking or deficient.

Elaborated code. An idea advanced by Bernstein (and much disputed) that middle-class speakers use context-free, complex forms of language.

Pragmatic rules. The unspoken rules that operate in interactions between people who share a common understanding.

Restricted code. An idea advanced by Bernstein (and much disputed) that working-class speakers use context-based, limited forms of language.

Language, social class and education

Many studies have speculated about the connections between these three aspects – mainly in order to explore ideas about different levels of achievement and the extent to which they can be ascribed to language skills. This is a complex topic and one that tends to be over-simplified. There is general agreement that language skills are vital to success in learning, and that a language-rich home environment is important, but whether children from different backgrounds use language differently because of their social class is highly disputed.

The work of the sociologist Basil Bernstein is sometimes quoted as 'proof' in this respect. He claimed that working-class speakers used a **restricted code** of language, which related to the here-and-now, while middle-class speakers used an **elaborated code**, which was much more explicit and independent of context. Aside from the problematic labels, his work unfortunately contributed to a **deficit model** of language being associated with working-class identity. In fact, what his work really showed was some of the differences between speech and writing: he showed pictures to children and asked them to describe what was happening in them. The working-class children used language that fitted with the fact that they shared the same physical space with the researcher, while the middle-class children spoke as if the researcher wasn't there. What you could say about this result is that it might show that middle-class children are more aware of the nature of assessment, and that it reveals the potential unnaturalness of school-based practices. You can read more about this topic in Chapter 4 of this book.

Communities of practice

The concept of **communities of practice** is another tool for exploring how language varies according to our particular social groups. The term describes people coming together for a particular purpose, and establishing ways of doing things and of interacting in order to achieve that shared purpose. Lave and Wenger (1991), who first developed the concept, identify three crucial strands: *mutual engagement*, which involves regular interaction, based around *a joint negotiated enterprise* and with group members using a *shared repertoire*. It's about the ways groups do things, the ways they talk, their beliefs and values, and power relationships between members.

You can apply this concept later when you look at occupational language and see how communities of practice operate in workplaces, but it can also be exemplified through the social groups that come together because of shared interests. Take supporters who come together regularly to watch their football team. Fans are often represented as the 'twelfth man' of a team, because – although they don't actually play – they are closely connected to the joint enterprise of their team's success.

There is a large community of those who are passionate about football. The practices of this community can be shown in the general register associated with the game. But there are also specific aspects of language that identify fans as part of a particular fan base. You can see the **pragmatic rules** of a specific community in the following description, which is from a blog. The writer, a university linguistics student, reflects on the nature of the supporters' language.

Language of football fans

When I told Tom about my first football blog post about language in football, he said 'what, like the chanting?' to which I replied 'no, but that would be interesting to write about *mind starts whirring*'. So here goes!

I am a Bristol Rovers supporter – and proud of it! At most of the games I go to, there is a considerable amount of chanting, aimed at various players, people and just passionately singing for the hell of it.

Win, lose or draw, the club's song 'Goodnight Irene' will be echoed around the stadium. From a personal perspective, I think that is a reflection of the passionate nature of our fans (gasheads). Other fans may do that at their home grounds, but we will do it home or away. I have been to two away matches with Rovers in the past year – the first was Torquay, and the second was last month at Birmingham in the FA Cup. At Birmingham, although we lost 3–0, from the first to the last minute, we sang and chanted – supporting our team. I think that the passion in chanting can come from the plosivity/plosiveness/plosivitude (can't decide which one is correct) of words we include. Needless to say, a lot of them are vulgarities and swear words.

Research idea

Research the language of sport as an example of a community of practice. What register is used? Which genres are part of the community's repertoire? What are some of the pragmatics of their communication?

REVIEW YOUR LEARNING

- Define the following terms: macro-level, micro-level, convergence, divergence.
- What is social network theory?
- What is a community of practice? Give some examples.

References

Cheshire, J. (1982). 'Linguistic Variation and Social Function'. In Romaine, S. (ed.) *Sociolinguistic Variation in Speech Communities*. London: Edward Arnold.

Eckert, P. (2000). *Linguistic Variation as Social Practice: The Linguistic Construction of Identity in Belten High*. Oxford: Wiley-Blackwell.

Fine, C. (2010). *Delusions of Gender*. London: Icon Books.

Labov, W. (1966). *The Social Stratification of English in New York City*. Washington DC: Centre for Applied Linguistics.

Lave, J and Wenger, E. (1991). *Situated Learning*. Cambridge: Cambridge University Press.

Milroy, L. (1991). *Language and Social Networks*. Oxford: Wiley-Blackwell.

Trudgill, P. (1974). *The Social Differentiation of English in Norwich*. Cambridge: Cambridge University Press.

Further reading

Investigate the following academic blog and write notes about any interesting pieces of research you find. The blog is run jointly by linguists at universities in York and London, and is part of a larger project called *From Sociolinguistic Research to English Language Teaching*:

http://linguistics-research-digest.blogspot.co.uk/p/about.html

This section of Chapter 3 will:

- help you to understand how regional language can be described
- explore representations of regional language
- give you some frameworks and concepts for analysing data and answering essay questions about this topic.

! REMEMBER

There is no such thing as 'accentless' speech – everyone has an accent.

! REMEMBER

In language study, the terms **standard** and **non-standard** have nothing to do with high or low standards, although you will have noticed that in this pair of words, 'standard' is still constructed as the norm. The meanings of the terms in language study are closer to ideas about mainstream and non-mainstream usage.

Key terms

Accent. The way that people pronounce sounds.

Descriptivism / Descriptivist. The belief that correctness is dependent on context and should be defined by what is appropriate in any context. Descriptivists take their norms from observing what the majority of people do, not what any particular authority says they should do. ▶

Introduction: Some definitions

An **accent** differs from a dialect. Accent refers to the way in which people pronounce sounds. Dialect refers to vocabulary and grammar (and sometimes accent as well), so it relates to a much wider idea of regional language.

Pragmatics tends not to have been explored very much in UK studies of language and region, but pragmatic variations are possible between speakers in different regions of the country. For example, there may be different rules of politeness in routines such as saying 'goodbye' when leaving a shop after having been served, or in the extent to which people are happy to engage in talk with strangers.

Historically, the accent with the highest prestige has been **Received Pronunciation (RP)** – so called because it was socially approved. Some writers prefer to call this accent **non-regional**, because it's the only accent that does not suggest the regionality of speakers – but instead suggests that they belong to a more privileged social class. This accent is thought to have developed during the 19th century, and its growth was associated with the public school system and Oxford and Cambridge universities. Certainly, its origins seem to be southern rather than northern, but nowadays speakers of RP can come from any region. In 1974, Trudgill – whose work was referred to on pages 60–61 – estimated that only 3% of speakers used RP.

The term **Standard English (SE)** is associated primarily with written language and with vocabulary and grammar, rather than with accent. Originally this was a dialect, but it has become an agreed standard language for writing. Both RP and SE have connections with the south-east of the country, because of the early growth of that area as the centre of government and commerce.

Prescriptivism and descriptivism

The two terms **prescriptivism** and **descriptivism** will recur throughout your studies, so understanding the difference between them is important. If you *prescribe* something, you say that something *should* be the case: when a doctor prescribes medicine, you are expected to take it. When you *describe* something, you say what *is* happening, not what *should* happen.

A prescriptive attitude to language states that features are absolutely right or wrong, regardless of context or actual usage – basing notions of correctness on what has historically been the case. But a problem with using historical precedents is that it is often the people in power who set the rules in a particular age.

A descriptive approach doesn't talk about 'good' and 'bad' – although these ideas can still be relevant where something is used inappropriately. Description is based on ideas about what people do, not what they should do. You will look at these ideas in more detail in Chapter 5, Language Change.

But even descriptive approaches to language can have problems in treating regional varieties fairly. For example, the phonemic alphabet of English sounds is based on the RP accent, so other accents are described by saying how they differ from RP. You will see below how this can cause problems for some regional speakers.

How do regional accents vary?

Accents can be studied in a great deal of detail. At both AS level and A level, you need to be familiar with the phonemic alphabet for English sounds, which you were introduced to in Chapter 1 (page 12). You were also directed to an interactive chart where you can practise and develop your skills.

But you do not need the level of phonetic detail used in the International **Phonetic Alphabet** (IPA), which is designed to describe variations between languages.

While there are aspects of accents that can be distinctive to them alone, there are some features that broadly characterize groups of accents. For example, a big difference between northern and southern accents is the **distribution** of two pairs of vowel sounds:

> /æ/ and /ɑ:/
> /ʊ/ and /ʌ/

The difference between the first pair can be heard in the northern and southern pronunciations of the words 'bath' and 'grass', where northern speakers say /bæθ/ and /græs/ and southern speakers /bɑ:θ/ and /grɑ:s/. This difference only applies to some words, however. For example, people at both ends of the country would say /kæt/ for 'cat' and /ænt/ for 'ant'. Everyone would also use /ɑ:/ in 'heart' and 'calm'. Variation in how different words are treated in this way is what is meant by the term 'distribution' – it describes *where in the language system* something happens.

The second pair of vowels also distinguishes many northern and southern accents, but for a different reason: the vowel /ʌ/ doesn't exist in many northern accents. This makes using the phonemic alphabet more difficult for northern speakers: because the alphabet is based on RP, you will see the vowel /ʌ/ labelled on the chart as the sound in the word 'up'. But this is only true for southern speakers: northern speakers will say /ʊp/. So when people talk about how many 'sounds' there are in English, they really mean in RP, because regional speakers will have different numbers of sounds in their **inventories**. Perhaps you can now see that even descriptive approaches aren't entirely without historical bias.

A window on history

The comments of Daniel Jones, an influential academic in the field of describing English pronunciation, can give us some interesting insights into historical attitudes to regional varieties. In the preface to his 1909 book, *The Pronunciation of English*, he says this:

> This book is intended for English students and teachers, and more especially for students in training colleges and teachers whose aim is to correct cockneyisms or other undesirable pronunciations in their scholars.

Jones revised his book in 1950, after 40 years of teaching at University College, London, and changed his preface to this:

> a new attitude was adopted in regard to the much-discussed subject of standard pronunciation. This was because […] it can no longer be said that any standard exists, nor do I think it desirable to attempt to establish

Key terms

Distribution. Where a feature is used, within the language inventory of an individual or group.

Inventory. A list of items. For example, in phonology, a list of the sounds used in a person's accent.

Non-regional. An alternative name for the RP accent.

Non-standard. Different from normal or majority usage.

Phonetic alphabet. An alphabet designed for transcribing the sounds of all of the world's languages.

Prescriptivism / Prescriptivist. The belief that there is an absolute authority determining what is correct usage; that correctness is something absolute and unchangeable, based on rules established in the past.

Standard. Used or accepted as normal or average. In language study, socially agreed usage that is familiar to most language users.

one […] I no longer feel disposed to recommend any particular forms of pronunciation for use by English people or to condemn others. It must, in my view, be left to individual English-speaking people to decide whether they should speak in the manner that comes to them naturally or whether they should alter their speech in any way.

Jones was a descriptive linguist, but also a man of his time. In the early 20th century, teachers of English were seen as 'missionaries' of speech, whose job it was to 'correct' aspects of regional language by removing them and replacing them with RP and Standard English, which were seen as hallmarks of refinement.

Activity

How much has changed since the time when Daniel Jones was writing? What are our contemporary attitudes to the idea of people changing their accents? Discuss this with other students, using the online article below as a starting point. This article is from *The Independent* and is about a teacher who was told to try to change her accent:

http://www.independent.co.uk/news/uk/home-news/teacher-told-to-sound-less-northern-after-southern-ofsted-inspection-8947332.html

When you have finished your discussion, write up your views in the form of an opinion article, imagining that you are addressing your school or college governors or council to help them devise a policy on this issue.

More accent variations

There are further sounds that characterize broad differences between regions. On page 60, you learned about the **post-vocalic /r/**, where some speakers pronounce the /r/ where it occurs in the spelling of a word after a vowel: for example, 'work', 'car', 'fur', 'surf'. In RP, the /r/ would not be pronounced, but in the West Country and parts of Lancashire, as well as in Scotland and Ireland, the /r/ would be sounded. Accents where the /r/ is sounded are called **rhotic**.

On pages 60–61, you also learned about Trudgill's research on the East Anglian accent, where he found that – in Norwich – speakers used /n/ where RP speakers would use /ŋ/ at the end of a word such as 'swimming'. This substitution is common to many regional accents. In prescriptive, judgmental statements about this feature, you will sometimes hear people talking about 'g dropping', characterizing this as 'sloppy speech'. This is not an accurate description of what is happening, because there was no 'g' to be dropped in the first place. Statements like this show that people are thinking about writing, rather than spoken language. Such speakers are simply substituting one sound for another; they are not losing anything.

Understanding some linguistic facts can also help to clarify the use of another sound, /h/, which doesn't exist at all in some regional accents, such as the older version of Cockney. Just because some English words are spelt with the letter 'h' at the beginning – for example, 'hospital' or 'holiday' – it doesn't mean that it is necessarily pronounced in speech. In fact, even RP speakers don't always pronounce an /h/ where it occurs in the spelling of a word – for example, in the words 'honour', 'hour', 'honest' and 'heir'. Those who would criticize regional speakers for supposed 'h dropping' don't criticize pronunciations of those words. Again, the idea of 'dropping' something that you never had in the first place doesn't make sense.

Key term

Rhotic. Accents where speakers produce the post-vocalic /r/, such as in many rural accents in the south-west region of the UK.

Did you know?

Many English words that have a letter h at the front when written but no /h/ when spoken come from French, where that sound is not pronounced. For example, honnête is French for 'honest'.

Glottal stops /ʔ/ also feature in many regional accents. Technically, a glottal stop is not a sound in itself but a lack of sound: it describes closing off the vocal cords to prevent sound coming out. This mechanism has a physiological function: it traps air in the lungs in order to help with a physical challenge, such as lifting a heavy weight. Stops are also used in connected speech – to demarcate boundaries between sounds. As a feature of regional speech, glottal stops function as alternatives for some plosives – for example, the /t/ in 'button' or 'butter'. In a Cockney accent, these words would be /bʌʔən/ and /bʌʔə/. As with the other sounds, it makes no sense to describe the glottal as 'lazy' or 'sloppy' speech, because in fact it takes a lot of energy to produce.

Some London speakers also substitute the fricative /θ/ with /f/ and /ð/ with /v/, so 'thin' is pronounced as 'fin', and 'with' as 'wiv'. English regional accents in the London area present a complex picture, however, as some aspects of London speech have been generalized to other areas of the country, with some aspects acquiring **overt prestige** and others **covert prestige**. **Estuary English** is an example of the former, and will be discussed later in this section. **Multicultural London English** is an example of the latter, and will be discussed in the final section of this chapter, on language and ethnicity.

Researching accent variation

Acquiring exactly the data that you want in as natural a way as possible is a constant methodological issue in social science investigations generally, and linguistic research is no different. In order to explore specific features of accent and dialect, Trudgill developed a complex and thorough method which involved recording people speaking in a range of different ways, to see whether increased formality of the context reduced the frequency of non-standard features. These different contexts included extended free talking (prompted by asking about a strong memory); reading a passage aloud; being interviewed; and reading a list of words. Trudgill's word list was carefully designed to include clusters of words that would highlight specific differences between varieties.

Once the data from the methods above had been collected from his informants, Trudgill told them exactly which **linguistic variables** he had been investigating. He then asked his informants whether they used the features in question. Information given by people about their own language use is called **self-reported usage** and can reveal some interesting insights. For example, in Trudgill's study, men tended to over-report their own usage while women tended to under-report, suggesting a connection with gender identity (but see the comment on page 61 about gender and social-class categories).

Regardless of how well any particular method worked, the reason why Trudgill and other sociolinguists employ a range of different methods is because none of us has only one style of language use: we all have a repertoire, which, for some speakers, could include a strongly regional style. We are all adept at accommodation and adaptation, and may therefore perform a range of identities through our linguistic choices, even across the course of a single day. This can depend on our audience, our physical location, the purpose of our speech and even the topic. For example, someone now living in a different region may unconsciously adopt features from a 'home' dialect when reminiscing or being nostalgic.

Key terms

Covert prestige. Status gained from peer group recognition, rather than public acknowledgement.

Estuary English. A recent accent variety used in south east England which combines RP with some aspects of regional southern accents. 'Estuary' refers to the Thames Estuary area.

Glottal stop. A closure of the vocal cords. This can be used to replace /t/ in some regional accents.

Linguistic variable. An item of language that is likely to vary and is therefore of interest to sociolinguists.

Multicultural London English. A recent variety combining elements of the language of different ethnic groups, particularly Afro-Caribbean English. The variety arose in London but has spread to different parts of the UK.

Overt prestige. Status that is publicly acknowledged.

Self-reported usage. People describing their own language use (as opposed to being recorded using language).

Link

See Chapter 7 for more information about different research methodologies.

Word	Possible pronunciations
BUS	/bʊs/ /bʌs/ /bʊz/
CAR	/kɑ:/ /kɑ:r/
BATH	/bæθ/ /bɑ:θ/
COT	/kɒt/ /kɔ:t/
FUR	/fɜ:/ /fɜ:r/
FAIR	/fɜ:/ /feə/
PUT	/pʊt/
PUTT	/pʊt/ /pʌt/
PAW	/pɔ:/
POOR	/pʊər/
SINGING	/sɪŋɪn/ /sɪŋɪŋ/ /sɪŋgɪŋ/
THREE	/θri:/ /fri:/ /tri:/
BOTTLE	/bɒʔəl/ /bɒtəl/
ABOUT	/əbɑ:t/ /əbaʊt/
THEM	/ðem/ /vem/ /dem/

Key term

Dialect levelling. The way in which dialect terms have been dropping out of use.

Link

If you are interested in the topic of language and region, you could think about writing something on this subject for the original writing element of your coursework folder. There are many informative, as well as persuasive, aspects of this topic that could lend themselves to an interesting article. For example, very detailed work is done in forensic fields by experts in speech and language variation. See the work of Tim Grant at Aston University: http://www.forensiclinguistics.net and Peter French at York University: http://www.jpfrench.com

Activity

Compile a word list that you think might capture some aspects of regional speech in your area. To get you started, and to give you some more practice in working with the phonemic alphabet, look at the words in capitals in the table on the left and then at the possible pronunciations. Try to work out which accent is represented in each case. Some of the words have more than one possible answer. You have been told about some of these in this section, but in other cases you have not – so you will need to pronounce each set of symbols carefully and see what kind of voice emerges. Answers are at the back of the book.

Research idea

Use your word list and one of Trudgill's more naturalistic methods, described on page 69, to research the accent of your local area. Try to involve people from different age groups if you can. If you ask them about some of the words and phrases they think are part of the local dialect, you could capture more than one source of data for your study. You could use this research idea either as your coursework investigation or as a pilot study for it. ●

Activity

There are many online sources where you can hear different accents and improve your listening and analytical skills. One of the best sites is the British Library's 'Voices' project, at the address below. Spend some time on the site and listen to the wide range of regional speech that has been collected by researchers.

http://sounds.bl.uk/Accents-and-dialects/BBC-Voices

Regional dialect vocabulary

Researchers have for some time noted a process of **dialect levelling**, where aspects of regional language – particularly vocabulary – have gradually been dying out. Nevertheless, certain aspects of cultural life still seem to have preserved some significant variation. One such area is regional food names (particularly different kinds of bread roll). Another area is vocabulary about people's personality traits or moods, along with more general terms for 'good' and 'bad'. Some names for items of clothing, children's games and rituals, and endearments such as 'love' and 'mate', also seem to vary according to region.

Activity

Below are some items from each of the categories mentioned above. Research their origins and see if you can add to this list for your locality.

If you are in a group context where there are people from different regions, compare your terms with theirs. For the children's items, you will need to search your memories or ask young relatives.

When you have compiled your lists, think about why these particular areas of lexis might have retained some variation.

You will also need to think about whether the terms you have noted are regional dialect (distinctive of a particular region) or **slang** (informal usage that is widely recognized). Note that terms can move from the former to the latter. For example, 'gobsmacked' was originally a north-west regional term, but has now become well known across the UK and beyond.

- Bread roll: barm cake, cob…
- Personality traits or moods: nesh, nowty…
- Good/bad: bostin', hangin'…
- Clothing: ganzie, daps…
- Children's terms: tag, fainities…
- Endearments: hinny, boss…

Key terms

Isogloss. A geographic boundary indicating where certain items of language are used.

Slang. Language that is used in informal contexts and widely recognized (unlike dialect usage, which occurs only in particular regions).

The earliest studies in this area were conducted by survey and involved recording what things were called in different parts of the country. Such differences were often recorded on maps using **isoglosses**, or lines drawn to show where one usage ended and another began. Lexical differences can still be explored now by asking people to select from a list a word or phrase that they would use (ranking words and phrases according to how likely they are to use them); by showing people pictures and asking them to name the objects or concepts; or by asking them to imagine particular scenarios and state what they would say.

Extension activity

Construct and conduct a survey of the regional dialect vocabulary of your area. You could do this in a group, with each person taking a different age group. That way, you could get a sense of whether usage is changing as years go by.

Agree a method from the options above. As part of your research, you could try to identify which terms people actually use and which they may recognize but not use. The British Library site, mentioned earlier, could be a useful starting point if you want to add further items to your list:

http://sounds.bl.uk/Accents-and-dialects/Survey-of-English-dialects

Regional dialect grammar

There seem to be very different public attitudes towards dialect vocabulary and dialect grammar. In fact, some people would probably argue that there is no such thing as dialect grammar – that it's all just 'bad English'. Dialect grammar exists because Standard English was once itself a dialectal system, and the way things are done in SE in some areas of grammar happen to be different from how they are done in other regional systems.

On the following pages are some of the areas of grammatical variation that still exist today. As with the accent variations we studied earlier, some of these variants are present in more than one dialect.

Key terms

Determiner. Determiners, as the name suggests, help to determine what a noun refers to. Determiners can be wide ranging in their reference, including quantity ('some', 'many'), definiteness ('the' or 'a'), possession ('my', 'our') and demonstrativeness ('these', 'those'). Demonstratives are also called **deictics**, or pointing words.

Preposition. A word that typically indicates direction, position, or relationship, such as 'into', 'on', or 'of'.

Progressive form. The 'ing' ending in words such as 'walking' and 'running', indicating ongoing activity.

Relativizer. Another word for a relative pronoun, for example, 'which', 'who' 'that', often used at the front of a subordinate clause.

Prepositions

Prepositions vary regionally – for example, dialect speakers in the south-west say 'where's he to?' (Standard English: 'where is he?') and Yorkshire dialect speakers say 'while' (SE: 'until') in phrases like 'ten while twelve'.

Pronouns

There are variations in personal pronouns. For example, in Liverpool, there is a plural of you – 'yous' – which is a subtlety that Standard English doesn't have. It used to have this, in the form of 'thee/thou' for the singular and 'ye/you' for the plural.

Some speakers of northern and midlands dialects still retain 'thee' and 'thou' as address terms for 'you'. Reflexive pronouns, which again are irregular in Standard English, are often regularized in regional dialect grammar, so the system that begins with 'myself' and 'yourself' continues in some regional speech with 'hisself' (SE 'himself') and 'theirselves' (SE 'themselves'). The SE versions are irregular, using personal pronouns to make those two exceptions to what is otherwise a system of possessives + 'self'.

The verb 'to be'

The Standard English past tense of the verb 'to be' is an irregular system, with 'was' used in the first and third person singular, and 'were' everywhere else. Cockney speakers will use 'was' throughout (so they would say 'we was') and some northern dialect users have 'were' throughout (so they would say 'I were'). Speakers of dialect in the south-west may also use 'be' throughout the present tense ('I be', 'you be').

Other verb forms

Dialects tend to simplify some systems, for example having an 's' on all present-tense verb endings, instead of just on the third person – for example, 'So I gets out of the car and I says…'.

Where in SE the verbs 'sit' and 'stand' are used in their **progressive forms**, 'sitting' and 'standing', some regional dialects use the perfective 'sat' and 'stood' instead: 'I was sat there', 'she was stood there'.

Regional dialect verb usage can sometimes reduce the number of different forms for marking tenses, for example using two rather than three: 'I do' and 'I done', rather than (in SE), 'I do', 'I did', 'I have done'.

Relativizers

It is an accident of history that modern English uses the relative terms 'that' and 'which' to join clauses together. 'What' was a **relativizer** from a different regional dialect; if chosen, it would have led to an expression such as 'that's the film what I saw' being regarded as correct.

Determiners

Standard English uses the **determiner** 'those' in expressions such as 'look at those people', where regional dialects sometimes have 'them'.

Double negation

This is a complex topic, because there are double negatives in Standard English as well as regional dialects. For example, if you write in your essay 'this is not an unreasonable idea' you are using a double negative, and no one would criticize this usage. Yet double negatives are stigmatized in regional dialect as 'bad English'. It follows that it's just some double negatives that attract criticism: the usual example quoted is 'I didn't do nothing', which sounds less like an academic and more like a miscreant.

Historically, double negatives – like another negative construction, 'ain't' – were in common use. For example, Chaucer uses three negatives in the example below (in italics); in his time, the piling up of negatives was simply an expressive strategy for emphasis:

> Ther *nas no* man *nowher* so vertuous
> Geoffrey Chaucer, 'The Friar's Tale'

A final type of negative construction – a particular use of never – can indicate a one-off meaning in regional expressions, such as 'I never ate that cheese', where SE would not use 'never' in this way.

Activity

Read the made-up text below, which includes a range of regional dialect constructions.
- See if you can describe all of the structures in a technical way.
- What impression do you think this kind of language creates in public perceptions?
- What kind of speaker do you imagine the narrator of this text to be?

The answers are all in the previous explanations.

> We was going shopping ten while twelve. We was stood there when I says to my friend, 'That's the man what I saw before'. My friend says, 'Where's he to?' I says 'Over there, next to them people'. We goes up to him and he gets hisself up and says, 'Why are you picking on me? I never done nothing'.

Attitudes to non-standard varieties

Attitudes to regional language clearly vary according to which aspect of language is under discussion. While many people appear to have some fondness for dialect vocabulary – perhaps seeing these terms as part of their family history – the idea of dialect grammar seems to be scarcely credited or even believed. And yet, based on a great deal of empirical evidence, Milroy and Milroy (2014) list many differences between the grammatical systems used by contemporary regional speakers in different parts of the country.

When grammatical structures are the topic of discussion in popular discourse, it seems that this usually centres on some point of disputation about 'correctness' in a prescriptive sense. You saw this in action in Chapter 1 (pages 24–25), where objections were raised to the use of 'was' instead of 'were'. In that case, as in others – for example, the issue of the double negative, above – language is being

Key term

Matched guise technique.
An experimental technique where a single actor puts on a different accent for different audiences, but keeps the content of the speech the same.

Link

Media coverage of accent issues is interesting, but you need to be aware that some media programmes can generate controversy as well as expose it. The following article includes some research on attitudes, but take a critical approach to the results: what has really been discovered?
http://www.itv.com/news/2013-09-25/28-of-britons-feel-discriminated-against-due-to-accent/

used as a Shibboleth, where objections to the language of an individual or group are really objections to the people themselves.

Attitudes to accent seem to share some common ground with those surrounding grammar, but with the difference that there seem to have been some changes in perspective as well as in the accents themselves.

Attitudes to accent

Much work on attitudes to accent was done in the 1970s by Howard Giles and his associates in the field of language and social psychology. The question of interest to Giles – whose work on convergence and divergence was discussed on page 60 – was how far responses to speakers were due to an individual's accent alone, or to his or her character.

To rule out the effects of different character traits, Giles famously conducted experiments where the same speaker performed a set speech to different audiences, using a different accent for each of the audiences. This method was called the **matched guise technique**. Many criticisms can be made of this method, including whether it is possible for one person to perform different accents convincingly. But his results raised some interesting questions that we are still discussing today.

Giles tested responses to different accents using three main parameters:

- status – testing how powerful and important the speaker appeared to be
- personality – testing what traits of character came across
- persuasiveness – testing how believable the person seemed.

His results showed a ranking order of this kind for status:

RP

National accents (e.g. Welsh, Irish, Scottish)

Regional rural accents

Regional urban accents

In terms of personality, RP was seen as self-confident, intelligent and ambitious, but also cold and ruthless. Northern-accented speech was characterized as honest, reliable, generous, sincere, warm and humorous.

The factor of persuasiveness was more complex to disentangle, because someone can seem persuasive because of social status, or friendliness, so persuasiveness isn't really an independent dimension. However, in one of the experiments the speech was about capital punishment, and when a questionnaire was used a week after the speech, only those who had heard the regional guises appeared to have been persuaded by the views proposed.

Over the years, various studies asking people to rate accents for particular qualities have produced similar results. Although RP is associated with high social status (in terms of wealth, level of education and employment), regional speakers are trusted more (being seen as more honest, reliable and friendly, as well as more humorous).

Estuary English

Some of the findings above may explain the rise of the new type of accent that has been called Estuary English. David Rosewarne coined the term 'Estuary' for this accent in an article in the *Times Educational Supplement* in 1984. He described the accent as 'modified regional speech' and placed it along a continuum between RP and Cockney. The idea of Estuary English has become well known outside linguistic circles, while many linguists see it more as an umbrella term covering a range of southern English dialects.

Key features that are generally accepted as Estuary include the following:

- Glottal stops, particularly in word-medial and word-final positions before a consonant: e.g. Gatwick Airport /gæʔwɪk eəpɔːʔ/. But a glottal stop before a vowel, e.g. /bʌʔə/ for 'butter', is seen as closer to the Cockney end of the spectrum.

- L-vocalization, in which /l/ is pronounced as a vowel or like a w: e.g. /fʊʔbɔːw/ for 'football'.

- Confrontational tag questions: 'I said I would, didn't I?'

Speakers of Estuary English are thought to be aiming for a 'classless' profile – avoiding the privileged and unfriendly connotations of RP while also, for regional speakers, sidestepping the tag of being ill-educated. There has been much debate about the precise demarcation of Estuary English, but there is general agreement that it represents a shift towards more centralized varieties. Estuary features can be heard all over the British Isles, which perhaps points towards the levelling of UK dialects. However, at the same time, some regional dialects seem to be resisting levelling. Watson's study of Liverpool speech (2008) has found that, contrary to indications that Estuary or hybrid accents are used UK-wide, Liverpool appears to be a 'dialectal island'.

REVIEW YOUR LEARNING

Carry out the set of activities below in order to review your learning in this section.

Activity

The following article from *The Times*, and the two weblinks below, all present ideas about public attitudes towards accent. This material shares the theme that both RP and regional accents are subject to stereotyping. The article suggests that some speakers are trying to adapt their RP accents in order to seem more approachable. The two poets, Tom Leonard and Emma Jones, both express views about regional accent prejudice and the nature of media representations.

Read (and listen to) this material and then carry out Activities 1–4 to add your own evidence to the mix.

- Tom Leonard, Unrelated Incidents: http://www.youtube.com/watch?v=gMo5cxzLdR4
- Emma Jones: http://youtu.be/TzOUJ4YKNJo

▶

1. Record some examples of TV advertising and analyse the ways in which different accents are used to sell products.

2. Survey some different news outlets and make notes about the accents of the announcers.

3. Record a public figure who uses RP and assess whether there are any features of 'Estuary' in his or her pronunciation.

4. Tom Leonard and Emma Jones make a point of writing their poems in **eye dialect**, representing regional accents by using the regular written alphabet. Find some written representations of their work and compare it with a phonemic version of the sounds they are suggesting. You could do the same exercise with any piece of eye dialect from a novel.

Key term

Eye dialect. Using the regular alphabet to represent sounds, rather than a phonetic or phonemic alphabet.

Voice coaches in demand to rub the polish off posh accents

Growing numbers of young adults, expensively educated in some of the best public schools in Britain, are seeking to soften the haughty-sounding accents that cost their parents thousands of pounds for them to acquire, voice coaches say.

The shamelessly posh upper-crust accents of *Downton Abbey* and *Sherlock's* Benedict Cumberbatch might show what life was like for a privileged few in the past, but in the present the trend is heading in the other direction.

George Osborne is among politicians who have been accused of toning down their accents to broaden their popular appeal. Recently he has been heard to pronounce 'British' as 'Briddish' and 'want to' as 'wanna'.

Henry Fagg, director of The Tutor Pages, a website that includes elocution teachers on its books, said that the 350 inquiries his website had received so far this year for help with elocution showed how an accent could hamper career progression in professions such as the media, law and medicine.

He said, 'Our experience of increased demand for this subject suggests that people now have an updated concept of what elocution is really for. Rather than taking elocution lessons to speak the Queen's English, the trend has been towards individuals from diverse backgrounds wishing to adapt their voices for success in a surprising variety of contexts – sometimes even by sounding not posh'.

The BBC newsreader Charlotte Green, once voted the 'most attractive female voice on national radio', has claimed that her accent is no longer in vogue at the BBC. 'Received pronunciation is on the wane', she has said. 'The BBC's days of employing people who sound like me are more or less over.'

[…] The violinist Nigel Kennedy rebelled against his middle-class background and adopted a London accent. BBC footage has shown him speaking with received pronunciation when he was seven and he has explained how the change to a less posh accent was driven by his peers. 'I also found that some of the jazz musicians I looked up to most didn't speak like my mum. So it just sort of changed by osmosis'.

Christine Hubbard, a professional soprano and voice coach who was privately educated, has noticed the trend. 'I was brought up with a cut-glass accent and all my peers were the same', she said. 'As I entered later teenage years and adulthood it became obvious that it was not always an advantage to speak well. It was therefore my first experiment to reduce my own accent, however, I am still able to use it.'

She is sought after, especially by young professionals such as police officers, teachers and social workers who are trying to hide the evidence of an expensive education to help them in the workplace. 'They have clients who might refuse to talk to them because they think they are stuck up'. Young people training for professions such as the law, on the other hand, approach her to make their accent more posh.

[...] 'I had inquiries from a maths teacher who felt his voice was very haughty and gave the wrong impression to students,' said Liam O'Sullivan, a voice coach. 'A lot of people feel the accents that many in this present Government have can make them seem out of touch. It gives them an air of superiority that makes them seem impervious to other people's feelings. 'Interestingly, I have never had an inquiry or student who wanted to speak with received pronunciation.'

Gledhill (2014)

Research idea

Any of the ideas above could form the basis of an interesting investigation (or a good starting point for a piece of original writing). Many further areas have been covered in this chapter, such as:

- identifying the features that make up a particular variety
- exploring differences between different groups within a region
- finding out why people use non-standard varieties
- examining people's attitudes to different varieties.

Each focus would require a slightly different methodology and can enrich our understanding of regional variation in different ways.

References

Gledhill, R. (2014) 'Voice coaches in demand to rub the polish off posh accents', *The Times*, Monday 7 April.

Jones, D. [1909] (1956) *The Pronunciation of English*, Cambridge: Cambridge University Press.

Milroy, J. and Milroy, L. (2014) *Real English: The Grammar of English Dialects in the British Isles*. London: Routledge.

Watson, K. (2008) 'Is Scouse getting Scouser? Exploring phonological change in contemporary Liverpool English'. In Grant, A. & Grey C. (eds) *The Mersey Sound: Liverpool's Language, People and Places*. Liverpool: Open House Press, pages 215–241.

Further reading

Coggle, P. (1993) *Do You Speak Estuary?* London: Bloomsbury

Hughes, A., Trudgill, P., and Watt, D. (2012) *English Accents and Dialects*. London: Routledge

Some pages by Clive Upton, who ran the Survey of English Dialects at Leeds University, can be found here:

http://public.oed.com/aspects-of-english/english-in-use/english-dialect-study-an-overview/

This section of Chapter 3 will:

- help you to understand the relationship between language and occupation

- show you some of the linguistic complexity within work contexts, as well as how organizations are represented

- give you some frameworks for analysing data and answering essay questions about this topic.

Introduction

Most of us don't experience lots of occupations in our lives, in the sense of being employed in many different jobs. Yet, at the same time, most of us have a sense of different workplaces, and could say something about how workplaces might vary. For example, we have images of some people in offices and others in laboratories, some people in factories, and others in fields. But how much do we really know about those different contexts?

We have a broad knowledge of workplaces, partly because we interact with them as part of our everyday lives. Attending school is compulsory for children; but it is also a workplace for some people who choose to be teachers. Going to a café or restaurant can be a leisure activity for customers; but working there is a career choice for some people who want to work in the catering and hospitality industry. Shopping involves us parting with money; but the retail sector is also a big employer, paying the wages of workers in many different roles.

Did you know?

Schooling was made compulsory for children in Britain only in 1870. Before that, the children of working-class parents were part of the workforce – labouring in factories, on farms, or as domestic servants or apprentices.

Activity

Make a list – in a group, if possible – of all of the workplaces with which you have had some contact. Don't forget to include your school or college! This doesn't have to be somewhere you have actually worked – also include instances where you may have been a customer.

When you've finished your list, think about any language use that you may have encountered in your listed workplaces. In particular, try to think of any examples of distinctive or typical language used by the employees in those contexts.

Aside from our actual experiences of workplaces, we also think we know about different occupational groups from the many representations we are shown in films and TV programmes.

Activity

Think about any films and TV programmes that you've watched where workplaces form the main setting for the storyline. Make a list of the different workplaces.

- Do any particular types of workplaces feature more than once? If so, what do you see as the main reason for using that particular occupational setting?

- Are some types of workplaces never featured? If so, why do you think that is?

- What impressions are you given by these representations of the various workplaces and the language used in those occupations?

There is some feedback on this activity at the back of the book.

Research idea

Language and occupation is a good area for potential investigations. If you do a part-time job, have a relative who works in a particular occupation, or are interested in how language is used to represent occupations – for example, in recruitment advertisements or in TV programmes – you could easily collect some good data for researching this topic.

Occupational lexis

When we think of occupational language, we tend to think of the lexical items that are part of that occupation's semantic field. This is because they are probably the most noticeable aspect of language use, especially if the terms are exclusive to that occupation and not part of our more general vocabulary. Such terms might also be memorable if we have had to puzzle over them – finding ourselves as much at sea as a beginner would be learning a foreign language.

Some occupations – most notably, law and medicine – not only use highly specialized lexis, but lexis that is heavily influenced by other languages. Many legal terms are based on French and Latin – these languages having been influential in the history of the legal profession, as well as in the UK's cultural history more generally (see the section on lexis and semantics in Chapter 1, pages 17–20).

 Activity

Below are 12 examples of **restricted** occupational lexis – specialist vocabulary that is only ever used in a specific occupation (in this case, the legal profession). Look up these legal terms in a dictionary with etymological information (most contemporary archives have this, including online sites such as OUP's www.oxforddictionaries.com).

- How many of these terms come from French or Latin?
- What do they refer to?
- What was their original meaning?

voir dire	estoppel	laches
prima facie	novation	waiver
sub judice	habeas corpus	tort
subpoena	covenant	fee simple

There is some feedback on this activity at the back of the book.

Key term

Restricted. Used only within a specific context.

As well as specialist terms that are only ever used in one profession, there are also terms that have a particular meaning within a profession, but a different and perhaps broader meaning within general usage. This is by far the more common case where occupational lexis is concerned. For example, again with reference to legal language, the terms 'action', 'party', 'execute' and 'seizure' have particular meanings that are quite different from everyday usage. Can you see how this is the case in the text below?

> They started *an action* against their neighbour, who in this case is the innocent *party*. The terms of the agreement must be *executed* and a general *seizure* must surely be the outcome.

So far, occupational lexis has focused on:

- restricted usage
- usage that is shared with more general functions, but where the occupational usage has a particular meaning.

A third aspect of occupational lexis is the direct opposite of these cases. There are some instances where words and phrases that were originally restricted to occupational contexts have now become part of general discourse – losing their original restricted meaning but still having traceable connections with it. Chapter 1 touched on this idea when looking at idiomatic expressions (page 21). Many idiomatic expressions in English started life more literally, as occupational references: for example, the phrases 'bringing home the bacon', 'balancing the books', 'a close shave' and 'spinning a yarn' all refer to different jobs.

Activity

1. What do you think the occupational references are behind the four phrases above?
2. English also has many idiomatic expressions that derive from sport. Try to work out which sports gave us the following phrases:

- 'out for the count'
- 'on a sticky wicket'
- 'he won hands down'
- 'reaching a stalemate'
- 'the ball is in your court'
- 'let's touch base'
- 'no holds barred'

Answers are at the back of the book.

A further, more subtle, aspect of occupational lexis is where employees use language that is part of everyday discourse, but they resort to it more frequently than people outside that occupation. You can see an example of this below, in the language of teachers' reports.

Activity

Identify some of the lexical items that are characteristic of teachers' professional discourse by analysing the reports below.

There is some feedback on this activity at the back of the book.

Hasan is a reserved member of the group, who displays a quiet interest in the subject. Hasan tries hard throughout lessons and generally succeeds in all tasks set. A good year with steady progress being made – well done Hasan.

William is a lively pupil, who is keen to participate during class discussion. William needs to listen more carefully if he is going to improve in this subject. Good progress has been made, but with a more concerted effort he could go much further.

Susan is a sociable pupil. She puts considerable effort into her work, but doesn't plan out her tasks in sufficient detail. The progress Susan has shown this year has been hindered by attendance issues.

Safiya is a conscientious and capable pupil. She always listens carefully and puts full effort into tasks. I am pleased with the effort Safiya has put in this year – well done.

Teachers' reports represent one type of communication within that profession. You would get a very different result if you collected some spoken data from a teacher's lesson, or if you analysed some worksheets that a teacher had written with pupils in mind, or if you recorded some staffroom coffee-break chat. As you saw in Chapter 2, language varies considerably according to such factors as audience, genre, purpose and mode.

The factor of audience for teachers' reports is especially complex. They certainly have parents as one major audience, but they are also read by pupils, and in some cases, the reports you have just been studying actually address the pupils themselves. But there are also further audiences inside the school – for example, teachers' own heads of subject, the year head, the head teacher, and school governors. There are also potential audiences beyond the school, such as local authority figures and Ofsted inspectors. The reports have to strike a balance between the needs of all these interested readers.

Working on a small sample of material, as is the case with the reports opposite, may be revealing of what we think we know from our experience of educational contexts. But to confirm those intuitions enough to create academic theories, a larger amount of data is necessary.

Modern language **corpora** are increasingly used to look at patterns in specialist domains. For example, Michael Nelson's research at Manchester University on business English compared a **corpus** of business language with a more general corpus, the British National Corpus (BNC), in order to investigate whether there was such a thing as business lexis. He found what he describes as 'a semantic field of business' involving a limited number of semantic categories: terms to do with 'business people, companies, institutions, money, business events, places of business, time, modes of communication and lexis concerned with technology' (Wilson 2000).

By comparing business English with the BNC, Nelson also showed what did *not* feature in business contexts. For example, while all the weekdays featured in business English, Saturday and Sunday did not. He also found little reference to personal issues, society, family, house and home, and personal activities. Taking one example of difference, in referring to places, business English included references to these sites:

premises, department, boardroom, depot, office, division, marketplace

but none of these:

town, county, village, opera, prison, castle, library, palace.

Also used far less in business was lexis referring to distinctly negative states. Words used to express deep, reflective and profound feelings were found to occur significantly less – the word 'truth', for example, was found to occur nine times less in business English than in general English.

Occupational grammar and discourse

Lexis is not the only language level that is useful when thinking about occupation. Aside from the vocabulary used by teachers in the reports opposite, you will have noticed that all four of the reports adopted a similar structure: an initial sentence beginning '[Pupil name] is', referring to his or her general character and demeanour; a sentence describing habitual behaviour in lessons throughout the year; and a concluding sentence either summing up in a positive way (for those showing good progress) or setting out what needs to be done in future (for those showing limited progress).

REMEMBER

You do not need the same amount of data for your investigation that a university researcher would need. Your study is a small-scale piece of research where you need to analyse a limited amount of data, in order to show that you can analyse in detail.

Key term
Corpus (plural corpora). A collection of searchable language data stored on a computer.

Key terms

Discourse community.
An alternative term for a **community of practice.**

Discourse structure. The internal structure of a text.

Ethnography / Ethnographic. The study of how a group of people communicate. Ethnographers are often part of the community they study.

Inference. Using assumed knowledge in order to determine meaning.

Research idea

In his book *Other Floors, Other Voices: A Textography of a Small University Building,* John Swales tests out his ideas about discourse communities by going to different spaces in an academic setting, where he notices the varied discourses used by different academic subjects. He calls his work a 'textography', because he mixes text analysis with **ethnography**.

You could investigate this idea in your school or college by looking at the different notice boards, textbooks, and displays in classrooms and corridors devoted to different subject areas. Do academic subjects speak the same language?

This can be termed **discourse structure**, because it is a structure that runs across sentences – weaving them into a pattern to form a cohesive text.

Many occupations use texts that have predictable patterns in this way. For example, texts such as a doctor's prescription; sheets showing earnings and expenditure in accountancy; a last will and testament; a marriage certificate; a police report, or a newspaper article all have predictable elements that are more or less flexible. All are occupational discourses, and knowing how to write them is part of the knowledge held by any **discourse community** or community of practice.

John Swales (2011) defined a discourse community as having members who:

- share a set of common goals
- communicate internally, using and 'owning' one or more genres of communication
- use specialist lexis and discourse
- possess a required level of knowledge and skill to be considered eligible to participate in the community.

Of course, members of a discourse community do not all communicate using fixed templates all the time. If they did, it would seem very robotic. In fact, discourses are constantly changing as members exercise their creativity in adapting and refreshing the language they use.

Another way to look at occupational grammar and discourse is to think about the functions that language can have for employees in a particular role. For example, a teacher with a class of young children will need to spend time managing behaviour, and this could lead to the use of large numbers of verbs in the imperative mood, in phrases such as 'be quiet' or 'work quickly' or 'play nicely'. The same structure could be present wherever someone is in a position where they need to give instructions: for example, a surgeon in an operating theatre, a pilot flying a plane, an instructor leading an aerobics class.

A different balance of grammatical structures might be in evidence in the language of employees whose job it is to find out what customers want: for example, the counter staff at a food outlet. While they might well be shouting orders behind them, to the chefs making the food, their interactions with customers are likely to be populated with question-and-answer routines.

Occupational pragmatics and power

Pragmatics refers to the idea of assumed meanings, where people know how things work because they share **inferences** – unspoken understandings. Being able to infer a meaning shows that you are already knowledgeable and don't need everything spelt out. Pragmatics and power are strongly interconnected because – as should be obvious from the previous sentence – there is power in knowledge. If you know the rules of a community, you can participate in it; if you don't, and you don't know how to acquire knowledge of the rules, then you are destined to be an outsider.

In some periods of British history, the area of pragmatics related to entire languages. For many years after the Norman invasion in 1066, the language of official life was French, so for example it was impossible to take a legal case to court without knowing French. If you couldn't speak French, you had to pay someone to speak for you. Being able to use Latin was also a sign of status and power for many centuries, because of its role in education and the Church. More recently, literacy itself – the ability to write and read – has played a role in marking professional status.

The references to power and privilege above may now seem old-fashioned, but have ideas about 'knowing the rules' and 'knowing the right language to use' ever really gone away?

Activity

Think about the power of different occupations, and how that power relates to language use.

- Are there still situations where we pay people to speak on our behalf?
- Which professions profit from our inability to 'speak the right language'?
- Have you ever felt that you didn't use the right language, or use language in the appropriate way, when interacting with certain groups of people?

Drew and Heritage (1993) suggest that members of a discourse community share **inferential frameworks** with each other, consisting of implicit ways of thinking, communicating and behaving. They also suggest that there are strong hierarchies of power within organizations, with many **asymmetrical** relationships marked by language use. One example of this is the idea that there are constraints on individuals dictating the language they are allowed to use.

We have seen some clear examples of this in recent years, where employees have lost their jobs for bringing their organization into disrepute by what they have written on social media sites such as Facebook or Twitter.

Activity

Identify an organization with which you are familiar. This may be somewhere you work part-time, or you could use your own school or college. You could also think about your use of social media, and the discourse communities that you are a part of there.

Are there ways in which individuals within the organization have different language rights? For example, consider:

- the ability to speak, or having to be silent in certain situations
- the use of names and titles
- aspects of taboo around certain language topics or expressions
- interactions with the world outside of the community – for example in the use of digital media to publish thoughts, views and experiences.

As well as the idea of power both within and beyond organizations, some researchers have pointed out the way in which employees can support each other in their tasks. For example, Koester (2004) shows how important **phatic** talk is, in getting jobs done. Workers need to establish interpersonal relationships and have interactions that are not just about work-related procedures. And although some employers are represented as discouraging talk that is not strictly work-related, Koester shows that being sociable and engaging

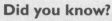
Did you know?

The Plain English Campaign has been lobbying since 1979 to make the language of official bodies easier to understand. It awards a 'Crystal Mark' to organizations that have made their documents more user friendly. Go to http://www.plainenglish.co.uk

Key terms

Asymmetrical. Unequal.

Inferential framework. Knowledge built up over time and used in order to understand meanings that are implicit.

Phatic. Language that is devoid of content but that supports social relationships.

Key term

Solidarity. A feeling of connection with others, mutual support.

in personal chat is an important aspect of effective working. As well as power, then, **solidarity** – the ability to connect with one's workmates – is an important dimension in workplace communication.

Occupational phonology and prosody

This language level receives scant mention in research on language and occupation. However, it is worth thinking about, because some occupational roles include particular requirements on individuals to use their voices in special ways. Teaching and lecturing are examples of this, as are those other professions that involve public performance of one kind or another: for example, delivering sermons; making railway announcements; commentating on sports events; speaking to camera as a journalist; chairing meetings; performing stand-up comedy. You can probably think of many more examples, and each one would be a valid source of data for your coursework investigation.

Occupation and international English

In an age when organizations are increasingly networked, it would be remiss not to mention the changing role of English in international workplaces. Employees can stay in one location but still use English in international interactions, because of the use of digital communication tools. Chapters 5 and 6 cover the topics of language change and international English, respectively. Perhaps nowhere are these topics more keenly felt than in work contexts, where native speakers of English are in communication with a wide range of different users of English, and where there are many more interactions in English that don't involve native speakers at all. In all of these interactions, participants have to negotiate how to understand each other – making judgements all the time about the best options of register and style.

International interactions are by no means simply about the language skills of people who are using English as a second or additional language. They are also about the ability of native speakers to develop useful language strategies for new situations where they are not understood, or where they do not understand the variety of English being used. A good example of this can be seen in research by Kim & Elder (2009) on the communication difficulties experienced by Korean pilots and air-traffic staff when communicating with their American colleagues. Far from the problems being caused by poor language skills among the Korean personnel, examples of miscommunication were often the result of native speakers not using the agreed phrases, but either abbreviating unhelpfully or elaborating unnecessarily, and sometimes employing idiomatic expressions.

Approaching data and essays on language and occupation

The way *not* to approach this topic is to think that you need to 'learn' about every occupation under the sun, and be able to discuss its linguistic peculiarities. What you *do* need is some awareness of the different language levels and how they might vary, with some examples of your own to illustrate that you understand different types of variation. You also need to understand how ideas about power and status relate to occupation, and how discourse communities work. As you read the other sections of this chapter and add the different sociolinguistic dimensions to your understanding of the whole field, you also need to recognize that none of the dimensions in this chapter exists alone: any employee has an identity beyond his or her work, such as having a family role; a gender identity; an ethnic identity; a regional identity and a network of social relationships. We all exist in a **nexus** of inter-relationships.

Writing an essay from a standing start is different from responding to data, where the data samples are designed to help ease you into the topic. You need to go beyond the language samples you have been given, but you also need to refer to them. However, rather than immediately analysing the data at a micro-level, think about some broad questions: What are the people in this example trying to do with language? And what do people in this occupation normally have to use language for? If you start with these broad questions in your mind, you will be able to make sense of the data, and you will therefore be able to write about the topic meaningfully.

> **Key term**
> **Nexus.** A cluster of connections.

REVIEW YOUR LEARNING

- What is restricted lexis?
- How might corpus research help us to understand occupational language?
- What is an inferential framework?
- What is a discourse community?
- How does the growth of international workplaces affect language use?

References

Kim, H., and Elder, C. (2009) 'Understanding aviation English as a lingua franca: Perceptions of Korean aviation personnel'. *Australian Review of Applied Linguistics* 32 (3)

Swales, John (2011) 'The Concept of Discourse Community', in Wardle, E. and Downs, D. (eds) *Writing About Writing: A College Reader*. Boston: Bedford/St. Martin's

Swales, John (1998) *Other Floors, Other Voices: A Textography of a Small University Building*. London: Routledge

Michael Nelson's Business English Lexis Site http://users.utu.fi/micnel/business_english_lexis_site.htm

Further reading

Drew, P., and Heritage, J. (1993) *Talk at Work: Interaction in Institutional Settings*. Cambridge: Cambridge University Press

Koester, A. (2004) *The Language of Work*. London: Routledge

Koester, A. (2011). *Workplace Discourse*. Continuum

This section of Chapter 3 will:

- help you to understand the relationship between language and gender
- show you how approaches to this topic have changed over the years
- give you some frameworks and concepts for analysing data and answering essay questions about this topic.

Key terms

Heteronormativity. A set of norms or expectations based on heterosexuality. For example, the idea that in a gay couple, one partner should be 'masculine' and the other 'feminine'.

Sex. A classification of people into 'man' or 'woman' based on biological characteristics.

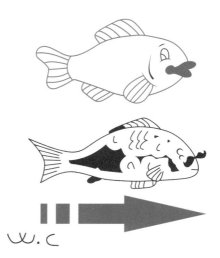

This toilet sign projects gender onto fish.

Introduction

Sex refers to biological differences, while **gender** refers to socially expected characteristics. For example, the fact that women can biologically produce children is an aspect of sex; expecting women to go all dewy-eyed about babies is an aspect of gender. But gender isn't just about women: there are also many ideas about masculinity, from concepts of 'real men' to notions of 'metrosexual'. Gender is closely connected with sexuality: for example, ideas about gender differences are often projected onto same-sex couples. This is called **heteronormativity**.

This isn't the first time that ideas about sex and gender have come up in this book. In Chapter 2 they occurred:

- on a T-shirt, where there was a mother-in-law joke
- in the texts about dogs (including the sex of the dogs themselves).

In Chapter 3, they have also occurred:

- in Colette's account, where she talks about male and female groups using language differently
- in research about social groups, in the section on 'jocks and burnouts'
- when discussing social class and accent research.

All of the variations in this chapter are interconnected, so the examples above should come as no surprise. All of the variables in this chapter are ways in which our society categorizes people, and as academic research is part of that society, it uses those categories too. Good academic research points out the connections between those categories, as well as looking at them one by one.

However, gender is a little different from some of the other variables, because it is so **salient** as a category. Gender seems to be a major organizing principle for the society that this book is describing. This means that the idea of identifying things and people as 'male' and 'female', and seeing these categories as different, pervades the culture and is difficult to escape. Perhaps this is partly because sex differences are associated with physical appearance, so are highly visible – although studies in fashion history show that we actively construct differences in the way the sexes look. Physical appearance may also have high salience in assessments of ethnicity and age, too. However, nothing is signalled visibly about our regionality; that is usually revealed when we open our mouths and speak.

You can see evidence of gender as an organizing principle all around you. Toy shops often separate girls' and boys' toys or, where they put them together, colour-code them differently, as is done with items of clothing. One toymaker recently claimed to be supporting equality by producing pink toy guns, for girls. Even simple objects like plugs and cables are said to have 'male' and 'female' versions, with the male ones having projections and the female ones acting as receptacles.

Activity

Record some material from the TV about the natural world and analyse it for gendered descriptions. But first, read 'The Sex Life of Seals', in Goddard & Mean (2009), page 9.

Is the world male? Gender and pronouns

Many changes over the years have made representations of the sexes fairer in official written material of all kinds. Some of those changes resulted from proof gathered by linguists and psychologists of the harmful results of always referring to people in the world as male – in other words, in using the male pronoun 'he' as a supposed **generic** form of reference. Researchers showed that children didn't process the term 'he' or 'man' as referring to both sexes, but as only referring to male figures. Early books aimed at writers and editors, such as Miller and Swift's 1981 *Handbook of Non-Sexist Writing*, did much to help writers think around the problem of not having a gender-neutral pronoun in English.

However, it is easy to still find examples of 'he' used by default, as in the extract below from *Study Skills for Dummies* (2009) about how to write academically:

Clarity: Make everything clear to the reader or listener to help him follow the proceedings. Assume he's an intelligent non-expert in your subject. Provide headings and a framework – a 'how to read' or 'how to listen' so that he can follow the stages in your argument.

Activity

Are the following phrases problematic? If so, what alternatives could you suggest?

A two-man tent	The man in the street	The average working man
Manning a stall	Mankind	To man up
Take it like a man	May the best man win	A family man

A useful concept in studying language and gender is that of **marking**. Marking in linguistics means that a language item stands out and is distinctive or unusual in some way. Marking often creates an additional or contrastive meaning, which tells you something about the original meaning of the term in question. For example, in the phrase listed above, 'a family man', the term 'family' modifies the noun 'man', marking the man as a particular type of man, someone who spends time with his family. This suggests that there are other kinds of men – men who don't do this. Otherwise, why bother to add the modifier 'family' in the first place?

So what is a 'family woman'? That phrase sounds odd because the traditional idea of a woman is that she's family-oriented, so it sounds like a **tautology**. Studying marking helps us to reveal some of the layers of hidden meaning that lie behind even our most basic words, such as 'man' and 'woman'.

Key terms

Anthropomorphism. Imposing human qualities on the animals and objects around us.

Generic. For general use or general reference.

Marking. In language study, identifying an item as different from the norm.

Tautology. Producing redundancy in meaning by saying the same thing twice.

Did you know?

Sweden has recently created a new pronoun to get round the problem of gendered pronouns: 'hen' is a neutral alternative to 'han' (he) and 'hon' (she).

Did you know?

In the early days of the Internet, people assumed that it would create a more egalitarian society, because the disembodiment of online presence would remove stereotyping. But some researchers have concluded that the absence of physicality makes us exaggerate differences even more. For example, the gender researcher Kira Hall says in her essay 'Cyberfeminism' that computer-mediated communication (CMC) has led, not to **cyborgs**, but to 'goddesses and ogres'.

Key terms

Cyborg. A blend of 'cybernetic' and 'organism' describing a part machine, part human individual.

Patronyms. Names that reflect male lines of inheritance.

You can see the same process of marking at work if you think about some of the modifiers that are regularly placed in front of the noun 'mother', such as:

- working mother
- unmarried mother
- stepmother
- foster mother
- surrogate mother

These modifiers tell us that the hidden norm for motherhood is someone who is not working, is married, and is biologically related to her child.

Activity

How does marking work in the following expressions? What do the modifiers 'male' and 'female' (or 'woman') tell us about the meanings of the words that they mark?

- male secretary
- male prostitute
- male doctor
- male nurse
- female secretary
- female prostitute
- woman doctor
- female nurse

After the Sex Discrimination Act of 1975, it became illegal to write a job advertisement in a way that implied people of only one sex could apply. However, there were some exceptions, where a job required a particular type of recruitment because of the under-representation of a group, or other special circumstance.

Activity

How have the following job titles changed so that they are no longer marked for gender?

- Headmaster/Headmistress
- Waiter/Waitress
- Air steward/Air hostess
- Fireman
- Chairman
- Salesman/Saleswoman
- Barman/Barmaid
- Policeman/Policewoman
- Weatherman/Weathergirl
- Dinner lady
- Nanny

Is the world married? Gender and address terms

Gendered marking also extends to terms of address – the names and titles we give to each other, both in public life and in our more intimate relationships. Kinship terms vary considerably between languages, as do social practices around naming and lineage. The English-speaking world has traditionally used **patronyms**, or names that relate to male lines of inheritance: the elements 's', 'son', 'O', 'Mac' and 'Ap' can be added to male first names to create English, Irish, Scottish and Welsh surnames– for example, Peters, Johnson, O'Brien, MacDonald, Pritchard (Ap Richard).

Icelandic and other Nordic societies can use **matronyms** (the mother's first name plus the term for 'daughter' or 'son' – in Icelandic, 'dóttir' or 'son'). In Spain, children can inherit names from both sides of the family and add them together to create surnames with multiple elements.

Societies also differ in their practices for using titles. The USA and some European countries, including the UK, have adopted ways to create equivalents to the title 'Mr', given to an adult male but not denoting marital status. In English this is 'Ms', which in some contexts has replaced 'Miss' and 'Mrs', but documents can still appear featuring all three. In Germany, 'Fraulein' ('Miss') has been quietly dropping out of use in favour of using 'Frau' as an equivalent to 'Herr'. Similarly, in France, 'Madame' has been replacing 'Mademoiselle' as an equivalent to 'Monsieur'. In Sweden, no titles are used at all. In official letters, people are addressed by their first names and surnames.

English has a wide range of informal terms of address that can be used to strangers where a person's name is unknown. These are commonly known as **endearments**. Many of these are part of regional dialects, as you saw in Section 3.2. But how do they work in terms of gender?

Activity

Look at the following table of terms, which were collected in 1983 in a study of naming (Goddard 1983).

- Which terms in the table are used only to men, and which only to women?
- Are there any terms in the table that are used solely by one sex (for address among themselves)?
- Are some of these terms more strongly regional than others?
- Who might use these terms to you, and how do they make you feel when they are used to you? Do you use any of them yourself?
- Are there any further terms that you could add to this list? (Note: think about use to strangers, not to family members.)

kid	dear	mate	love	son	lad	flower	friend
sunshine	chum	sweetheart	boss	darling	gorgeous	boy	petal
chief	squire	poppet	grandad	grandma	princess	lover	mush
mister	mac	buddy	pal	missus	pet	hen	hinnie
dad	guv	baby	angel	sugar	honey	duck	lamb

However you have experienced these terms, their semantic content is fairly benign. But there are address terms that are abusive, with much more offensive content. Historically, many more terms of abuse have been aimed at women than at men, particularly around ideas of sexual promiscuity. This area will be explored in more detail in Chapter 5, where you will have a chance to think about the possibility of changing negative terms.

Connotations and collocations

Connotations are the associations that we have for a term, which can include the idea of who is normally the referent when a word or phrase is used. For example, who 'flounces', 'struts', 'shrieks' and 'nags'? Who 'strides', 'marches',

Did you know?

The second most common source of names in Sweden is the landscape. Go to http://www.nordicnames.de/wiki/Surnames to see some examples. What are the main sources of surnames in English or in another language that you know?

Key terms

Endearment. A term used to address someone without using the person's name.

Matronyms. Names that reflect female lines of inheritance.

Key terms

Collocation. The regular occurrence of a word or phrase alongside others.

Concordance line. A line of text from a corpus, showing where the searched item occurred within a sentence or utterance.

Lexical priming. The way in which some words appear to be ready-made for certain meanings, as a result of their habitual use in the same contexts.

'bellows' and 'criticizes'? Who is 'buxom', who is 'muscular'? Who is 'slender', who is 'ripped'? The connotations that are built up around a term, including who it might be applied to, contribute strongly to meaning.

Hoey (2005) uses the expression **lexical priming** to describe the way in which words and phrases come with a kind of undercoat layer, built from habitual usage in the same contexts. John Sinclair, an early proponent of the use of language **corpora**, talked of the importance of analysing 'the company that words keep', or their **collocations**.

Activity

The following is a list of films from the last few years with terms for men and women in their titles. What types of nouns and modifiers are used in the film titles for each gender? What connotations do these have? How do they represent men and women in terms of characteristics and roles? Can you add to this list?

Women	Men
Exploding Girl	The Wolf Man
The Time Traveler's Wife	Repo Man
The Astronaut's Wife	Solitary Man
The Dead Girl	Iron Man 2
My Best Friend's Girl	A Single Man
The Other Boleyn Girl	A Serious Man
Factory Girl	Yes Man
A Good Woman	Spiderman 3
The Good Girl	Harvard Man
Birthday Girl	Family Man
The 24 Hour Woman	The Perfect Man
Kit Kitteridge: An American Girl	The Man
	The Ladies Man
	Cinderella Man

The table on page 91 is the result of a brief search of the British National Corpus (BNC), a collection of searchable language items consisting of 100 million words. The corpus is free for a 50-line random search, and often this is enough to reveal some interesting patterns, or collocations. The search in this table was for the phrase 'old lady'. The BNC is available at: http://www.natcorp.ox.ac.uk

The phrase 'old lady' represents an interconnection between gender and age. Representations of gender change according to age, although Dale Spender, in *Man Made Language*, quips that only men are allowed to grow up – women remain as 'girls' until they become 'old girls', something perhaps borne out by the film titles above. But even with the few **concordance lines** opposite, you can see some collocations that look familiar. All of the examples focus on appearance, but two different kinds of figures appear – a 'little old lady' who is 'scrawny' and 'wizened', or a 'nice old lady' with her hair 'in a bun'.

In the 50 lines that were available, 'old ladies' didn't seem to be having a good time – with suggestions of poverty, abandonment, illness and death prevailing. However, you need to realize that language corpora are determined by the texts that they contain, so if they contain a lot of news articles and novels about old age, those texts are not likely to be full of good news about ageing.

She was a rather nice	old lady	all dressed in black, with her white hair in a bun
A scrawny little	old lady	
A wizened	old lady	almost totally obscured by a black chador
The little	old lady	who went to Salvation Army, always wearing a hat

From a gender perspective, there is evidence from corpus work on other language items that terms for women are less positive than those for men. For example, Paul Baker explores two dictionary equivalents – 'bachelor' and 'spinster' – and reports his findings on the words that collocate with these, and the discourses implied, in a chapter of *Gender and Language Research Methodologies*, a collection of linguists' research. To show the differences he found, the title of his chapter refers to 'eligible bachelors' and 'frustrated spinsters'.

Discourses about men and women

What images of men and women do we build by our habitual use of the sorts of language items you have been studying? As you saw in Chapter 2, the concept of discourses is all about building up notions of 'reality' through repeated ways of talking and writing – and therefore thinking and behaving. So what shared assumptions do we have about the way men and women 'are'?

Activity

Below is the front of a packet of throat lozenges called 'Manflu Lozzers'. The text on the back has also been reproduced for you on page 92. How does 'Manflu' present familiar discourses about gender (masculinity and femininity)? Analyse the text and write up your analysis in a formal way. Refer not just to the ideas in this chapter, but apply the work you have done on the language levels and text analysis in Chapters 1 and 2.

reproduced for you on page 92

Research idea

A 50-line search of the BNC is enough for you to start to see the collocations of terms. You will also be able to see the sources of the examples (there is a clickable link for each example, taking you to an explanation of its source). You may have your own ideas for terms you want to explore, but if not, choose two terms that would appear to be male/female equivalents, such as boy/girl, master/mistress, gentleman/lady, and assess the results. Do the equivalent words hold the same weight in meaning? Are different collocates evident? What discourses about men and women are shown in the citations?

The text on the back of the lozenge packet includes the following:

> *Misery? No! Try these Ultimate Lozenges – with up to 10 minutes of love and attention in every single one.*

> P.S. Permission not to take the bins out unless hot drinks, chicken soup and back rubs are provided. Try **MANFLU Hot or Shot** drink!

Do men and women speak different languages?

Unfortunately, this area of language study has more myths than facts. This is probably because, like the case of old ladies having a good time, facts are not very newsworthy. Would the following headline sell many newspapers?

BREAKING NEWS! MEN AND WOMEN ARE LARGELY THE SAME!

The idea of 'difference' in language sells because, as was suggested at the start of this section, it taps into the differentiations we make in other ways between the sexes. It provides miles of media copy, from advice columns on 'how to talk to your man' and 'what your woman really means' to articles about evolutionary psychology suggesting that modern men might not speak much because their hunter ancestors needed to be silent to catch the dinner.

The modern history of language and gender can be viewed as occurring over a number of stages, and as part of larger cultural patterns that also affected research on the other variations in this chapter. The 1960s saw new liberal movements demanding greater equality in Western societies, so areas of academic research started to focus on language as a possible source of disadvantage.

An influential book on this theme was Robin Lakoff's *Language and Woman's Place* in 1975. Her conclusions were that women were disadvantaged by having to adopt forms of language that made them sound unconfident – for example, hesitation, approval-seeking tag questions, and euphemistic politeness terms. She called this 'talking like a lady'. At the same time, work such as Dale Spender's collection of research in *Man Made Language* suggested that women were trapped in a world of language that was not of their making, because men had historically controlled the meanings, to the extent that the strongest taboo term, and therefore one avoided by women, referred to a part of their own bodies.

The 1970s saw the beginning of portable tape recorders, so for the first time researchers could collect real data. However, because this was a new phenomenon, there was a tendency to generalize large results from very small amounts of data collected in specific contexts. Research focused primarily on American speakers – often the researcher's own social circle – or college students. Informants tended to be from white middle-class communities. Yet the results from these specific groups were taken as insights into how all men and women behave.

An example of this process was a single study of interruptions between men and women who knew each other well, reported in Thorne and Henley's 1975 collection, *Language and Sex: Difference and Dominance*. Because in this one study men interrupted women more than the other way round – in reality one man

Did you know?

The idea that men and women might speak different languages is a very old story based on a mistake. Early anthropologists studying language and culture in what is now the Caribbean, thought they had discovered men and women speaking different languages within the same society. It turned out that one group of men (the Caribs) had killed the men in another group (the Arawaks) and abducted the Arawak women. So they really were speaking different languages, but not because of gender.

Did you know?

Some of the views about male and female talk are just folk-linguistics – popular cultural beliefs about language that have been passed down through generations. An example is the notion that women talk more than men. Modern research shows that the amount of talk we produce depends on the context we are in. If you record a group of men at work or in a pub talking about sport, you will find that they are not lost for words.

accounted for most of the interruptions – this was regarded as a universal trait that could be applied to all male–female interactions.

Later studies moved away from the idea of male domination and female deficit, towards more exploration of ideas of difference. Deborah Tannen's 1990 book *You Just Don't Understand: Men and Women in Conversation* posited the idea that there are male and female 'cultures', a little like the communities of practice you learned about earlier (see page 64), with their own rules, shared meanings and ways of doing things. In single-sex groups, men and women understand each other; but when they come together, there are misunderstandings. Tannen looked more carefully at the whole area of simultaneous speech, because she had experience of different ethnic groups whose rules of interaction varied in their levels of directness. She showed that there were what she called 'high engagement cultures', such as her own Jewish community, who overlapped each other's speech to show enthusiastic agreement. Tannen showed that not every example of simultaneous speech was an interruption, and made some connections between gender and ethnicity that were a welcome step forward.

Tannen's idea about the sexes was that they were socialized into seeing themselves as having very different roles and positions in life, and that they were trained to use different linguistic strategies in interactions. She broadly claimed that men monitor their interactions for signals of power and status, and women monitor theirs for signals of alignment and **solidarity**. Taking a number of **speech events** – questions, consultations, apologies, problem sharing and troubles talk, reporting experiences – Tannen claimed that men and women could use exactly the same words but have very different understandings of them. For many people, Tannen's ideas offered insights into how communication could break down in mixed-sex interactions. But there were also criticisms of this approach. One criticism was that men and women normally don't grow up in different communities in the way suggested, so they can't be so unaware of each other's meanings. Another was that there is a power factor in the way that 'difference' is used in societies, and this was being ignored. Ideas about who is allowed to have a public voice and what they are allowed to say still needed to be explored.

Then and now

Studies of male and female speech start from the perspective that there is no such thing as generic 'men' and 'women', but men and women in different regions, with different social status, of different ages and ethnicities, and so on. In addition, there are different contexts of language use: what is the talk for, where does it happen, what is it a part of? In other words, gender studies need to be much more closely connected with the other social variations in this chapter.

There is also a difference in how the connection between language and gender identity is understood. Previously, language was seen as the result of gender: I am male or female, therefore I use language in this way. Now language is seen as constructing gender: I use language in this way, which constructs a certain kind of gender identity. This newer idea fits with ideas in other subject areas about the 'self' as having multiple identities based on the discourses that you use and that are in play at any particular time. Gender is something that you *do*, not something that you *are*.

> **Key terms**
>
> **Speech event.** A spoken interaction of a recognizable type. For example, a lecture or a phone call.
>
> **Vocal fry.** A vocal effect where the speaker produces a rasping, creaky sound by blowing air through the vocal cords.

> **Did you know?**
>
> Linguists have identified a female version of what used to be called 'creaky voice', where speakers produce a low staccato vibration at the end of an utterance. This was previously seen as an aspect of American male speech, intended to make the speaker sound serious. This same effect, now termed **vocal fry** because of its raspy bubbling sound, has appeared in the speech of female American public figures, like the Kardashians and Britney Spears.

> **Link**
>
> Read the whole *New York Times* article 'They're, Like, Way Ahead of the Linguistic Currrrve', which interviews linguists for their interpretations of vocal fry: http://www.nytimes.com/2012/02/28/science/young-women-often-trendsetters-in-vocal-patterns.html?pagewanted=all&_r=0

Gender and occupational language

Gender and work offer an interesting connection, because if gender is a performance, then perhaps a certain kind of performance can be learned by people in work contexts, regardless of their gender. For example, Kira Hall reports in *Language and Desire* that some of the most successful sex-chat workers in the community she interviewed were a different sex and ethnicity from the identities they performed. Who is to know, on the phone or online?

Anna Hultgren's 2008 study of British and Danish call centres showed that a stereotypical female 'script', not very different from Lakoff's original picture of politeness, compromise and rapport, was the model expected of workers. Cameron critiques this model in her study of call centres, *Good To Talk?*, seeing this type of company-imposed style as requiring workers to subjugate themselves to callers and adopt a submissive position which opens them to abuse.

REVIEW YOUR LEARNING

- What is 'marking' and how is it relevant to the study of gender?
- Choose some terms of address and explain how they relate to gender issues.
- What are some of the connotations that construct ideas about gender?
- Define the following and explain how they relate to gender: discourse, deficit, difference.

Further reading

Baker, P. (2008) *Sexed Texts*. London: Equinox

Cameron, D. (ed.) (1990) *The Feminist Critique of Language*. London: Routledge

(This text includes reference to some of the older books and articles mentioned in this section of the chapter).

Cameron, D. (2008) *The Myth of Mars and Venus*. Oxford: Oxford University Press

Goddard, A, and Mean, L. (2009) *Language and Gender* (2nd edn) London: Routledge

Harvey, K. and Shalom, C. (eds) (1997) *Language and Desire: Encoding Sex, Romance and Intimacy*. London: Routledge.

References

Baker, P. (2008) '"Eligible" bachelors and "frustrated" spinsters: Corpus linguistics, gender and language' in J. Sunderland, K. Harrington and H. Stantson (eds) *Gender and Language Research Methodologies*. London: Palgrave

Cameron, D. (2000) *Good To Talk? Living and Working in a Communication Culture*. London: Sage

du Boulay, D. (2009) *Study Skills for Dummies*. Chichester: Wiley & Sons

Goddard, A. (1983). *Addressing without naming: a sociolinguistic study*. University of Manchester MA Thesis.

Hall, K. 1996. 'Cyberfeminism' in Herring, S. (ed.) Herring, S. *Computer-Mediated Communication: Linguistic, Social and Cross-Cultural Perspectives*. Amsterdam: John Benjamins.

Hoey, M. (2005) *Lexical Priming*. London: Routledge.

Hultgren, A. (2008) 'Reconstructing the Sex Dichotomy in Language and Gender Research: Some Advantages of Using Correlational Sociolinguistics' in J. Sunderland, K. Harrington and H. Stantson (eds) *Gender and Language Research Methodologies*. London: Palgrave

Introduction

Ethnicity is a concept that relates to aspects of a person's cultural identity. It is different from **nationality**, which refers to the more technical issue of which nation or nations you formally belong to (that is, what is on your passport). Nationality is more of a legal concept, while ethnicity is more to do with who you see as your community. This could involve several factors, including religious beliefs and language, as well as your family relationships or other close connections. In a label such as 'British Asian', the first term relates to nationality while the second relates to ethnicity.

The terms 'black' and 'white' are very broad labels that don't make distinctions between ethnic groups, but try to suggest similarities – sometimes in a very crude and over-simplifying way – by focusing on skin colour. All of the terms that surround ethnicity need serious thought, because there are some complex issues to unravel.

The term 'ethnicity' has quite a complicated history. It was intended to replace the word 'race', which had acquired negative associations with ideas about racial superiority and inferiority, and with racism. But 'ethnic' has come to mean 'non-white' in many people's minds; 'ethnic food' could suggest curry or couscous, but is unlikely to be used for fish and chips. In fact, the term 'ethnic' should refer to everyone: just as everyone has an accent because of the way they pronounce words, everyone has an ethnicity because of their family ties. Everyone is part of an ethnic group of some sort, regardless of skin colour or nationality. Now, you will see the term 'race' in academic texts: for example, a 'raced text' would be a text that uses ideas of race in a manipulative way.

Where ethnicity is perhaps most useful is in its reference to the family heritage that many people share – linking them historically and culturally to places where their relatives may once have lived.

As identity is so intimately connected to language, it is hardly surprising that the intersection of ethnicity and language is such a fertile area of sociolinguistics. Different ethnic groups often use language in ways that reflect solidarity and affiliation to aspects of their heritage, but there is also a wider linguistic repertoire to draw upon, signalling different elements of identity when speaking to different people. For example, all of us choose different styles and/or registers when we talk to different audiences, and select elements of our linguistic repertoire with which we perform an identity, but with ethnic background as another variable, more choices exist.

In a world and a country where there is more contact and mixing between different ethnic groups than ever before, the language linked to ethnic background rapidly changes, so this section of the chapter will take a look at some patterns in language use, trace their origins and consider where they are going now. As with other forms of variation in language use, there are many different ways in which language users are judged by others. This can involve judgements about whether a particular use of language is 'correct' or 'incorrect', how 'white' or 'black' someone sounds, and how 'nerdy' or 'street' a speaker might be. We will also be thinking about ethnicity and textual representations.

This section of Chapter 3 will:

- help you to understand the relationship between language and ethnicity
- give you some frameworks and concepts for responding to exam questions about this topic
- show you how ethnicity is one of many sociolinguistic variables that may come into play when people make language choices.

 REMEMBER

The study of ethnicity is required at A level, but not at AS level.

■ **Key term**

Nationality. An aspect of identity that refers to the country of a person's birth or citizenship.

Early immigration and language

Immigration to Britain is not a recent phenomenon – for many centuries people have moved to Britain, bringing with them their own mother tongues. The Anglo-Saxons (the tribes from northern Europe who settled in Britain and gave us what we now know as English) arrived in the 5th century. French became a significant language in Britain after the Norman invasion in the 11th century. In the early 1500s, African musicians are recorded as living in Britain, and during the 16th and 17th centuries, the slave trade meant the arrival of more African people.

Historically, one of the largest ethnic groups to settle in England has been the Irish, and there is some linguistic evidence of Irish affecting the Liverpool accent and dialect, but little elsewhere. Other groups to arrive have included the French Protestant refugees, the Huguenots, who arrived in London in the 17th century, and Jewish refugees from Russia, who settled in large numbers in the late 19th and early 20th centuries. In the 20th and 21st centuries, many people from the Caribbean, India, Pakistan and Bangladesh have settled in the UK, while there are also communities from many other parts of the world, including Turkey, Cyprus, Somalia, Portugal, Colombia and Eastern Europe.

Interestingly, many of these immigrants tended to settle in the inner city – especially East London – and where there were concentrations of a particular ethnic group, the English language often absorbed some influences from these new arrivals. However, it is debatable whether these groups had any significant impact on the English spoken more widely. What seems to have happened in most cases is a rapid 'Anglicization' of the incomers' language use, so within a generation or two at most, they would have been speaking English. There is evidence of some lexical influence from Jewish settlers on the slang of London English (and beyond), with the spread of terms such as *kosher* (which has a specific cultural meaning in Yiddish relating to the suitability of food for eating by Jews, but broadens out to mean something similar to 'OK' or 'legitimate'), and *nosh* (meaning 'food').

Creoles and crossing

With the large-scale arrival of Caribbean people in the UK from the late 1940s onwards (as part of a post-war drive to recruit workers for Britain's growing public services), new forms of English started to be heard in many predominantly urban areas. While the new arrivals were not all from Jamaica, the variety of English developed by second- and third-generation speakers later became known as London Jamaican.

English had been a large part of the Caribbean's linguistic heritage for over 500 years before that – its history inextricably bound up with that of slavery and liberation struggles – and the **Creole** spoken by many Jamaicans had its roots in English and the various West African languages spoken by slaves taken from Africa during the period of the slave trade. While the first generation of Caribbean immigrants tended to speak the variety they had brought with them, younger speakers who were born and/or brought up in the UK often developed a more mixed form of language.

In the 1960s and 1970s, the contact between Jamaican-English young people and their white working-class neighbours at work and at school, and the increasing number of mixed-race relationships, meant that people of different ethnic

---

Link

The following language map of London provides an interesting snapshot of the most widely spoken second language (to English) in each of the London boroughs: http://randomlylondon.com/map-other-english-borough/

Link

Information about the etymology of some borrowed words and about the contact English has had with other languages can be found in Chapters 1, 5 and 6.

Link

You can learn more about Creoles in Chapter 6.

Key term

Creole. A variety that has developed from a 'pidgin' or trade language to become a stable language used by speakers as their mother tongue.

backgrounds were exposed to each other's varieties of English. A degree of 'crossing' was evident in some situations, when speakers who had access to both London English and Jamaican English might shift from one style to another, depending on who they were with. So a young white speaker might use more traditional London English with a white peer group and shift into a lexis more influenced by Jamaican English with black friends.

This cross-cultural mixing gave rise to significant changes in youth culture, as well as language. Interestingly, some white or Asian young people *without* a black peer group started to use non-standard Creole-influenced speech at around this time, too. Ben Rampton notes that 'Creole was widely seen as cool, tough and good to use. It was associated with assertiveness, verbal resourcefulness, competence in heterosexual relationships, and opposition to authority' (2010).

Work by Roger Hewitt (1986) and Mark Sebba (1993) identified a new development in the 1980s, that of 'Black Cockney' – a style, rather than a discrete variety – used by young black speakers in London, while John Pitts (2012) noticed a different shift among some young black English speakers who felt that mainstream society was ignoring and constraining them, towards a **resistance identity** through language. As he put it, there was a move from 'sounding like Ian Wright to sounding like Bob Marley'. As you will see from other sections in this chapter and other chapters in this book, the role of language to express identity is crucial in this and goes beyond where you are born and the colour of your skin to the sense of who you are and how you want to be seen.

Activity

Read the language case study below about Shahnaz, and then answer the following questions.

1. What different influences can you find on the ways in which Shahnaz uses language?
2. What functions do they have for her and for the people she is speaking to? Are they used to express certain meanings?
3. Are there ways in which the process she describes – choosing terms from her repertoire for different audiences and people – is similar to what everyone does, regardless of how many varieties they have in their repertoire?
4. How many of these might be related to ethnicity?
5. How important is ethnicity on its own in discussing an individual's language use?

Shahnaz is a black British woman in her early twenties. She was born and raised in South London, went to a state secondary school and then sixth form college, before studying for a BA at the University of Manchester. Here she talks about some of the factors that affect her language use.

> Both my parents were born in the UK, therefore I am second-generation Jamaican diaspora. I, personally, don't have a lot of contact with my family in Jamaica and have never been there.
>
> My parents do not speak **Patois** unless they are with their Jamaican friends and family and it is usually used in a colloquial manner, usually in jest.

Did you know?

As well as research into different non-standard forms of English used by ethnic minorities, there is a strand of research that looks at what are called **super-standard forms** used by some white speakers. Bucholtz (2001) for example, looks at the language of 'white nerds' who deliberately distance themselves from white peers who are more willing to adopt 'cooler' black speech styles.

Key terms

Patois. An alternative term for creole, sometimes spelt 'patwa' to distance the language from apparent connections with Europe, and to suggest how it should be pronounced.

Resistance identity. An identity that goes against mainstream culture.

Super-standard forms. Language use that deliberately intensifies the standard forms of mainstream culture.

Key terms

British Black English. A wide-ranging label, but often referring to a variety used by some speakers within the Caribbean community in the UK.

Multicultural Urban British English. A label that refers to the way in which Multicultural London English has spread to other large conurbations in the UK.

Research idea

Investigations into the language use of different generations can be a great way of using your own family as a source of language data. If you have relatives who have come from different countries, different parts of the UK, or who have a distinctive variety of English, you could record them and make use of their language in a study of linguistic variation. •

My nan speaks with a Patois accent. However, her lexicon is English-based — when my nan was in Jamaica her family was considered lower middle class, and more 'British' sounding words were encouraged.

In formal situations I use Standard English; sometimes I may even use a more Standard version of English, especially if I was speaking to upper-class people at university who I did not know. However, if I am familiar with someone (even if they are upper class) I will slip back into my vernacular, which I would class as 'slight BBE' [**British Black English**].

When I was in Manchester a lot of people said I had a strong South London accent. I lived in a house with Londoners in my final year of University and was told that my accent was the strongest (relating to BBE).

I think I spoke with a more Standard English variety in Manchester because I was reading a lot of articles and books, and we would often have debates relating to scholarly material. However, at home we often used to mimic African accents in jest, which ultimately became part of our vernacular. We would use words such as 'chale' (Ghanaian Twi word for 'friend') 'sha' (a West African expression similar to 'hun' or 'honey') and 'kai' (usually an expression of shock). We also used common Nigerian Pidgin English phrases like 'You no de tell lies' (You're not lying). With my Somalian friend she was also Muslim so at times we would use words like 'Walahi' (similar to Swear Down/I swear it's true) and 'habibi' (darling).

I only usually speak Patois when I am imitating my nan or a person I know that has a strong Patois accent, or if I am using humour or reciting lyrics from Jamaican music. I only really have one close Jamaican friend as my close friends come from other backgrounds (Asian, other Caribbean Islands, Nigeria, Somalia, Syria, etc.) so at times I may use a form of Nigerian Pidgin English with them, or variations of their languages and words I have picked up.

Hybrid forms and Multicultural London English

While language contact between different ethnic groups in the 1960s through to the late 1990s was often a case of mix and match, one distinct variety that has emerged is British Black English (BBE), which is a form that many members of Britain's Caribbean-heritage community have as part of their repertoire of styles. BBE combines elements of Standard British English with **Creole** (or **Patois**) forms. BBE varies from region to region, reflecting the local varieties spoken in places such as Leeds, Birmingham and Bristol, for example. More recently, work by Cheshire et al (2008) has identified a new form of English emerging (predominantly among young people) from the melting pot of London's inner city and taking root far beyond: **Multicultural London English (MLE)**. Given that it has now been identified in many other areas, some linguists are also starting to describe such forms as **Multicultural Urban British English**.

Strictly speaking, MLE is not a discrete variety of language (like Cockney or Scouse), because it does not have a uniform set of features shared by its speakers. Rather, it is a pool of language characteristics adopted to differing degrees by its users — depending on age, ethnicity, region and identity. MLE is more than just 'slang' — although elements of its vocabulary are slang terms and have moved into wider use – because it also consists of phonological, grammatical and discourse characteristics, such as those below:

- Vocabulary: 'bare' (a lot/very); 'beef' (disagreement, conflict); 'choong' (attractive); 'ting' (girlfriend or thing); 'endz' (local area); 'on road' (on the streets)

- Phonology: most noticeably the diphthong vowel sounds of words such as 'face' and 'like' are pronounced /fes/ and /lɑːk/

- Grammar: there are few syntactical differences, but the use of 'dem' as a plural marker (as in 'man dem' for 'men', or 'boy dem' for 'police' – perhaps derived from 'the boys in blue') and 'man' as a new pronoun referring to oneself (as in 'man paid for my own ticket') are broader grammatical differences in MLE

- Discourse features: 'innit' as a tag question, 'you get me' as a confirmation check; 'this is me' as a quotative (as in 'I went over to his place and this is me "What you doing?" and this is him "Not a lot, just playing Xbox".')

This pool of linguistic features varies from place to place, so a young person in East London might use some vocabulary items that are not in common use among MLE speakers in another part of London, while MLE speakers in Nottingham might use phonological features that are more common to that area than London. Local ethnic populations also have an impact on the pool of features, so a higher proportion of Ghanaian- or Turkish-heritage English speakers in an area might produce more influence from those mother tongues.

Significantly to linguists, MLE is quite different from previous contact languages in the UK, because the numbers are very different and, for perhaps the first time, the influence of the native language is not as strong a force as the influence of the second languages – meaning that the process of Anglicization is less noticeable – instead, a form of convergence is taking place between a number of different influences and creating a genuine and organic hybrid form of English. For those dismissing it as 'Jafaican', it should be clear that there's nothing fake and only a touch of Jamaican about it.

However it is defined, MLE is an important new area of research and study for linguists and has come under intense scrutiny in the media, revealing as it does so much about the changing nature of British society and the language we use.

Code switching and style shifting

Moving between different styles of language is not just an aspect of language and ethnicity: it is a common characteristic of most forms of daily communication. All speakers and writers have linguistic choices to make about which level of language to use in a particular situation. The notion of **linguistic appropriacy** is central here: in other words, which form of language is suitable or appropriate for a given situation. However, because of the centrality of ethnicity to many people's linguistic identity, switching and shifting between different forms of a language – or even totally different languages in the case of bilingual speakers – perhaps carries a greater significance.

Code mixing refers to the occasional insertion of vocabulary items from one language into another, while **code switching** can be used to describe how speakers move from one language to another for more extensive periods

Link

For a detailed and insightful exploration of MLE from some of the linguists who researched it, read some of the following posts from the Linguistics Research Digest: http://linguistics-research-digest.blogspot.co.uk/search/label/Multicultural%20London%20English

To look at links to argument and discussion about MLE, read the posts on the EngLangBlog: http://englishlangsfx.blogspot.co.uk/search/label/MLE

Key terms

Code mixing. The inclusion of words and phrases from one language in another.

Code switching. Switching between different languages in a sustained way.

Linguistic appropriacy. The way in which language choices reflect ideas about what is appropriate for any given context.

■ **Did you know?**

Yiddish speakers sometimes say 'Kein Ayin Hora', which means 'no evil eye', when they are saying something that appears to be tempting fate – for example, talking about the high achievements of someone in the family.

■ **Did you know?**

Using different levels of formality at a job interview and when speaking with friends can be seen as a form of code switching. Switching based on ethnicity is just a different facet of this.

of time. For example, in Gautum Malkani's novel *Londonstani*, a speaker shifts from English to Punjabi at the end of the utterance: 'Even if he doesn't die, the wedding insurance covers serious illness. Koi gal nahi.' This is the equivalent of saying 'no worries' or 'touch wood' as a way of commenting on what has gone before.

■ **Activity**

Why do people code switch and code mix? Consider each of the following reasons and think about situations when you might have switched between different styles or codes:

● Identity
● Intelligibility (making yourself understandable to others)
● Keeping up with family culture and heritage
● Fitting in
● For fun and play
● To mock someone or something
● To give someone a secret message that others can't understand

Representations of ethnicity

As you have already explored in Chapter 2, language can create and shape representations around us, and the ways in which language represents ethnicity is a particularly interesting case in point. This area is of concern because many words used to label different ethnic groups have not been chosen by the groups themselves, but by others who have often been hostile or dismissive of the people labelled by these terms.

You will look more at the changing meanings of words and ideas around the ownership of language in Chapter 5 on language change, but the most extreme examples of racial epithets are rarely found in the mainstream media and tend to be confined to the more extreme ends of social media.

However, representations of ethnicity can be made through a more subtle (and some might say insidious) use of language. Take the following two examples from newspaper reports about crime.

1. The suspect is described as of medium build, with brown hair and wearing dark blue jogging bottoms and a dark hooded top.

2. The suspect is described as Asian, of medium build, with brown hair and wearing dark blue jogging bottoms and a dark hooded top.

The second example refers explicitly to the suspect's ethnicity, and by implication the first extract assumes that the suspect's ethnicity is white, because it is not marked. Highlighting ethnicity in one case and not another creates a danger that certain ethnic groups appear to be singled out and associated with crime. This becomes more dangerous and politically charged when a whole community is damned for the actions of a few of its members. While the perpetrators of sexual abuse in the widely reported Rotherham case were described as 'mainly of Pakistani origin', no mention of ethnicity was made in relation to the numerous (white) perpetrators of sexual abuse in the Yewtree cases (associated with Jimmy Savile).

■ **Research idea**

Taboo in language is an interesting area to research. For example, have you noticed how asterisks are sometimes used to blank out the letters of supposedly offensive words in news articles? Is there a system to this in different newspapers? Why is it done? Does it stop us from filling in the gaps?

There is also an argument that, as with gender, the English language itself has some historically entrenched double standards connected to ethnicity, with positive associations for 'white' and negative ones for 'black'. For example, a 'white lie' is not a very bad one; however, one of the worst financial crashes in recent history was termed 'Black Wednesday' (in 1992).

The banner on the right celebrates the resounding victory of the West Indies cricket team over England in the 1984 test series by reversing the connotations of 'black' and 'white':

Representation in the media

Paper 2 of the English Language A level focuses on language diversity and change, along with language discourses, so as part of that you could be asked questions about the ways in which ethnic varieties of English are used, viewed and represented; and you could be asked to do a directed writing task about the topic.

Historically, Creoles have been perceived by some as 'broken' or 'incorrect' English, a discourse that persists in the representation of other non-standard forms, dialects, **sociolects** and **ethnolects**. MLE has sometimes been referred to as 'Jafaican' (fake Jamaican) and 'ghetto grammar' by non-linguists, and associated with gangs, violence and poor education by others.

What does this use of the word 'Blackwash' imply?

Activity

The following article excerpt was written by a non-linguist, Ed West, and offers a personal perspective on language change and variation in London. Once you have read the text, answer the two questions below and discuss with a partner or small group of students the ideas raised; then complete the directed writing task underneath.

1. What attitudes does West express towards young people's use of what he terms 'Jafaican'? What examples could you pick out to illustrate his views?

2. What problems does West identify as being associated with speaking 'Jafaican'?

Write an opinion article defending MLE, drawing on any of the material you have worked on in this chapter (or any other chapters in this book). Before writing your article you should state your intended audience.

'Jafaican' may be cool, but it sounds ridiculous

by Ed West

I was surprised a few years ago to hear an acquaintance more left-wing than me (admittedly that's not saying much) saying he was moving out of London because he'd just had kids and 'didn't want them growing up talking like Ali G'.

And Paul Weller said the same thing in an interview with the *Telegraph* a few years later, about his choice of school for his kids, although perhaps having mixed-race children made him feel bolder about facing any accusation of racism.

And I don't think an aversion to Jafaican (fake Jamaican), which according to the *Sunday Times* will have completely replaced Cockney by 2030, is racial. The West Indian accent from which it came is fairly pleasant, nice enough for various drink makers to use it to flog us their products. However, its by-product is rather unpleasant, sinister, idiotic and absurd.

Imagine that an Englishman were to start speaking in an inexplicable French or German accent – people would probably take the trouble to wind down their car windows to shout abuse at him. Yet enough people talk with an affected West Indian accent for it to become an accent, Jafaican, partly thanks to Radio One's Tim Westwood, and despite the Sacha Baron-Cohen character, Ali G, mocking the phenomenon.

It's unusual for a small minority to actually change a city's accent, in this case one that is supposed to date back to the time of Chaucer (although how similar a *cokenay* of that time would have sounded to modern-day cockneys is hard to know). The only previous British accent to have been significantly changed by immigration is Scouse, which took on a distinctive Irish sound in the late 19th century, but the Irish made up well over of a third of the city. West Indians are barely 10 per cent of the London population.

Multiculturalism probably played a part. Jafaican's rise may have been accelerated by the 1975 Bullock Report into education, 'A Language for Life', which heralded the start of multiculturalism in the classroom. It recommended that 'No child should be expected to cast off the language and culture of the home as he crosses the school threshold, and the curriculum should reflect those aspects of his life', and recommended that teachers were expected to have an understanding of Creole dialect 'and a positive and sympathetic attitude towards it'.

Never mind that speaking Creole would not have been much of an advantage for a young black kid trying to get on in London; there seems to have been a general approach in teaching that accents were authentic and should not be ironed out.

And the replacement of Cockney with Jafaican may reflect something more profound. Accents and fashions display underlying insecurities and cultural aspirations; the rise of Received Pronunciation reflected a desire by the lower-middle class and provincials to embrace the values, lifestyles and habits of the British upper-middle class. In London the adoption of Jafaican, even among the privately educated, reflects both a lack of confidence in British cultural values and an aspiration towards some form of ghetto authenticity.

Anyway, what are house prices in North Yorkshire like at the moment?

West (2011)

You might also want to revisit this text after reading Chapters 5 and 6 about language change, and language in the world.

REVIEW YOUR LEARNING

- What is the difference between ethnicity and nationality?
- Identify three cultural groups who have immigrated to the UK.
- How is language connected with identity?
- What is MLE and what have researchers said about it?
- How is representation connected with ethnicity?

References

Bucholtz, M. (2001). 'The Whiteness of Nerds: Superstandard English and Racial Markedness', *Journal of Linguistic Anthropology* 11(1). American Anthropological Association.

Cheshire, J, Fox, S, Kerswill, P, and Torgersen, E. (2008). 'Ethnicity, friendship network and social practices as the motor of dialect change: linguistic innovation in London', *Sociolinguistica* 22. Special issue on Dialect Sociology. pp. 1–23. Hewitt, R. (1986). *White Talk, Black Talk: Inter-racial Friendship and Communication amongst Adolescents*. Cambridge: Cambridge University Press.

Pitts, J. (2012). 'Spinning the crisis: Riots, Politics and Parenting', a lecture given at University of Bedfordshire Luton campus, 31 May 2012. Available at: http://www.youtube.com/watch?v=Gd3SJ6qakyY

Rampton, B. (2010) 'Crossing into Class: Language, Ethnicities and Class Sensibility in England', draft paper available at: http://www.academia.edu/1220312/Crossing_into_class_Language_ethnicities_and_class_sensibility_in_England_2010

Sebba, M. (1993). *London Jamaican: Language systems in interaction*. London: Longman.

West, E. (2011) '"Jafaican" may be cool, but it sounds ridiculous' *Daily Telegraph* 7 June 2011: http://blogs.telegraph.co.uk/news/edwest/100091088/jafaican-may-be-cool-but-it-sounds-ridiculous/

Further reading

Fox, S. 'Ethnicity, Religion and Practices: Adolescents in the East End of London' in Llamas, C. & Watt, D. *Language and Identities* (2010) Edinburgh: Edinburgh University Press

Harris, R. and Rampton, B. (2003) *The Language, Ethnicity and Race Reader*. London: Routledge

This chapter will:

- help you to understand how children's language develops from 0–11 years
- give you some frameworks, concepts and case studies for analysing and exploring data and answering essay questions
- explain the key academic arguments about this topic.

Key term

Critique. A critical analysis that pays attention to all aspects of a text or topic, seeing different perspectives.

! REMEMBER

Children do not produce language in a vacuum, so don't ignore the context they are in when you discuss any data you are presented with. For example, who are they talking to or writing to? Are they at home or at school, and what effect do such factors have?

As with Chapter 3, this chapter is divided into different sections, 4.1 and 4.2, each with their own aims and learning reviews. Section 4.1 concentrates primarily on spoken language, and 4.2 on written language. However, it is important not to regard these modes as separate in children's own experience of language – even though you might be studying them separately. As you work through the material, you will find references to how the modes connect.

A level assessment

Child language acquisition (CLA) is a required topic for A level, but not for AS level. It is examined on A level Paper 1, Section B. Language acquisition can also be a rewarding area to explore for your investigation coursework: see Chapter 7 for further information about this.

You need to answer one question about CLA, from a choice of two. Each question will have some data for you to consider, as a starting point for writing an essay. The essay will ask you to 'evaluate' an idea that is put forward. This means that you need to **critique** the statement or question you are given, weighing up how far it can be said to be true and also how it might not be accurate in all cases or circumstances.

The data accompanying each of the questions will be different in each case. It could appear as spoken language, written language, or – as young children are now early users of new communication tools of all kinds – it could be multimodal language from digital contexts. For that reason, this chapter includes a wide range of data produced by children.

Relevant Assessment Objectives

Essay questions about language topics require you to know about the area, which is assessed through AO2: 'Demonstrate critical understanding of concepts and issues relevant to language use.'

These questions also require you to apply relevant aspects of linguistic methods, such as the levels you are now familiar with; to use terminology relevant to the topic; and to write coherently. All of these things are rewarded through AO1.

Development of children's spoken language

When you think of how children's language develops, you will probably think of children gradually moving from making sounds to speaking words, putting words together into longer utterances, and then on to areas such as reading and writing. All of those individual elements are of course what most children acquire at some point, but a very important aspect of their language development is related to how children use language in real-life communication. After all, while we can study language in an abstract way by breaking it down into different levels, the reality of everyday communication is very much a mixture of different elements.

While the development of words and meanings (lexis and semantics), grammar (syntax and morphology), sounds (phonology), spelling, handwriting and keyboard use (**orthography** and graphology) are important elements of a child's language acquisition, one of the most crucial areas of study is what they use language *for* and how they learn to understand what language can *do*. This is an area of language study that spans pragmatics and discourse, and includes such aspects as the functions of language, the implied meanings of what people say and write, the contexts that people communicate in, and the structures of interactions with other people.

In the AQA English Language A level, the questions you are set will always provide you with data as a starting point, so this chapter will match that approach. In each section, you will be introduced to ideas about how children's language develops and be given data to explore to see how those ideas relate to what children actually do. The questions on this topic are designed to make you think about the data you see in front of you and apply your ideas, rather than just offload all the information you know about the topic.

For example, what do you make of the short extract of data below? This data set shows the utterances of three children – Ruby, Stan and Liam, who are siblings – at various stages of their development. All of the utterances are requests for biscuits – an important morning ritual in their household.

This section of Chapter 4 covers children's spoken language and will:

- help you to understand how children's spoken language develops
- give you frameworks for analysing and exploring data
- introduce you to researchers' studies of children's spoken language.

Key term

Orthography. The spelling system.

Activity

Look at how the language use of the children develops as they get older – not just in what they say, but in what they mean. Think about the following:

- What are the children trying to do with language?
- What kinds of words and structures are they using?
- How is this changing as they get older?

Data set: the pragmatics of asking for a biscuit

Context: Different conversations with parents shortly after breakfast, over a three-year period.

  a Ruby: dat (*pointing at biscuit tin, age: 1 year 6 months*)
  b Ruby: biscuit, daddy (*age: 2 years*)
  c Stan: I want a biscuit, daddy (*age: 3 years 6 months*)

d Stan: Can I have a biscuit, daddy? (*age: 3 years 9 months*)

e Stan: Please can I have a biscuit, daddy? (*age: 4 years 2 months*)

f Liam: I'm hungry, daddy (*age: 4 years 9 months*)

g Liam: Stan's had a biscuit. (*age: 4 years 9 months*)

As you can see from this set of extracts, the words themselves remain largely the same ('biscuit', 'daddy', 'have', 'I'), but both the syntax and pragmatics become more sophisticated. Why is this? On a basic level, as children get older, they use more words and put them together into increasingly sophisticated structures. So, the child in utterance **a** is not able to use more than a single word (which might not even be viewed as a proper word), while the child in utterance **g** can use 5 words in a conventional clause structure. Also, **d** and **e** show that the children can go beyond statements to questions.

On a different level, something else is starting to happen. As children get older, their parents and caregivers are less prepared to respond to blunt and apparently rude demands or requests. They expect children to recognize the 'rules' of politeness: an understanding that develops through interacting with others. **Politeness** is an important element of pragmatics and is very much a part of other types of language acquisition too: think about English tourists abroad pointing at items in shops and saying 'that one'.

In a very short data set like the one above, there is already quite a lot to think about in terms of how children's language develops, and that's before you have even started to study the topic in detail. Working from the data outwards, you might want to start thinking about questions such as why the girl in utterance **a** says 'dat' rather than 'that', why the children revert to statements in the later examples, and why they become less direct as they get older. All of these will be looked at in more detail in this section of the chapter, and linked to different concepts and studies that attempt to shed light on how children's language develops.

Children are born unable to speak or to understand the words spoken around them, but within five to six years most of them will be speaking fluently in their mother tongue. Some will be speaking more than one language and, even within a matter of a few weeks from birth (and some research suggests even before birth), many children will respond in different ways to different types of language used around them.

Something has clearly developed in that time, and linguists generally agree that children's language develops in a way that's markedly different from how adults or older children might learn a foreign language. However, there are many disagreements and different explanations for how children's language develops. Do they have some inbuilt tendency to tune into language, some ability to grasp its rules system, or do they pick up language from what is used around them? As you work your way through this chapter, many of these ideas will be explored and you will have the opportunity to assess the different evidence and reach your own conclusions.

In this section of the chapter, you will look at the first sounds that children make, the first words they speak, and how the meanings of these words are understood. You will also look at how children put these words and parts of words together into meaningful patterns and combinations, as well as how they come to understand how language is used around them to achieve different things.

Key term

Politeness. An aspect of pragmatics that refers to the cultural rules of a community and regulates how social relationships are negotiated. Everyday use of the term 'polite' tends to be associated with surface aspects such as table manners and saying 'please' and 'thank you'. These aspects are connected with the academic concept but it goes much deeper than this, including all aspects of cultural rules about appropriate language use in social engagements.

Along with looking at what children say, you will look at what is said to them and the ways in which input and interaction might influence the language of children. This is a key area of the AQA English Language A level specification, which brings in wider debates and research about the nature of children's language development and offers you the chance to assess the different ideas and evidence before coming to your own conclusions.

In Section 4.2, you will move on to explore the transition that children make from spoken language to written language. This includes how they read and how they start to write, and how they use other modes of communication such as social media, texting and email.

Sounds and words

Here, you will look at the first steps that children take in their use of language. You will look at early words, meanings and sounds.

 Activity

Look at the examples of children's language below. They are all taken from three children in the same family as they grew older. Make a note of what you observe about each utterance and how they develop as the list progresses.

● What changes are taking place?

● What is the language being used for?

Data set: developing over time

1. 'Dat.' (*context: pointing at a cup*)
2. 'Horsey!' (*context: pointing at a photo of a horse*)
3. 'Me want one.' (*context: watching their brother get a sweet*)
4. 'There's a band of mouses.' (*context: describing a picture in a children's book*)
5. 'What you doing?' (*context: talking to dad as he makes dinner*)
6. 'Not eat that daddy.' (*context: talking to dad, who is pretending to eat a book*)
7. 'Doctor made my ear better.' (*context: describing a trip to the doctor*)
8. 'I just putting her back.' (*context: the child has been asked not to play with someone else's doll*)
9. 'The goodies are going on their ship cos they've caught a baddie.' (*context: playing with their brother and some toy figures*)
10. 'Don't do that because you'll hit the men and they'll fall over.' (*context: telling their brother what to do in a game of soldiers*)
11. 'Ruby walks down stairs backwards, but when she's more older she can walk down them forwards.' (*context: talking about how his little sister goes down the stairs*)

You might have noticed many things about the utterances above, including the following:

● Some of the 'words' don't seem to be 'proper' words at all.

- The utterances seem to get longer – there are more words – as you read from 1–11.
- Some of the utterances seem to be incomplete – words are missing.
- Some of the utterances make sense but sound 'wrong'.
- Some of the utterances seem to use 'rules', but in cases where you wouldn't expect them to be applied.
- The utterances become more sophisticated and convey more complex information.
- Many of the words seem to be linked to the world immediately around the child.
- Some of the words seem to be linked to imaginary worlds and play.
- The utterances seem to have a range of functions: from demands, questions and statements to more advanced comments about what might happen in the future.

Words and meanings

One of the key things that you've probably noticed in the above data is that over a short space of time (generally between the ages of about 1 and 4) children's language rapidly develops from something that might not even be classed as 'proper' words to long and quite sophisticated utterances, conveying a number of different ideas. It's this speed of language development that is so remarkable, and there are competing explanations about how it happens.

Another key discussion point relates not to what children can say (**production**) but what they can understand (**comprehension**), and it is generally agreed that children are much more advanced in their comprehension than their production (that is, they can understand far more than they can say).

In the very early stages of language development, children normally make a range of different sounds, as described in the table below.

Sounds in the pre-verbal stages ▶

Pre-verbal stage	Main features	Approximate timings
Vegetative	Reflex crying noises	0–4 months
Cooing	Open-mouthed vowel sounds	3–6 months
Babbling	Repeated consonant–vowel sounds and combinations of these	6–12 months
Proto-word	Babbling sounds that seem to match actual word sounds – a grey area between pre-verbal and grammatical stages	9–12 months

A child's first recognizable word usually appears at about 12 months of age, but this varies, depending on the child. Some children will not utter a single word at all, but instead will start speaking using two- or three-word utterances at a later date.

Once children reach 18 months, they will often have a **productive vocabulary** of around 50 words: that is, 50 words that they can say. They will understand many more than 50 words, but this is harder to test. By the age of 24 months, most children will have reached a 200-word productive vocabulary, and by

Key terms

Comprehension. The ability to understand language, which might differ from how much an individual can produce.

Production. The language that people can produce, which might be different from how much they can understand.

Productive vocabulary. Vocabulary that can be put to use.

36 months it will be around 2,000 words. Learning new words is something most people do all their lives, but the speed of children's acquisition of lexis is staggering; most linguists put the figure at something close to 10 words a day.

The first words that children produce tend to fall into quite similar categories, and many researchers – along with many parents – have logged the early language of children. Nelson (1973) placed the early words of children into four categories: naming, action, social, and modifying (descriptions). She found that far and away the largest category was naming words, with around 60% of a child's first 50 words being nouns.

Others, such as Bloom (2004), have argued that this supposed noun bias in early children's vocabulary merely reflects the relative frequency of nouns in the vocabulary (nouns outnumber verbs by about 5:1 in most dictionaries).

Environment plays a significant part in determining which individual words are spoken by children at this age – children growing up in the countryside perhaps use different words from those growing up in a city – but the general pattern that many early words are nouns is true for children of all backgrounds.

The table below gives examples of common patterns in children's early words (Saxton, 2010).

Food and drink	bread, cookie, drink, juice, milk
Family	mama, dada, baby
Animals	dog, kitty, duck, cow, horse, bunny
Parts of the body	nose, mouth, foot, ear, hair, hand
Clothing	hat, shoe, coat, nappy
Vehicles	car, truck, bike, boat, train
Games and routines	bye-bye, night-night, upsidaisy, peekaboo, hi, shhh
Toys	ball, book, doll, teddy, bubbles
Familiar objects	chair, cup, spoon, bottle, key, clock, flower, door
Actions	eat, go, up, down, sit, off, back
Descriptives	hot, cold, allgone, dirty
Sound effects	yum-yum, ouch, moo, woof

◀ **Words in the vocabularies of children younger than 18 months**

Stretching words

At this early stage of development, children are trying to do a lot with a little. Children's early words are often **overextended** to cover more things that have similar properties or similar functions to the actual object. An example is a child referring to any kind of round fruit as an 'apple', or labelling rats, squirrels and rabbits as 'mouse', presumably because they share similar characteristics. On other occasions, words have their meanings **underextended** to cover a narrower definition of a word's meanings. In this case, a child may have a clear idea what a banana is, and use the word when faced with a real banana on a plate, but will not be able to see that a picture of a banana in a book or a photograph of a bunch of bananas can be labelled in the same way. Children often use quite specific meanings for objects around them, and the mislabelling they apply sheds some light on how they learn to link words and their meanings to objects.

Key terms

Overextended / Overextension. Applying a label to more referents than it should have. For example, a child saying 'sea' to label any body of water.

Underextended / Underextension. Applying a label to fewer referents than it should have. For example, a child saying 'milk' to refer to milk in their own cup, but not a picture of some milk in a book.

Key terms

Analogical overextension. Extending a label from one item to another by connecting their functions or how they are perceived. Although the connections may have some logic to them, they differ from existing categories.

Categorical overextension. Inappropriately extending the meaning of a label to other members in the same category. For example, a child calling all leafy green vegetables 'cabbage'.

Hypernym. The name of a category. For example, 'vegetable' is a hypernym, and 'carrot', 'cabbage' and 'onion' are all hyponyms.

Hyponym. The name of a category member. For example, 'carrot' is a hyponym of the category 'vegetable'.

Mismatch statement. In child language studies, when a child makes a connection based on what is normally the case, but isn't the case on this particular occasion.

Predicate statement. An alternative term for mismatch statement.

There are several theories about extension. Rescorla (1980) noted three forms of overextension:

- **Categorical overextension** is the most common form, and best exemplified by the example of the apple above: the label of 'apple' is stretched to include other types of fruit within a similar, larger category. The same type of extension might relate to the example of the word 'mouse', where the other animals are similar in appearance. In this form of overextension, the **hyponym** 'apple' is perhaps taken to stand for the **hypernym** 'fruit', and it is only when a child has picked up other hyponyms within the same category (such as 'orange', 'pear', 'melon') that these overextensions start to disappear.

- **Analogical overextension** is found in about 15% of Rescorla's cases, and is related more to the function or perception of the object: a scarf might be called 'cat' when a child strokes it, or a cement mixer might be termed a 'football' because of its apparently similar shape and rolling action.

- **Mismatch** or **predicate statements** are a third form of overextension noted by Rescorla, and they account for about 25% of the overextensions in her study. These are statements that convey some form of abstract information. An example quoted in Rescorla's research is a child using the word 'doll' when referring to an empty cot. This may appear to be a complete mislabelling of the item, but appears to be linked to the fact that the doll could usually be found in the cot, but wasn't on this occasion.

The possible reasons why children make these overextensions is something you will look at in more detail when you study different theories, later in the chapter, but it would appear that children are still trying to make sense of how words map to objects and types of object in the real world.

Activity

Analyse the following examples of children's language and the contexts that gave rise to them. Try to explain which form of extension is taking place within each example.

There is some feedback on this activity at the back of the book.

Data set: object mapping

Child's words	Context of utterance
Tiger	Used when looking at pictures of tigers, lions and leopards in a picture book
Socks	Used when referring to gloves
Duck	Used when talking about feeding ducks, pigeons and other birds in a park
Cat	Used when pointing at the door where the cat normally waits
Shoes	Used when referring to own pair of shoes but not when talking about any other type of shoe

Building meanings

Aitchison (1987) identified the three stages below in children's acquisition of words and their meanings. This table offers a useful overview of the processes outlined so far in this topic.

Labelling	• Associating sounds with objects in the world around the child • Linking words to things • Understanding the concept of labels
Packaging	Starting to explore the extent of the label – often the stage during which overextensions and underextensions occur most frequently
Network building	• Making connections between the labels they have developed • Understanding opposites and similarities, relationships and contrasts

◄ **Aitchison's model showing the three stages of children's acquisition of words and their meanings**

As an example, *labelling* might mean attaching the label 'cat' to a particular animal. *Packaging* would consist of establishing what makes this animal a cat, as opposed to a bird or a snail – for example, four legs, size, fur. *Network building* would consist of the child making connections between 'cat' as a label and the cat as a member of the broader category 'animal'.

As Aitchison's model makes clear, children's acquisition of words and their meanings is not simply a question of remembering labels that they have been taught. It is an active and deductive process that involves the child making sense of his or her surroundings and then mapping out connections between words and the world. The competing theories behind child language development are explored later in this section, but much of what you have read here will be useful in looking at whether children learn language through imitation, or if certain processes are inbuilt.

Sounds

Even when children are starting to use more words, they still struggle to pronounce them as an adult might, and there are certain key patterns to the sounds that children use.

Process	Explanation	Example
Addition	Adding an extra vowel sound to create a CVCV structure	*hɔːs* becomes *hɔːsiː* *dɒg* becomes *dɒgiː*
Deletion	Leaving out the last consonant of a word, so a word like mouse becomes mou (mow)	*kæt* would be pronounced *kæ* *pɪg* would be *pɪ*
Reduplication	The repetition of particular sounds and structures	*choochoo* *weewee*
Substitution	One sound is swapped for another, easier sound	*ræbɪt* becomes *wæbɪt* *sɪŋ* becomes *tɪŋ*
Consonant cluster reduction	Children find it difficult to produce consonant clusters – groups of two or more consonants – so will reduce them to smaller units	*draɪ* becomes *daɪ* *frɒg* becomes *fɒg*

◄ **Pronouncing sounds**

►

| Deletion of unstressed syllables | The removal of an entire unstressed syllable from a word | *banana* becomes *nana* *pyjamas* becomes *jamas* *pretending* becomes *tending* |
| Assimilation | A process in which substitution occurs, but the sound changes because of other sounds around it, e.g. a sound is substituted with one that is closer to others in the word | *dɒgi:* becomes *gɒgi:* |

Activity

Look at the examples of child language below. Try to identify which processes are at work in the bold words. The adult target word is given in brackets next to each example. In some cases, there might be more than one process in each extract.

a   **maʊ** (mouse).

b   Can I play on the **puter** (computer), daddy?

c   The bunny **eated** the **kæwət** (carrot).

d   We went on a **ɔ:si:** (horse) ride.

e   I want my **bæŋkɪt** (blanket).

f   My **bʊt** (book).

g   It's a **bæbɪt** (rabbit).

There is some feedback on this activity at the back of the book.

Putting words together

As children grow older, their language skills develop and they begin to piece together longer utterances. Typically, a child of 18 months would be able to put together two-word phrases such as those below, while a child of 24 months or older might be producing some of the utterances seen in the data examples related to the Activity on page 113.

Data set: 18 months

a   'Sit chair.'

b   'Mummy pushchair.'

c   'My cup.'

d   'Shut door.'

However, length of utterance – in other words, how many words a child strings together – is not the only factor you need to consider when studying child language.

Linguists use the term 'mean length of utterance' (MLU) when analysing what children say. MLU is used to work out the average length of a child's utterances across a sample of data and takes into account not just the individual words but the morphemes as well. In an expression such as 'I eating', the child is using two words but three morphemes. 'Eating' can be split into two morphemes: 'eat' and '-ing', where the **free morpheme** 'eat' carries the main meaning, and the '-ing' **bound morpheme** indicates the progressive aspect – showing that the child can talk about his or her action as continuous and ongoing.

You can see that the complexity of what a child is saying is not based just on how many words are used, but also the grammatical units within those words. It is children's use of these morphemes that can often help us to grasp what is going on inside their minds.

Activity

Look at the utterances below. Count up the number of morphemes used in each one.
Answers are at the back of the book.

Data set: 24 months

- **a** 'What you doing?'
- **b** 'Not eat that daddy.'
- **c** 'Where's man going?'
- **d** 'The mans are laughing.'
- **e** 'The soldiers falled over when they got hitted.'

One of the most noticeable developments in the language of children is the progression from proto-words to the one-word stage, and then from the one-word stage towards two, three, four and more words in an utterance. Basically, as children get older, they produce longer and more complicated utterances. In fact, most linguists use the numbers of words as the names of the stages themselves: proto-word; one-word/holophrastic; two-word; telegraphic; post-telegraphic. These are all explained in the table below.

It's important to realize that these stages should only be seen as a loose framework and not a straitjacket for every utterance from every child. It is not uncommon for children to bypass the one-word and even two-word stages and to go on to produce telegraphic utterances as their first spoken language. Also, many children do not limit their utterances to just one stage at a time: many will vary their utterances depending on context. It's therefore a good idea to look at as much data as possible – and to consider the context fully – before making judgements about children's abilities.

Stage	Main features	Example
Proto-word	Consonant–vowel–consonant–vowel sounds that are similar to actual words, but applied inconsistently to **referents**	*Goggie* – this could mean 'dog' but would have to be applied consistently for this to be clear
One-word / holophrastic	Single words that relate consistently to identifiable referents	*Daddy*
Two-word	Utterances consisting of two words in a range of patterns	*Daddy go.* *Where mummy?* *Drink allgone.*

◄ **Typical stages in a child's acquisition of language** ►

Key terms

Bound morpheme. A morpheme that does not exist as an independent word but adds meaning to a free morpheme, For example, the free morpheme 'help' can have the bound morphemes 'un', 'ful' and 'ly' added to it to create the 4-morpheme word 'unhelpfully'.

Free morpheme. A morpheme that can exist as an independent word.

Key terms

Gestalt expression. The term gestalt is German for 'shape' or 'form' and refers to the way in which children at a certain stage can compress a string of words into a single utterance. For example, while an adult would say 'what is that?' a child might say 'wassat?'

Holophrase / Holophrastic stage. Holophrase means 'whole phrase' and, as it suggests, refers to the stage of language acquisition where whole phrases can be expressed via a single word. Also called the **one-word stage.**

One-word stage. Also called the **holophrastic** stage, this refers to the stage of language acquisition where a single word can stand for a whole expression.

Segment. To be able to segment something is to perceive the boundaries or breaks between the units. This is a skill that is gradually acquired. Adults may not be aware of how they run words together in speech. For example, a child once asked a teacher how to spell 'sponner': he'd heard 'Once upon a time' as 'One sponner time'.

Two-word stage. This involves children using two words to create mini-sentences, with the word order often resembling adult speech.

Telegraphic	Utterances consisting of three or more words, in which key content words are used while grammatical function words are omitted	*Where daddy gone?* *That my doll.* *Give doggie biscuit.*
Post-telegraphic	Utterances where grammatical words missing from the telegraphic stage start to appear, and **clauses** begin to be linked into longer sentences	*We went to the park and played on the swings.* *That's my dolly cos granny bought it for me.* *That baddy got eaten by the dragon.*

One-word/holophrastic stage

Most children will say their first word at about one year of age, but identifying this stage is often a little problematic. When children say a word, is it actually a word? How do we know? And what if they mean more than they say? What happens if they say two words together as if they're a single word? A sound – to put it simply – can only become a genuine word if it is used consistently to relate to something. If a child says *dada* when dad comes into the room, that might sound like a word, but what if the child then says that 'word' when mum or the dog walk in? Once a genuine word has been uttered, you also face the problem of trying to identify what the child actually means.

Many early utterances are termed **holophrases**. Holophrastic means 'whole phrase', and it's a stage during which children use what sound like one-word utterances to convey more than one word's meaning. For example, if a child says 'doggie' when the family dog enters the room, the child might be just labelling the animal with a word, but it's equally likely that the child is trying to convey something like 'look, there's the dog' or 'the dog's come in'. It's quite possible that most one-word utterances are in fact holophrases – one notable exception being when parents sit with young children and ask them to name and label objects in picture books, as in the example below.

> **Parent**: What's that?
> **Child**: Dog.
> **Parent**: That's right. Now, what's that?
> **Child**: Sheep.

Phrases can also consist of two words that the child has put together after hearing them spoken. Utterances such as 'inthere' or 'wassat' can be termed **gestalt expressions**: they sound like one word and almost function as short sentences ('put it in there' or 'what is that?'). The most likely explanation for these gestalt expressions is that the child has yet to **segment** the sounds into separate words, so some elements of adult speech such as 'Shall we put your top on?' or 'Have you got your shoes on?' become 'topon' or 'shoeson'. Alternatively, it might be argued that the child is picking up 'chunks' of language and using them as units to communicate meaning.

Two-word stage

At the **two-word stage**, syntax comes into play and the child is likely to combine words into a range of patterns to create mini-sentences. The word order of these two-word expressions is often very close to adult syntax. Brown (1973) noted that many of the two-word utterances fit into a common set of patterns, often with one word being a doer and another being what is done ('I walk', 'mummy eat'), an action and a thing being acted upon ('drink juice', 'eat apple', 'get baby') or an object and its qualities ('drink allgone', 'nappy wet', 'daddy sad').

As with the holophrastic stage, many of these two-word utterances may have wider or more detailed meanings that the child cannot yet express. It is when children move into the next stage – telegraphic speech – that a more varied pattern of grammatical structures starts to emerge.

Another child language researcher, Braine (1963), noted that at the two-word stage, children use patterns of two-word utterances that seem to revolve around certain key words. He called this a **pivot schema**. 'Pivot' words combined with what he called 'slots'. So, a word like 'allgone' would act as a pivot and be combined with a range of other words to create two-word expressions, such as '*allgone* dinner', '*allgone* milk', '*allgone* daddy'. These two-word patterns can be very productive for a whole range of functions, and help to develop a child's range of communication at this stage.

Telegraphic stage

Beyond the two-word stage, children move into what is known as the **telegraphic stage**, adding more words to their utterances, but often omitting apparently less meaningful grammatical words such as **auxiliary verbs**, determiners and prepositions.

Activity

Below are four short extracts of telegraphic language. What kind of things do you notice in the language being used, and what is being missed out? What patterns do you observe?

There is some feedback on this activity at the back of the book.

Data set: telegraphic speech

Example 1 Context: girl watching train go by a few minutes after her mother has left for work.

Age: 2 years 4 months

Ruby: Mummy go work on train.

Example 2 Context: imaginative play with teddy bears and figures.

Age: 2 years 8 months

Adult: What are you doing?

Stan: I giving blanket to monkey.

Example 3 Context: looking over balcony and finding fisherman who's been there for last three mornings isn't there.

Age: 1 year 10 months

Mattie: Where man gone?

! REMEMBER

Don't think about language development just as a process of adding words to other words. Think about what is meant, not just what is said.

Link

For more detail on the two-word stage and the patterns noted by Brown, William O'Grady's *How Children Learn Language* is recommended.

Key terms

Auxiliary verb. These are verbs that help other verbs and include the verbs 'be', 'do' and 'have'.

Pivot schema. The use by children of certain key words as a 'pivot' to generate many utterances.

Telegraphic stage. A stage where children produce abbreviated speech that, like SMS messages in the modern world, misses out the grammatical structures and markings that are not essential for understanding.

Did you know?

The telegraphic stage is so named because of the way it resembles the language of telegrams, where you had to pay by the word so people missed out the less important words from a message.

Example 4 Context: watching TV with father and asking question about girl on CBeebies.

Age: 2 years 6 months

Liam: What her doing?

Questions and negatives

In the two-word and telegraphic stages, the typical sentence structure used in declaratives begins to be manipulated by children as they explore the world around them and the language that describes it.

An important aspect of syntax is the way in which it can be altered to create questions and negatives, and children quickly make use of a range of methods to either ask who, where, when, what or why, or to say no. Linguists Ursula Bellugi and David McNeill carried out many observations on children during the 1960s and 1970s, and theorized that children progress through distinct stages as they develop, and apply rules to the creation of negatives and questions, such as where to place the negative word or particle (such as *not* or *don't*) or how to invert subject and verb (such as changing 'Mummy has gone to work' to 'Has Mummy gone to work?').

Beyond the telegraphic stage

As children pass through the telegraphic stage, the missing words – the determiners, the auxiliary verbs and the prepositions – start to appear in the right places, and a range of more complex grammatical features are used. The **post-telegraphic stage** sees the appearance of more confident use of forms such as the passive voice, different **tenses** and **aspects**, and a wider range of clause structures. **Noun phrases** are also built up into more detailed structures.

Beyond the telegraphic stage, the post-telegraphic utterances of children start to resemble the patterns of adult speech. Clauses are linked with conjunctions to create complex and compound sentences, while different types of clause crop up to serve different functions.

Key terms

Aspect. This refers to the way in which certain grammatical markings on verb forms indicate whether an action or state is ongoing. For example, the 'ing' form in 'looking' suggests continuous action: the 'ing' ending is called a 'progressive'.

Post-telegraphic stage. A developmental stage that goes beyond children's use of abbreviated speech.

Tense. This refers to the way in which verbs can indicate time, for example the 'ed' ending on a verb such as 'look' indicates past time.

Activity

Read the data set below and look at what the children are doing with language. How are the utterances becoming more complex? What kind of linking is going on between the clauses, and how are they starting to express more complex relationships between different ideas?

There is some feedback on this activity at the back of the book.

Data set: post-telegraphic stage

Example 1 Context: imaginative conversation with father.

Age: 2 years 9 months

Stan: My head falled off and rolled around but I put it back on again.

Example 2 Context: talking while playing.

Age: 3 years 6 months

Liam: The goodies are going on their ship cos they've caught a baddie.

Example 3 Context: conversation with father about baby sister.

Age: 4 years 9 months

Stan: Ruby walks down stairs backwards, but when she's more older she can walk down them forwards.

Example 4 Context: talking while playing.

Age: 4 years 6 months

Stan: Don't do that because you'll hit the men and they'll fall over.

Example 5 Context: conversation in car with father.

Age: 4 years 10 months

Liam: If the baddies attacked the castle and the goodies weren't there, what would happen, daddy?

Example 6 Context: conversation with father.

Age: 4 years 11 months

Stan: The other game which Liam was playing was really tough.

Tense and aspect

Another feature of the post-telegraphic stage is children's increased skill at dividing events into distinct time frames. As you have seen from the examples above, auxiliaries are often left out at the two-word stage, but become increasingly important when questions, negatives and accounts of past events need to be formed.

Looking back at Example 2 from the telegraphic speech data set ('I giving blanket to monkey'), it is clear that the child is trying to create the present progressive 'I am giving', which uses an auxiliary verb to mark the present tense, and an *-ing* inflection to mark the progressive aspect. Even without the auxiliary verb, the meaning is still fairly clear, but when slightly more complicated sequences of events need to be recounted, the auxiliary verb is more important.

Take, for example, the difference between 'I have found it' and 'I found it'. In the first example, the auxiliary verb marks this as a present-tense construction, while the use of the main verb in the past participle form *found* shows that this is a present-perfect construction. The action of finding has been completed but is still relevant to what the child is doing now ('I have found it and now I'm digging with it'). The second example, 'I found it', is a simple past-tense construction, recounting that the event has finished and is perhaps no longer relevant. The use of an auxiliary verb allows the child a subtler palette from which to draw his or her descriptions of what is happening and what has been done.

Activity

Read the data set that follows and look at the ways in which the child has tried to indicate different time frames through his use of tense and aspect. How would you describe linguistically what he is doing and how it differs from the standard adult version?

Suggestions are provided in the feedback at the back of the book.

Data set: time and tense

> *Example 1 Context: talking while playing.*
> Ages: 2 years 8 months to 2 years 9 months
> **Liam**: I couldn't found it.

> *Example 2 Context: talking to father about TV programme.*
> Age: 5 years 7 months
> **Liam**: Look at what some people have did.

Passive voice

Another grammatical structure that appears as the child develops is the passive voice, which children often understand from a fairly early age, but whose structure makes it more difficult for them to construct. The passive voice places the thing or person receiving the action of the verb at the front of the sentence.

Data set: passive voice

> *Example Context: talking while playing with toy soldiers.*
> Age: 4 years 2 months
> **Stan**: The baddy's been got by the goody leader.

In this example, Stan successfully forms a passive construction by applying the action of the verb (to get) to the subject of his sentence (the baddy), and adding the agent of the verb (the goody leader – the person who has performed the 'getting') at the end.

'Virtuous' errors and logical mistakes

Another aspect of grammar that children develop as they get older is their use of **morphology**. When studying the early utterances of young children, you may come across some or all of the features in the following data set. These **virtuous errors** are not mistakes as such, because they have an underlying logic to them. They can tell us a great deal about what children are picking up and understanding from the language around them, and how they are trying to apply rules to their own language.

> **Key term**
>
> **Virtuous error.** A mistake that has an underlying logic, showing that learning has taken place.

> **Activity**
>
> Read the examples in the data set below. What 'virtuous errors' are the speakers making in each example?
>
> There is some feedback on this activity at the back of the book.

Data set: virtuous errors

> **a** 'I runned.'
> **b** 'There was three mans.'
> **c** 'I eating.'
> **d** 'This goody is more braver than that one.'
> **e** 'He's hitting him with a hitter.'
> **f** 'They shotted their arrows at the baddies.'
> **g** 'Daddy go work.'

Overgeneralization

If the child hasn't heard the expressions in the examples above, where do they come from? One answer seems to be that children start to apply to their own language, rules that they have observed in action in other people's language. If children have heard the -ed sound being used to tell a story about events that have already taken place – in the past tense – they might start applying the -ed ending to all the verbs they use. Of course, most of the time this will produce perfectly acceptable past-tense verbs, such as 'walked', 'pushed' or 'opened', but English grammar isn't always so simple and many of the most widely used verbs tend to have irregular past-tense forms. Hence, a child saying 'runned', 'seed', 'eated' or 'holded' is not creating nonsense but rigidly applying rules: what linguists call **overgeneralization** (or over-regularization). They may be errors, but they're logical errors. You will look at some possible theoretical explanations for these patterns later in this chapter.

Pragmatics and interaction

As children grow older and achieve more competence in language, there are still obvious ways in which their speech differs from that of older children and adults. Language is not just a straightforward system of communication but a web of connections between people, what they want to say and the contexts that surround them. A child who has acquired a sophisticated grasp of tense and voice might still struggle to know that adults don't like to be interrupted when talking on the phone, or that telling a grandparent that 'mum doesn't like your cooking' might not be a good idea.

In Chapter 1 you looked at different language levels, and it is pragmatics that is most relevant to this area of language development. Pragmatics concerns things like implication and the social conventions connected with communication.

Activity

Work with a partner, if possible, and consider the problems which a child might face in understanding the following scenarios. Think about how the intended meanings are being communicated.

- A boy drops his empty crisp packet on the floor and his dad says 'There's a bin over there'.
- A girl hears her mum say 'Come on, we'd better get our skates on or we'll miss the bus'.
- A child accidentally drops a phone in the toilet and her older sister says 'Oh thanks very much!'

As adults, most of our communication takes place using spoken conversation, and this has its own unwritten rules and structures, such as **turntaking**, staying on the same topic and paying attention to others' face needs. Children are often quite capable of conducting two-way conversations, and indeed have been trained for this since they were babies with ritualized games such as 'Peek-a-boo' and 'Walkie round the garden', but do not always know how to open conversations or how to balance their needs with those of others.

Politeness, too, is something that is acquired through interaction, but also through explicit teaching ('say "please" if you want ice cream'). But politeness is

Did you know?

Jean Berko Gleason carried out an experiment in 1958 to test children's use of the -s plural. She found that when faced with a picture of an imaginary animal called a 'wug', children tended to create the plural 'wugs' when asked to complete the statement: 'This is a wug. Now there is another one. There are two of them. There are two…'. Of the four- to five-year-olds tested, 76% formed the regular -s plural, and 97% of the five- to seven-year-olds did the same. Berko Gleason also used other nonsense words, such as 'heaf', 'cra', 'tor' and 'lun', with broadly similar results. You can find a YouTube clip of the test by searching for 'Jean Berko Gleason and Wugs'.

Key terms

Overgeneralization. Applying a rule and assuming that every example follows the same system, without realizing that there are exceptions.

Turntaking. The way in which participants take turns at talk in interactions.

not just about saying 'please' and 'thank you', it is about shaping your language to avoid imposing on others, and also to make others feel good about themselves.

Activity

Review what you have learned so far by answering the following questions:

1. What are the main stages of language acquisition that children go through?
2. In what ways is children's early production of sounds different from that of adults?
3. What kinds of 'virtuous errors' do children often make, and how might these be explained?
4. What areas of pragmatics are important to children's later language development?

How do they do it?

In the previous parts of this chapter, you have looked at the ways in which children develop from very early stages of language – cooing, babbling and then saying one or two words – to much later stages where they can ask questions, explain complicated events and use the unspoken rules of adult interaction, such as politeness and humour. But how do they do it?

This has been a subject for debate for centuries, and modern linguistics is a field in which the arguments about children's language acquisition are still hotly debated. In this section you will look at some of the key arguments about child language and be pointed towards further reading and potential ideas for your own investigations, which will help you to learn more about the nature of children's language development.

One of the key arguments is whether children's language comes from the environment they grow up in and the language they hear around them, or is something inbuilt. For years, the main debate was polarized between those who advocated a 'nature' approach and those who argued a '**nurture**' approach. In the nurture camp were **behaviourists** such as B. F. Skinner (1957), who argued that children's language was just like any other form of conditioned behaviour in the animal world, and that they would hear language used around them, attempt to use it and be either positively reinforced by their parents (in the form of praise and attention) or negatively reinforced (in the form of punishment or correction). By selectively reinforcing accurate – or relatively accurate – speech, parents would therefore help to condition a child's words, phrases and utterances towards the correct adult version of speech.

The 'nature' camp, in the form of Chomsky (1959) and fellow **nativists** who have followed him, argued that this approach could not explain how children's language develops – partly because what children hear around them is not a useful model to pick up (Chomsky referred to this as the 'poverty of the stimulus') and partly because children are capable of saying completely new things they couldn't have heard before. Language development must therefore be something that is built in (**innate**) to all humans. For example, according to the behaviourist model, a child would not say something like 'I falled over and hurted my knee at nursery' because they would not have heard this being said and would not have been positively reinforced by parents to say it. But most

Key terms

Behaviourism / Behaviourist. Within studies of language acquisition, a notion of learned behaviour as a set of responses to stimuli.

Innate. Something in-built, already in place.

Nativist / Nativism. A belief that language acquisition relies on an in-built capacity for language in humans.

Nurture. The idea that language development results from being socialized by people around the learner.

children *do* pass through stages of language where they make such 'virtuous errors' (as you have already seen on pages 118–119), so it would appear that they are generating their own language in some form or other.

These overgeneralizations (such as 'sheeps', 'falled', 'mouses' and 'runned') are all evidence to nativists that humans have an inbuilt grammar and are showing the workings of these inbuilt rules in their language production (an ability termed a **language acquisition device** or LAD by Chomsky).

As Saxton (2010) explains, 'Nativists argue that the grammar-acquiring capacity is dedicated exclusively to language. Non-nativists, on the other hand, consider grammar to be simply one of many mental achievements acquired by general-purpose cognitive learning mechanisms.' These 'mechanisms' might be things such as the ability to spot patterns and make contrasts, or grasp the probability of one thing following another, so might not, in fact, be anything to do with language in and of itself. Aitchison (1983) refers to this kind of mechanism as 'puzzle-solving equipment', and the idea contrasts with Chomsky's view that specific language knowledge is inbuilt in all humans.

Chomsky's ideas have been very influential and have come to dominate linguistics for several decades, but more recent approaches to the study of children's language have challenged his view that all humans have an inbuilt universal grammar, and instead have argued the following:

- The child's language environment provides much richer language data than Chomsky acknowledged.

- Parents and caregivers interact with children to give them input and relevant context, helping them to acquire language.

- If there is an inbuilt capacity for language, it is not the product of a specific language-related facility, but something that is linked to many other areas of understanding and development.

In fact, the split between ideas about nature and nurture is probably a much less pronounced one than it was in the 1950s, with most child language researchers (linguists and psychologists) in broad agreement that nature and nurture combine in some form or other to explain child language development.

Social interaction

One area that has attracted a great deal of interest since the 1980s is the social interaction model. According to interactionists, the language used by parents and caregivers to children (**child-directed speech – CDS**) has its own recognized characteristics, such as the following:

- More pronounced intonation, drawing attention to key morphemes or words.

- Simplified vocabulary, which helps to establish key words ('dog' rather than 'Labrador and Springer Spaniel cross').

- Repeated grammatical 'frames' that help to draw attention to new elements within those frames (e.g. 'What animal lives in a kennel? What animal lives in a stable? What animal lives in a sty?').

- Simplified grammar – shorter utterances.

- Tag questions used to initiate turn-taking.

- Actions that accompany speech: pointing, smiling, shrugging shoulders, etc.

Key terms

Child directed speech (CDS). The speech that parents and caregivers use to children.

Language acquisition device (LAD). Chomsky's idea of an innate capacity for language learning in humans.

- 'Recasting' of children's mistakes to make them more grammatically accurate.
- More obvious lip and mouth movements to help younger children copy.

Interactionists also point to ritualized scenarios, such as dinner times, nappy changes and bath times, in which children 'learn their lines'. They also suggest that games such as 'Peek-a-boo' or 'Round and round the garden' help children to acquire turntaking skills.

Parents and caregivers often expand, recast and develop their children's utterances rather than explicitly correct them for grammar or vocabulary. This helps the child to develop at a natural pace, while providing models for communication, as in the data set below.

Data set: doggies

Child: It's a doggie.

Father: Yes, it's a big brown doggie, isn't it?

Child: Brown doggie?

Father: Yes, a brown doggie.

Critics of the social interaction theory point to cultures around the world such as Samoa and Papua New Guinea, in which interaction with CDS is not believed to take place. They argue that children in these environments do not seem to be impeded by the lack of verbal interaction. Others, such as Wells (1986), Hart and Risley (1995), Thiessen et al (2005) and Henrichs (2010) have all found a positive correlation between interaction with children at an early age and their subsequent educational and/or linguistic achievement.

Activity

The following extract has been taken from a conversation between Tom (2 years 7 months) and his mum as they play with a farm-themed jigsaw.

- Which characteristics of child-directed speech do you notice in the text?
- What evidence can you find here for the different theories you have studied so far?

There is some feedback on this activity at the back of the book.

Transcription key

(.) normal pause

(3.0) numbers in brackets indicate length of pauses in seconds

? indicates a questioning intonation

Tom and the chickens

Mother: how many chickens are there?

Tom: (2.0) there's many chickens (.) one (.) two (.) three (.) four (.) one (.) two (.) three (.) four (.) five (.) six (.) seven (.) eight (.) nine (2.0)

Mother: hmm (.) shall I count them now?

Tom: yeah

Mother: one (.) two (.) three (.) four (.) five

Tom: yep

Mother: and we saw chickens this morning didn't we?

Tom: we did

Mother: at Pascale's house (.) she's got some pet chickens

Tom: has (.) have (.) has (.) has she? I (.) I stroke one chicken

Mother: you did (.) didn't you? you stroked it

Tom: yeah

Mother: Pascale had to hold it still and then you stroked the feathers didn't you?

Tom: yeah

Mother: what did it feel like?

Tom: it feels shy (2.0)

Mother: it felt shy?

Tom: yeah

Mother: did you feel shy or did the chicken feel shy?

Tom: the chicken feeled shy (2.0)

Mother: it was nervous wasn't it (.) it was a bit scared of us but when Pascale held it it was alright (.) and what did the feathers feel like? were they scratchy or were they soft or were they tickly or were they? (3.0) what did they feel like? (2.0) bumpy?

Tom: they feel feathers!

Mother: they were like what? they felt like feathers?

Tom: yeah

Mother: I thought they felt really soft

Tom: I (.) I stroke one

Building blocks

A more recent focus in work on children's language is on what are called **constructions**. A construction is a 'chunk' of language, perhaps taking the form of a short phrase such as 'juice allgone', or mini-sentences like 'I want milk.' or 'Where's the cat?' through to less literal examples like idioms or metaphors such as 'down in the dumps' and 'under the weather'.

As Ibbotson (2012) explains:

> Young children begin by learning very local patterns, e.g. *Where's the X?, I wanna X, More X, It's a X, I'm X-ing it, Put X here, Mommy's X-ing it, Let's X it, Throw X, X gone, I X-ed it, Sit on the X, Open X, X here, There's a X, X broken.* The 'X' here is the variable element, a slot that can be filled by different items, such as Where's the toy/book/dog? Once a child has heard variation like this in their language, they build up more abstract constructions by analogizing across exemplars – this means finding similarity in the way things work or the way things sound. The idea is that these reliable patterns (called slot-and-frames) give the child a foothold into learning more complex syntax.

Where construction-based approaches differ from the nativist model is in their focus on real language as it is used in conversation between parents and children (hence its other title, the **usage-based approach**). Unlike in Chomsky's 'poverty of the stimulus', construction-based models see very rich language in the child's environment, taking the form of thousands and thousands of words a day spoken to, or around, a child. This language offers the basis for some of what the child draws on in his or her early utterances.

Instead of picking up single words and then learning to combine them according to a pre-programmed set of abstract grammatical rules, this model suggests that children pick up 'chunks' of language and create very productive structures from them, adapting them to generate new and creative forms of their own.

Key term

Construction. In language acquisition, constructions are ready-made chunks of language that can be used productively to express many ideas. This model is also called a **usage-based approach.**

Link

The Human Speechome Project can be found at http://www. media.mit.edu/cogmac/ projects/hsp.html

Key terms

Cognitive. This refers to thinking processes in the brain.

Object permanence. The idea that objects exist even when they cannot be seen.

Seriation. The idea of objects being in a series.

This model – assisted by the now widespread use of digital corpora, including Deb Roy's Human Speechome Project – places more of an emphasis on the influence of children's environment and the linguistic interaction they receive, and less emphasis on the application of abstract rules to language. This model suggests that children's early language is quite narrow in its range and focused very much on lexis – words and groups of words – with more abstract rules about grammar appearing later on. It also takes elements from the **cognitive** field, focusing on children's apparently inbuilt ability as human beings to draw connections and parallels between the language patterns they have heard and to apply that understanding to their own language output, perhaps in a fairly limited way at first, but expanding as they grow.

What is also interesting is that construction-based approaches have identified quite close connections between the forms used in speech to a child and the order in which they appear in the child's language. So, the order in which children produce 'wh-' questions (such as 'What's that?' and 'Where's mummy going?') can be predicted from the frequency with which these forms appear in the language used to children by their caregivers. Likewise, the order of negation that children use (words like 'no', 'not' and 'don't') can be predicted, along with the frequency of errors such as using 'me' instead of 'I' (for example 'Me done that' or 'Me like it').

So does this mean that children are simply copying the language around them? No. According to this kind of research, while the input and output match quite closely, children are not simply parroting what they hear, but making use of it in their own way: seeing patterns, drawing parallels and being creative with the language they are exposed to. If the language data they hear is very specific, what children seem to be able to do is generalize this, hence the appearance of virtuous errors such as 'mouses', 'runned' and 'goed'.

Cognitive theories

Followers of the cognitive approach see language acquisition as part of a much wider development of understanding and knowledge in children. They differ from nativists in that many nativists see language acquisition as separate from cognitive development. There is much discussion about the strength of the link between language and thought, but to simplify the debate, you could look at two positions: those of Piaget (1964) and Vygotsky (1934).

The Swiss psychologist Jean Piaget's work with children has led to a number of highly influential strands of thinking in children's psychological development. His cognitive approach suggests that language acquisition is part of a child's wider development: language comes with understanding. In other words, a child cannot linguistically articulate concepts that he or she does not understand. Meanwhile, the Russian psychologist Lev Vygotsky put forward similarly influential views on the connections between language and thought.

Piaget argued that children need to understand a concept before they can use the language terms that refer to that concept. So the concept of the past would have to be grasped before a child could start to use the past tense, and a concept such as **seriation** understood before a child could use comparatives and superlatives, such as 'bigger' or 'biggest'.

The idea of **object permanence** plays a part in this too. Once a child has realized that everything has a separate identity and life of its own, even when he or she can't see it, there seems to be a leap in conceptual understanding that affects language development. The rapid growth in vocabulary that occurs in the third year of a child's life might be linked to this. Pronoun use might also be linked to this conceptual leap forward – perhaps because children start to recognize the symbolic function of words and the power they now have to name all those objects around them.

Vygotsky, on the other hand, viewed language as having two separate roles: one for communication and one as the basis of thought. He saw language in this second role as a helpful tool for developing understanding, and believed that language and thought become closely related after a relatively short time. In a sense, it could be argued that children's developing language might help them in their grasp of some concepts, because it could help them to divide up and categorize the world around them.

Both approaches might appear to be common sense, but there are exceptions that suggest otherwise. Some children with cognitive problems still manage to use language way beyond their apparent understanding, while others with advanced cognition skills struggle with language. So the two concepts – cognition and language – do not seem to be as inextricably linked as Piaget and Vygotsky might have thought. While there are clearly connections between language development and other aspects of a child's overall development, perhaps language is distinct in a sufficient number of ways to make it unique.

Vygotsky's ideas about how children's understanding and language develop are also interesting because of his view that interaction is important, and there is some clear crossover here with the social interactionist model described above. For Vygotsky, children's increasing grasp of language and ideas does not develop in isolation but through interaction with others, or what he termed a More Knowledgeable Other (MKO), which could be a parent, teacher or older sibling. Through shared activities and talk, children and MKOs would 'co-construct' knowledge and language. This idea is taken up again in Section 4.2.

> ### Did you know?
>
> Children given a range of cups of different shapes and sizes have been found to develop their understanding of vocabulary more quickly than toddlers given only similar-looking cups. Work at the University of Iowa by Perry et al (2010) suggests that the range of different shapes and sizes helps children to grasp the possible range of objects that the word 'cup' can refer to.

REVIEW YOUR LEARNING

- Outline a range of theories about children's acquisition of language.
- Why did Chomsky propose the idea of a language acquisition device, and what evidence is there against his idea?
- Outline the main aspects of child-directed speech (CDS) and assess its importance.
- How does the language that children hear around them support their development?

References

Aitchison, J. (1983). *The Articulate Mammal*. Harper Collins.

Aitchison, J. (1987). *Words in the Mind: an introduction to the mental lexicon*. John Wiley & Sons.

Bloom, P. (2004). 'Myths of Word Learning'. In D. G. Hall and S. R. Waxman (eds.), *Weaving a lexicon* (pp. 205–224). Cambridge, MA: MIT Press.

Braine, M. D. S. (1963). 'The Ontogeny of English Phrase Structure'. *Language*, 39: 1–14.

Brown, R. (1973). *A first language: The early stages*. Cambridge, MA: Harvard University Press.

Chomsky, N. (1959) 'A Review of B. F. Skinner's *Verbal Behavior*' in *Language*, 35, 1: 126–58.

Crystal, D. (1989). *Listen to your Child: a parent's guide to children's language*. London: Penguin.

Hart, B. and Risley, T. R. (1995). *Meaningful differences in the everyday experience of young American children*. Baltimore USA: Paul H Brookes Publishing.

Heinrichs, L. F. (2010) 'Academic language in early childhood interactions: a longitudinal study of 2- to 6-year-old Dutch monolingual children'. Amsterdam Centre for Language and Communication (ACLC).

Ibbotson, P. (2012). 'Child Language Acquisition' in Clayton, D. (ed.) *Language: a student handbook on key topics and theories*. London: English and Media Centre.

Nelson, K. (1973). 'Structure and Strategy in Learning to Talk', monographs of the *Society for Research in Child Development*, 38.

O'Grady, W. (2005) *How Children Learn Language*. Cambridge: Cambridge University Press.

Perry, L. K., Samuelson, L. K., Malloy, L. M., & Schiffer, R. N. (2010). 'Learn locally, think globally: Exemplar variability supports higher-order generalization and word learning'. *Psychological Science*, 21(12), 1894–1902.

Piaget, J. (1964), 'Part I: Cognitive development in children: Piaget, development and learning'. *Journal of Research in Science Teaching*, 2: 176–186.

Rescorla, L. (1980). 'Overextensions in Early Language Development', *Journal of Child Language* 7: 321–35.

Saxton, M. (2010) *Child Language: Acquisition and Development*. London: Sage.

Skinner, B. F. S. (1957). *Verbal Behavior*. Acton, MA: Copley Publishing Group.

Thiessen, E. D., Hill, E. A. and Saffran, J. R. (2005). 'Infant-Directed Speech Facilitates Word Segmentation'. *Infancy*, 7: 53–71.

Vygotsky, L. [1934] (1986). *Thought and Language*. Cambridge, MA: MIT Press.

Wells, G. (1986). *The meaning makers: Children learning language and using language to learn*. Portsmouth, NH: Heinemann.

Further reading

Crystal, O'Grady, Saxton: see above.

Stilwell Peccei, J. (2005). *Child Language*. London: Routledge.

Introduction

People often think of children's literacy as very separate from their speech development, perhaps because reading and writing are viewed as taught skills – unlike speech, which is acquired without the same kinds of deliberate intervention by 'professionals' such as teachers. Yet, when you start to think about even very young children's daily experiences, their routines can involve explicit literacy experiences, such as looking at books or seeing adults write shopping lists, fill in forms, or read some instructions.

You may think of your own literacy use in a very narrow way – confining it to your academic study or to handwritten contexts. But typing a reminder note or to-do list on your phone, constructing and posting tweets, posting statuses on Facebook and sending text messages are all activities that involve reading and writing. Like you, children have a wide range of literacy experiences, even if they are not able to participate in quite the same way as more experienced users. These may include seeing letters and images around them; the images may range from logos and signs to the moving images on computers and TV screens. To consider literacy as just words and as wholly book-based, therefore, is to miss the point that literacy is a broad concept that is all around us all the time.

Being literate is about making meanings from signs, including linguistic ones, as well as calling upon our personal cultural experiences. Part of children's early literacy development is to acquire the knowledge of how literacy is used, essentially joining a **community of practice** – a group of people who share knowledge and cultural practices over time. The different groups that children become a part of – family, school, and the wider society – all have their part to play in literacy development, although there might be differences in how they define and view literacy.

To illustrate early influences on literacy, on the next page are two A level English Language students' memories of their early language acquisition. You can see that their recall of their early development does not separate learning to speak from enjoying books, nursery rhymes and television programmes.

Activity

Create your own memory map of your early years. What books and nursery rhymes did you enjoy? What television programmes, films or DVDs can you remember liking? What features of these did you enjoy? For example, it may have been the rhymes, the interactivity and actions, or the characters, that you recall.

This section of Chapter 4 covers children's writing and will:

- help you to understand the relationship between children's reading and writing development and their acquisition of spoken language

- help you to explore the features and patterns of writing development and consider the different modes and genres that children understand and use

- give you frameworks for analysing and evaluating data

- introduce you to researchers' studies about children's early literacy.

! REMEMBER

You need to see literacy as defining a wide area of meaning-making activity involving the use and interpretation of symbols. But you will come across many different definitions of literacy, some of them very narrow.

Did you know?

Literacy might be seen as an essential skill in our society, but some societies are primarily oral cultures, where literacy has a minimal role. Therefore you need to distinguish the idea of **illiteracy** from **non-literacy**.

Key terms

Illiteracy. Failure to become literate.

Non-literacy. An oral society is non-literate, i.e. it has no system of literacy.

Two students' memories of their early language acquisition

Link

For more ideas about approaches to language and new technologies, including ideas about young children's toys, read Goddard, A. and Geesin, B. (2011) *Language and Technology*. London: Routledge.

Activity

Focus on your own communication practices now. Think about the different experiences of communication that you have had over the past week. Include your experiences of being a viewer, not just a producer of communication, for example in watching or reading TV programmes, films, videos, DVDs, and digital texts of all kinds on phones, tablets and other computer-based devices.

Can you identify which of your experiences were of oral communication, and which involved literacy skills? Or are those modes intertwined, particularly in text involving new technologies?

Charting the development of writing

Activity

Look at the three examples of a child's writing on page 129. What do you notice about the ways in which the writing develops as the child grows older? Use the following prompts to help you organize your ideas.

- How would you describe the genres of these pieces of writing?
- What ideas is the child trying to communicate?
- How is each text organized?
- What lexical and grammatical features are in evidence?
- What is noticeable about spelling, punctuation and handwriting?

There is some feedback on this activity at the back of the book.

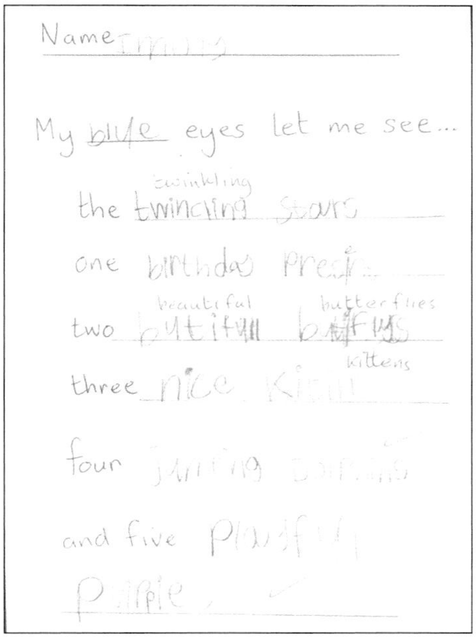

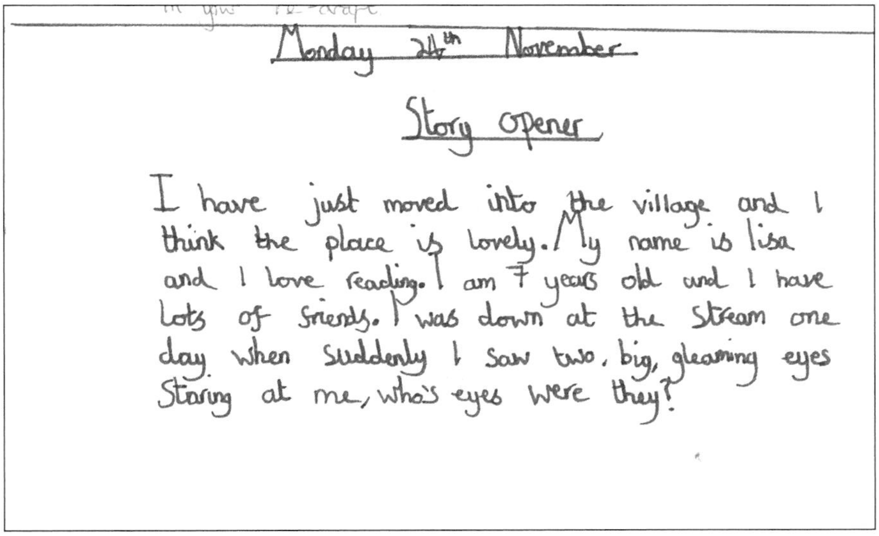

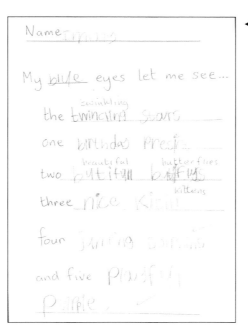

◀ **Imogen's writing (at 4, 6 and 8 years old). The writing at age 4 (on the far left) translates as: Alfi liked the dark; Alfi talked to the dark; the dark talked back.**

What is writing?

When we think of writing it is often the technical aspects that are uppermost in our minds, and writing certainly does involve physical dexterity and technical expertise: all writing through history has used a technology of some kind, whether that was a stonemason's chisel, a quill pen, or a computer mouse.

From Imogen's writing, above, you can see that children have much to learn and their competence in writing develops over time – with practice and experience. But, ultimately, it's not just about mechanical skills. It is as much about the following aspects, and more:

- using a common, agreed code of symbols (**graphemes**)
- recognizing that graphemes need to be combined to make words that a language user can understand
- combining words and sentences to convey ideas

Key term

Grapheme. Graphemes are visual symbols, for example alphabetic letters.

Research idea

Once you have studied literacy development in this chapter, you could either explore how your own writing developed (if you have access to your own primary school books) or alternatively collect sample writing from parents, children or primary schools. From these, you can create a longitudinal study of individual literacy development, investigating the development of an individual's communication skills and applying relevant language methods to analyse these (see Chapter 7 for information about the investigation).

Clay's principles of development ▶

! REMEMBER

There is always a time lag between doing research and publishing articles and books. Always think about whether ideas still apply, or whether there have been big changes in society that have affected communication.

Yetta Goodman's principles of development ▶

- recognizing that writing has an audience (even if it's oneself)
- using recognizable discourse and genre conventions
- manipulating language to achieve specific purposes.

Early writing

The term 'emergent literacy' is often used to describe children's early scribbles or representations of written symbols. It was proposed by New Zealand researcher Marie Clay some time ago to describe children's interactions with the written word in books and when imitating writing themselves. Clay identified a number of key principles that children seem to adopt in their early writing. Her ideas are still influential, helping parents and educators to recognize that writing skills develop – and should be valued – long before a child can produce formal texts. However, you need to remember that she was researching and writing in the 1970s, and this was long before the advent of computer use in schools or at home. So when you read her ideas below, think about how far they still apply to contemporary literacy practices; Clay was really talking about writing composed with a pen, not a keyboard.

Clay's principles of development included the following:

Recurring principle	When a child only knows a limited number of letters, he or she may use these repeatedly to create a message.
Directional principle	Reading and writing from left to right and then using a return sweep to start the process again.
Generating principle	When a child starts to realize that there are only a limited number of letters to use, but that these can be mixed and matched in different ways. The child begins to recognize that there are patterns that can be used to convey a message.
Inventory principle	A child begins to package knowledge together into lists of the letters and words that he or she knows.

The idea of emergent literacy suggests that children move beyond simple mark-making and begin assigning meaning to the symbols and images that they are using to represent their understanding of the world. Yetta Goodman's (1986) research into children's emerging print awareness characterizes children's early writing as following three principles:

The functional principle	The notion that writing can serve a purpose and has a function for the writer.
The linguistic principle	The notion that writing is a system that is organized into words and letters and has directionality.
The relational principle	Children start to connect what they write on the page with spoken words – understanding that the written alphabetic system carries meaning.

Activity

Using the following text, think about what this child knows about writing. Use Clay's and Goodman's principles to help you make your observations. For example, think about the direction of the writing and the formation of the scribbles.

Oliver, aged 3, wrote the following at nursery. The explanation underneath, given by the nursery teacher, came from asking Oliver what his marks and scribbles meant. She then turned his oral explanation into a written message aimed at his parents.

◀ **Oliver's early writing**

You can see that Oliver's early writing still resembles a drawing, yet within it are letter-like forms, written in strings. Oliver's next stages – creating words, sentences and texts – will be encouraged during his school experiences within a more formal framework of literacy teaching. To illustrate this, below is Francesca's early writing (aged 4), which was written at home, while sitting with her mother at the kitchen table. The orange mark was contributed by her two-year-old brother, who was colouring in at the table with her. Unlike Oliver, Francesca doesn't have a message but is simply practising the letters that she has learned at nursery school.

◀ **Francesca's writing**

Francesca is a little ahead of Oliver in both age and educational experiences, and this is shown in her ability to shape letters more recognizably. Like Oliver, her text is multimodal and the layout suggests a familiarity with the layout of books aimed at younger children. She leaves a large space at the top of the page, placing her writing at the bottom underneath a picture. She creates mainly capital letters but combines consonants and vowels – showing an understanding of relationships between symbols and sounds (**grapho-phonemic** knowledge).

Influences on early literacy development

Francesca's writing also highlights the role of adults in helping children to acquire and develop writing skills. The following transcript of the conversation between Francesca and her mother, while the writing was in progress, shows that literacy is not performed in isolation but is often supported by verbal interaction. This conversation also shows that the mother had an input into her daughter's text. She checks that Francesca understands different letter cases by requesting that Francesca adds the lower case 'e' at the top of the page.

Supporting Francesca's writing

Mum: you try

Francesca: okay [*draws the letter e*] I did it [*smiling and laughing*]

Mum: /i:/ (.) beautiful

Francesca [*continues writing on the page, watched by her younger brother*]

Here informal learning is taking place. Literacy is reinforced in a domestic context – not only through the ritual activity of sitting down to write and draw, but in the mother's response to Francesca's efforts. In recognizing Francesca's reproduction of the 'e' grapheme, her mother is supporting her in her attempt to match conventional notions of what the grapheme should look like. The crucial role of the child's environment, including the idea of support by key adults, has been identified by many researchers, but a key figure in this area was the Russian scholar Lev Vygotsky, who was mentioned in Section 4.1.

In Vygotsky's **social constructivist** view, teachers (and parents) act as more knowledgeable others, offering **scaffolding** to help children learn. Vygotsky sees children as active participants in their own learning, but as needing individually tailored support at crucial times. An important concept proposed by Vygotsky was the idea of a **Zone of Proximal Development** (ZPD), which describes a recurring process: children reach a stage which they can attempt with support, then are able to perform unaided. The idea of ZPD focuses attention on an individual child's needs, rather than thinking that all children need to reach a government-driven definition of development based on large-scale testing.

Literacy is often a shared experience, as illustrated by Francesca's context: she is learning about literacy but so too is her two-year-old brother George. In adding his scribble to Francesca's writing, George is demonstrating his own early experimentation with written language. However, not only are both children learning about the mechanics of writing, they are also likely to be exploring written language in different forms at home and becoming aware of the different purposes that it can be put to. This is a **functional** approach to understanding literacy – placing emphasis on the social contexts to a child's learning and applying a developmental model.

Transcription key:

[brackets indicate non-verbal communication]

/ / forward slashes indicate a phonemic symbol

Key terms

Functional. Emphasizing what something is for, its purposes.

Grapho-phonemic. The relationship between symbols and sounds.

Scaffolding. An idea from Vygotsky's theory of learning that structures need to be in place to help learners on to the next stage.

Social constructivism. The idea that reality is socially constructed and that groups construct knowledge for each other.

Zone of proximal development. In Vygotsky's theory of learning, the difference between what a learner can do without help and what they can do with help.

Activity

Look at the following teacher's feedback to Isobel, aged 8, over the course of Year 3 in her literacy activities.

- How does the teacher respond to Isobel's writing?
- What aspects of literacy does the teacher reinforce?
- What evidence is there of the teacher scaffolding Isobel's development?

A teacher's written feedback on Isobel's writing

1. A super piece of writing Isobel.

2. A very good start.

3. Well done Isobel – a very informative piece of writing.

4. Super Isobel. Well done.

5. What a lovely character. I can't wait to see her in your story.

6. Well set out and excellent wording Isobel.

7. Great, add in more description of the characters, e.g. the dragon and how they feel/what they think in your redraft.

Community literacy

In the 1970s, Shirley Brice Heath conducted an ethnographic investigation of American pre-school children and their families. She focused on three distinct local communities, situated near each other but different in terms of social class and ethnicity. Heath found that these communities offered contrasting literacy experiences for children. The more affluent and middle-class community developed their children's literacy in a more formal way, explicitly using books and placing value on children participating in literacy activities.

By contrast, literacy in the other communities did include book reading but with more limited imaginative discussion and verbal commentaries around these activities. What she observed in these communities was a different kind of literacy, based around oral storytelling, where stories about the people and things from their everyday lives and communities matter more than creating fictional worlds. Once at school, children from the more middle-class literate community were more successful, because the type of literacy that they were familiar with (reading and writing fictional stories) conformed more to schools' expectations. She argued that schools should look to the home and community practices and value the rich types of literacy taking place in these contexts, incorporating these more into school policies and curricula.

The influence of books

Children are likely to be exposed to books in various different forms from very early on – often helping to support their spoken language acquisition and containing speech-like qualities and repeated patterns to entertain them, as well as supporting their learning of language. Later on, once they start formal education, reading is taught and supported by materials that increase in difficulty as the child becomes more proficient.

Although your main focus is on writing, it's important to understand how reading links with writing, starting from the earliest books that children share with adults

Research idea

Interview some older members of your community. Ask them about their early experiences of literacy. Possible questions could be about books and bedtime rituals, or other literacy experiences that they can remember, such as letters to and from friends and family, oral stories, literacy around everyday objects, such as breakfast cereal packets and magazines. You could record these interviews and transcribe them. This could make an interesting investigation on the nature of literacy: see Chapter 7 for information about this aspect of coursework.

and which enable them to learn about the world they live in. Aside from directly instructional purposes, books introduce young children to story-telling, creativity and playfulness with language, as well as to the structures of the written mode more generally. And stories of all kinds give us ideas for our own writing.

Activity

Collect a selection of children's first books and categorize them. Choose your own categories, but some ideas could include the way they expect children to interact with them (for example lift-the-flap, touch/feel, press/sounds), or types of characters (human, animal, monster). Identify some of the linguistic features that writers choose and think about why they have chosen them. For example, how does the writer:

- expect the reader to interact or react?
- structure the story or sections?
- use rhyme and other phonological devices?
- depict characters?
- represent spoken language features?
- combine pictures and text?
- use semantic fields and word classes?
- use rhetorical devices such as repetition and parallel structures?
- create cohesion through lexical repetition, syntactical repetition and connectives?

If you survey the texts of children's writing that you have already looked at in this chapter, you may notice similarities in layout, such as the emphasis on pictures rather than words, and more unconventional arrangements of text and images. You could hypothesize that early readers influence the structure of children's own texts.

Multimodal literacies

Children's early literacy experiences are multimodal: they don't separate their experiences into discrete modes by regarding speech as different from writing or from visual aspects. Their storytelling may be physical rather than written, as they act out roles and use props and toys to represent either their imagination or to demonstrate their awareness of the rituals, roles and daily practices around them. Their storytelling may also be visual – using drawing to represent their ideas and personal versions of their emerging understanding of the world.

By studying his own children, Gunther Kress (1997) found that children naturally behave multimodally. He observed the ways in which children use objects and mix these with toys to construct 'worlds' in which they can act out narratives in play. You've already explored Vygotsky's ideas, among others, about the importance of socio-dramatic play when looking at children's spoken language development. Here, you can focus on this type of play as part of a broader literacy practice, considering cultural influences from books, television, films and other media.

Activity

Below is a transcript of Joel, aged 3, playing with his aunt. This 'pirate' game has become a repeated ritual and a feature of the aunt's visits. In this scenario, they are in Joel's mother's bedroom.

How have Joel's experiences of books, TV and other types of representation influenced his understanding of pirates? You could think about:

- particular books and media that could have influenced Joel's and his aunt's game
- the objects that they could be using as their dramatic 'props'
- how the language used by Joel and his aunt draws on **sociocultural** knowledge about 'pirate' narratives and representations.

There is some feedback on this activity at the back of the book.

Key term

Sociocultural. Related to social and cultural factors.

Joel and his aunt playing their pirate game

Aunty: oh ar oh ar (.) now I'm looking for a little pirate boy here (1.0) I'm looking for a pirate boy and I've heard he's called JOEL (.) does anyone know where I can find this little boy Joel

Joel: but we need to find the treasure first (.) and then we get a (.) then we get | a

Aunty: | this one can't be a pirate (.) he's much too small (.) he's way too small

Joel: but I bigger

Aunty: would you be a good pirate do you think

Joel: but we need to (.) we need to find the treasure and then get in the boat and then find the treasure (.) and then you get when you get (.) when you see the pirates

Aunty: okay (.) are you up to the task because you look a bit small to me (1.0) get on my boat let's go find some treasure (1.0) oooo these waves are so high (.) swish swish swish

Joel: I'm going this way (1.0) I can find some treasure

Aunty: where do you think this treasure is (.) what have you found | there

Joel: | there's writing look (.) can you put these on [*picking up his mum's beads*]

Aunty: do you think you should put them on (.) or should I put them on

Joel: er I put them on then you put them on later (.) then get you have yeah (1.0) where can we put this on (.) where can we put this on the neck | la

Aunty: | I think it's a little bit too small to be a necklace

Joel: but I but I want a necklace when (.) you put this on

Transcription key

(.) normal pause

(3.0) numbers in brackets indicate length of pauses in seconds

| vertical lines show simultaneous speech

In the activity above, you explored the way in which books and media representations influenced an episode of spoken play. In the following text, you can see how the same influences are at work in a written text. This is five-year-old Cameron's representation of Doctor Who, in both a written version and a storyboard, where he uses multimodality to present the narrative.

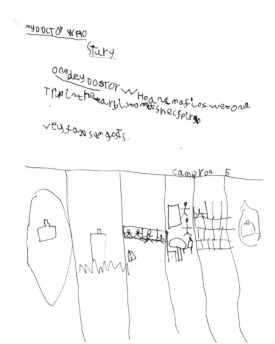

One day Dr Who and Martha
Jones went on a trip in the
Tardis to meet Shakespeare
and they found some ghosts.)
◄ Dr Who and Shakespeare
(One day Dr Who and Martha
Jones went on a trip in the
Tardis to meet Shakespeare
and they found some ghosts.)

The written text summarizes the story viewed on television into a compound sentence using adverbials ('One day', 'on a trip', 'in the Tardis'). He has captured the main plot elements and uses words lexically relevant to *Dr Who*. Cameron has not elaborated on the story descriptively, using pictures to show the stages of the story and help the reader to visualize the events. Cameron's graphological choice of a storyboard is interesting. It is unlikely that he has been taught this; perhaps he has used his cultural experiences of watching or reading comic-strips and cartoons. This shows how strong the links can be between cultural experiences and literacy.

As well as absorbing the influences of multimodal media and reproducing ideas drawn from them, children nowadays are often writing from a very young age in a multimedia environment. This can mean that whole definitions of aspects of literacy that have remained unquestioned for many years have had to be redefined. For example, what is a 'page' in a digital environment? We don't 'turn over the page' when we read on a computer screen. We can click through from one screen to the next, reading in a **non-linear** way. So children may still be learning the traditional conventions of paper-based writing, but they are also learning that writing can be produced, as well as received, in many different ways – some of those ways being very fluid.

For example, writing has traditionally not been an interactive medium: the whole idea of writing being 'on the move' – or of someone being on the other end of your writing as you compose it – is a recent phenomenon. You saw in Chapter 1, and you will see again in Chapter 5 (on language change) that new forms of communication are making us re-think many of our established notions about language rules and conventions. They are also affecting different age groups in different ways, with older people having to learn new language strategies from younger people, who have suddenly become more expert in some respects than their elders.

Key term

Non-linear. In studies of literacy, non-linearity refers to new forms of literacy such as webpages, where we don't read line by line but often click through to further pages.

Activity

Below is an example of collaborative multimodal dialogue, based around a computer game. Alfie is 4 years and 7 months old. He is talking to his aunt Debbie about how to play *Temple Run* on a tablet computer.

- Who is in the role of the teacher in this interaction?
- How is the teacher's language helping to scaffold the learner's understanding of this multimedia environment?
- How are speaking, listening, reading and writing all in play in this episode?

Alfie and his aunt Debbie playing *Temple Run*

Debbie: okay and then what do you do after that

Alfie: just press tha::t (2.0)

Debbie: okay and then (2.0)

Alfie: temper temper

Debbie: temple run

Alfie: temple run 2 or temple run 1

Debbie: what's the difference between them

Alfie: that one's got one monster and that got em **nine**

Debbie: **ni::ne** oh wo::w (.) which one do you prefer (.) which one are you

Alfie: I'll do that one | first (3.0)

Debbie: | okay all right

Alfie: just wait (2.0)

Debbie: what's it doing now

Alfie: it's downloading

Debbie: okay (2.0) wow [*screeching noise from the game*] right so what's happening now

Alfie: um (.) you have to jump | now

Debbie: | oh no what's what's chasing her now then

Alfie: er angry hungry monkeys

Debbie: so how far have you got with this (.) what's your best score (.) ooh (.) so how far have you got with this (.) what's your best score (.) ooh that's good

Alfie: that's 1900 points

Debbie: yeah and you're tippin it as well aren't you (.) why d'you tip it?

Alfie: to get (2.0) to get the points without

Debbie: ooh what did you do then

Alfie: slided

Debbie: you slided over (.) yeah

Transcription key

(.) normal pause

(3.0) numbers in brackets indicate length of pauses in seconds

| vertical lines show simultaneous speech

:: elongated sound

[ ] square brackets indicate non-verbal aspects

bold indicates a stressed syllable

Given the proliferation of digital devices across society as a whole, it is not surprising that schools and other educational organizations make use of the affordances of new technologies to encourage children to write. New technologies can be particularly useful to help children who are reluctant to write because they lack confidence after experiences of failure and criticism, perhaps because they have learning difficulties. Children of all abilities can use new communication tools to produce professional-looking texts, allowing them to access the adult world on a new footing and engage in dialogues that were not possible when writing was limited to publication merely on classroom walls.

Activity

Below are some examples of texts that children are now producing using computers to record and share their learning activities with other classmates, teachers or parents. These are posts written by children from different year groups for publication on the school website. The Year 6 children are reflecting on key events, whereas the Year 2 children are recording their findings about insects at the same time in a computer room at school. The teacher provided the starter options 'my bug is' and 'my bug has', before asking the children to add some facts to complete their chosen sentence.

- Do these replicate familiar genres of writing? If so, in what way?
- What are children learning about literacy in producing these texts?

There is some feedback on this activity at the back of the book.

Children's posts on a primary school website

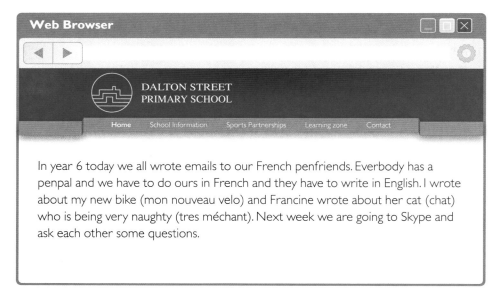

In year 6 today we all wrote emails to our French penfriends. Everbody has a penpal and we have to do ours in French and they have to write in English. I wrote about my new bike (mon nouveau velo) and Francine wrote about her cat (chat) who is being very naughty (tres méchant). Next week we are going to Skype and ask each other some questions.

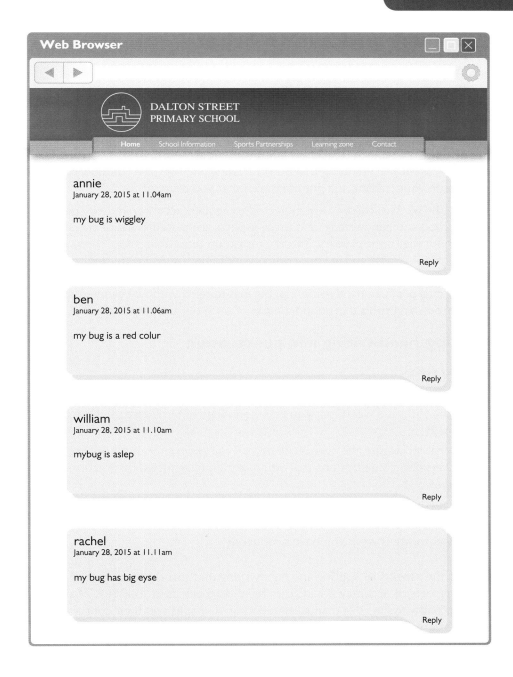

Web Browser

DALTON STREET
PRIMARY SCHOOL

Home   School Information   Sports Partnerships   Learning zone   Contact

annie
January 28, 2015 at 11.04am

my bug is wiggley

Reply

ben
January 28, 2015 at 11.06am

my bug is a red colur

Reply

william
January 28, 2015 at 11.10am

mybug is aslep

Reply

rachel
January 28, 2015 at 11.11am

my bug has big eyse

Reply

Research idea

1. Survey school websites or visit a primary school to find out how they use digital and new literacies in the classroom. You could collect resources from different year groups to investigate if children's use of computers and the activities they undertake change as they become more competent readers and writers.

2. Investigate some of the tools that are available to support children's writing development. For example, Crick software (www.cricksoft.com) produce a technology called 'Clicker', where children can select key words on a tablet in order to write a story. They can also choose to have the words they've selected spoken aloud by a computerized voice app. If you know of any schools that are using tools like these, you could research how they are used and what skills they might be developing.

See Chapter 7 for more information about the investigation coursework.

Becoming an accurate writer

Just as literacy is sometimes defined very narrowly as being about spelling, punctuation and handwriting, so the term 'accuracy' is often associated with those same things. But accuracy can refer to a wide range of different ways in which writers match what they produce to a target: for example, in their use of lexical or grammatical features. There are also, of course, differing views about not just the importance of accuracy, but sometimes about what is correct. For example, when you are using a word-processing package, are you offered some versions in your spelling and grammar tool that you dismiss?

Having said all that, children are expected to acquire accuracy in their spelling, punctuation and handwriting, and these aspects are tested in national tests throughout their school years. You are tested on these things too: there are marks in your exams and in your coursework folder (in AO5) to credit you for your accuracy in these areas. And currently in public examinations, entrants are expected to produce handwritten, paper-based texts with no recourse to the word-processing tools that support most of us in our daily writing tasks.

Spelling, handwriting and punctuation

 Activity

1. How do you spell a word that you haven't heard before?
2. What about a word that you have seen before but forgotten how to spell?
3. What strategies and resources do you call upon in both these cases? Consider all the options that you might employ, including practical ones.

When you have finished your list, close your eyes and write out your name and address using the 'wrong' hand.

How accurate is what you have produced?

One of the aspects of spelling and handwriting that sometimes surprises people is that aspects of accuracy are in your 'hand' as much as in your eye. That is, you develop pathways in your manual sequencing of shapes and their connections that are derived from writing out those sequences over and over again. One interesting question, now that we are using keyboards probably more often than we handwrite, is whether we have developed a keyboard version of this 'hand' knowledge. Clearly, people who can touch-type have already done this, as they use the keyboard without looking at it.

 Extension activity

The national curriculum now contains very specific guidelines about the stages that children are expected to reach in their development of spelling, punctuation and handwriting skills. These government documents are easy to access at the link below, and they will give you an insight into the external targets that teachers and children are expected to meet in these areas of language development. Working from this site is better than from any textbook outline, because the requirements change frequently:

https://www.gov.uk/government/collections/national-curriculum

Make some notes from the documents about the spelling, punctuation and handwriting requirements for Key Stages 1 and 2.

How is spelling taught?

Although writing is a very different system from speech, there are correspondences between the sounds and symbols of English up to a point, so calling on knowledge from spoken language (for example, in sounding out a word) can be helpful. But, as you saw in Chapter 1, there are 26 alphabetic letters and around 44 phonemes, so there is no one-to-one correlation. In reality, spelling skills are developed through a range of strategies, including knowledge of sounds, but also:

● recognition of the individual profile of words (e.g. 'elephant')

● familiarity with common letter strings (e.g. '-ight', '-ful', '-ly')

● an awareness of word families and relationships between words (e.g. 'walk', 'walking', 'walked', 'walker')

● an understanding of morphology and affixation (e.g. 'unhelpful', 'undone', 'unnatural')

● recognition of homophones (e.g. 'there'/'their')

● an understanding of etymology and meanings (e.g. 'fond' and 'phone' both have an /f/ when spoken but the 'ph' in 'phone' has its origin in a Greek root meaning 'sound' – 'telephone', 'microphone', etc). You looked at this in Chapter 1.

Stages of spelling development

Spellings are not just taught: they are of course also 'caught' through the reading that children do. But how can spelling development be judged?

Richard Gentry (1978) proposed five spelling stages, believing that identifying these could help teachers to nurture children's ability by helping them with cognitive strategies. These stages represent something different from the 'Key Stages' of the national curriculum documents: the stages below are developmental and don't correlate with specific ages.

 ▼ **Spelling stages**

Stage	What can a child do at this stage?
Pre-communicative	Imitate writing by scribbling, showing an understanding that symbols have meanings and messages
	Use a range of symbols (numbers, letters, lower and upper case) and present some decipherable letter shapes but not make sound–symbol connections
Semi-phonetic	Link letter shapes and sounds
	Show an awareness of word boundaries and how writing is organized on a page
Phonetic	Understand that all phonemes can be represented by graphemes, making sound–symbol connections consistently
	Have a sight vocabulary
Transitional	Combine phonic knowledge with visual memory
	Show an awareness of combinations of letters and letter patterns
Conventional	Demonstrate knowledge of the spelling system and rules, using mostly correct spelling
	Spell using a large sight vocabulary
	Know about word structure

You saw in the earlier part of this chapter that errors made by children are often the result of a rule learned or a pattern that has been noticed, rather than a deficit in their knowledge. Spelling errors are exactly the same: you can see that the mis-spelling patterns on the left below are a result of things learned on the right.

Aspect of misspelling	Definition – and what has been learned
Insertion	Adding extra letters – the child has noticed that sometimes letters are doubled
Omission	Leaving out letters – as above
Substitution	Substituting one letter for another – often close in the way they look or sound
Transposition	Reversing the correct order of letters in words – showing that the child knows what letters the word contains
Phonetic spelling	Using sound awareness to guess letters and combinations of letters
Over- or under-generalization of spelling rules	Over-generalizing of a rule where it is not appropriate to apply it, or under-generalizing it by only applying it in one specific context – in either case, knowledge of the rules is being shown
Salient (key) sounds	Only writing the key sounds in a word and missing out letters – the most noticeable elements are being memorized

 Activity

Below is a selection of Harriet's spellings when aged 7–8. Describe her spelling strategies. Can you relate them to Gentry's stages, or to the aspects above?

There is some feedback on this activity at the back of the book.

Child's spelling	Actual spelling
suddnly	suddenly
peculier / perculiar	peculiar
cloke	cloak
kitchin	kitchen
discusting	disgusting
(golf) corse	course
shale	shall
exspensis	expensive
twincling	twinkling
butifull	beautiful
kitins	kittens
fraindly	friendly
becuase	because
correg	courage
bissnis	business
cheerfull	cheerful
intelgent	intelligent

Handwriting

Will handwriting eventually disappear as a general aspect of writing skill and become a specialized art form? Perhaps – although personal handwriting still carries an idea of authenticity – for example, when we sign cheques or other official forms. For this specification, you will be required to sign a form to say that your coursework is your own. Handwriting is also a sign of personal engagement: we handwrite personal messages in greetings cards.

In a curious turnabout, digital devices also have fonts and tools that create an impression of personal handwriting practices, even though they are mechanically produced.

For example, here is a font called 'chalkduster', which presumably got its name from an idea of teachers' handwriting on a board. And below is a PowerPoint theme called 'Inkwell', evoking a school context from former times. Do we hanker for the past, and is this just another form of intertextual play for grown-ups?

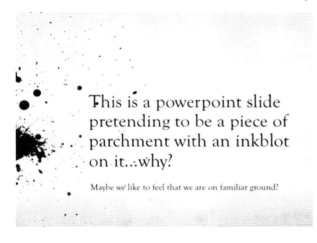

This is a powerpoint slide pretending to be a piece of parchment with an inkblot on it...why?

Maybe we like to feel that we are on familiar ground?

In the meantime, we still expect children to develop their fine motor control and their hand–eye co-ordination well enough to produce legible handwriting on paper – eventually. You can look back at Imogen's texts in this chapter and recognize how her writing has changed, resulting partly from formal instruction and partly as an active, creative process where she has chosen her own style.

Punctuation

Like handwriting, punctuation has also changed its status in recent years because of digital writing. Regardless of whether children can use full stops in their own writing, they can certainly recognize them from the many website addresses and emails that they will encounter from a young age. Some children will also make punctuation pictures in the form of **emoticons**, but this aspect will be very age-related because more recently, devices have ready-made images (see Chapter 5 on language change).

Punctuation isn't grammar but it can signal grammatical boundaries, such as clause or sentence units. It can be used to separate items in a list (with commas), point to information coming next (with colons) and show that two parts of a sentence are in equilibrium; it can be used expressively, to represent aspects of phonology and prosody such as question intonation (?), raised pitch and/or

Key term

Emoticon. A blend word, consisting of 'emotion' and 'icon', which refers to symbols that express the attitude of a writer in digital contexts where non-verbal elements are missing.

volume (!), someone speaking (" "), a trailing off of speech or thought… and more.

Grammar

Chapter 1 discussed the importance of cohesion, or the way in which aspects of structure, including grammatical structure, enable a text to knit together and be perceived as a whole entity. Key aspects of cohesion in writing include **reference**, substitution, repetition, variation, and connectivity. Young writers have to learn how to make references from one part of their text to another without endlessly repeating the same linguistic items: for example, people's names can be replaced with pronouns such as 'he', 'she' and 'they'; place names and time references can be replaced with **deictic** expressions such as 'there' or 'then'; and clauses can be joined in more sophisticated ways than simply adding one to another by using 'and'.

Extension activity

Make detailed notes about cohesion by consulting the book by Halliday and Hasan in the references list at the end of this chapter.

Katharine Perera's (1984) work on children's writing, particularly on how they develop grammatical expertise, shows that young people go on acquiring progressively more sophisticated grammatical structures for some considerable time, through and beyond their teenage years. But a significant turning point is their shift from what seem to be more speech-like structures, such as **co-ordination** (the use of 'and' as a connective), towards the more complex and varied links typical of formal writing, such as **subordination**, where one clause is reliant on another.

The table below is a very simplified version of Perera's work, which used the research of Barry Kroll as a starting point.

These phase-related ideas can be a useful starting point in thinking about children's writing, but it is important to remember that children can demonstrate characteristics of different phases in their written work. Remember also that before children write anything at all, they need to feel that they have something to say.

Key terms

Co-ordination. Joining elements together by using a co-ordinating conjunction, such as 'and' or 'or'.

Deixis. The act of pointing to something by using certain language items. Deictic expressions refer to aspects of space (spatial deixis, for example 'over there'), time (temporal deixis, for example 'yesterday') and person deixis (who is being referred to, for example 'they').

Reference. Reference within a text is a general term for the various ways items are related to others.

Subordination. A subordinate clause is one that depends on another to make complete sense.

Phases in children's writing ▶

Stage	Age (years)	Characteristics
Preparation	Up to 6	Basic motor skills are acquired alongside some principles of spelling
Consolidation	7–8	Children are able to express in writing what they can say
Differentiation	9–10	Awareness of writing as separate from speech emerges; a stronger understanding of writing for different audiences and purposes is evident, and becomes more automatic
Integration	Mid-teens	This stage heralds the 'personal voice' in writing and is characterized by evidence of controlled writing, with appropriate linguistic choices being made consistently

Activity

The extracts below, written by the same child, were produced two years apart. Although not in the child's handwriting, the texts have been reproduced using the original spelling and punctuation.

Compare these samples of writing, paying particular attention to the structures that the child is using and to the range and purposes of the punctuation.

A Terrible Day (aged 8)

It all started one morning when the alarm clock rang very loud and I fell out of bed and bumbed my head. I got dressed and had breakfast my sister got a toy in her breakfast and I got nothing. and I lost my toothbrush so my Mum told me of. when I was brushing my hair my brush broke. when I was on my way to school my car broke down and I had to walk to school. Then I dropped my bag and its strap broke in half. when I got into school I had to do a hard test and I got all my spellings wrong. in the playground I had a fall out with my best fraind, and I fell over and hurt my knee.

A Space Adventure (aged 10)

Somewhere in deepest, darkest space travelled a team of explorers on board. No one could of predicted the mayhem and misfortunate happenings lying ahead. This was only the beginning…

The crew inside the spaceship wasn't a big crew, there was only 4, but they were always arguing; they could never agree on anything! They were called Katie, Jessica, Tom and James and all they thought about was themselves. Nevertheless, they were stuck together.

Suddenly the ship made a sudden jolt and everyone was thrown of their feet and fell with a bump to the floor.

'What was that?' asked Katie

'It wasn't me!' replied Tom

Becoming a creative writer

As children grow older, they also develop skills in checking, editing and correcting their work – learning that writing is a process. These processes might be separated further into:

- thinking and reflecting about their ideas
- planning and composing how best to convey them
- writing down, revising and editing them.

You can see in children's writing from different stages how the latter skills begin to appear. In the early years, a child's writing may be very personal and relate to the world of the child. As children and their writing ability mature, writing may become more engaging as they become aware that they are writing for an audience other than themselves. Children need to learn to craft and shape material and exploit all the creative resources of language.

Understanding genre

From an early age, children are engaged with specific writing genres, usually by their caregivers and usually ones related to their own experience. If you think of key events when you were younger, such as parties, you might recall the invitations sent out on your behalf and the birthday cards that you first signed and then contributed to writing, using genre conventions ('Dear Emily, Happy birthday, Love Jenny'). Other early home-writing experiences might have been writing a list for Father Christmas or a note for the Tooth Fairy. Children begin to learn that genres have their own linguistic patterns or specific shapes in terms of discourse structure. Children first need help to master a genre and then they can play with it and explore its creative aspects.

Activity

Below are two pieces of writing in specific genres. What makes the writing characteristic of these genres?

There is some feedback on this activity at the back of the book.

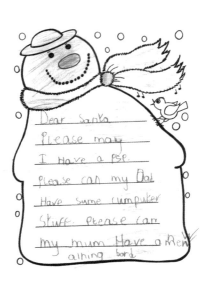

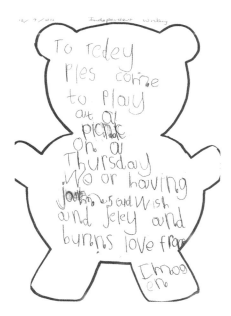

Luke's letter to Santa (age 7). Transliteration: 'Dear Santa. Please may I Have a PSP. Please can my Dad Have some cumputer Stuff. Please can my mum Have a new aining bord [ironing board].'

Imogen's party invitation for her teddy (age 4). Transliteration: 'To Tedey. Ples come to play at a picnic on a Thursday. We or having jam sandwish and jeley and bunns love from Imogen.'

The genres used in children's early writing at school

Key term

Genre theory/theorists. How different genres of writing are structured and how people learn to produce them.

A useful way to help you evaluate children's writing is to use some of the categories devised by **genre theorists**, such as Jim Martin and Joan Rothery, who researched young children's writing in Australian schools in the 1980s. They found that early writing within school fell into some distinctive groupings: *observation/comment, recount, report* and *narrative*.

The table below outlines the key generic elements found in their research.

Category	Features
Observation / comment	The writer makes an observation ('I saw a tiger') and follows this with either an evaluative comment ('it was very large') or mixes these in with the observation ('I saw a very large tiger').
Recount	Usually a chronological sequence of events. A typical example would be a recount of a school trip. The structure of a recount usually follows a set pattern: **Orientation – Event – Reorientation** The orientation sets the scene, perhaps the journey to the place or the name of the place visited. The reorientation at the end of the recount completes the writing.
Report	A factual and objective description of events or things; it tends not to be chronological.
Narrative	A story genre where the scene is set for events to occur and be resolved at the end. It also has a set pattern: **Orientation – Complication – Resolution – Coda** The coda, which identifies the point of the story, is not always added. Because of the structural complexity, few children will achieve the whole structure early on, despite their experience of reading stories that follow this narrative structure.

◀ **Generic elements of children's writing**

Since the 1980s, much work has been done in the **genre theory** field to categorize more extensively all the different written genres that children are expected to learn during their school years in their different subject areas. Here is a summary from the work of Frances Christie, a colleague of Martin and Rothery:

- *Narratives*: which introduce characters in some setting, unfold a series of events leading to a complication (sometimes more than one), and offer some evaluation, eventually bringing about some resolution; these are found in storybooks and literary texts of many kinds.

- *Recounts*: which reconstruct experience in temporal sequence, and which are found in early writing of personal experience, though they are also found in the writing of history among older writers and readers.

- *Procedures*: which direct behaviour in undertaking activities, and which are found in games, recipes, manuals and science experiments.

- *Reports*: which classify some phenomenon and describe it, used in the social and the natural sciences.

- *Explanations*: which identify some phenomenon or historical event and explain how or why it occurs, or what its consequences are. They are also used in the social and natural sciences and in the humanities such as history.

- *Expositions and discussions:* which are both argumentative genres, involved in exploring issues and arriving at opinions on the basis of evidence. While the discussion involves some examination of different arguments for and against a position before adoption of a particular position, expositions take up one general position and argue it at some length. *Argumentative* and/or *persuasive* genres are found in many subjects and areas of knowledge.

Other ways to classify children's writing

Katharine Perera used her classroom investigations into young children's writing development to suggest a further broad categorization of texts – those that are structured **chronologically** and those that are **non-chronological** in the way they work. Chronologically organized texts are those that rely on action words (verbs) and on linking ideas using temporal connectives such as 'then'. Non-chronological texts rely on logical connections between ideas, rather than a sequence of events, and so are harder for children to write. Non-chronological texts often use connectives based on logical or causal relationships, such as 'therefore', 'so', or 'because'.

Key terms

Chronological. Structured with reference to time.

Non-chronological. Not structured with reference to time but shaped by other factors.

Activity

Firstly, try to apply any of the genre frameworks you have covered in this chapter to the following two texts (written by a 4-year-old in her Reception class).

- Which text exemplifies which category?
- What evidence is there in the texts to support your choices?

Then go back over all the samples of children's writing in this chapter and see whether you can classify them in terms of genre. Refer to any of the genre frameworks that you have learned about, and give examples of language features to support your analyses.

There is some feedback on this activity at the back of the book.

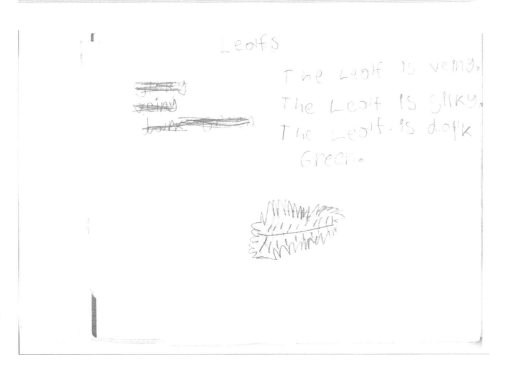

Two texts written by a 4-year-old. Transliterations: 'Leafs. The leaf is veiny. The leaf is spiky. The leaf is dark green.' and 'On Saturday my dad did some painting. I helped my dad and then I went to play with my toys and then I had my tay (tea). I went to bed.'

REVIEW YOUR LEARNING

- Give a brief definition of literacy.
- How is writing connected with reading, speaking and listening?
- What are the key skills that children need to become successful writers?
- What is emergent writing?
- What are some of the characteristics of early writing?
- What do adults do to support children's literacy development?
- Name and describe some genres of writing that young children produce.

References

Christie, F. (2013). 'Genres and genre theory: a response to Michael Rosen', on website http://www.interstrataltension.org/?p=1159

Clay, M. (1975) *What Did I Write? Beginning Writing Behavior.* Auckland: Heinemann Educational Books

Gentry, J. Richard. (1982) 'An Analysis of Developmental Spelling in GNYS AT WRK.' *The Reading Teacher* 36: 192–200

Goodman, Y. (1986) 'Writing Development in Young Children.' *Gnosis* 8 March 1986. Birmingham: Questions Publishing Company

Halliday, M. A. K. and Hasan, R. (1976) *Cohesion in English.* London: Routledge

Heath, S. B. (1983) *Ways with Words: Language, Life, and Work in Communities and Classrooms.* New York: Cambridge University Press

Ibbotson, P. (2012) 'Child Language Acquisition' in *Language: a student handbook on key topics and theories.* London: English and Media Centre

Kress, G. (1987) *Before Writing: Rethinking the Paths to Literacy.* New York: Routledge

Martin, J. & Rothery, J. (1980) Writing Project Report No.1. *Working Paper in Linguistics* No 1 Department of Linguistics. University of Sydney: Sydney

Perera, K. (1984) *Children's Writing and Reading: Analysing Classroom Language.* Wiley Oxford: Blackwell

Further reading

Christie, F. and Derewianka, B. (2008) *School Discourse. Learning to Write across the Years of Schooling.* London and New York: Continuum

Gillen, J. (2003) *The Language of Children.* London: Routledge

Karmiloff-Smith, A. (1994) *Baby It's You.* London: Ebury Press. (There is also an excellent DVD on which this book is based)

Kress, G. (1993) *Learning to Write.* New York: Routledge

Marsh. J. and Hallett, E. (eds) (2008) *Desirable Literacies: Approaches to Language and Literacy in the Early Years.* London: Sage

Pahl, K. and Rowsell, J. (2012) *Literacy and Education.* London: Sage

This chapter will:

- explain the nature of language change
- examine reasons for change
- give you examples of change and offer you the chance to explore your own case studies
- explore attitudes to change and guide you in your analysis of arguments about language.

Relevant Assessment Objectives

Language change as a topic is assessed on A level Paper 2 (Language Diversity and Change). It also features as an aspect of text analysis on Paper 1, Section A, but it is not the main focus. Paper 2 differs from Paper 1, with respect to language change, because it treats the topic as an area in its own right.

Paper 2 Section A

You are required to write one essay, from a choice of two options. One option will always be on diversity and the other will always be on change. The essay questions will always ask you to 'evaluate' an idea. This is because at A level you are expected to realize that things are not cut and dried: there are different attitudes to issues of language use. You are also expected to demonstrate your understanding that, in language study, one area is strongly connected with another. You should have become aware of this while working through this book, and it should have been especially evident in Chapter 3. There is more about this below.

The essay questions are equally weighted for AO1 and AO2:

- AO1 credits your understanding of the language levels and the terms associated with them, plus the coherence of your writing.
- AO2 credits your knowledge of the concepts and issues relevant to the subject area. Language diversity and language change are important concepts, and raise many issues.

Paper 2 Section B

There are two compulsory questions in this section, which is called 'Language Discourses'. The first question asks you to analyse two texts, and your analysis is credited through a range of Assessment Objectives:

- AO1, as above.
- AO3 credits your ability to understand how language features build into patterns of meaning and are shaped by context.
- AO4 credits your ability to move between the texts and make connections between the ideas they express.

The second question asks you to write an article by using the ideas in the texts and expressing your own views. This is assessed as follows:

- AO2 credits your knowledge of the concepts and issues that you are writing about.
- AO5 credits your writing skills.

How are diversity and change connected?

In many elements of this course there is overlap between topics. In the case of language change, an obvious crossover is with language diversity. Change is generally taken to mean change over time (sometimes referred to as **diachronic variation**) while diversity is more to do with the different uses of

Key term

Diachronic variation.
Variation through time.

English at a given time (**synchronic variation**). Of course, it isn't always that straightforward and the two can be quite closely linked; for example, if a new word or phrase starts to appear in the language, it might be seen as an aspect of change, but the use of that word by different groups of people (younger, middle-class females in the US, as an example of a group) might also be seen as an aspect of diversity. Be aware of this as you work through this chapter and think of ways in which you can apply your understanding of both topics to help you achieve a better, more comprehensive overview of the whole subject.

Key terms

Citation. A reference to an example of language use or research.

Synchronic variation. Variation across society at a single point in time.

Activity

To give you a practical starting point for thinking about these connections, find the meanings and the first **citations** (the earliest recorded use) for the following list of words and phrases. Use any dictionary that includes etymological information (about word origins) – or, if that fails, try a general Internet search. Most dictionaries now have this information, but if you want a place to start, try the Oxford dictionaries website: http://www.oxforddictionaries.com

For slang terms, you could also use the Urban Dictionary website: http://www.urbandictionary.com

What do these words tell you about how English has changed in the past few decades?

- YOLO
- hashtag
- jeggings
- credit crunch
- gas guzzler
- bae

There is some feedback on this activity at the back of the book.

The changing face of English

One of the most interesting areas of study for English Language A level is the topic of change, and how the English language came to exist in the first place – developing over the centuries into the language that we use now. It is a huge topic and one that has exercised the minds of experts for nearly as long as there has been a language recognized as 'English'. It has led to frequent and often angry debates about what 'English' is, what it should be, and what it is becoming.

A major focus of this chapter is on those arguments, and contemporary debates about different expressions, but you are not expected to know every debate about every different language item. Your job is to see the bigger picture, which will show you that, while a lot of the arguments stem from different views about *how* language is used, many of them also relate to *who* is using it. This once again shows that your study of English language is not something that happens in a vacuum, but relates to much wider ideas about society, identity and community.

Another part of that same big picture is *why* language changes. We will look at some of the driving forces of language change: what causes language to change?

What English was

Perhaps the simplest way of seeing how English has changed would be to look at examples from different time periods. Read the examples on the next page and make a note of some distinctive aspects of their language use. How much of

> **! REMEMBER**
>
> As with other areas of language study, language change is full of interesting questions that you could address in your investigation (see Chapter 7).

each text can you understand, and how old do you think they are? In the case of the first text, a modern 'translation' has been provided underneath. See if you can match some of the Old English words with the modern ones.

Old English (Anglo-Saxon)

> ælc þæra þe ðas min word gehyrð & þa wyrcð byþ gelic þam wisan were se hys hus ofer stan getimbrode.
>
> Þa com þær regn & mycele flod & þær bleowun windas & ahruron on þæt hus & hyt na ne feoll; Soðlice hit wæs ofer stan getimbrod.
>
> & ælc þæra þe gehyrþ ðas mine word & þa ne wyrcð se byþ gelic þam dysigan men þe getimbrode hys hus ofer sandceosel.
>
> Þa rinde hit & þær comun flod & bleowun windas & ahruron on þæt hus & þæt hus feoll & hys hryre wæs mycel.

A modern 'translation' of the above extract

Everyone who hears my words and carries them out will be like the wise man who built his house on stone.

The rain fell there, and big floods came, and the winds blew and beat on that house, but it did not fall, because it had been built on stone.

And everyone who hears my words and does not carry them out will be like the foolish man who built his house on sand.

The rain fell there, and floods came, and the winds blew and beat on that house, and it fell, and his misery was great.

Middle English

> Bifil that in that seson on a day,
> In Southwerk at the Tabard as I lay
> Redy to wenden on my pilgrymage
> To Caunterbury with ful devout corage,
> At nyght was come into that hostelrye
> Wel nyne and twenty in a compaignye
> Of sondry folk, by aventure yfalle
> In felaweshipe, and pilgrimes were they alle,
> That toward Caunterbury wolden ryde.

Early Modern English

> The great question, long debated in the world is, whether the rich or the poor are the least miserable of the two? It is certain, that no rich man ever desired to be poor, and that most, if not all, poor men desire to be rich; from whence it may be argued, that, in all appearance, the advantage lieth on the side of wealth, because both parties agree in preferring it before poverty. But this reasoning will be found to be false: for, I lay it down as a certain truth, that God Almighty hath placed all men upon an equal foot, with respect to their happiness in this world, and the capacity of attaining their salvation in the next; or, at least, if there be any difference, it is not the advantage of the rich and the mighty.

The dates for these texts are:

- Old English – end of the 7th century (taken from the *Lindisfarne Gospels*)

- Middle English – end of the 14th century (taken from Chaucer's 'Prologue' to *The Canterbury Tales*)
- Early Modern English – beginning of the 18th century (taken from Jonathan Swift's sermon 'On the Poor Man's Contentment').

As you can see, the English written in the Anglo-Saxon period (widely regarded as the first form of English) has some common vocabulary but seems different in its appearance and structure from that used in the present day. There are many reasons for that, including **internal** and **external factors**.

For example, the nature of English word order has changed over the nearly two millennia of its existence, and this is an internal, syntactic change. But, equally, the use of writing technology has changed from the quill and ink of Anglo-Saxon times to the computer-mediated communication (CMC) of the present day, and this is an external, graphological change. Note that Anglo-Saxon text uses the letter ð, which in modern texts is 'th'.

While the extracts of language may look very different, some of the reasons why the language has changed from one form to another remain quite similar, even in today's language. And that should not really come as a surprise, because language remains a tool for humans to communicate ideas, emotions and intentions, as well as a means of expressing personal and group identity, whenever they were born – be it in the 6th century or the beginning of the 21st.

What changes in English?

In this section you will look at examples of how English has changed – and continues to change – over time. To do this, you will need to build on ideas first discussed in Chapter 1, and in particular the language levels referred to there.

Vocabulary: lexis and semantics

One of the most obvious changes in the English language over its nearly 1,600-year history is the sheer number of words that it has added to its vocabulary. In terms of raw figures, English has somewhere between 650,000 and 1 million words in its vocabulary – and it is estimated that up to 70% of those words come from other languages (termed **borrowings**).

How has English grown so rapidly and picked up such an enormous vocabulary? You will look at this in more detail in the next section, but one of the main reasons is that English as a language has spread around the world and managed to absorb many foreign words as it has come into contact with them (ultimately making them its own).

Key terms

Borrowing. Incorporating words and phrases from another language.

External factor. A factor to do with external forces. For example, many French terms came into English after the Norman conquest of 1066.

Internal factor. A factor to do with the internal structure of the language system. For example, English used to have different singular and plural forms of 'you': 'thee' and 'thou' to address an individual or to express closeness, and 'ye' and 'you' to address groups or to express respect to a powerful individual.

Link

The British Library has a historical timeline of English that you may find interesting and useful: http://www.bl.uk/learning/langlit/changlang/across/languagetimeline.html

Activity

Look at the list of words below and, using the Oxford English Dictionary online, find the origin of each word. Where have they come from, and when did they first appear in English? Why do you think these words entered the English language? What does this tell you about the cultural history of English?

- abacus
- pyjamas
- hashish
- trek
- kamikaze
- alcohol
- tattoo
- bicycle
- skill
- dog

Link

Ritchie, H. (2013) *English for the Natives* offers a very clear and accessible summary of the early history of languages around the world and the origins of English.

Key terms

Acronym. Initials that can be pronounced as words (e.g. SIM).

Blending. Using parts of existing words to form a new word.

Compounding. Adding two existing words together to create a new word.

Functional theory. The idea that language changes because society does.

Infix. A particle added to the middle of a word.

Initialism. Initials that cannot be pronounced as words (e.g. DVD).

Prefix. A particle added to the front of a word.

Suffix. A particle added to the end of a word.

While English has been good at borrowing words (and of course, 'borrowing' here is used incorrectly, as it has no intention of giving them back), it has also been good at coming up with its own new words made up of existing parts. You saw in the introductory chapter that, in earlier times, English speakers drew on Latin and Greek in order to create new terms for new inventions. This phenomenon of course continues today, and there is no limit to the range of languages that can be used as a source. Many new words are formed by the processes of **compounding** and **blending**.

Words such as 'bromance' (a close friendship between two male friends), 'treggings' (leggings made to look like trousers) and 'sharknado' (a terrifying and rather stupid mixture of *shark* and *tornado* for the title of a 2013 film) are all formed by taking elements of one or more words and putting them together, so they are blends. Compounds often begin life as two separate words, before being hyphenated or put together into a single word (such as 'laptop', 'headache', 'mousemat'); while some remain as compounded lexical items, generally treated as if they are a single word (such as 'couch potato' and 'pole dancer').

Activity

Using a sample of new words from one of the following online sources, identify which ones have been formed by compounding, and which by blending.

- Buzzwords: Macmillan Dictionaries site at: http://www.macmillandictionary.com/buzzword/recent.html
- Oxford Words blog new words 2013 at: http://blog.oxforddictionaries.com/2013/11/language-review-2013/
- Collins Dictionary new words 2014 at: http://www.collinsdictionary.com/submissions/latest?page=2

Vocabulary also changes because new objects are invented, and new ideas become popular, and they need words to label them. According to one key idea about language change – the **functional theory** – language changes to suit the needs of its users. So, to take an example from music technology, in the 1970s music appeared in the format of LPs, cassettes and even 4-tracks, so these terms were widely used. But as music moved into the digital era, new terms had to be coined to apply to the new forms of music – CDs in the 1980s, MP3s in the 2000s, digital downloads and streams in the 2010s – while older terms dropped out of use.

Another common pattern with vocabulary change is the abbreviation of some words or phrases. This can involve clipping the front, end, or both from a word ('refrigerator' to 'fridge', 'disrespect' to 'diss', 'promotional' to 'promo'). A popular process has also been to turn words or phrases into **acronyms** or **initialisms**. Acronyms are pronounced as words: 'self-contained underwater breathing apparatus' became 'scuba' in the 1950s, 'buy one get one free' offers are often termed 'BOGOFs', while 'massive open online courses' – 'MOOCs' – are growing in popularity now. Initialisms are pronounced as individual letters: United Nations as 'UN', 'for your information' as 'FYI' and British Broadcasting Corporation as 'BBC'.

Morphology plays its part, too – with **prefixes**, **suffixes** and **infixes** all contributing to the creation of new words. Prefixes such as 'anti-', 'dis-', and 'un-' can all be placed on the front of existing words to create new terms and new meanings, so the rise of fascism in the 1930s gave rise to anti-fascism in opposition to it, while the verb 'to friend' arrived with Facebook and gave rise to the tricky process of getting rid of a 'friend', or 'to <u>un</u>friend'. Suffixes are tacked onto the ends of words, so terms such as 'hipster<u>ism</u>' and 'stor<u>ify</u>' have cropped up to label new trends or online activities. Infixes slot into the middle of existing words, often to provide an ironic twist, as for example in 'hoo-bloody-ray'.

Activity

1. What processes do you think were used to create the following new words?

IMHO	In my humble opinion
SIM	Subscriber Identity Module
Mansplain	An ironic way of describing how some men explain things to women
Chick noir	A violent and dark genre of literature aimed at women
App	Application
Malware	Malicious software
Springador, Labradoodle and Puggle	Cross-breeds of dogs
Cyberbullying	Online bullying and abuse

2. Aim to list ten additional examples of new words from the past year or two, and then describe the processes that you think led to their formation.

There is some feedback on the first activity at the back of the book.

Word meanings also change over time, and this is connected to the field of semantics. Existing words may gradually pick up new meanings or undergo a very rapid switch. In the case of gradual changes, because words are shifting in meaning very slowly, they can mean different things to different people at the same time. While older members of a particular speech community may generally understand a word to have one meaning, the youngest members of the same community may have a very different meaning for the same word, and those in the middle will perhaps understand both meanings and/or tend to use one more than the other. Good examples of this kind of difference can be found below.

Activity

1. Use an online dictionary, or dictionaries, to identify different meanings for the following words – and also when new, and very different, meanings started to evolve for them.

- sick
- bad
- mental
- heavy
- literally
- enormity
- disinterested
- opinionated

2. The same process can operate for phrases, especially idiomatic expressions where the meaning is not literal. For example, what about the following phrases?

- 'It'll all come out in the wash': does this mean that an issue will be brought out in the open, or be washed away?
- Is it 'The proof is in the pudding' or 'The proof of the pudding is in the eating'?
- Is it 'He did it off his own bat' or 'He did it off his own back'?
- Is it 'Locking the stable door after the horse has bolted' or 'Bolting the stable door after...' (provide your own ending – various are possible).

3. Can you think of other examples of words or sayings where the way you say something and/or your understanding of the meaning may differ from that of older people?

Key terms

Amelioration. A process whereby a word or phrase develops more positive connotations. For example, 'nice' used to mean ignorant (from the Latin 'nescire' meaning 'to not know').

Determinism. The idea that language determines the way we think and behave.

Pejoration. A process whereby a word or phrase develops more negative connotations. For example, 'cunning' used to mean knowledgeable.

Reflectionism. The idea that language reflects the society that produces it.

Sapir-Whorf hypothesis. The idea, derived from the work of Edward Sapir and Benjamin Lee Whorf, that our language constructs our view of the world and that it is difficult or even impossible to think beyond it.

Some of these semantic changes gradually add more positive or negative connotations to the word. For example, while 'sick' has generally had quite negative associations – illness and disease – its slang meaning is unequivocally positive. In such cases, the meaning is said to have undergone **amelioration**. The reverse is true for other words, which move from a neutral or positive meaning towards a more negative one, and this is known as **pejoration**. This is the case with 'silly', which originally meant 'holy' or 'blessed' and now has connotations of stupidity and foolishness. Historically, words associated with less powerful groups in society – the working class, women, ethnic and sexual minorities, people with disabilities – have often acquired pejorative connotations. This shows you, again, that language is never neutral: it is a human construct, reflecting the interests of those in power in society.

Who owns meaning?

Language is used to label and represent individuals and groups of people, but the 'ownership' of these labels is often a vexed question. In recent years, the American football team Washington Redskins has faced pressure over its use of an allegedly disparaging racial term for its team name, and many other debates have raged about potentially (or obviously) offensive terms such as 'nigger', 'queer' and 'paki'. You will look at the debate around 'political correctness' and language later in this chapter, but a major issue here is the power of language to shape, influence and (perhaps) control the way we think. If words used to describe the less powerful groups in society (as outlined above) pick up negative connotations over time, is this because of worsening social attitudes towards these groups, or are the words themselves so steeped in negativity that they cause people to feel a certain way about the people who are labelled?

The linguistic debate around two positions – **reflectionism** and **determinism** – can be used to explore this. Linguistic reflectionism suggests that language simply reflects the needs, views and opinions of its users. The argument is that to change language, you need to change attitudes.

Linguistic determinism (associated with the **Sapir–Whorf hypothesis**) maintains that language controls our perceptions of reality – influencing us to think in certain ways. The argument is that to change attitudes, we need to change language.

The Sapir–Whorf hypothesis is named after two American academics, the anthropologist Benjamin Lee Whorf, and the linguist Edward Sapir. Their original contention was that language controls and determines the way we think – hence the term 'determinism'. Nowadays, this is seen as too strong a claim, for if this were true, we would never be able to think beyond our language and create new terms. A weaker version of the same idea is called **linguistic relativity**, which claims that language exerts a powerful influence over how we think and behave.

It is important to recognize that not every linguist agrees with either of these claims. For example, John McWhorter refutes this idea in his book *The Language Hoax: Why the World Looks the Same in Any Language* (OUP 2014).

A relatively recent phenomenon in semantic change has been the process of **semantic reclamation** of negative words by the groups labelled by them. This is a complex process, and so it is worth thinking through with the help of a practical case study example. The term 'slut' is an interesting example of attempted semantic reclamation, and the following article from an Australian language blog explains some of the arguments around the use of this word. This article, from the Superlinguo blog, refers to a phenomenon known as 'slutwalking', a form of protest that involves women dressing in a 'slutty' style to draw attention to male sexual violence and double standards over dress codes and attitudes to women.

Link

Geoffrey Hughes (in Hughes, G. 1989, *Words in Time*, Oxford: Blackwell) provides an interesting exploration of the way in which many words have changed their meanings over time (including 'churl', 'villain', 'noble' and 'gentle'), and also looks at social and linguistic reasons for pejoration and amelioration.

Key terms

Linguistic relativity. The idea that language shapes our thinking but does not completely control it.

Semantic reclamation. Taking language that has had negative connotations and trying to overturn them by using the language in new ways.

Activity

Read the blog article below and then answer the following questions:

1. What are the key arguments about the use of the word 'slut' and its different meanings?
2. How has the word been used differently in the past, and how does this cause problems now?
3. What do you think of the argument that slutwalks are helping to 'reclaim' and 'reappropriate' the word?

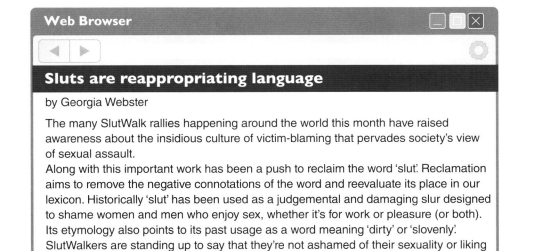

Web Browser

Sluts are reappropriating language

by Georgia Webster

The many SlutWalk rallies happening around the world this month have raised awareness about the insidious culture of victim-blaming that pervades society's view of sexual assault.

Along with this important work has been a push to reclaim the word 'slut'. Reclamation aims to remove the negative connotations of the word and reevaluate its place in our lexicon. Historically 'slut' has been used as a judgemental and damaging slur designed to shame women and men who enjoy sex, whether it's for work or pleasure (or both). Its etymology also points to its past usage as a word meaning 'dirty' or 'slovenly'. SlutWalkers are standing up to say that they're not ashamed of their sexuality or liking sex, and that being a slut should not invite judgement or violence.

I'm a feminist and a linguist, so this idea of 'slut' reclamation is fascinating on both those levels. There's been much debate online and offline about what it means to call yourself (or others) a slut, and about whether it's possible to entirely reclaim a word and strip its negative or malicious intent and control.

The process of language reappropriation is one where a word that was at one time a pejorative used to malign, control or victimise, is brought into acceptable (or even preferable) usage.

It's not necessarily a straightforward process, but sluts everywhere should be heartened by the examples of other words successfully reappropriated so far in our social and linguistic history. There are some notable examples of reappropriated words and language in common usage: 'gay' was previously considered an insult but is now strongly favoured as the preferred term to describe homosexuality.

In Australia, 'wog' began as a racist term during the wave of Southern European immigration in the 50s and 60s. Through the phenomenon of Mediterranean-Australian performing artists taking ownership of the term 'wog', its original pejorative nature has been defused […] Similarly, 'crip' has been reclaimed by sections of the disabled community.

Let's look at how exactly this semantic shift occurs. To reappropriate a word or phrase, a deliberate intervention is made into its common or **hegemonic** (for the cultural studies majors amongst us) usage. This common usage as a word of oppression, hurt or victimisation is challenged and reevaluated. The word may attain a neutral or acceptable connotation and become absorbed into broader cultural use. It may even attain a positive connotation within informed and aware groups.

Language reappropriation usually takes place within the oppressed community affected by the word's original meaning. Often, use of the word outside that community retains its derogatory meaning. An example of this is the word 'nigga' – a still-controversial term reclaimed by parts of the African-American community, which is not generally accepted when it's used by a person outside that community.

This reminds us that we shouldn't forget our ol' friend context […], which plays a huge part in our linguistic interactions. Word meaning is decoded within a context – how it's conveyed, by whom, when, where and why all have effects on the intent and receipt of a word.

The SlutWalks happening around the world are working as a deliberate intervention into the way the word 'slut' is used. Women and men are working to redefine a 'slut' as someone in control of their sexuality, who enjoys sex and who doesn't invite sexual, physical or emotional violence by virtue of their promiscuity.

Key terms

Broadening. A process by which words acquire a broader reference. For example, 'hoover' can be used as a general label for vacuum cleaners, but it was formerly the name of a particular brand.

Hegemonic. Culturally dominant.

Narrowing. A process by which words acquire a narrower reference. For example, 'deer' used to refer to animals in general, not to a specific animal.

Link

You can find out more about similar arguments connected with sexist language, and campaigns to reform it, in Goddard, A. and Mean, L. (2008) *Language and Gender*, London: Routledge.

Other historically contentious terms have been reclaimed in one way or another, and a look at a source such as http://englishlangsfx.blogspot.co.uk/search/label/racist%20language should allow you to find many of the debates concerning these terms and why they have been challenged, changed or even embraced.

Word meanings can also change in other ways, **broadening** to pick up wider and less specific meanings, or **narrowing** to become more limited in range. Words can also undergo semantic shift where they move from one domain to another. An example of semantic shift is the word 'navigate', which was originally only applied to ships, but is now used for other forms of transport or even in a metaphorical sense on a website. Examples of broadening are words such as 'dog' (originally just one breed of dog) and bird (originally just a young bird in a nest). Narrowing is the reverse process and usually involves a word becoming more specialized as time goes on. An example of this is 'meat', which once meant all forms of food, not just one type.

Look at the bar graph on the right, which is from a study by the linguist Justyna Robinson about the changing meanings of the word 'awesome' in the UK. The vertical axis shows the frequency of use of a particular meaning; and the horizontal axis shows people's ages. A mean is derived from adding up all the examples of use and dividing by the number of informants. As you can see from the results, for many people up to the age of 18, this word means 'great', while for people over 60, it means either 'terrible' or 'impressive'. For those in the other age groups, there is a greater mix of different interpretations, suggesting that the meanings have been in a state of flux for some time.

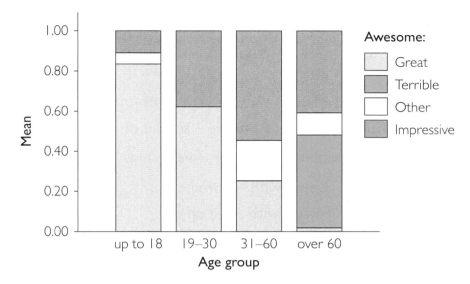

Activity

1. Look up the original meaning of 'awe' in an etymological dictionary. Are there any connections in sense between the meaning as understood by younger speakers and those of older people?
2. Do you think the results would have been different if Robinson had done her research in another country – for example, the USA?

Grammar: syntax and morphology

One of the most significant long-term changes in the history of English has been its movement from a language whose grammatical meanings have been determined by word endings, towards a language where word order controls meaning. In Old English, **inflections** (**morphemes** on the ends of words) would indicate whether a word was acting as a **subject** or **object**, **agent** or **patient**, in a clause. For example, you would be able to tell whether 'the queen' was carrying out the verb or receiving the verb's action in a clause by the ending used on the noun – *cwen* for subject and *cwene* for object – regardless of where 'the queen' appeared in the sentence. Present-day English makes use of word order to allocate these roles to words and phrases. In a clause such as 'the queen congratulated the performers', the roles of agent (the queen) and patient (the performers) are clear, because of where they are positioned in relation to the verb.

With this shift towards syntax rather than morphology controlling meaning, English has also made less use of inflections. In Early Modern English (1500–1700) it would have been common to see inflections such as 'can*st*' and 'play*eth*' used on verbs, but these have largely died out and present-day English tends to use a more restricted set of inflections.

Key terms

Agent. An alternative word for the **subject** in a sentence.

Inflection. A morpheme on the end of a word to indicate a grammatical relationship or category. For example, many nouns in English add an 's' to indicate plurality.

Object. The thing or person on the receiving end of the action of the verb.

Patient. An alternative word for the **object** in a sentence.

Subject. The thing or person carrying out the action of the verb.

Link

The Oxford English Dictionary *English in Time* web pages have some more detailed explanations of grammar changes over time, and a wealth of examples drawn from real data: http://public.oed.com/aspects-of-english/english-in-time/

Changes to English grammar have been relatively few and far between in recent years. This is perhaps unsurprising: while new words and meanings are relatively easy to understand, grammatical change can often be more confusing. But changes are still taking place, and perhaps the supposed errors of today are examples of language change in action. It may be that written language is undergoing a very similar process of informalization to that which has been apparent in speech for some time, and that written language is picking up some of the characteristics of informal spoken language. If you look at the examples below, you might be able to see how a supposed grammatical 'error' can develop when a sound becomes similar to another sound and is then 're-analysed' and written as it sounds.

Must have – must've – must of

Should have – should've – should of

That process could then establish a pattern that others follow:

Bored with – bored of

Fed up with – fed up of

Activity

Look at the examples of English from different time periods below. What do you notice about the ways in which the grammar is different from contemporary English? How can you describe these changes linguistically?

- 'I tell thee, churlish priest, / A ministering angel shall my sister be / When thou liest howling'. (William Shakespeare, *Hamlet*, c.1602)
- 'I like it not' (William Shakespeare, *Romeo and Juliet*, c.1597)
- 'The curse is come upon me' (Lord Alfred Tennyson, 'The Lady of Shalott', 1832)

There is some feedback on this activity at the back of the book.

Phonology

The sounds of English have changed hugely over time, and linguists have spent much effort reconstructing how the language might have sounded back in the Old English and Middle English periods. One major event – although 'event' is probably a misnomer for a three-century-long process – was what linguists refer to as the Great Vowel Shift (GVS). Over approximately the 14th to the 17th centuries, vowel sounds in English changed. A sentence from David Crystal's *The Stories of English* (quoted in Harry Ritchie's *English for the Natives*), 'We do say it's time to go now', demonstrates just how radical a shift in sound this was, with Crystal suggesting that this would have been pronounced before the GVS as something like:

weɪ dəʊ sɑː ɪts tiːm tuː gɔː nuː

Link

A tutor at a Dutch university took a 16th-century poem by John Skelton called 'Speke, Parrot' and recited it as it would have sounded at the time. The students produced images as backdrops and you can hear (and see) the result on YouTube: http://www.bbc.co.uk/news/blogs-trending-29536411

While the GVS is largely outside the time frame that you need to cover in detail for your A level course (1600 to the present day), it is useful to know the background to the major changes in English and understand the impact that they have had on what we say and write now.

Phonological change is not just a historical phenomenon, but one that occurs all the time. While regional and social variation were topics for Chapter 3, some changes can be linked to the topic of language change – among them the style of speech that is known as 'uptalk'.

 Activity

Read the newspaper article below from 2006 and think about the ways in which this changing style of speech is being reported. Is this a feature of language that you have become aware of or been made aware of by other people?

The rise of the interrogatory statement

by Stefanie Marsh

My sister lives in Los Angeles, and has picked up this irritating verbal tic, 'uptalk', which means that she uses an interrogative tone even when making statements such as: 'I never want to talk to you again (?)' In the old days I could pretend to listen to her on the phone while actually reading a book — I would do this by keeping one ear on her intonation and lobbing a well-placed 'in principle, I would say yes', after every one of her high notes. These days when I do that she sighs and says flatly: 'It wasn't a question, Stefanie.'

But uptalk has spread far beyond California and the dur-brained Valley Girls who are supposed to have invented it. An article in last week's *New York Observer* confirms that 'high-rise terminals' have infected the East Coast, while psychology professors writing in the Toronto-based *Globe* and *Mail* talk of an 'epidemic' in Canada. We won't even talk about Australia.

In this country, uptalk is still a burgeoning trend. John Humphrys has not yet stooped to introducing the '*Today* programme?' Nevertheless, it is spreading – especially among women – and, more worryingly, is being championed by the most cunning and manipulative section of society: and yes, I do mean children. They get it from the television, apparently. I, for one, am glad that I don't come home to a six-year-old who talks like Philip Seymour Hoffman imitating Truman Capote.

A few years ago I would have been able to say: I have some bad news for you six-year-olds. Because, back then, the view held by experts was that uptalk was a symptom of self-doubt: framing your statements as questions was thought to indicate a desire for approval. Research by DiResta Communications in 2001 found that uptalk was 'destroying the credibility of millions of professionals who are unknowingly falling victim to this increasingly common form of speech'. DiResta claimed that uptalk was the result of having either foreign parents or low self-esteem. The bottom line was that nobody could take you seriously as a boss when you pronounced 'You're fired!' as 'You're fired?' But the experts have changed their minds; the prevailing wisdom now holds that incorporating high-rise terminals, or HRTs, into your speech is actually a means of controlling your interlocutors, of compelling a response, if only an internal one, and of establishing common ground.

New studies show that people who use uptalk are not insecure wallflowers but powerful speakers who like getting their own way: teachers, talk-show hosts, politicians and facetious shop assistants. Mark Liberman, a phonetician at the University of Pennsylvania, who has been monitoring George W. Bush's speeches on his fascinating weblog Language Log, points out that the President has started peppering his Iraq speeches with HRTs. Why? Not,

Looking ahead

You will look in more detail at how people feel about language change and variation in the section on language discourses later in this chapter, and the text by Stefanie Marsh on the right would be a good one to think about.

Key term

Intonation. Tunes, created from variations in pitch, that convey meaning in the speech of a particular language.

apparently, because Bush's confidence is failing him. Rather, it has more to do with an aggressive need to direct conversation. Liberman quotes from a linguistics paper published last year in which scientists counted the number of HRTs used in real-life conversations: 'In four business meetings... the chairs (sic) used rise tones almost three times more often than the other participants did. 'In conversations between academic supervisors and their supervisees, the supervisors used rise tones almost seven times more often than the supervisees. So maybe the problem with "Valley Girls" and other youth of the past couple of decades,' continues Liberman, 'is really that they're, like, totally self-confident and socially aggressive?' This news seems to have percolated down to primary schools ages ago. Parents: you are being had.

The Times, 28 March 2006

The article you studied in the Activity above focuses on **intonation**, which is an aspect of prosody. But phonology can also be considered from the perspective of speech practices and routines – the pragmatics of our social rules about when and where we make sounds.

Activity

Think about and discuss the following questions.

1. Have there been changes in our social rules about speech and silence? What impact have mobile phones had on our ideas about where we speak and when?

2. Have there been changes to the routines we follow in our greetings? For example, how do you respond to the opening 'Hi, how are you?' in exchanges with strangers and friends?

3. What about farewells? Do you often hear 'Have a nice day/evening/weekend'? How do you feel about changes to these aspects of interactions?

Graphology and orthography

These two language levels have also undergone change over time. An obvious difference between older versions of English and that used today is the disappearance of some letters (such as æ, ð, ʃ) and the appearance of more keyboard-based symbols (such as hashtags (#), asperands (@) and emoticons and emojis).

Graphology has changed, often as a result of new technologies offering greater affordances for titles, borders, graphics and font changes. The move from text on the page to hypertext immediately allows page elements to become interactive, so with a single click or by touching an icon on a screen, graphology can become multidimensional.

Spelling, too, has undergone change – with the gradual drift towards a widely recognized spelling system following the general standardizing flow of English, helped along the way by dictionaries and universal education. But, more recently, the growth of **computer-mediated communication (CMC)** and the rise of spellchecks and predictive text have led some critics to argue that spelling standardization is breaking down. Are young people becoming less accurate in their spelling because of technology? It seems to be a familiar argument in the media, but one that you can perhaps explore in more detail by looking at some examples suggested in the section on language discourses in this chapter.

Why does English change?

The English language has changed as its users have changed. From its earliest origins in the 5th century to the present day, it has functioned as a tool for its users, and as their needs have changed, the language has changed too. Or at least that is one explanation. But, as with other areas of English language study, there are many different opinions to evaluate.

Activity

Look at the following list of possible factors in language change. Think about how each of these might influence a change in language. Can you think of examples of new words and meanings that have come about as a result of any of them?

- Movement of people from one place to another
- Technological change
- Changing social attitudes to different groups in societies (e.g. women, gay people, religious minorities)
- Education
- War
- Politics
- Religion

Language as a tool

One simple way of looking at language change is to consider language as a tool for communication, and then to think about the ways in which the nature of communication has changed over time. A common misconception is that written language is 'proper' language and spoken language is some kind of casual attempt to imitate it. But when you consider how much of normal communication in a given day is written, compared to that which is spoken, you can see that spoken English is extremely important.

In the earliest human societies, it is believed, spoken language evolved to accompany and augment body language and gesture, and it is this essence of spoken language – connected to the here and now, closely related to immediate context and rooted in face-to-face communication – that was probably important for a long time. As soon as humans started to use written forms of communication (the pen and the printing press, for example), language itself

Link

John McWhorter's lecture *Txting is killing language. JK!!!* offers an engaging and accessible take on the impact of technology on communication, and can be found here: http://www.ted.com/talks/john_mcwhorter_txtng_is_killing_language_jk

moved into a different dimension. We could make language last for longer by writing it down. It could also be carried over longer distances, copied for others to read, and planned and edited in a way that isn't always possible with spoken language. These are ideas connected to mode, which you have looked at as part of Chapter 2, and they are equally important in this chapter too.

The linguist John McWhorter notes that for a long time spoken language has had the opportunity to become more like written language (people speaking as they would write, in longer, multi-clausal sentences), but until the advent of digital technology and computer-mediated communication (in the form of mobile phones, text messaging and social networking), written language has not always had the chance to be influenced by spoken language.

In a number of important ways, English has changed to suit the needs of its users. With the birth of writing, longer and more complex structures could be put on paper, when previously they would have relied too much on memory. With the growth of CMC, abbreviated keyboard forms of communication have proliferated alongside features such as emoticons and emojis – designed to replace the body language and facial expressions of face-to-face talk.

Logical progression or random fluctuation?

The functional theory proposes that language changes to suit the needs of its users, so as new words and modes of communication arrive to suit our changing world, older words drop out of use. This model would suggest that there is a certain logic to language change: as a landscape changes, so a map has to change to reflect it, and language might be seen as mapping reality in a similar way. Crystal (2011) says 'All living languages change. They have to. Languages have no existence apart from the people who use them. And because people are changing all the time, their language changes too, to keep up with them. The only languages that don't change are dead ones.'

> **Key term**
>
> **Random fluctuation theory.**
> The idea that language change is not a logical and ordered process.

However, there are instances where the change is less logical, something that the **random fluctuation theory** proposes. Take the slang expression 'pwned' (pronounced variously as *powned*, *pooned* or *pawned*), for example. It means something along the lines of 'beaten or humiliated in an argument or game' (as in 'That noob got pwned on CoD' or, translated into non-gamer speak, 'That novice player was humiliated while playing Call of Duty'). It is believed to have derived from a typo in the word 'owned' (a slang expression meaning something very similar). This common error – 'p' and 'o' being next to each other on the QWERTY keyboard – then grew in online popularity before spreading into spoken language. You might have heard of 'pwned' but then again you might not, and that links to another important area of language change as a topic. Change often follows a clear pattern, but that doesn't mean it has to be regular.

The spread of a new form of language (a slang term, for example) might be rapid and widespread (think about the word 'chav', which took off in use over the early 2000s and is now widely understood), while others may exist only among very small groups of people and rarely spread beyond them. Language change consists of two distinct stages:

- Innovation – the creation of a new word, phrase, meaning or way of saying something, sometimes initially perceived as a mistake.
- Diffusion – the spread of a feature from the original user to a wider population.

Curves, waves, spikes and twerks

Linguists have often found that changes follow the pattern of what is called an s-curve, where the new form of speech is just one of many in existence, competing against others for prominence. The new form, be it a word, phrase, new meaning or way of speaking, gradually increases in use before rapidly taking off.

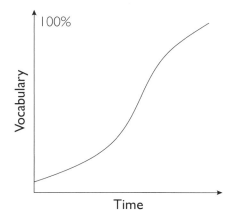

◀ **Changes in vocabulary follow an s-curve**

The s-curve describes a situation where a new form is slow to take off, at first. Then there is a kind of tipping point where the rate of increase starts to accelerate rapidly, shown in the steep upward climb of the curve. By the time the curve flattens out again, the innovation has become dominant but the older form may still be in existence and continue to be used in some specific contexts.

Another way of explaining how changes spread is through the **wave model**.

◀ **The wave model of change**

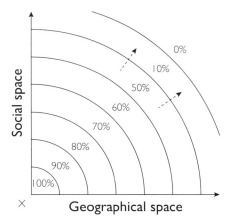

The new form of language starts at a centre and its use gradually spreads like ripples on a pond towards users further away from the centre. As the ripples spread, they may become weaker and this might be reflected in fewer people using the new feature further from the centre. On one level the wave model might be related to geographical distance, but other factors might also be significant – age, ethnicity, social class and gender, for example – and the use of CMC also means that changes can spread almost instantly across huge distances. For example, a new slang term starting life in a multi-ethnic and largely working class area of South London might spread quickly to similar young people in East London and Essex and then beyond through social media and popular culture, but might be much less recognized among those over 30 or from a different background.

Of course, not all new forms of language take off at all. The success of a new expression or even a new way of talking or writing depends not just on the usefulness and appeal of the innovation itself, but the influence of the initial users. For example, once a word has been approved for a dictionary, it will gain a degree of official status (overt prestige), but equally if a word is used by an influential member of a particularly fashionable speech community, such as young American rappers or singers, the language feature might gain covert prestige.

Digital technology can also be used to track 'spikes' (sudden increases) in word use. The social network Twitter has proved particularly interesting in recent years, because it allows linguists to track users' locations as well as access a huge database of billions of words from tweets all over the world. In 2014, a BBC Radio 4 study found that the use of swear words spiked on Twitter at 9pm on 1 September. Why? This was a few minutes after the transfer-deadline-day move of Manchester United striker Danny Welbeck to Arsenal. In the same survey it was found that Redcar and Cleveland Twitter users had the most swear words, while Orkney Islands tweeters used the fewest. Other online spikes have been found for new or obscure words being looked up or searched for, such as 'twerk' for Miley Cyrus's dancing at the Video Music Awards in 2013, and 'caliphate' for the rise of Islamic militants in 2014 and their declaration of an Islamic state in Iraq and Syria.

The driving forces of language change

What are the main external forces of language change? These have remained largely the same over the history of English, but have perhaps developed at different speeds, with many arguing that some forms of change are much more rapid now than ever before.

Movement of people

Individuals, groups and even whole communities move from one place to another, bringing with them their own vocabulary. Through contact, the new words are picked up by other speakers and the overall vocabulary grows. This can be a movement within a country or between countries.

Technological change

New inventions need new names. New words are created to label these new objects and ideas (podcast, laptop, smartphone). Older words might be recycled to have new meanings. The 'cloud' used to store data is not a real cloud in the sky (as the *Daily Mail* helpfully explained to its readers at the height of the celebrity hacking scandal in 2014); the word 'tablet' has been repurposed to refer to small computers; and 'track', used to describe a path or road, has also been used to describe a song on a record, CD or now a digital file containing one song. Sometimes terms can be recycled more than once. In the Bible, tablets were made of stone and some had the Ten Commandments inscribed on them. This meaning was in currency long before they became something to swallow. In a way, the digital tablet harks back to an ancient form of graphology – one still seen on gravestones.

War

While wars are usually devastating for those involved, they are often intense periods of word creation and adoption. World War I gave us 'shell shock' (now referred to in our abbreviation-happy times as PTSD, for post-traumatic stress

Did you know?

There are many examples of food names that have come into English as a result of population movements, particularly the waves of immigration into America: for example, spaghetti, pizza, sushi, hamburger.

disorder) and 'tank', while World War II provided loan words from German and Japanese respectively, such as 'Blitzkrieg' (lightning war) and 'kamikaze' (divine wind).

Politics

Political campaigns and major events often influence language. A sensational political controversy of the early 1970s gave rise to the term 'Watergate' (originally the name of a building complex broken into by US President Richard Nixon's undercover operatives) to denote the subsequent wide-ranging scandal. However, the suffix '-gate' has become a **libfix** (suffix liberated from its original word) that is hugely productive – being added to new words to denote any kind of scandal or political outrage ('plebgate' being a high-profile example in the UK in 2014).

Attempts by politicians to control language discourses, and redefine the way in which the general public views their policies and those affected by them, have become apparent in terms such as the unpopular 'poll tax' of the late 1980s (originally named the 'community charge' by the Conservative government); the switch from 'Disability Living Allowance' to 'Personal Independence Payment' in 2013; and many other 'rebrandings'. The rise of 'isms' and 'phobias' to describe political and social movements or reactions against them is also interesting to observe, with terms such as 'racism' and 'sexism' only really gaining prominence in the 1930s and 1960s respectively, while the Greek '-phobia' suffix (denoting fear) has given us 'homophobia' (hostility towards gay people) and 'Islamophobia' (hatred of Muslims).

Youth culture

The emergence of the 'teenager' as a distinct demographic group (and word) in the 1950s led to a spike in terms associated with youth culture. With various youth subcultures forming, spreading, dying out and then being revived years later, we have terms such as 'teddy boys', 'mods', 'rockers', 'hippies', 'skinheads', 'rudeboys', 'gangstas', 'emos', 'goths', 'grungers', 'nu-ravers', 'metalheads', as well as the perpetual battle between the 'townies', 'chavs' and 'neds' and their rivals the 'alternatives', 'freaks', 'nerds', 'geeks', 'neeks' and 'boffs'.

Expressiveness and creativity

In some of the cases you have looked at in this chapter, the need for a new word or a different meaning for an existing word is obvious, but do we really need yet another new term for 'good' or 'bad'? Apparently so, if the proliferation of slang terms for approval and disapproval is anything to go by.

Activity

Look at the list below of slang terms expressing approval. Using online dictionary sources, find out when these words first appeared. Why do you think there are so many different terms for the same thing? Can you think of other areas of language where we have multiple terms for the same idea?

- cool
- groovy
- gnarly
- bodacious
- awesome
- rad
- phat
- sick
- wicked
- peak

Link

The Language of War by Steve Thorne (2006, Routledge) provides a range of fascinating examples of how war influences language.

Key term

Libfix. A 'liberated' suffix, or one which has been taken from its original context and applied to new situations. Libfixes are creations of their time. For example, after the launch of the Russian spacecraft 'Sputnik' in 1957, there was a growth in the West of terms ending in 'nik' – beatnik, peacenik, refusenik – to label people associated with dubious causes.

Link

Other libfixes are discussed in this article by Neal Whitman, including '-zilla' (from 'Godzilla'), '-gasm' (from 'orgasm') and '-stock' (from 'Woodstock'): http://theweek.com/article/index/249302/a-linguistic-tour-of-the-best-libfixes-from--ana-to--zilla

Link

The slang lexicographer Jonathon Green charts the growth of key social trends and social groups in this excellent article for the BBC News Magazine: http://www.bbc.co.uk/news/magazine-27405988

Deutscher (2006) offers the suggestion that some changes in language are for reasons of expressiveness:

> Expressiveness refers to speakers' attempts to achieve greater effect for their utterances and extend their range of meaning. One area in which we are particularly expressive is in saying 'no'. A plain 'no' is often deemed too weak to convey the depth of our unenthusiasm, so to make sure that the right effect is achieved, we beef up 'no' to 'not at all', 'not a bit', 'no way', 'by no means', 'not in a million years', and so on.

The examples above, and others you may have listed, suggest that we are always on the search for inventive new ways of saying things that are common to much human experience. An alternative explanation might be that different youth subcultures and **communities of practice** tend to use particular terms as markers of social identity at a given time, and that these terms function to express a shared evaluation of what is perceived as good or bad.

Deutscher also notes that language changes for what he terms reasons of economy and analogy:

- Economy: the tendency to save effort in communication – for example, shortening longer words, and using ellipsis to remove unnecessary grammatical elements and to take short cuts in pronunciation.

- Analogy: the tendency to regularize language use. For example, when new nouns are coined, they almost always follow a regular pattern of pluralization, adding '-s' rather than '-en' or changing the root form, while verbs tend to adopt a regular past tense ending such as '-ed'.

So it would appear that in many ways there are logical reasons *why* language changes and fairly logical patterns as to *how* it changes, but many different factors are at work and it can be extremely difficult to pinpoint just one overarching reason.

Change from above

Historically, language change has often come from 'below': if large numbers of people use a particular feature of language, it tends to catch on and enter the mainstream as time goes by. But more recently there have been attempts to regulate language use for different reasons and by different organizations.

For example, the Plain English Campaign (http://www.plainenglish.co.uk) has urged government organizations and businesses to avoid what it describes as 'gobbledygook, jargon and misleading public information' and to use straightforward English wherever possible, awarding 'Crystal Marks' to show its approval.

Laws have also been passed to punish those who use abusive or threatening terms. Where racial discrimination is involved, this can be regarded as an aggravating factor, leading to harsher punishments and recent cases of Internet-based sexual harassment through language use have resulted in jail sentences.

However, unlike France, which regulates its language through an 'Academy', the UK has no single organization that adjudicates on 'correct' English. Instead, there is a wide range of decision-makers and gatekeepers: lexicographers, educators, journalists, linguists and, above all, users of English.

Activity

Look at the table below, which has been taken from *Speaking for Ourselves: A teacher's guide to disability and oral history,* by Alex White, Philip Mann and Richard Rieser.

1. Why are the expressions in the right-hand column preferable to those in the left?

2. What does this kind of extract suggest to you about ways – other than those you have looked at so far in this chapter – in which language can change?

Avoid	Use instead
(the) handicapped	disabled people
afflicted by suffers from victim of	has (condition or impairment)
confined to a wheelchair wheelchair-bound	wheelchair user
mental handicap subnormality	learning disability / learning difficulty
cripple invalid	disabled person
spastic	person who has cerebral palsy
able-bodied	non-disabled

Some have referred to the policing and replacement of apparently offensive language as **political correctness (PC)**, but this is a term that has picked up quite pejorative connotations and is often misused (sometimes deliberately); a more positive way to refer to PC is **language reform**. In its earliest form, as part of the political and social activism of the 1960s and 1970s, the language reform movement sought to challenge language that represented women in derogatory or unequal ways, or ignored their existence. As it grew, areas such as ethnicity, sexuality and disability were also challenged. The thinking was that if negative language could be challenged – if people could be made to think about their language choices and the implications of them, or if the words themselves could be replaced – then attitudes towards these groups would be altered; social and political change would then follow. Some on the right of the political spectrum have complained that language reform challenges traditional language choices for no good reason, while some on the libertarian left have argued that top-down models of language control are repressive in nature.

Activity

Read the following newspaper article, which offers a perspective on the need to change offensive terms for people with disabilities.

Comment on the ways in which this writer represents the issue. How does she present her views about the need to challenge problematic language? What is your response to these views?

Key terms

Language reform. A term used, usually by liberal commentators, to support the idea of consciously changing language because it is considered unfair to different groups.

Political correctness. A term used, usually by conservative commentators, to object to the idea of consciously changing language because it is considered unfair to different groups.

Link

The first section of this chapter looked at the ideas of linguistic reflectionism and determinism, so you can relate these directly to the arguments about language reform.

More than words

Careless talk may not nowadays cost lives as it might have during the war, but there is a price to pay for continuous thoughtless usage says Penelope Friday

It's almost impossible to go through a single week without hearing a remark which implies something negative about, or trivialises, disability. Insults such as 'You spaz!' or 'What a retard' are immediate examples that come to most people's minds, but their very offensiveness makes them in some ways less of a threat to people with disabilities than commonplace phrases which abound in the English language. How often do you hear someone comment 'Oh, that's so lame' or 'how short-sighted of you', both of which sayings reference disability in a negative way? This use of language, however, is not only associated with healthy, able-bodied adults.

Many disabled people not only use disablist language but also criticise those who seek to change it, calling suggested alternative phrases 'political correctness gone mad'.

Intriguingly, often the same people can see the offensiveness of 'that's gay' – a homophobic phrase also commonly used to demean something or someone – and yet don't follow the same argument relating to remarks like 'that's so lame'. Both phrases imply that the subject or object under question is rubbish. Change the first word in each sentence to 'I'm' or 'You're' and the problem becomes clearer. 'You're gay' would mean 'You're rubbish' – and what message does that send about homosexuality?

Similarly, 'I'm so lame' implies uselessness more than it does an uneven gait.

Language has repercussions. It doesn't exist in a vacuum, and it both shows a society's beliefs and helps to shape them. Often, people use the argument that 'everyone says it' – as if the majority are never wrong. Newsflash: fifty years ago 'working like niggers' was a socially acceptable saying in regular use. Were the people who fought against its use wrong to do so? Probably when that phrase first began to drop from common parlance, many people said: 'Oh, how ridiculous: it's not meant in a derogatory way.' Yet now, few people would deny it is racist. The language of the time demonstrated society's feelings about racial differences; changing the use of language helped to change opinions.

I'm sure people who use phrases such as 'how short-sighted' or 'turn a deaf ear' don't intend to degrade people with disabilities, and would be offended if it were suggested that they were doing so. However, the regular use of disablist language has a drip-drip effect. A drop of water spilt onto a rock doesn't wear away the stone – yet a steady drip of water has, over time, precisely this effect. Each word which devalues the life or experiences of disabled people is like a drip of water adding to society's unspoken, and probably unconscious, feeling that disability lessens a person's worth.

Restrictions on change

While the pace of language change is probably quicker than it has ever been before, with digital technology allowing people to communicate across huge distances very quickly, it is perhaps surprising that English isn't changing more than it does. One key reason for this is that English has a widely recognized standard form which allows a high degree of intelligibility between English users. Standard English is not an official language as such, but a widely accepted dialect of English that is used in formal written texts. The existence of a standard form appears to offer a core for English, so the innovations around the periphery of the language – new words, meanings and sounds – can continue to alter without having a significant impact on the core.

However, different varieties of English exist around the UK and beyond, in areas where English is spoken as a first or second language, or as a lingua franca, and a major topic of discussion in this field is the continuing role of a form of Standard English and whether there is still the need or even the desire to have a stable and intelligible form of English used everywhere that English is used.

Another limiting factor on the pace of language change is how people feel about it: this is something that will be looked at in more detail in the next section.

Attitudes to language change

The fact that language is debated all around you all the time is good news for you as a student of English Language. What is perhaps less straightforward is how to pick these arguments apart to reveal what motivates them, and that is what this section will look at in more detail. But first, let's look in more detail at how you might analyse such extracts and engage with the idea of language discourses that is central to your study of this topic and others.

Activity

Read through the seven extracts below. All express different ideas about language use and how it is changing or has changed in the past. What do you notice about the key concerns and the language used to articulate them? Are there any subtexts to the views put forward? Can you group them together in any particular ways?

1. 'This is nothing but idiot speak. If you hear your children using it, it means they are brainless morons. Next stop = tattoos, binge drinking & ASBOs.' (Comment on a newspaper website after an article about teenage slang)

2. 'It is the relentless onward march of the texters, the SMS (Short Message Service) vandals who are doing to our language what Genghis Khan did to his neighbours eight hundred years ago. They are destroying it: pillaging our punctuation; savaging our sentences; raping our vocabulary. And they must be stopped. This, I grant you, is a tall order. The texters have many more arrows in their quiver than we who defend the old way.' (From an article on texting by John Humphrys in the *Daily Mail*)

3. 'It adds nothing to Britain's language but it's here now, like the grey squirrel, destined to drive out native species and ravage the linguistic ecosystem.' (From an article by Matthew Engel about American English in the UK in the *Daily Mail*)

4. 'You can hear this Jafaican crap on buses, in benefit centres and McDonalds across London - anywhere but where money is earned. As if these kids didn't have little enough chance in life as it is, speaking a patois derived from some of the most pointless countries in the world is hardly going to help.' (From a comment after an article on Multicultural London English in an online newspaper)

5. 'The English language is an incredibly rich inheritance. Yet it is being squandered by so many young people of all races and backgrounds. Across London and other cities it is increasingly fashionable for them to speak in an inarticulate slang full of vacuous words such as "innit" and wilful distortions like "arks" for "ask" or tedious double negatives.' (From an article by Lindsay Johns in the *London Evening Standard*)

6. 'If you allow standards to slip to the stage where good English is no better than bad English, where people turn up filthy… at school… all those things tend to cause people to have no standards at all, and once you lose standards then there's no imperative to stay out of crime.' (From Norman Tebbit, former Conservative minister)

7. 'We are plagued with idiots on radio and television who speak English like the dregs of humanity.'

Link

Language in the statements above is being used as a Shibboleth: see Chapter 1 (page 15).

What you might have noticed is that, while the concerns quoted in the Activity above are about how people use language, they are also about many other things – for example, social class, race, money, politics.

One of the important points to establish early on is that in Section B of Paper 2 you are being presented with texts that offer you views about language. Your job is to analyse how these views are being put across to the reader, and to do this you will use many of the skills that you have developed as part of Paper 1. This time, though, you are also being asked to engage in more detail with what is being said about language and to offer a response to it. What kinds of ideas are being signalled about language? What kinds of attitudes are being expressed? Can these be related to any other debates about language?

Extract 1 in the Activity above is a good starting point:

This is nothing but idiot speak. If you hear your children using it, it means they are brainless morons. Next stop = tattoos, binge drinking & ASBOs.

Lexis/semantics: By using a semantic field of crime and anti-social behaviour, the writer immediately makes a connection between language and wrongdoing. Judgements are also being made about intelligence through the use of the terms 'idiot' and 'moron'.

Key term

Clause of condition. A clause introduced by conjunctions such as 'if' or 'unless', suggesting that something will happen only if certain conditions are met.

Grammar: Thinking about the grammar of the extract, you can see that a real sense of certainty is apparent in the first sentence, achieved through the single clause and the lack of modality. There is no hedging using modal verbs (might/ may) or adverbs (perhaps/maybe), just a statement of apparent fact. This certainty is conveyed in the second sentence with a **clause of condition** ('If you hear…') and the main clause following on from this.

Discourse: On a discourse level, the use of a final sentence beginning with 'Next stop' implies a straightforward route from one thing (language use) to another (crime).

Graphology: The use of the signs '=' and '&' also suggests an easy equation and a sense of a writer not willing to waste time on such trivia by writing his comment out fully.

By applying a close analysis of the language used, you can start to make some observations about the attitudes on display, the agenda behind them and the positioning adopted by the writer. But that's not all. By looking at other examples, such as Extract 6, you might also start to see connections.

If you allow standards to slip to the stage where good English is no better than bad English, where people turn up filthy... at school... all those things tend to cause people to have no standards at all, and once you lose standards then there's no imperative to stay out of crime.

This is very similar in its approach – mapping out a connection between 'bad English', low social standards, poor education and crime. It is perhaps more tentative in its style (with the verb phrase 'tend to' suggesting a degree of caution) but the idea is essentially the same.

The other extracts can be looked at using a similar approach. If you can critically analyse the language being used, wider issues start to appear. Why are so many of the writers so worried about the decline and degradation of language? Why are so many of them convinced that young people are at fault? Why do so many of them make a direct link between so-called 'bad English' and low moral standards?

Activity

Focus on the remaining extracts and analyse them using the same frameworks.

There is some feedback on this activity at the back of the book.

Standard and non-standard

Before looking at the arguments about language use, it's important to establish what is being argued about. As outlined above, language is often treated as a proxy battlefield for arguments about many other social issues, but on the surface at least, the debates about language often focus on what is perceived to be 'correct' or 'incorrect' English. These are loaded terms and tend not to be used by linguists, because they carry with them a sense that there is a right and wrong form of English, when the reality is more complex. Instead, linguists tend to talk about language being standard or non-standard.

Standard English has developed as a prestige written dialect of English over several centuries – its growth and form influenced by the power of the South East of England as a centre of trade and political power. While many different regional varieties of English exist, each with their own variations in lexis and grammar, the written variety that has become Standard English is recognizable to most users of English. You explored some of the non-standard varieties of English in Chapter 3.

Standardization – the process of developing and maintaining Standard English – can be broken down into a number of stages: selection, elaboration, codification and implementation.

The *selection* of the East Midlands dialect as the standard was linked to the area's power, particularly the existence of key universities, cathedrals and the capital itself.

The *elaboration* of Standard English involved using this prestige form in an increasing range of functions and roles: government, science and education.

Codification took the form of establishing rules of spelling, drawing up definitions of word meanings and agreeing norms of grammar usage. This last one has remained something of a sticking point ever since, because some of the earliest

Key term

Standardization. The process by which a form of language is developed and used as a common code.

grammarians (the writers of early 'grammars' of English) often turned to Latin for grammar rules, meaning that the realities of English grammar were often not addressed head-on, while many of the other 'rules' were more to do with personal taste than clarity or effective communication.

Having established a standard, *implementation* was then required to control and maintain it. The promotion of Standard English as the prestige form was built up through the publication of books, pamphlets and newspapers, which all made use of it, and often through the dismissal of non-standard forms as inferior or uneducated. In particular, in the 18th century, grammarians were quick to put forward their ideas for the rules of English, and these have been influential on many modern-day prescriptivists.

However, the 'rules' of English are not rules about how English actually works; they are more like a set of conventions, like the rules of etiquette.

Many of the arguments about language that occur now are linked to the changing nature of English – a changing nature that some writers and early language experts wanted to stop. In the early 1700s, the writer Jonathan Swift unsuccessfully called for an 'English Academy' to regulate language use. In compiling his famous dictionary of 1755, Samuel Johnson admitted that his initial plan to write a dictionary that would help regulate and control English, to 'embalm his language, and secure it from corruption and decay' was as pointless as trying to 'lash the wind'. Standard English is still not officially prescribed, but discussed and debated by its users.

Decline, decay and doom

Ever since English has existed as a language, there have been complaints about it changing. Jean Aitchison (2012) reports that 'A 14th century monk complained that the English practised strange stammering, chattering, snarling and grating tooth-gnashing: "strange wlaffyng, chytering, harryng, and garryng grisbittyng"', while in 1909 S. K. Ratcliffe complained that 'The language is going to pieces before our eyes, especially under the influence of the debased dialect of the Cockney' and in a *Times* leader article from 1983 it was claimed that 'As we approach 1984 nobody can ignore the fact that we are on our way both by design and by default to a progressive and irreversible deterioration in the use of language.' Perhaps that is a natural, generational response to seeing things change. After all, we will all see the language that we used as young people change as we get older. Such change might be viewed by some as an inevitable, even positive, process, but seeing and hearing the language that we grew up with change in front of us is likely to cause some kind of reaction. The scale of that reaction can then be multiplied by millions when we think about the sheer number of people who use English and what they see and hear on a daily basis.

A key thread in much of the discussion of language change is that standards of English are slipping. In his 2012 book *You Are What You Speak*, Robert Lane Greene refers to this as **declinism**: a perception that English is in an irreversible decline from a once-great peak. Lesley Milroy described the same thing as a **complaint tradition** when she wrote about Standard English in *Authority in Language* in 1989. The blame for decline and the trigger for complaints is often laid at the door of young people, technology and immigration. But as Greene points out, the picture of decline is an odd one when so many *more* people read and write these days than ever used to in the past. Literacy rates are much *higher* in the 21st century, so where does this perception of decline come from?

Key terms

Complaint tradition. A tradition of complaining about the state of the language.

Declinism. The idea that language is in constant decline.

In a series of important lectures for the BBC in 1996, the linguist Jean Aitchison put forward a set of metaphors for explaining how such perceptions of decline, decay and collapse can exist, and referred to what she called a 'crumbling castle' model. Those with the crumbling castle worldview looked upon English as a language that had reached a peak of perfection, from which it was now in decline. Attacking such a prescriptive view, Aitchison (a descriptivist herself) argued:

> This view itself crumbles when examined carefully. It implies that the castle of English was gradually and lovingly assembled until it reached a point of maximum splendour at some unspecified time in the past. Yet no year can be found when language achieved some peak of perfection, like a vintage wine. The 'beautiful building' notion presupposes that rigid systems, once assembled, are better than changing ones. This is untrue. In the animal world, flexibility is a great advantage, and animals that adhere to fixed systems often lose out. The ever-shifting nature of language keeps it flexible, so it can cope with changing social circumstances…

Along with a sense of decline, many of the concerns expressed about language change and diversity (as exemplified by the quotations at the start of this section) suggest ideas about destruction, conflict, pollution, infection and stupidity. Equally, positive representations of change and diversity tend to use metaphors of evolution, progression and the natural world. These ways of thinking about and describing language become the kinds of language discourses that you will be asked about in Paper 2, Section B of the A level, and you will often see that when writers discuss language they tap into these wider discourses, contextualizing their views in a wider frame of reference.

Greene and Aitchison also outline other models for describing prescriptive views. Greene talks about some commentators' finger-wagging approach as **sticklerism**: the tendency to 'correct' and criticize others' language use, whether it's in need of correction or not. Journalist and broadcaster Lynne Truss is one such stickler, according to Greene, and her popular book on punctuation, *Eats, Shoots and Leaves,* is held up as an example of the kind of book that is designed to make its readers feel bad about their own use of language.

Along with the 'crumbling castle' model mentioned earlier, Aitchison refers to the 'damp spoon' and 'infectious disease' metaphors as ways of explaining prescriptive concerns over language change. The damp spoon is what she describes as some people's 'queasy distaste' for certain usages, like 'seeing a damp spoon dipped in the sugar bowl or butter spread with the bread-knife'. By equating views about language use to wider ideas about manners and social etiquette (even in a rather old-fashioned metaphor about sugar bowls and bread-knives, which younger people might find hard to relate to) Aitchison makes another valuable point about the links between language and social practice: language is closely tied to social customs and its use (or abuse) often presses the same buttons as seeing someone picking their nose in public.

The 'infectious disease' model suggests that many prescriptivists view language change as something harmful that can be transmitted unwittingly from one person to another. Aitchison counters that many forms of change are deliberately picked up by users who make choices over what they want to say and write. To cast change as an infection is also to present it as ultimately harmful and this too is a view that can be challenged.

Link

The text of Aitchison's lecture on 'The Web of Worries' is available here: http://www.independent.co.uk/life-style/reith-lectures-is-our-language-in-decay-1317695.html and the original audio can be found here: http://www.bbc.co.uk/programmes/p00gmvwx

Key terms
Sticklerism. An intrusive concern with correcting others' language use.

Activity

Looking back at the extracts on pages 171–172, can you identify any ways in which the language choices suggest a particular perspective on language change or signal a wider discourse? For example, can you see any extracts which present an idea of decline, erosion or infection?

Describing language

The alternative position to prescriptivism is that of descriptivism. Descriptivists view language change as natural and inevitable, and instead of judging changes as harmful or destructive, tend to describe what these changes are, who uses them and how they come about. Modern linguistics is largely based on this descriptive tradition, and that is why you will rarely find linguists describing a particular use of language as 'wrong' or 'incorrect'. Of course, some ways of using language might be more appropriate in one context than in another (for example, using formal Standard English in a university or job interview, rather than a more colloquial style) and descriptivists are not advocating a free-for-all where there are no standards, but promoting an awareness of different types of language and their value.

Descriptivists look to usage as their guide, rather than artificial rules. If a language feature is regularly used, it cannot be 'wrong'. It might be non-standard and seen as inappropriate for formal usage, but a deficit model is not applied.

It is too simplistic to cast the descriptive versus prescriptive debate as a matter of black and white, where prescriptivists are fussy outdated pedants, bemoaning every shift in language, and descriptivists are open-minded progressives, embracing the inevitable evolution of language, because there are many grey areas. It is probably more accurate to place views along a continuum line:

Prescriptive   Descriptive

One metaphor that might be applied to the debates about language is that of a tug of war: there is always a tension between the forces of innovation and conservatism (change and stability) just as there is always a tension between the views of descriptivists and prescriptivists about what is happening, or should be happening, to language. As in a tug of war, one side may achieve dominance for a while, before the other side pulls them in the opposite direction. In this tug of war, the contest never ends.

 Activity

Using a copy of the above continuum line, indicate how you feel about each of the following examples. How prescriptive or descriptive do you feel about each one? What do you think motivates your feelings for each expression?

1. New blends and compounds (e.g. cronut, spork, photobombing, upcycle)
2. Rising intonation

3. Use of 'like'
4. Different terms to mean 'good' and 'bad'
5. American English vocabulary (e.g. movies, soccer, trash, restroom), and routines such as 'How are you? I'm good', or 'Have a nice day'.

The following newspaper article offers strong views about language in use and is indicative of the kind of texts that you will face in the Paper 2 exam. In the exam you will have two texts rather than one, but the texts will not be in opposition to each other; they may well share the same views but express them differently.

Activity

1. Carefully read the article and try to identify and evaluate:
   - how the writer uses language to present her ideas and express her attitudes
   - how the writer addresses the reader and represents herself
   - how the writer's views fit with what you know about prescriptive and descriptive attitudes to language.
2. Write a response to the Lynne Truss column in which you justify taking a descriptive approach to language study. Use any of the ideas, examples and quotations that you have encountered in this chapter (and/or in any others) in order to argue your case.

Lynne Truss has a grammatical axe to grind

In her weekly column, Lynne Truss argues that if something isn't done about compound words, English is doomed.

So here we are in yet another new year, and I have an especially trivial linguistic point to make. I feel it is time to take note of a lamentable development in written English, which I have decided to blame (mostly) on our effing word-processing software, because that's the kind of girl I am. The other day I received an email that included the oddly pidgin-type sentence: 'It maybe time to act on this.' I puzzled over the grammar of this for quite a while. I tried saying it to myself in a Sitting Bull accent, but I felt that the natural grammar in that case would have been, 'Maybe it's time to act on this', so I was still stumped. Did my correspondent merely mean to write, 'It's maybe time to act on this?' And then I realised that

her computer – ever eager to stick its oar in – had perhaps spotted the word 'may' contiguous with the word 'be' ('It may be time to act on this') and simply rectified the unnecessary space between the words. No sooner had I reached this conclusion than I realised that the true explanation might be even worse: my friend thought 'maybe' was just a quicker and easier way of writing 'may be' – and the English language as we know it was hereby doomed, and we might as well all go off and kill ourselves.

Has anyone else noticed this happening? The compound word has, of course, an honourable tradition, and we would be lost without it. In American English, it has long been standard to write, 'You don't love me anymore' or 'Will you be free anyday soon?' British English, which is highly porous, has adopted this practice unthinkingly – and largely this is a harmless development, because 'anymore' means precisely the same as 'any more'. But there are many existing compound words (such as 'maybe') that have established themselves in the language already, and have quite specific uses. 'Everyday' is a lovely adjective, meaning humdrum, ordinary or unremarkable. 'Anyway' is a useful 'sentence adverb' (I think), by means of which a writer can airily change the subject. 'Throwaway' pertains to remarks uttered sotto voce; 'Comedown' is quite interestingly related to 'comeuppance'. (When I was a child, by the way, I heard the word 'comeuppance' such a lot when we watched TV that I once lisped, 'Will he get his uppings, mummy?' Needless to say, I never lived it down.)

So I think we should be vigilant. We need to be able to write:

'Is there any way you can do this?'

'I will love you every day of my life.'

'That was super natural, in my opinion.'

'I've got no body!'

'One self is better than two.'

'Can I have any one of these?'

'Let's think about some times.'

And so on.

Obviously one hates to be a stick-in-the-mud about English. But occasionally it's important to speak as you find. When I was deeply mired in linguistic debate a few years ago (for which I was seriously unqualified), it became clear to me that the academic study of the English language (and this includes the lexicographers) was entirely concerned with looking cool and broad-minded and 'descriptive', when what was required was some positive action to remedy literacy levels, and so on. A 'descriptive' linguist is one that monitors the changes in language, and in case you think there is any other kind of linguist, there isn't. 'Prescriptive' does exist as a term in linguistic circles, but only as a powerful juju word used against bad people who model themselves on King Canute.

Ooh, I don't usually rant, I'm sorry. But New Year seemed like a good opportunity to let rip for once. It does seem weird to me that we hear all the time about a crisis in literacy, and at the same time there are well-paid academics just sitting back and enjoying the show. Imagine if other academic fields were dominated entirely by a 'descriptive' ethos: we could have 'descriptive' epidemiologists, perhaps, who just sat back with a clipboard and monitored the way we all died from contagious diseases. Or 'descriptive' architects, who collected large salaries for watching and making detailed notes while all the buildings fell down.

The Telegraph 5 January 2014

REVIEW YOUR LEARNING

- How are language diversity and language change connected?
- Give an example of language change from each language level.
- What are 'compounding' and 'blending'?
- What is 'semantic reclamation'?
- Give three reasons why language changes.
- Give three metaphors that people use to express ideas that language is in decline.

References

Aitchison, J. (1996) 'Is our language in decay?' Reith Lectures http://www.independent.co.uk/life-style/reith-lectures-is-our-language-in-decay-1317695.html

Aitchison, J. (2012) *Language Change: Progress or Decay?* (4th edn). Cambridge: Cambridge University Press

Crystal, D. (2011) *A Little Book of Language*. Yale University Press.

Deutscher, G. (2006) *The Unfolding of Language*. London: William Heinemann Ltd

Engel, M. (2010) 'Say no to the get-go! Americanisms swamping English, so wake up and smell the coffee', *Daily Mail*, 29 May http://www.dailymail.co.uk/news/article-1282449/Americanisms-swamping-English-wake

Goddard, A. and Mean, L. (2008) *Language and Gender*, London: Routledge

Hogg, R. and Denison, D. (eds) (2008) *A History of the English Language*. Cambridge: Cambridge University Press.

Hughes, G. 1989, *Words in Time*, Oxford: Blackwell.

Humphrys, J. (2007) 'I h8 txt msgs: How texting is wrecking our language', *Daily Mail*, 24 September, http://www.dailymail.co.uk/news/article-483511/I-h8-txt-msgs-How-texting-wrecking-language.html

Johns, L. (2011) 'Ghetto grammar robs the young of a proper voice', *London Evening Standard*, 16 August http://www.standard.co.uk/news/ghetto-grammar-robs-the-young-of-a-proper-voice-6433284.html

McWhorter, J. (2014). *The Language Hoax: Why the World Looks the Same in Any Language*. Oxford: Oxford University Press.

Ritchie, H. (2013) *English for the Natives: Discover the Grammar You Don't Know You Know*. London, John Murray

Robinson, J. (2010) 'Awesome insights into semantic variation'. In Geeraerts, D, Kristiansen, G and Peirsman, Y (eds.) *Advances in cognitive sociolinguistics. Cognitive Linguistics Research (45)*. Mouton de Gruyter. pp. 85–109

Thorne, S. (2006). *The Language of War*. London: Routledge.

Truss, L. (2014) 'Lynn Truss has a grammatical axe to grind', *The Telegraph*, 5 January http://www.telegraph.co.uk/journalists/lynne-truss/10547372/Lynne-Truss-has-a-grammatical-axe-to-grind.html

Webster, G. (2011) 'Sluts are reappropriating language' http://www.superlinguo.com/post/6208420513/sluts-are-reappropriating-language

White, A., Mann, P. and Rieser, R. *Speaking for Ourselves: A teacher's guide to disability and oral history,* http://worldofinclusion.com/res/scope/Scope_Speaking_for_ourselves_GUIDE.pdf

Further reading

Aitchison, J. (2012) *Language Change: Progress or Decay?* (4th edn) Cambridge, Cambridge University Press

Crystal, D. (2004). *The Stories of English*. London, Penguin.

Deutscher, G. (2006) *The Unfolding of Language*. London, William Heinemann Ltd

Graddol, D., Leith, D., and Goodman, S. (1996). (eds.). *English: history, diversity and change*. London: Routledge, in association with The Open University.

Greene, R.L. (2011) *You Are What You Speak: Grammar Grouches, Language Laws and the Politics of Identity*. New York, Delacorte Press

Hitchings, H. (2011) *The Language Wars: A History of Proper English*. London, John Murray

Trousdale, G. (2012) *Language Change* in D. Clayton (ed.) *Language: a student handbook on key topics and theories*. London, English and Media Centre

This chapter will:

- explain where and how English is used around the world

- help you to understand how this situation came to be and where it might lead

- explore issues around identity, culture and history connected to English use in the world

- explore attitudes to international English and guide you in your analysis of arguments about language.

Relevant Assessment Objectives

As with language change, this topic is examined formally in Paper 2 of the A level (Language Diversity and Change). As you saw in Chapter 5, Paper 2 of the A level specification is in two sections. Section A, Diversity and Change, requires you to write one essay, from a choice of two questions. One question will always be on diversity and one on change.

As noted in Chapter 5, the essay questions will ask you to 'evaluate' an idea. This is because, at A level, you are expected to realize that things are not cut and dried: there are different attitudes to issues of language use. You are also expected to demonstrate your understanding that, in language study, one area is strongly connected with another. You should have become aware of this while working through this book, particularly in Chapters 3 and 5. International English is certainly about diversity, but it is also about change – because the use of English by ever greater numbers of speakers is an aspect of recent history. More will be said about this as the chapter proceeds.

Section A essays are credited via AO1 and AO2:

- AO1 credits your understanding of the language levels and the terms associated with them, plus the coherence of your writing.

- AO2 credits your knowledge of the concepts and issues relevant to the subject area. Language diversity and language change are important concepts, and raise many issues.

International English could also feature as a topic on Paper 2 in Section B (Language Discourses). This is because it is a topic that generates very different views and attitudes, as you will see in this chapter. There are two compulsory questions in this section. The first question asks you to analyse two texts, and your analysis is credited through a range of Assessment Objectives:

- AO1, as above.

- AO3 credits your ability to understand how language features build into patterns of meaning and are shaped by context.

- AO4 credits your ability to move between the texts and make connections between the ideas that they express.

The second question asks you to write an article by using the ideas in the texts and expressing your own views. This is assessed as follows:

- AO2 credits your knowledge of the concepts and issues that you are writing about.

- AO5 credits your writing skills.

How much do you need to know?

International English is a huge topic that academics can spend their whole careers studying. Obviously, at this level you are not expected to know everything about all the diverse forms of English that exist globally; rather, you will be working with very broad ideas. However, it is important to have an understanding of:

- some reasons for the spread of English around the world
- some facts and figures about English use around the world
- some of the linguistic characteristics of different varieties of English around the world (including your own case studies and research into specific varieties)
- how and why English is used around the world in the modern era, and attitudes towards its use
- the key arguments that are raised about the use of English as a global language.

This chapter picks up from where Chapter 3 left off. In that part of the book, you looked at how different individuals, groups and communities use language, and how those different people are represented by language. In this chapter we move away from the UK and out into a world where English is used by many hundreds of millions of people. You will look at how and why English spread around the world to become such a dominant presence, how English has absorbed words from many of the languages that it has come into contact with, and how people feel about English as it spreads around the world and comes back to its place of origin in many different forms.

As with all of the other areas of language change and diversity that you have looked at so far, people have strong feelings about English around the world. There are many who argue that there is no such thing as 'English' any more, but many different 'Englishes'. There are others who argue that if English is allowed to fragment too far into other forms, it will be harder for the world to communicate. Yet others say that even though English may be dominant as a world language now, it may not last very long. Some of these arguments are linguistic but others are more about identity and politics.

You will consider all of these arguments in this chapter and learn more about the background to the spread of English – looking, too, at how arguments about the topic are presented by different writers and commentators.

What's the right label?

The different terms that you might encounter connected with English in the world include the following:

- World Englishes
- English as a lingua franca
- Global English
- International English.

None of these terms is wrong, but they have all come from slightly different traditions. **World Englishes** refers to the different English varieties that have been in existence for some time, which have often arisen because of colonial rule in the past: for example, Singaporean English and Indian English. World Englishes are spoken by large numbers of people in many post-colonial societies, and these varieties have their own distinctive versions of Standard English. 'World Englishes' is a useful label, but it doesn't describe all the contexts for the use of English in the world.

English as a lingua franca (ELF) is a more recent coinage. The term 'lingua franca' was defined in Chapter 1 as a language that speakers have in common,

> **Key term**
>
> **English as a lingua franca.**
> The role of English as a bridging language in interactions where it is not everyone's first language.

where it is no one's first language. This was the case for Latin in medieval Europe, and it is now the case very frequently with English: it can serve as a useful common communication system between speakers of different languages. People using ELF tend not to be in contexts where English is part of the local community, and many ELF conversations are conducted in virtual contexts, where there are no geographical boundaries in any case. The ELF label is useful, but sometimes it can seem to imply that ELF is just one language, when in fact every time people come together their joint use of English will be shaped by each person's skills and repertoire. There can be native speakers in ELF interactions, too. They will be shaping their own language choices to fit the group situation.

Global English blurs the distinctions of the two labels above and represents the extensive scope of English use in modern times. But the label can, again, make it seem as though there is just one unified form of English when there are clearly many. Also, the term 'global' can sometimes make the rise of English sound a little like world domination!

International English can be a useful catch-all phrase to describe all of the above situations, if you think of World Englishes as forms of English that 'went abroad' some time ago. There is nothing wrong with any of the terms above, but you need to be aware that they describe slightly different things, so try to match your choice of term with the situation you are talking about.

How international is English?

Before we look at the use of English in different parts of the world, it is important to recognize the international nature of the English used by native speakers in the UK. This is because when people object to English being used in different parts of the world, sometimes they argue that the English of native speakers is 'pure' and shouldn't be 'corrupted' by people using it in new ways. You saw the way that people use different discourses of this kind in the previous chapter; and both Chapter 1 and Chapter 5 ask you to do etymological work on how some words came into English. Now you need to build on that previous work and think about all of the different languages that have contributed to modern English. You can use this knowledge to counter arguments about the supposed 'purity' of the English language.

Key terms

Global English. The idea of English as a worldwide language.

International English. The idea of English as a language that is used in international contexts of all kinds.

Did you know?

There's a difference between the numbers of native speakers of a language and the total number of its users. In terms of native speakers, there are more native speakers of Mandarin Chinese and of Spanish than there are of English.

Activity

Using a range of online resources and books, try to find five words in modern English that have come from each of the languages, or groups of languages, listed on page 183. For each example, write some notes for yourself about why you think the word was borrowed, and when. Later, if you give an example of such a term when you are writing an essay, you will be able to say something meaningful about it.

If you are working in a group context, you could choose different words and pool your results.

Here are some suggested sources:

- The Oxford English Dictionary at www.oed.com
- The British Library's Changing English site at http://www.bl.uk/learning/langlit/changlang/across/languagetimeline.html

- Yourdictionary.com at http://grammar.yourdictionary.com/word-lists/list-of-english-words-of-foreign-origin.html
- Crystal, D. 2003. *The Cambridge Encyclopaedia of the English Language*. Cambridge: Cambridge University Press
- The ITV Series, *The Adventure of English*, narrated by Melvyn Bragg, covers the history of English in earlier episodes and the international growth of English in later programmes

Language or groups of languages:

- African languages
- Chinese
- German
- Japanese
- Hungarian
- Arabic
- Indonesian
- Hindi or Urdu
- Turkish
- Hebrew

English in the world: some historical background

> The current status of English is unprecedented. Simultaneously, it has a preeminent global role in science, commerce, politics, finance, tourism, sport, and even screen entertainment and popular music. With no challenger comparable to it, it seems almost untouchable…
>
> Nicholas Ostler, *The Last Lingua Franca*

How did English go from being a relatively localized language spoken by between 5 million and 7 million people in 1600 (nearly all of them in the UK) to a language spoken by between 1.5 billion and 2 billion people across at least 75 different global territories in the present day? The answer is both simple – English speakers moved around the world during a period of colonial expansion, global trade and invasion – and more complex.

Is there something about the magpie history of English – its tendency to pick up words from nearly every language that it's come into contact with – that makes it attractive to others? Is there something in its grammar that makes it easier to learn than other languages? Is there anything linguistic at all in the appeal of English, or is it all due to the doors it unlocks into trade, education and popular culture? And, even with its global popularity at an all-time high, will English retain this position in the world or go the same way as other languages, such as Latin in Roman times or Persian from the 11th century, which have occupied similar positions in the past? You will look at some of these ideas and evaluate different explanations as this chapter goes on, but first you will need to look at the key developments involved in English making its way around the world.

Dispersal and migration

One clear way through which we can distinguish between the different ways in which English has spread is to separate them into two distinct categories. In the first category, which includes the first **diaspora** or dispersal, English spread from the British Isles (where it was spoken in England, Wales, Scotland and Ireland) to the areas that are now the USA, Canada, Australia and New Zealand. In these countries, English speakers settled in large numbers and established new **first language (L1)** varieties of English.

Did you know?

In practice, English is the national language of the USA, but it has no official status. At state level, there is considerable variation in the languages that have status. For example, in Louisiana, French has equivalent status to English; in New Mexico, Spanish does.

Key terms

Diaspora. The dispersal of people (and their languages) to different parts of the world.

First language (L1). The first language learned by an individual, usually in childhood.

In the second diaspora, smaller groups of English speakers settled in areas such as South Africa, South Asia and parts of Africa, and the result was very different. In these territories, English was often used as a means of communicating not just between the English settlers and traders and the local people, but also among the local people themselves (many of whom spoke different languages, depending on the area they were from). This meant that English was not an L1 variety but used initially as a lingua franca, then later acquired a degree of power and status, often being adopted as an official language and gaining what is called **L2** status, use as a **second language**.

In terms of numbers, it is often difficult to pin down exactly how many people speak English in each category, but David Crystal (in Denison and Hogg, 2008) estimates that there are around 400 million L1, over 400 million L2 and somewhere between 600 million and 700 million ELF speakers – giving a total of around 1.5 billion speakers of English in some form or other. And this is growing all the time. Sometimes these finer distinctions between L1 and L2 don't work, because they were devised at a time when things were more static, so the phrase **English as an additional language (EAL)** is useful.

The first dispersal of English dates back to the early 17th century, in the case of English settlers moving to the USA and Canada, 1770 to Australia and 1790 to New Zealand; while the second dispersal occurred at various points between the late 15th century in West Africa, 1600 (South Asia, including India and Pakistan) and the late 18th century in South Africa and South East Asia (including Singapore and Malaysia).

The arrival of English in the territories noted above was not a simple case of the language appearing and then becoming widely used. As you might imagine, the arrival of English as a language often coincided with the arrival of people, political power, trade, religion and violence. The relationships between the native populations and the English settlers or traders were often characterized by the use of force and the subjugation of the local people and their languages. Imposing English on newly conquered territories was not just a linguistic decision but a political one too. In many former colonial territories where English is still used – Ghana and India, for example – there are very different opinions about how the use of English should be viewed. Some see it as a reminder of a violent, oppressive colonial regime, while others see it as a useful tool. Some see it as both.

Pidgins and creoles

Along with the two types of dispersal, a rather different process led to what are called **pidgins** and **creoles**. Pidgins are a form of contact language that act as a lingua franca, so are a type of communication adopted by people who share no common language. Unlike other lingua francas (Latin, English, Mandarin Chinese, for example), pidgins are made up of elements of different languages. In the case of the Caribbean, pidgin languages developed because of the history of slavery. During the slave-trade period, in which West African people were forcibly shipped to the USA and Caribbean to work on plantations, the slave-traders found it useful to prevent rebellions and uprisings by dividing the slaves from others who spoke the same language. The slaves, with their wide range of languages, and the mainly English-speaking slavers and sailors, then developed a contact language to communicate. This continued in the Caribbean between the slaves and the plantation owners, so a basic and stripped-down form of communication was developed. The longer it went on, the more the pidgin developed.

Key terms

Pidgin. A trade language, usually not the language of either of the speakers.

Second language (L2). The second language learned by an individual.

Did you know?

The term 'pidgin' is thought to have come from the name of a trade language based in Papua New Guinea, called 'Tok Pisin'.

Once a pidgin becomes a native language – for example, when children are born to pidgin speakers – it develops into a creole and picks up a wider vocabulary and more complex grammar. Creoles can develop very much like other varieties of English around the world (although there are, of course, creoles of other languages such as Dutch, French, Spanish and Arabic too). Jamaican Creole, for example, exists in a range of forms along a continuum from Standard Jamaican English (the **acrolect**) to the **basilect** (most colloquial form) with the **mesolect** in the middle.

Pidgins, and to some extent creoles too, have tended to be viewed by many (including some speakers themselves) as inferior forms of language – 'broken English' as some have called them – but this is an unhelpful deficit view. Pidgins fulfil a communicative need at a given time and change fairly quickly, so they are a practical and functional form of language. Creoles, with their wider range of vocabulary and grammar, often have many of the characteristics of 'full' languages.

> ## Key term
>
> **Acrolect.** A term used to refer to a standard or official language variety in contexts where creole is spoken. A **basilect** is at the other extreme, referring to the most informal style that speakers use. A middle style of language, between standard and colloquial varieties, is termed a **mesolect**.

Activity

Prepare – preferably with a partner – a short case study on one particular variety of World English from the list below. Try to find and present information on the origins of English in that territory, the development of the language there, its key linguistic characteristics, and its current status. Include as much information as you can find on the other languages that are spoken there.

- USA
- Canada
- Hong Kong
- Singapore
- New Zealand
- Nigeria
- Australia
- Pakistan
- Cameroon
- Jamaica
- India
- Kenya
- Zimbabwe

Models of World Englishes

While the history and development of English in countries around the world is largely straightforward to understand, the models for explaining the relationship between English in the UK and English elsewhere can be quite contentious.

One of the problems has been that visual representations, like language, are never neutral. A frequent way of representing different Englishes around the world has been via concentric circles, where native speaker English is in the centre, World Englishes are on an outer ring, and all other (more recent) developments of English as a lingua franca appear furthest away. This kind of representation was originally devised by a linguist called Braj Kachru (1992), as a way of sorting the different Englishes into groups. This was important to do at the time, because all of the different types of English were being lumped together, and newer varieties were being seen as deficient. You will see this kind of representation in many books and articles. However, the problem with it is that it can suggest a kind of in-group privilege in being in the 'inner circle', with those on the periphery furthest away from the 'real thing'. Are native speakers really at the heart of the language – from which everything else derives? Many changes are happening to English a long way away from England – and over which UK English speakers have no control.

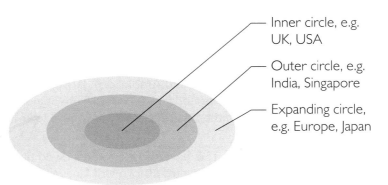

Inner circle, e.g.
UK, USA

Outer circle, e.g.
India, Singapore

Expanding circle,
e.g. Europe, Japan

Kachru's 'Circles of English' model ▶

Kachru has since revised his original model by breaking the circles apart and having them as overlapping rings. Meanwhile, there are many other representations that you could think about and research.

Activity

Find some further diagrammatic representations of different Englishes online and evaluate their representations. A good place to start is Google images, which will offer you many examples and then take you through to particular pages where each diagram appeared. Here are some starting points for locating and thinking about different kinds of representation:

- Search for 'McArthur's Circle of World Englishes' on Google images.

This is very comprehensive looking – but is there really such a thing as 'World Standard English'? If so, what is it?

In Google images you will see many further options, including Kachru's overlapping circles. Are there any other kinds of representations? Here are some more ideas:

- Search for 'English as an International Language Modiano' on Google images.

Modiano (1999) proposed putting English as an international language (EIL) in the centre of the diagram, with the different Englishes around the edge having equal status. But does this tell us anything about the connections between the varieties?

- Search for 'Spread of English According to Strevens' on Google images.

Strevens (1980) represents Englishes using 'family tree' structures. Is this an improvement on the idea of circles, or not?

Choose two different representations from your searches and write an analysis of how they compare. What are some of the positive and negative aspects of each? If possible, present your findings to your classmates.

The representations that you have looked at so far are based on geographical regions. But there are other representations that focus more on language users' own experiences, and on the process by which varieties of English become established in a region or country. For example, the model opposite (adapted from Schneider, 2007), considers how **post-colonial** varieties of English have evolved, so time is important as a factor here, along with a range of other social and political considerations.

Key term

Post-colonial. The time since former colonies gained their independence.

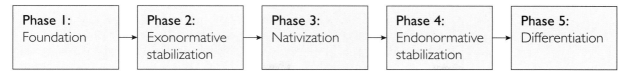

| Phase 1: Foundation | Phase 2: Exonormative stabilization | Phase 3: Nativization | Phase 4: Endonormative stabilization | Phase 5: Differentiation |

Schneider's dynamic model

In each of the stages, Schneider considers how a new variety of English develops, from the foundation stage, in which English first appears in a new territory, through to the stage of **exonormative** stabilization, where English begins to be used. At this stage, the English speakers in the country still look outside (hence *exo*normative) for the norms and standards of their English variety. After a period of nativization, in which the old and new languages become more closely linked, there follows a stage of **endonormative** stabilization, often when the country has gained independence and the English being spoken there has developed its own sense of standards and norms (hence *endo*normative). The final stage of differentiation involves the new variety developing its own regional and social differences.

Key terms

Endonormative. Looking within the immediate community for the norms of language use.

Exonormative. Looking beyond the immediate community for the norms of language use.

Activity

Below is an article by Afua Hirsch of *The Guardian* on different views about English in Ghana. Read the article and then:

- summarize the different opinions put forward in the article by Kofi Agyekum, Delalorm Semabia and Kofi Amenyo

- explain how these factors seem to influence the development of English in Ghana: popular culture, politics and education

- see if you can apply or relate any of the models for World Englishes to the views in the text.

Ghana calls an end to tyrannical reign of the Queen's English

Voice of colonialism gives way to local form of English that's 'flexible and fun' as opposed to giving language 'a good beating'

Question: 'Have you eat?' Reply: 'No I go eat after small small.' This is just one of the turns of phrase Ghanaians employ, in the words of one local commentator, 'to give the Queen's English a good beating'.

But as Ghanaians join their West African neighbours – following the examples of Nigerian Pidgin and Sierra Leonean Krio – in speaking their inherited colonial tongue with growing creative licence, a row is breaking out about what really is the proper way to speak English.

On one side of the fence are the old-school Ghanaians who were taught throughout their education to mimic received pronunciation – or BBC English, as it is popularly known – with varying degrees of success.

On the other side, a backlash is growing against the old mentality of equating a British accent with prestige. Now the practice has a new acronym, LAFA, or 'locally acquired foreign accent', and attracts derision rather than praise.

'In the past we have seen people in Ghana try to mimic the Queen's English, speaking in a way that doesn't sound natural. They think it sounds prestigious, but frankly it sounds like they are overdoing it,' said Professor Kofi Agyekum, head of linguistics at the University of Ghana.

'There has been a significant change now, away from those who think sounding English is prestigious, towards those who value being multilingual, who would never neglect our mother tongues, and who are happy to sound Ghanaian when we speak English.'

Ghana has nine indigenous languages that are officially sponsored by the government, including Akan languages spoken widely in the south. A further 26 languages are officially recognised and at least double that number are also spoken. Unlike its francophone neighbours, which were forced under colonialism to teach only in French, Ghana has always maintained the use of African languages in its primary school education.

But the idea that sounding 'British' carries prestige also has a long history in Ghanaian society, manifesting itself in the country's struggle for independence in the 1940s and 50s, when an ideological difference emerged between an Oxbridge-educated Ghanaian elite and more radical, left-leaning leaders.

Now, more than 50 years later and more than 200 years after the abolition of the slave trade saw an influx of Christian missionaries imposing British language and literature, Ghanaians are embracing a new standard: Ghanaian English.

'The idea that intelligence is linked to English pronunciation is a legacy from colonial thinking,' said Delalorm Semabia, 25, a Ghanaian blogger. 'People used to think that if you speak like the British then you are as intelligent as the British. But now we are waking up to the fact that we have great people here who have never stepped outside the borders.'

'The best example of Ghanaian English on the international scene is [former UN secretary general] Kofi Annan's clear diction,' said Ghanaian columnist Kofi Amenyo. 'The man maintains the Ghanaian features in his pronunciation and yet succeeds in being easily understood by the peoples of the world.'

For Ghana's younger generation, though, the move towards Ghanaian English is less about elder statesmen, and more about music and technology.

'In the 90s many local artists wanted to sound like Usher or Jay-Z, but now they are taking local names and branding themselves locally,' said Semabia. 'Little by little, people are embracing the use of our own languages – for example, now we can Google in Akan.

'For us, English is our language – we want to break away from the old strictures, to personalise it, mix it with our local languages, and have fun with it. The whole point of language is that it's supposed to be flexible and it's meant to be fun.'

Afua Hirsch, *The Guardian*,
10 April 2012

Link

Chapter A4 of Jennifer Jenkins' *World Englishes: A resource book for students* offers a more detailed survey of variation around the world.

How English varies around the world

Applying your knowledge of the language levels introduced in Chapter 1 and developed in Chapter 3 (particularly when looking at different regional and social varieties of English) will also help you in thinking about some of the key variations between different forms of English around the world. There will, of course, be some variation within these countries, as there is in the UK itself, but some of the key patterns are outlined below.

Phonology

A common difference among many English speakers is the accent they have. As you have already seen, there is a range of accents around the UK and it's therefore not a surprise to find many different accents around the world. There are also many phonological features of English that vary from variety to variety around the world.

One common feature is the pronunciation of the sounds /θ/ and /ð/ in words such as 'mouth' and 'that'. Jamaican English speakers, for instance, often pronounce 'thing' as 'ting' and 'this' as 'dis'. Indian speakers of English sometimes use distinctive types of the consonants /t/ and /d/, called **retroflex** – pronounced with the tip of the tongue curled back. Another common consonant variation – most often heard in Hong Kong or Singapore – is the similarity in sound between /r/ and /l/, so words such as 'low' and 'row' would sound the same. This is because the sounds are perceived as variants of the same phoneme, rather than as different phonemes.

Vowel sounds, too, vary around the world. As Jenkins explains, many New Englishes do not differentiate between short and long vowels, so the vowel sounds in 'sit' /sɪt/ and 'seat' /siːt/ are different in English RP but would be rendered as the short sound in Nigerian or Ghanaian English. Many English words include the use of the **schwa** sound /ə/, the unstressed vowel that occurs at the end of the word 'butter', which would be this in RP: /bʌtə/ and this if you have a northern accent: /bʊtə/. The schwa would be replaced by the full vowel sound /bʌtɜː/ in some forms of African English.

Another pattern in phonology is determined by whether the speaker's native language is **stress-timed** or **syllable-based**. English is widely viewed as having a stress-timed intonation. This means that speakers place a stress on a syllable after a certain amount of time has passed. Syllable-based languages such as French, Yoruba and Hindi have a pattern in which all syllables are given the same regular stress. If you know more than one language then this will be something that you have learned, perhaps without even being aware of it. Even if you don't know any languages other than English, you will still be aware that in an utterance such as 'How are you doing?' in which each of the syllables is not given the same amount of stress, you will emphasize the first syllable in *doing*. If you try giving each syllable the same amount of emphasis, you will sound rather unnatural. Just changing the syllabic stress within a word can make it difficult to understand: for example, try saying 'tomato' with a stress on the first or third syllables rather than the second.

The result of all this on different world varieties of English can sometimes be challenging. Knowing the words and the grammar doesn't always mean that clear communication will take place between two speakers of different varieties of English.

Vocabulary

As you have already seen, English has borrowed a huge number of words from other languages, and it is no surprise to find that users of different world Englishes often mix English with their native tongues, sometimes taking an English word and adding an ending. An example is the Hindi English word *filmi* to describe something dramatic (as in a film). An example of a compound of two English words that reflects an existing local concept is the Hindi *air dash* (a fast local flight). Also, local language terms may be used unchanged, interspersed in an otherwise English conversation.

Another area of vocabulary is where different meanings exist for the same word in other English-speaking countries. If you were to hear an Australian say he had to take off his thong, would you be confused and worried? An Australian 'thong' generally means what UK English speakers might refer to as a 'flip-flop' rather than an item of underwear. In the case of American English, you are probably very familiar with some semantic differences.

Link

There is some evidence that syllable-based languages are having an impact on some patterns of speech in the UK, specifically that of Multicultural London English (MLE), which you looked at in Chapter 3.

Key terms

Retroflex. A particular way of producing the sounds /t/ and /d/ with the tip of the tongue curled back and touching the roof of the mouth.

Schwa. The sound /ə/, sometimes called the middle or central vowel in English because of where it is produced in the mouth.

Stress-timed. Intonation that is based on applying stress at regular intervals.

Syllable-based. Intonation that is spread across syllables evenly.

Activity

Partner up each UK English term on the left with the correct US English term on the right.

UK English	US English
Flat	Cookie
Wardrobe	Suspenders
Biscuit	Zucchini
Lift	Potato chips
Tap	Movie
Petrol	Apartment
Post	Elevator
Film	Truck
Trousers	Sidewalk
Crisps	Gas
Toilet	Mail
Pavement	Faucet
Braces	Restroom
Lorry	Pants
Courgette	Closet

Perhaps a less obvious area of vocabulary use is that of idiom. In Chapter 3, mention was made of the research by Kim and Elder into misunderstandings between Korean pilots and air-traffic staff when communicating with their American colleagues. The use of idiomatic expressions ('take a rain check', 'get a heads up', 'I was gutted') often relies on a shared cultural background or understanding which cannot always be assumed in interactions between people from different countries, whether or not they speak English fluently in other ways. Interestingly, it is perhaps the native English speakers who have the problem here. This is a point we will return to when we look at Jennifer Jenkins' idea of a 'lingua franca core' at the end of this section.

Grammar

Differences in syntax are perhaps less pronounced than those for morphology when looking at grammar in different world varieties of English. This is probably because a shared syntax is still something that is required to maintain a core of intelligibility to most English constructions. Endings of words tend to be the features that are different, however. Some of these include:

- not marking plural endings on nouns (e.g. 'she has two shoe')
- not marking agreement in third-person verbs (e.g. 'he walk ten miles to college')
- limited marking of past tense (e.g. 'he walk here yesterday')
- using present progressive forms on verbs that wouldn't normally take them in UK English (e.g. 'she is a very good footballer, I am thinking').

There are many more individual differences in world varieties of English, which you can explore in more detail as part of a case study, as suggested earlier in the chapter; there is a wealth of accessible further reading. Material aimed at learners of English can also offer insights into some of the areas that may cause particular difficulty. For example, prepositions in English can often be complex or idiomatic and, to compound the problem, can vary a lot between UK regions as well.

The lingua franca core

Jennifer Jenkins suggests that – given the huge range of variations found in New Englishes around the world – the focus for English teaching should be on those features that most affect the intelligibility of speakers. Do all potential English speakers around the world want to learn the types of English spoken in the UK? Are there some aspects of the English spoken in the UK that are not needed by speakers of English as a lingua franca?

Jenkins has identified some elements that she judges as essential for intelligibility and others that are seen as peripheral. Most consonant sounds (except for /θ/ and /ð/) and the contrast between long and short vowel sounds (as in the difference between bɪt and biːt) are seen as important, while word stress and stress timing are not judged as being so significant. To the purist, these accommodations towards foreign speakers of English might be seen as a degrading of standards, but in reality, how significant are they?

Attitudes to English in the world

> The English... have as much control over English as the Italians have over pizza and Indians over chicken korma.
>
> Anonymous *Daily Telegraph* message board commentator

> How English develops in the world is no business whatever of native speakers in England, or the United States, or anywhere else. They have no say in the matter, no right to intervene or pass judgement. They are irrelevant.
>
> Widdowson, quoted in Zamel et al (2002)

Whatever the views of the commentators above, and regardless of the facts of English usage around the world, many people have very strong opinions about how English should be used. In this section, you will look at some of the language discourses around World Englishes, and build on your work from Chapter 5 to consider how to analyse, evaluate and respond to such views.

Alternative views

One of the first distinctions to make about opinions on English usage is that there is often quite a big difference between what the general public have to say about the issue and what academics think. Public discourses – particularly in the UK – often represent the English language as the property of the English people, and the foreign users of it – be they Americans, Nigerians or Indians – as imperfect borrowers of 'our' language. As A level English Language students, it's important for you to have the linguistic skills to analyse, evaluate and perhaps challenge such views, but to do so you will need to understand the academic discourses too.

Link

Look back at the grammar part of Section 3.2, Language and Region, to remind yourself about some of the variations within the UK.

Link

Many of the other features of the lingua franca core and arguments about it are identified in Setter (2012) and Jenkins (2009).

David Crystal suggests three different views about the ways in which English is developing around the world, and what might happen to it in the future: his own and those of Graddol and McArthur. Crystal's own view is that the momentum of English's growth has become 'so great that there is nothing likely to stop its continued spread as a global lingua franca'. He characterizes Graddol's view as being rather different: 'the current global wave of English may lose momentum'. McArthur's view is that English is going through such radical change around the world that it is fragmenting into 'a family of languages'.

Another view is that of the linguist Nicholas Ostler who postulates that English will go the same way as other powerful languages in history. He argues that as American and British power declines around the world, English will lose its pre-eminent role. Not only that, but instead of another language taking its place, technology will intervene, allowing us to translate any language into any other language, so that 'everyone will speak and write in whatever language they choose, and the world will understand'.

A different perspective again comes from the linguist Mario Saraceni. He challenges the idea that English has 'spread' from England to the wider world, and instead prefers to describe it as a 'relocation' of English. Saraceni argues that the very notion of 'spread' presupposes a 'centre–periphery' relationship between the 'inner circle' and 'expanding circle', one that he sees as problematic. By relocating and 'de-Anglicizing' English, 'the psychological umbilical cord' between England and English around the world is cut and people wherever they are – India, Malaysia, the USA or England – can do what they want with the language. Practically speaking, what does this mean? At the most basic level, it means that the books that English is taught from should get rid of their pictures of 'red double-decker buses or post-boxes', for a start.

 Activity

The following article by Michael Erard in *New Scientist* magazine in 2008 outlines a number of different academics' and linguists' views on the future of English. Try to summarize in your own words the key points from each of the following people mentioned in the article:

- David Graddol
- Jürgen Beneke
- Braj Kachru
- Paul Bruthiaux
- Jean Paul Nerrière
- Jennifer Jenkins
- Barbara Seidlhofer
- David Deterding
- Lisa Lim
- Suzette Haden Elgin
- Mark Pagel

English As She Will Be Spoke

Our language is evolving fast. How will it sound in 500 years, asks Michael Erard

The ghosts of English past are useful for predictions, but to get a full sense of where English is going we must also consider the ghosts of English present. The future depends heavily on where influences are coming from. For the foreseeable future, the most dramatic changes will be made by people learning English as a second language. 'The new language which is rapidly ousting [that] of Shakespeare as the world's lingua franca is English itself – English in its new global form,' wrote David Graddol, a language researcher and managing director of The English Company in a 2006 report for the British Council.

This means that the dominance of English won't be overturned by other world languages such as Chinese or Spanish. Instead, the new global form of English is already becoming a loose grouping of local dialects and English-based lingua francas used by non-native speakers to communicate with each other. The vast majority of interactions in English are between non-native speakers – as many as 80 per cent, according to Jürgen Beneke of the University of Hildesheim in Germany. Graddol predicts that by 2010 there may be 2 billion people on the planet speaking English, of whom only 350 million will be native speakers. By 2020 the number of native speakers will have declined to around 300 million. At that point English, Spanish, Hindi-Urdu and Arabic are predicted to have an equal number of native speakers.

Whether they are local creoles (such as Singaporean English, which combines English with Chinese, Tamil and Malay) or regional Englishes (such as the English used on the European mainland), non-native Englishes are already becoming less intelligible to each other. This fragmentation happens to all languages, says Braj Kachru, professor emeritus at Ohio State University in Columbus, who is one of the world's pre-eminent scholars of English as a world language. 'There have always been mutually unintelligible dialects of languages such as Arabic, Chinese, Hindi and Latin,' he says. 'There is no reason to believe that the linguistic future of Englishes will be different.'

Paul Bruthiaux of Asian University in Chonburi, Thailand, agrees. 'Even when spoken by highly educated speakers addressing the international media in television interviews, for example, Kenyan, Indian or Singaporean speakers are difficult to understand, largely for reasons related to the way their English is stressed,' he says.

Bruthiaux writes persuasively that one strength of English is that the English-speaking world does not have a central standards body, as French has its Académie Française. Without a language police, the norms of English native speakers will become less important to the language's evolution. The reality of English is that its future is on the tongues of non-native speakers, says Jean Paul Nerrière, a French former IBM executive who worked in Japan in the 1980s and 1990s, and discovered that his Japanese counterparts were more comfortable conversing in English with him than with native speakers. 'I was speaking a kind of English they could understand,' he says.

He named what they spoke 'Globish', and reckons that it has a basic vocabulary of 1500 words. Nerrière is working on a book of Globish for native English speakers, in which he warns us to speak in simple sentences and avoid idioms. But he is not advocating that non-native speakers take over; native speakers should still make the rules. 'I'm not saying the trend is towards 'Me, Tarzan, you Jane' English,' Nerrière says. 'We want to speak simple English, but correct English.'

This suggests that English may follow the path not of Latin but of Arabic, a language that was spread with Islam over 500 years and evolved into multiple local dialects, the speakers of which all feel united by the literary Arabic of the Koran. What may keep the world of English from dissolving entirely into mutual unintelligibility is scientific and technical writing, as well as worldwide media.

Realistically, though, the English of the future will probably look and sound like some stripped-down forms of English that are already around. Already, non-native speakers are stripping out parts of English that cause misunderstandings with other non-native speakers, regardless of what native speakers think about the changes. 'If you heard me talking with a Chinese citizen or a guy from Valparaiso [in Chile], you might think we were not talking in English,' Nerrière says. 'But you'd be surprised how easy it is between us – and how inhibiting it is when an anglophone shows up. Everyone freezes.' Jennifer Jenkins, a linguist at the University of Southampton, UK, studies the mispronunciations of non-native English speakers to see which ones create communication problems. These stumbles need to be fixed, but she says that English teachers may some day decide not to fix others that don't cause problems. As a result, it's easy to see how certain sounds may eventually drop from the English that is used as a lingua franca. Jenkins's findings make Marckwardt's predictions about English consonants seem absurdly conservative. For instance, she finds that the 'th' sounds of 'thus' and 'thin' are often dropped and replaced with either 's' and 'z', or 't' and 'd.' Another consonant that causes problems is the 'l' of 'hotel' and 'rail', which is often replaced with a vowel or a longer 'l' sound as in 'lady.'

What's more, clusters of consonants are simplifying, surviving intact at the beginnings of words but vanishing elsewhere. You may hear 'frien' and 'sen' for 'friend' and 'send'. It may become common to hear 'succeed' as 'suss-see' and 'accept' as 'assep', and teachers may even promote those pronunciations once they recognize that their students may never have a conversation with a native English speaker.

A similar set of observations has been made by Barbara Seidlhofer, a linguist at the University of Vienna in Austria, who also studies verbal interactions between non-native English speakers. She notes that they don't distinguish between mass nouns (like 'information' and 'furniture') and countable nouns (like 'ball' and 'onion'); some day it may be reasonable to talk about 'informations' and 'furnitures.' The conflation of types of nouns 'is extremely common in new varieties of English around the world', agrees David Deterding, a linguist at Brunei Darussalam University in Brunei, who studies Singaporean English.

If you're a proficient speaker of English, you may look on these new forms with horror, thinking: they're not changing English, they're ruining it. But Latin wasn't ruined in a day. It changed slowly over generations, sound by sound, word by word, and people probably complained about every step. Alternatively, you might consider that new speakers are actually making the language more streamlined and consistent. Only native speakers are attached to exceptions, anyway.

For instance, the third-person singular (such as 'she runs' or 'he writes') is the only English verb form that adds an -s at the end. Seidlhofer has found non-native speakers often drop this -s. They also simplify verb phrases, saying 'I look forward to see you tomorrow' instead of 'I am looking forward to seeing you tomorrow'. And they overuse some prepositions as in 'emphasise on' and 'discuss about', which come from the phrases 'emphasis on' and 'discussion about'.

All this means that English is under more pressure to change, from more directions, than Latin or Arabic ever were. Rather than look for single factors that have the biggest impact, Lisa Lim, a linguist at the University of Amsterdam, the Netherlands, who studies the evolution of Singaporean English, stresses what she calls the 'ecology of language'. This allows you to consider all the sources of change, from predictable ones (such as the speed at which irregular verbs become regular) to complex, unpredictable external events such as wars, migrations or the rise of rival global languages like Mandarin. The Internet looms large in this ecology, as does the direction of the world economy.

Suzette Haden Elgin, an American linguist and science fiction writer, says: 'I don't see any way we can know whether the ultimate result of what's going on now will be Panglish – a single English that would have dialects but would display at least a rough consensus about its grammar – or scores of wildly varying Englishes all around the globe, many or most of them heading toward mutual unintelligibility.' How long will it take for us to know which path English is on? 'My guess – a wild guess – is less than 100 years. How much less, I can't say.'

A recent paper in *Science* (vol 319, p 588) suggests that Elgin may be right. A team of mathematical biologists led by Mark Pagel of the University of Reading, UK, found that when a new language splits from its mother language, such as the divergence of Proto-Polynesian from Proto-Fijian in around 1500 BC, it generally undergoes a burst of rapid change in its vocabulary. All over the world this abrupt 'punctuational' change is occurring with local Englishes, and the shifts are occurring quickly enough to be visible in a human lifetime. The future of English is taking shape right now, in the mouths of billions of people who grew up speaking something else.

New Scientist, 29 March 2008

The public discourses about English in the World are often less subtle, reflecting the view that people can feel resentful about new users of English having rights of 'ownership'.

Activity

A flavour of this strength of opinion can be seen in the three extracts below, which are online responses to an article in the *Daily Mail* about the future of English around the world. The article drew on Mario Saraceni's views about 'de-Anglicizing' English which suggested that the language will be used however its users see fit.

You can read the original article at http://www.dailymail.co.uk/news/article-2056444/Dont-teach-Queens-English-foreign-language-students-linguist-urges.html

Using the skills of critical language analysis suggested in Chapter 5, analyse the three responses and decide:

- how the writers use language to express their views about the subject matter
- how the writers use language to position themselves and their audience
- how the views fit into (or challenge) wider discourses about language
- how you feel about the issues yourself.

Utter nonsense. I've taught English as a second language to many people and they all wanted to speak 'proper' English, English they could use in the UK and anywhere else they needed to use it. This is typical dumbing down by someone with too much time on his hands and a patronising attitude towards those who wish to learn English.

XXXX, Cambridge, 3/11/2011 01:03

If we do as this 'expert' suggests then all sorts of variations will appear and the ability to communicate will be lessened, not improved. Take regional dialects and variations within the UK alone. It can be hard to understand our fellow Brits at times!!! What a load of nonsense again from a so called expert...

XXXX, 2/11/2011 8:50

Err.... and his country of origin is? How dare he tell us how to speak and to abandon the correct usage of our beautiful language simply to dumb down and pander to those too lazy to speak it properly! I wonder how many French/Italian/Spanish academics would urge their country to speak sloppily! !!....Nul!

XXXX, Eastbourne, November 2011

Not all viewpoints are expressed in such strident terms as those in the *Daily Mail*. There are examples of public discourse that take a different, more humorous approach.

 Activity

Read the article below, which is from *The Times* in 2004, and:

- identify the views of the writer
- analyse the ways in which the author uses playful language to express his views
- evaluate the use of humour here: is it more or less effective than a serious approach? Give reasons for your answer.

Hold on to your arse

This perfectly good English word is under threat from a US import. Brandon Robshaw won't take it sitting down

In recent days I've twice seen the word arse replaced by the trashy American import ass, both times in broadsheet newspapers. This is an error we are growing more and more accustomed to seeing. And it's worse than just a misspelling. Ass is not merely pronounced differently — even in parts of the UK where a short 'a' is sounded, such as Scotland and the North of England, arse rhymes with 'farce', not 'gas'. No, the point is that ass is actually a different word.

As the writer Anthony Burgess has pointed out, 'ass' was originally a mealy-mouthed euphemism. Puritanical American colonists couldn't bring themselves to utter the a-word, so opted instead for an inoffensive synonym for donkey. Obviously, though, ass is not a euphemism any more. Over the years, or centuries, it has acquired connotations of its own and now sounds far lewder than the word it was supposed to replace. Arse is rude, but ass is dirty. Hearing the word 'ass' in its original sense now tends to cause something of a double-take. Biblical stories involving asses make one feel slightly uneasy, and Bertie Wooster, when describing this or that acquaintance as 'a silly ass', sounds incongruously foul-mouthed.

For reasons best known to themselves, Americans have an obsession with the bottom, and ass is used in contexts where the British equivalent would never be considered. It can refer to 'women' ('He's out chasing ass every night'); life ('He saved my ass back there'); or reputation, position or personal safety ('My ass is on the line here'). It can be used as a suffix to intensify insults ('dumbass, stupidass') or simply to spice up ordinary utterances and make them sound more offensive ('You can kiss my ass goodbye' instead of 'I'm off'). We say half-baked, they say half-assed, and so on.

Not that there is anything wrong with this, if you happen to be American. All countries have their own pet ways of swearing. The French think prostitutes are rude. The Spaniards always have to drag your mother into it. If the Americans want to say ass all the time, then why not? That's up to them. The question is, why should the American usage be creeping into British English when we have a perfectly good word of our own? One reason must be the prevalence of American or American-influenced spellchecks. If you type 'arse' in Microsoft word format, you will invariably get a squiggly line under it, and many people obey the spellcheck without thinking. A more potent reason is probably the glamour of Americanisms. People choose the US form more or less consciously because it sounds rougher, raunchier, more down and dirty. Arse belongs to the domain of pantos and seaside postcards; whereas ass is the stock-in-trade of colourful lowlife characters in Scorsese and Tarantino films.

This is one example of American hegemony we must resist. Not the worst or the most pressing case, but one that it is both possible and worthwhile to fight. When you tinker with the swearing system of a language, you tinker with its soul. Arse is an ancient word, dating back to Chaucer ('with his mouth he kissed hir naked ers') and beyond. To my ears, at any rate, it is a funnier, friendlier and, in its own way, sexier word than its US replacement. It is often said that you can't arrest linguistic change; Dr Johnson conceded in the preface to his dictionary that 'fixing the language'

was impossible. While in broad terms this is true, there is no reason in the case of a specific word why a rearguard action (no pun intended) can't be fought successfully.

It's clear that the Americanisation of English will proceed apace. We're going to lose 'programme' in favour of 'program', and the verb 'practise' is going to be noun-ised into 'practice', and 'schedule' will soon be universally pronounced with a hard 'c', and we'll all be saying and writing 'bagels' instead of 'beigels'. That much seems inevitable. But with a little conscious effort from writers, both amateur and professional, and from sub-editors, can't we hang on to our arses?

The Times 31 July 2004

REVIEW YOUR LEARNING

- What different situations do the labels 'World Englishes' and 'English as a lingua franca' describe?

- Identify some words in English that have come from different languages, and explain their origins.

- Give two reasons why English has spread around the world.

- What are pidgins and creoles?

- Outline one variety of World English in as much detail as you can.

- Identify and outline the views of two academics about English in the world.

References

Hogg, R and Denison, D (eds). (2008). *A History of the English Language*. Cambridge, Cambridge University Press.

Schneider, E. (2007). *Postcolonial English: Varieties around the world*. Cambridge: Cambridge University Press.

Erard, M. (2008) 'English As She Will Be Spoke', *New Scientist*, 29 March

Hirsch, A. (2012) 'Ghana calls an end to tyrannical reign of the Queen's English', *The Guardian*, 10 April http://www.theguardian.com/world/2012/apr/10/ghana-calls-end-queens-english

Jenkins, J. (2009) *World Englishes: a resource book for students*. London: Routledge

Kachru, B.B. (1992) 'Teaching World Englishes' in B.B. Kachru (ed.) *The Other Tongue: English Across Cultures*, 2nd edition, Urbana, IL: University of Illinios Press.

McArthur, T. (1998) *The English Languages*, Cambridge: Cambridge University Press

Modiano, M. (1999). 'International English in the Global Village', *English Today*, 15, 2, 22-27.

Ostler, N. (2010) *The Last Lingua Franca*. London: Allen Lane

Robshaw, B. (2004) 'Hold on to your arse', *The Times* 31 July

Strevens, P. (1980). *Teaching English as an International Language*. Oxford: Pergamon Press.

Zamel, V and Spack, R. (2002). *Enriching Esol Pedagogy*. London: Routledge.

Further reading

Crystal, D. (1997) *English as a Global Language*. Cambridge: Cambridge University Press

Jenkins, J. (2009) *World Englishes: a resource book for students*. London: Routledge

Omoniyi, T. (2010) *Language and Postcolonial Identities: An African Perspective* in Llamas, C. & Watt, D. *Language and Identities*. Edinburgh: Edinburgh University Press

Ostler, N. (2010) *The Last Lingua Franca: the rise and fall of world languages*. London: Allen Lane

Saraceni, M. (2010) *The Relocation of English*. London: Palgrave

Setter, J. (2012) 'English Around the World' in D. Clayton (ed.) *Language: a Student Handbook on Key Topics and Theories*. London: English and Media Centre

What is 'non-exam assessment'?

Non-exam assessment is the official term for coursework, and you will see this in specification documents. The term reflects the fact that you direct your own study and work in your own time, rather than at a set time in an exam room. Because it's rather long-winded, you will see it abbreviated to NEA. However, in this chapter and the next, we will use the more familiar term 'coursework'. This is likely to be used by your teachers when they have conversations with you about your plans and your progress. The most important thing to understand is what the work consists of, rather than worrying too much about labelling.

The coursework for English Language A level is a folder consisting of two distinctive types of work. The whole component – that is, the whole folder – is called 'Language in Action' because it requires you to be an active researcher, initiating your own plans rather than simply responding to others' directions, as would be the case with a written exam paper. The two types of work required for the folder are:

- a language investigation (2,000 words excluding data)
- a piece of original writing and commentary (1,500 words in total).

This chapter covers the investigation. Original writing is discussed in Chapter 8.

The folder is marked out of 100 and the mark contributes 20% to your final A level result. Your teachers are the first assessors of your work, and they agree all the students' marks within the department of your school or college. Those marks are forwarded to the exam board and are monitored. This is called 'moderation,' and it is a process that ensures students are treated fairly, regardless of where they study.

Teachers are not simply the markers of your work. They also have a responsibility to support you throughout the process of completing the coursework. This doesn't mean that they plan for you, manage everything you do in detail, or act as proofreaders of the final result. What they can do is to explain the nature of the task, making sure that what you are planning to do fits with the coursework requirements, particularly the marking criteria. They can also regularly review your work with you and ask questions about how you are approaching things, showing you what the marking criteria require. But coursework should, by its very nature, be your unaided work, and both you and your teacher have to sign a form to declare that it is your own. This is called authentication. Teachers also have to complete a record form to show that they have seen the progress of your work.

The comments above should help you to recognize the importance of using your teachers as a resource. It is usually the case that, where students don't bring their work to show their supervisors on a regular basis, the final product is not as good as it could have been if they had taken advice. Also, if you suddenly arrive with completed work that your teacher has never seen before, he or she will have difficulty signing the form to authenticate it as your own. If the form isn't signed, you cannot submit your work.

This chapter will:

- explain the nature of non-exam assessment
- help you to understand what an independent investigation involves
- give you many ideas for developing your own investigation
- explain how your investigation will be assessed.

! REMEMBER

Although your teachers mark your work, you should not think of them as your main audience. If you do, you will not write everything that you need to because you will think they already know it. Think of a person who is interested in language but not an expert, and focus on that person as your audience.

On the other hand, if you have relied on your teachers to the point where they feel that you have not made your own decisions, they will not be able to award you a high mark. Coursework involves guidance from teachers, but also independence.

This all sounds rather forbidding when written down as a set of rules and procedures, but the reality is that coursework is often the most enjoyable and rewarding part of the course for students, because it allows you to pursue your own interests. Having some rules simply ensures fairness of treatment.

> **Did you know?**
>
> The term 'investigation' comes from the Latin 'investigo', meaning to track or to search.

What is an investigation?

The general idea about investigating something is that you want to find out some answers to a question. You don't investigate something that you already know all about. This applies as much to your language investigation as it does to large-scale operations such as the American FBI (Federal Bureau of Investigation) or CSI (Crime Scene Investigation). Your investigation is a piece of genuine research, where you collect evidence and find some answers to a question or questions about language.

After formulating a research plan, your job is to collect some material in order to investigate your chosen area. Investigation requires a number of skills and these are rewarded through the following Assessment Objectives:

Assessment Objective 1 (AO1)

Apply appropriate methods of language analysis, using associated terminology and coherent written expression.

As it suggests, this Assessment Objective rewards you for the way in which you approach your research – the methods you use to collect and to analyse your data. You need to show that you understand the terminology you are using. You also need to organize your writing well, in the research report that you are required to write. This will be explained further below.

Assessment Objective 2 (AO2)

Demonstrate critical understanding of concepts and issues relevant to language use.

Any topic which you decide to research will involve considering concepts about language. Concepts are academic ideas – theories, proposals, suggestions about the way language works. For example, if you decide to research children's language, you will need to think about what academics have said about that area. Each of the chapters in this book has put forward concepts about language.

Issues are the consequences of our ideas about language. Again, whatever topic you choose will have issues associated with it. To take the example of children's language, our concepts about how children learn language will produce issues about how we behave towards them. You will be aware of many newspaper articles about how we should teach literacy skills to children, because this is an issue that is often debated.

Assessment Objective 3 (AO3)

Analyse and evaluate how contextual factors and language features are associated with the construction of meaning.

Whatever topic you are researching, you will need to identify and analyse some features of language. Having a method for how you do this, and knowing how to label features, are credited through AO1. AO3 recognizes your ability to analyse features and link them with aspects of context. As soon as you ask yourself what the language features are doing in the texts or data you have collected, you are covering context. Evaluation means standing back and thinking about how the component parts of what you're analysing add up to an overall meaning or interpretation. This aspect might particularly come to the fore when you are writing your conclusion to the study.

What is a research report?

The research that you undertake needs to be written up in the form of a report. The AQA specification suggests that you should include the following sections:

Introduction

In this section you need to state your aims and say something briefly about why you chose that particular topic and focus.

Methodology

Here you need to explain how you collected your data and how you selected areas for analysis. You also need to show that you have read around your topic by referring to any academic theories and theorists who have helped to shape your research plans.

At university level, a review of the **secondary sources** that you have read is called a 'literature review'. This is not structured book by book, as a review would be. It really means discussing the reading you have done in such a way as to highlight the ideas from the books or articles that are relevant to your topic.

Analysis

This section of a research report is often split into sub-headings, reflecting the different areas of language use that are being covered. Your analysis needs to relate to your research aims, and to go beyond description of what is in your data to consider why it is there / what its function is – in other words, the larger aspects of context that surround language use.

Conclusion

This should involve an evaluation of your findings. Don't be tempted to repeat an account of what you have done, because you have a limited word count and you need to be concise and precise.

References

This should list all of the references that you have used in your report. See Chapter 1 for information about how to reference your sources, including any that are web-based. You can also use the References sections throughout this book as a model.

Link

You can remind yourself about all of the AOs by looking back at Chapter 1.

Key term

Secondary sources. Books and articles where researchers and commentators put forward different theories and ideas about language.

Appendices

Your data needs to be included here. Appendices contain any of the workings that you've used to produce your analysis in the main part of the report.

Preparing for your investigation

Seeing what needs to be included in your research report should have helped you to understand the work that is involved in investigating a topic. But although the research report may look very logical and tidy, investigative work itself is never predictable, and can be very messy.

This is a good aspect of it, and one of the reasons why investigating is an interesting activity: genuine research needs to take you in whatever direction your inquiries lead you. For that very reason, you have to be well organized and do some forward planning. Below are some of the ways in which you can do that.

Building an archive

Keep careful notes of everything you read. Note down details of any quotations that you think might prove useful from secondary sources – see Chapter 1 (page 11) for advice about the level of information that you need to record. As well as ideas and quotations from secondary sources, there are other items that you need to keep a record of.

Sometimes, an idea or experience can occur in passing – you could be on a bus when an idea pops into your head. Buy a notebook, so that you can jot ideas down, or use a notes app to write on your phone or tablet. You could be walking past a piece of advertising that you think is intriguing. If you have a camera on your phone, take a picture of it. You might see something in a newspaper but you can't get a copy of it immediately. Go to the Internet later and see if you can find the story online. Set up a way to store digital links so you can retrieve them for subsequent use. Language students were restricted in the past by not having very sophisticated tools for recording and archiving data, so make the most of the fact that there are so many resources around you.

Below are some examples of language seen in passing, each of which could form the basis for an interesting collection and ultimate investigation.

In Chapter 1, you saw a set of symbols from East Coast trains (page 29), where the reader had to work to interpret the references. Meanings that are in the form of signs and symbols are complex forms of communication, because they are heavily reliant on shared cultural assumptions. But they also need to be recognizable to people who might share neither the culture nor the language of the producer.

Activity

The sign on the left was on the side of a swimming pool in Vancouver, Canada. How does this sign work? What are its component parts – and how does each part contribute to the overall message? How is this sign different from the East Coast symbols on page 29?

Investigations naturally involve the researcher as an analyst, but you can also derive results from testing out ideas on different groups of readers. For example, might different people find the 'No diving' sign effective, upsetting, or

How does each part of this sign contribute to its overall message?

funny – and why? If you decided to do an investigation about signs and notices, it would be a good idea to find some that were not just images, because that would mean that you couldn't write about other levels of language (see Chapter 1). But, on the other hand, it is also a good idea to choose a limited amount of data, because you are required to analyse in detail – and there can be a lot to say about a small text, if it is a good choice. Your teacher is there to help and advise you. Look at the discussion about language and images in the next section.

Another example of something noticed and photographed in passing is shown below: a packet of hydrocolloid dressings, supplied in a hotel in San Diego. It was noticeable because of its use of different narrative voices in the text.

Link

If you are not sure how much there is to say about everyday, seemingly unremarkable texts, then read David Graddol's semiotic analysis of a wine label (Graddol 1996).

Activity

Who is the narrator on the front of the hydrocolloid dressings packet? How would you describe the narrator's style on the back?

What is the narrator's style on both sides of this packaging?

Hydrocolloid is usually used in hospitals for serious things like third degree burns and leg ulcers. But you shouldn't feel guilty about using it on something as small as a blister. There is enough hydrocolloid to go around.

Language and images

As a language student, you are not expected to know about the history of art, or about the complexities of photographic processes, in the way that a student of fine art or media studies might. On the other hand, you certainly cannot ignore images: graphology is one of the language levels that you are expected to understand and use when analysing texts.

In semiotics, images are regarded as a type of language in themselves – there is a language of images. For example, there are many books and articles on the language of clothes and different styles of dress. As a language student, your approach needs to be that images are part of an overall message. Think about the part that they play alongside the verbal elements to make meaning. You wouldn't read an advert in real life by concentrating on the language and ignoring the image; we don't read books with children in that way, either. So think about the way in which we process texts as readers – your analytical approach should mirror the way that happens.

In fact, as Lemke (1998) has pointed out, we don't even read the verbal language and then the images, and put them together in a simple addition. Images and language interrelate: readers move between them, back and forth, to derive meaning. Lemke calls this process **multiplicative meaning** – likening it to a multiplication sum, rather than one of addition.

Research idea

Have you noticed how many objects 'speak' to us – from the backs of vans asking us if they are being driven sensibly, to coffee cups telling us that their contents are hot? An investigation into the voices of (and on) inanimate objects would be interesting. But such an investigation would require good observational skills, to spot the examples, and good organizational skills, to archive them.

Key term

Multiplicative meaning. The process by which one part of a text does more than just add to the meaning of another part. For example, readers understand images in the context of the words that surround them, and vice versa.

Copying data

There is nothing more upsetting than losing your data. Make copies of your collection and house it somewhere out of reach of a family pet who might regard it as food, or the house-proud adult who might regard it as litter. But don't forget to include it in the submission of your final investigation: you'd be surprised how many students forget to hand in their data. This makes it very difficult for markers and moderators because they are unable to check whether what you have said is a good interpretation. You might think that not being checked would be a good thing, but it's not – a lack of data looks rather suspicious. And if you've done a really good analysis, you might not get the credit.

Being pro-active

Being pro-active means taking the initiative, rather than waiting for something to happen. Waiting until you are told to do something is being reactive (the opposite of pro-active). Examples of taking the initiative include:

- doing your own searches in order to find useful secondary sources
- doing a **pilot study**, where you try out some possible research methods
- attending meetings with your supervisor having done some preparation, so that you can ask questions rather than waiting to be told what to do
- having a Plan B.

> **Key term**
>
> **Pilot study.** A study done in advance of a main study in order to test out different approaches.

What is a Plan B?

A Plan B is an idea of what you might do if your first plan fails. Failure means failing to get off the ground. It doesn't mean discovering that your initial thoughts were wrong – that would be a result! A failure to find the things that you expected is not a failure: you are not trying to 'prove' something in a scientific experiment. You are exploring language use, and that can result in not finding what you set out to find. That's absolutely fine.

Failure to get off the ground means failing to start. It could be that you planned to record someone and, for some reason, that can't happen now. It may be that someone promised to send you some data, and they didn't. Or you wrote to a magazine or newspaper and heard nothing. The point is to give yourself a time limit by which your plans should have started to take shape. But you need to be realistic and abandon a plan that looks like it's not going to go ahead. The worst situation to be in is to be in a state of paralysis, because you have invested all of your ideas in the one plan – Plan A, sink or swim.

Plan B needs to be something that you are still interested in doing, but one that requires a change of direction. Many students find that their original Plan A can become a Plan B with some thought and discussion with their supervisor. Or it may be the case that you need to abandon your first idea and go with a fresh topic. When you work through the ideas that follow in this chapter, make a list of several possibilities that you might be interested in, not just one.

> **! REMEMBER**
>
> Your topic doesn't have to be unique. There is nothing wrong with choosing something that many people have done before. Your investigation will be new because it will be your own take on the idea, with your own data.

Realistic time planning

You will only have time to change tack if you have set yourself a realistic set of deadlines for each stage of your work. Plan each stage carefully, particularly if you are planning to do any transcription work on a speech recording or video clip. Set a deadline by which you expect to hear from any people you are relying on to contact you. If nothing happens, don't hang on 'just in case' they reply: prompt them or change your method of communication (a phone appeal is harder to ignore than an email). If that doesn't work, change your plans – or do without their help.

Make sure that you know about the internal deadlines set by your school or college, and don't assume that exam board deadlines are the ones to guide you. Your teachers need time to mark and moderate your work. Internal deadlines are very important for another reason: supervising teachers have to complete a kind of log, showing the development of your work. If you miss internal deadlines that they set you, this will show up on your record card.

Being ethical

Any research has an effect on the people involved in it. Obviously, if you are planning to investigate some advertising, no individuals are likely to be affected. But any work with people needs to respect the rights of the individuals involved. There are various aspects to ethical approaches and you should think about each of these before you start your investigation.

Potential harm

Your research should not be damaging to anyone. This is particularly relevant when you are planning to work with young children, people with learning difficulties, or anyone who is vulnerable. You need to obtain informed consent from carers or parents.

Think about the participants in your study: what will taking part in your research feel like from their perspective? If you are going to work on the area of language and disability – for example autism, or dyslexia – it is very difficult to carry out an investigation without knowing the individual personally. You can't just invite yourself into a stranger's home: if you are not going to study someone you know personally, then a great deal of preparatory work will be required.

If you are thinking of doing any kind of 'testing', ask yourself whether this is really necessary. Some of the best research arises from being integrated into the normal routines of life and not from a laboratory-style approach. Research integrated into someone's everyday life is called an ethnography and this is a very valid method – see below.

Informed consent

People who are the subject of research need to know what they are letting themselves in for, so you must be as open as possible about what you are doing, and they need to give permission for you to use data that results from their involvement.

Research can sometimes face the problem of the **observer's paradox**, which refers to the fact that the presence of the researcher, or knowledge of the detailed outlines of research plans, can distort the very thing that is being researched. Everyone is aware of that problem. You don't need to go into a lot of detail in explaining your plans, but you do need to explain your methodology to anyone involved (see below). If you are planning to do some recording, the fact that people know they are being recorded shouldn't be a problem if you record for a reasonable amount of time: as time goes on, people become less self-conscious. You don't have to transcribe everything you record.

Looking ahead

In some school contexts you may need to obtain a criminal record (CRB) check: you need to enquire about this with the school.

Key term

Observer's paradox. The paradox that the only way to collect natural speech is to observe it – but the very act of observation is likely to destroy its naturalness.

It may be the case that it is impossible to record but you still want to explore how spoken language works. For example, you are not allowed to record in a courtroom, and you might have difficulty gaining permission to record in a café where you wait at tables or a shop where you serve behind a counter. The best plan in these cases would be to fix on something specific, where you don't need a record of the whole interaction – for example, the way in which people use terms of address or politeness terms – and then use a notebook to record usage. When you collect data in this way, you don't have to explain what you are doing to the people you encounter.

The right to withdraw

If people don't like the experience they are having by participating in your investigation, they have the right to withdraw, with no negative consequences to themselves.

Confidentiality and privacy

No one in your investigation should be recognizable or traceable. This means that you must not use their real names, or give away their location details or access details (including their physical and virtual addresses, phone numbers or any other personal details).

There are some inherent difficulties here, given that an interesting area of research for you may well be social media sites or other digital locations where people often seem happy to post many personal details. Issues of permission are hazy about how Internet material should be used, but a rough rule of thumb is that material from sites that are password-protected need permissions to be sought, while sites that are open access do not. People may be happy to grant permission but there may be practical difficulties in removing all their personal details, in which case you need to explain in your methodology section that this has been the case.

In reality, the readership of your work will be quite restricted – the teachers in your school or college and the exam board moderators. If you decide to publish your work more widely, you may have to think again about the approach you have taken.

Finding a topic to investigate

Now that you have been introduced to the main areas that you need to think about when preparing for an investigation, turn your attention to the all-important question: what topic should I choose?

There are many sources to help you devise a topic. But the key point to make right at the start of this process is that you should choose something that isn't completely familiar ground. It's fine to choose to extend a mini-project which you may have started earlier in your course and become interested in, but avoid playing it safe and sticking to an aspect that you feel you know well, and that you may have been over time and again. You will soon become bored, because you will feel that you are not really learning anything new. You need to stay with your investigation for a long time, so choose something that will excite you and keep your interest.

Don't be worried about taking risks: an engaged, committed research report that doesn't have neat and tidy findings because it was trying something challenging will be much more rewarding for people to read than a bored-sounding account going through the motions.

 Activity

The following pages describe some good places to start when thinking about choosing a topic. Look at the ideas under each heading and make some notes for yourself about those ideas that interest you and which you regard as possible investigations.

The specification document

There are plenty of suggestions in the specification itself, which is available online so you can access it anytime. Go to the AQA site (www.aqa.org.uk) and search for 'English Language A level'.

Your course

Regardless of the stage of the course that you have reached, think back to what you have done so far. Write some notes for yourself as you answer the following questions:

- Which aspects have you particularly enjoyed learning about?
- Which aspects have you found most intriguing – leaving you wanting to know more?
- Which aspects have you read about (beyond the material that was given to you in class)?
- Which aspects gave you some new insights into the way language works?
- Which aspects did you find you were good at?

Recognizing the enjoyment factor is important. Studying is often described as labour ('work' and 'effort'), which it undoubtedly is, but it should also be pleasurable. Wanting to know more about a topic shows that your interest has been stimulated – especially if you have started reading around the subject – and this is an opportunity for you to explore issues and fill in more details. If an aspect you've studied has opened your eyes to something that you'd never thought about before, then that is worth pursuing. And maximizing your talents is not a bad idea, either.

This book

The chapters of this book have covered a lot of topics – there are some examples in the left-hand column of the following table. As you read through the list, think about where you might find some suitable data if you were to choose each of those topics for your investigation. Make a large copy of the table and write notes about any possible sources in the right-hand column. Leave space in each box for additional notes.

Topics	Possible sources for suitable data
Informal speech	
Online communication	
Political speeches	
Varieties of text	
Language and representation	
Texts through time	
The language of advertising	
Language and culture	
Language and social groups	
Accent and dialect	
Language and gender	
Language and occupation	
Language and ethnicity	
Language acquisition	
Language change	
International English	

Your own resources

While completing your copy of the above table, you might already have thought about some very specific resources that you have access to. For example, you may be part of a special interest group, such as playing music, swimming or rowing. But your other examples could have been general ideas about where to source suitable data.

Now you need to think in more detail about the actual resources you have, or have access to. Answer the questions below and then add some more detail to your previous checklist.

Do you have:

- any relatives or friends in particular occupations?

- any experience of doing part-time work?

- a particular interest or hobby?

- material from when you were younger – for example, your first school readers, stories you wrote, comics?

- any young relatives who are at the early stages of acquiring language?

- any connections with any local primary schools?

- someone in the family with a form of language impairment?

- a local dialect that is still used in the area, perhaps also in your own family?

- knowledge of more than one language, or relatives who are bilingual?

- stores of texts and other kinds of digital communication on electronic devices?

- collections of any kind – for example birthday cards, magazines?

- particular types of literary text that you enjoy?

Your resources are also your own attitudes and values, which are harder to list in a simple way. Ask yourself what makes you feel moved about language use – excited, but perhaps also angry and passionate about issues. Thinking about your feelings is as important as thinking about ideas more intellectually. This could be a starting point – not only for your investigation, but also for your original writing. There's nothing to stop you exploring an area for your investigation, then writing about this same topic in the other elements of your folder, with a persuasive, informative, or creative purpose in mind.

Devising a research question

Once you have fixed on a general area, you need to give your research a focus. The best way to do this is to arrive at a title. This might seem like something you could do later, but it isn't: having a title really pins things down and helps you to stick to the point. So don't miss out this stage.

The fact that in research we talk about 'research questions' doesn't mean that your title has to ask a question. In some textbooks you will see advice about asking a research question and then setting up a **hypothesis**. A hypothesis is a speculative forecast about what you expect to find. The term really comes from science and from laboratory work, and some people find it useful if they are doing the kind of research that involves testing. There's nothing to stop you doing this, but you don't have to set your title up in the form of a question, or use the term 'hypothesis'. The problem for people who set themselves questions is that sometimes they feel that they have to 'prove' something, as if they were doing an experiment on mice – finding an 'answer' to a 'problem'. This doesn't really fit many of the topics which you might now have on your list of possible ideas.

Some useful ways to set up your title include terms such as 'study', 'examination', 'exploration', 'analysis', 'inquiry', 'comparison'. Here are some examples, using ideas from the AQA specification:

- A study of features of the Devon dialect, based on a survey
- An examination of the writing of two children aged 8
- An exploration of how travel guides represent a particular community
- An analysis of the language of sports commentary
- An inquiry into turn-taking in real-time writing online
- A comparison of the language of two wedding ceremonies from different cultures

Scope and focus

The titles above seem quite specific, but more thought is needed in each case about the **scope** and **focus** of each study. After setting up your title, you would say more about these two aspects in your introductory 'aims' section.

A focus describes an aspect of the academic area. Think of focus in terms of what a camera lens does: you set up a picture, but then the focus is the part that is given special attention in close-up. In the examples above, there is some suggestion of focus: the dialect of Devon (specific variety); children's writing (specific mode); travel guides and sports commentary (specific genres); online writing (specific type of computer-based communication); wedding ceremonies (specific ritual).

> ### Key terms
>
> **Focus.** The area where most attention is concentrated.
>
> **Hypothesis.** A proposed explanation for how something will work.
>
> **Scope.** How far a study extends, how much is covered.

More focus than this would be needed in the introductory section, however. Which area of Devon? Why two children aged 8? Which travel guides and which community? Which sport, what type of commentary? What type of real-time writing and by whom? Which cultures?

If focus is the area that is in close-up, then scope refers to how widely the whole picture is framed. In practice, scope tends to be reduced as researchers proceed, because they realize that they have taken on far too much and need to reduce their coverage. The best research, however, takes this on board from the start. You can already see in a title referring to 'two children aged 8' that this person has a more realistic sense of what is possible than someone who said 'a class of 30 children aged 8'. But of course there would need to be a specific rationale for why the study had been set up in this way: were the children of different abilities? Had they been taught differently? Had they been told a story and asked to write it down, in order to see how an oral account was turned into a written one?

How much data?

This question is not easy to answer because it obviously depends on the research question and on the focus. But a general rule is that if you are analysing texts or discourses (that is, long stretches of language), you need to narrow your scope and be particularly selective in your choice of data.

If your data is rich in language features and you can give an explanation of why you chose your selection, then you don't need very much at all. Areas where the choices are very wide – for example, gender and advertising – need more work to select the right material and justify the selection. For example, if you want to compare the ways in which advertising targets men and women, you need to find the same or similar products, choose a publication, identify the examples, then, perhaps having listed them and said a little about the range you've found, choose two to analyse in detail. A study involving several publications, different time periods, different products, and a sheaf of adverts would be a non-starter. Note also that studies of gender don't always have to compare men and women. Gender has so many other categories refracted through it, as should be evident from Chapter 3, that categories within gender can be usefully contrasted too – for example, age or ethnicity.

Where you are not analysing texts but collecting examples of language use, your scope might need to be wider. Another example from the AQA list is the language of shop names. This might need quite a few examples if you are to find patterns of use. This type of study is closer to the earlier example of Devon dialect, which uses a survey method, than it is to a text analysis.

Choosing research methods

The term **methodology** refers not just to how to do things ('method') but discussing and justifying those methods ('-ology').

When you write your report, your methodology section needs to cover four areas:

- Any relevant ideas from reading about your chosen topic.
- A description of the method of research you used.

Key term

Methodology. The study of different ways to research ideas.

- Details about your data – how, why, when you collected your material, how you selected from it.
- How you arrived at certain areas to prioritize for analysis.

You need to be concise, because you want to be able to write at sufficient length in your analysis section, so you need to focus on *relevant* ideas from your reading, and facts about your methods and data. It is worth spelling out in a little more detail why you have chosen certain areas to use as your headings for analysis, because this sets up the analysis section that follows in your report.

Text analysis

If you are analysing texts, it won't surprise you to learn that your research method is a text analysis. You could also call the analysis of any texts – spoken, written, or multimodal – a discourse analysis. In Chapter 1 the terms 'text' and 'discourse' were discussed, and there was some information about writing a text analysis (see pages 9–10). The focus on that page was on writing an exam answer, but the skills of analysis are the same wherever they are applied.

There are further research methods that will suit different kinds of investigations.

Questionnaires

Questionnaires can elicit people's attitudes to language, as well as their linguistic repertoires (as in the example above, about Devon dialect). But don't be fooled into thinking that this is an easy way to collect data: writing a good questionnaire is a time-consuming, skilled task.

Try out your questions in a **pilot study**, because they may be interpreted in ways that you hadn't expected. If you're intending to carry out a questionnaire online, you will need to make it brief, as many survey requests arrive in people's inboxes these days, so you are in a competitive situation.

A brief survey followed up by a more in-depth method, such as an interview, with willing participants, can be a useful mix of methods.

Interviews

Interviews can be highly structured, where you ask people exactly the same questions, or semi-structured, where you have a plan for your questions but are happy for your interviewee to change direction. Your choice needs to be tied to the aim of your research – but, whatever your aim, don't underestimate the skill involved or the need for a pilot stage, as described above.

Note-making

Note-making can be useful, as suggested earlier, where you want to be able to note down some specific aspects of language use but you are unable to make a recording.

In your notes, write down as much information as you can about times, places, participants, and so on. Observational notes can be particularly useful where the participants involved might react strongly to recording equipment, where they might find it very inhibiting, or where you are trying to capture something delicate. An example might be where you are working with a shy special needs pupil and are in a close one-to-one collaboration in a small space.

Did you know?

The word *logos* was used in ancient Greece to refer to an opinion or basis for a view, as well as discourse or speech – since that's how judgements were expressed. All of our modern words ending in '-ology' therefore refer to bodies of knowledge, or views about a subject.

REMEMBER

Self-reported usage in surveys involves what people say they do. This isn't necessarily the same thing as what they *really* do.

REMEMBER

All the methods listed here can be mixed: you are not tied to any one method alone.

Corpus searches

The use of language corpora can be both a useful support to analysis, particularly of lexical items, and a research method in its own right. A language corpus is a collection of millions of words from real texts, stored on computer databases.

There are many different corpora, each with its own distinctive contents, but one of the most commonly used general corpora is the BNC, the British National Corpus, hosted by Oxford University. Free searches are available for up to 50 random examples of language in context, with details of the sources alongside. Try a free search on a word to explore its connotations and collocations.

Link

The BNC can be found at http://www.natcorp.ox.ac.uk

Ethnography

Ethnography involves a research method where the researcher is part of the community that is being studied. The term comes from anthropology, where researchers often want to live alongside the people they are studying, because they want to tell their story 'from the inside'. If you are describing the way a community works and uses language, and you are a part of that same community, then you are taking an ethnographic approach. This might be the case, for example, where you are describing language use within your family, or the language that is part of a particular cultural routine or custom.

Recording and transcribing

Recordings of all kinds represent further ways to collect data. Speech will, of course, need to be transcribed, as will anything recorded from the TV or from online collections such as YouTube. In transcribing video or film clips, you need to produce a **storyboard** which gives enough detail of the non-verbal aspects of the interaction for a reader to see how the speech relates to the other aspects of communication, including the context. The same applies to TV advertising.

Key term

Storyboard. A set of images to represent the action within a moving text such as a TV programme or advertisement.

Transcribing speech can be a painstaking exercise and you need to allow yourself enough time to do it properly. You don't necessarily need to transcribe everything you've recorded, and the transcription markings you choose to use depend on what you are researching. Conventions vary, but some commonly used markings are given in Chapter 1 (page 14). These were developed in a field of analysis called Conversation Analysis, which can be taken to very technical levels.

Internet dialogues can also be saved, and these are already in transcript form. If you use chatlogs or similarly archived digital files, remember that the logs describe the results of the interaction, not the interaction itself. This means that while participants may have intended to write something at a certain point, their line ended up in a different place because of the speed of interaction. This makes turntaking very different from that of speech.

Experimentation

Setting up test conditions is of course a very valid approach to research. The experiments in the 1970s by Howard Giles and his colleagues on attitudes to accent relied heavily on testing audience responses in matched guise experiments, where a single speaker used the same words but spoke in different accents. Without those experiments we wouldn't have developed such a rich field of knowledge about accent prejudice.

Activity

Now that you have read about some different methodologies, go back to your list of ideas for investigations and see whether you can suggest possible methods for each of them. Note that there is no fixed answer, in the sense that there is more than one approach for investigating an area. This activity will help you to think through the pros and cons of each method or methodological mix.

Analysing your data

After collecting your data, you obviously need to analyse it. This means setting up some headings for yourself, in order to gather together the points you want to make in an organized way. Your headings will clearly need to relate to your research question and to what you can see in your data.

Analysis is different from description. Description answers the 'what?' question; analysis answers the 'why?' question, to explore why certain features might be in the data (possibly along with other 'wh' questions, such as who uses the language, when it occurs, and so on).

Activity

To trial the idea of analytical headings, as well as bringing back into view some of the work you have done so far on titles and research methods, look at the three examples of data outlined on pages 214–215. For each example, imagine that the data is to form part of the basis of an investigation and then:

- devise a title for your investigation
- specify what other data you might need in order to proceed with your plan
- identify an appropriate research method or mix of methods, as well as any further reading or research ideas you have encountered in this book
- outline a set of headings for your analysis, with, for each heading, some ideas about what you would cover.

Example 1: Football match reports at http://www.bbc.co.uk/sport/0/football/29341997

Example 2: A roadside diner menu

The Route 6 roadside diner

Burger menu

The Straight Talker
Our basic burger, just as nature intended and no messin' – 100% pure beef in a fresh-baked burger bun.

The Skyscraper
Our triple-decker – three juicy beefburgers in a tower, with lettuce, tomato, gherkin and mayo between each storey, all in a lightly toasted bun.

The Downhomer – our country-style beefburger, with rich onion gravy. Crunchy homefries replace the bun and are cooked fresh with every order.

The Southern Comforter – a southern-fried chickenburger in a cornbread fritter, with three sides of coleslaw, sweetcorn relish and a sweet chilli dipping sauce.

The Alamoburger – a hot 'n spicy Texan burger of slow-cooked pulled pork, with a rich and gooey barbecue sauce. Choose a regular bun or a corn tortilla.

The Full Dollar – everything you expect, and more, inside a fresh burger bun. 100% pure beefburger with thin 'n crispy bacon and melted Monterey Jack cheese, as well as all the trimmings of lettuce, tomato, gherkin and mayo.

Example 3: An online chat between a phone service provider and a customer

The customer below is complaining that his mobile phone doesn't work, because there is a technical fault in the company's system. (The company and the communicators have both been anonymized. Note that there is only enough space here for the opening, but the rest of the conversation proceeded in the same way.)

Transcription key

[ ] Square brackets indicate company name and other specific details

info: at 11:27:11

Welcome to [name of phone company]. Someone will be with you soon.

info: at 11:27:13

You're through to [ ] : Robert

[ ] : Robert: at 11:27:17

Hello, it's [ ]: Robert here. What can I do for you?

Andrew Benson: at 11:28:22

4 days of no coverage, replaced sim, phoning [ ] but no answer over 30 mins. No phone, no business, utterly fed up.

[ ] : Robert: at 11:28:47

I'm sorry for the inconvenience and can feel how upsetting this may be for you.

[ ] : Robert: at 11:28:56

This is not the level of service we want you to receive and I'm very sorry we've let you down this way.

Andrew Benson: at 11:29:02

and....

[ ] : Robert: at 11:29:21

Please help me with the post code of your area. So, that I can check the coverage for it.

Andrew Benson: at 11:29:54

[postcode] But I know what it will say. Same message for 4 days

[ ] : Robert: at 11:31:07

I can see that the mast close to your location is experiencing a high level of demand for service.

[ ] : Robert: at 11:31:27

Hence, you're facing this network problem.

[ ] : Robert: at 11:31:45

We're working on it to get this matter sorted soon.

Andrew Benson: at 11:37:04

How much refund and compensation for lost business am I entitled to?

Drawing conclusions

Pick out the main points from your study that you want to emphasize. Don't repeat everything you have said in your investigation; focus on the headlines – the main ideas that you want your reader to remember about your research.

Looking ahead

The investigation is a good example of the type of independent research work that students are expected to do at university. If you are interested in taking language study further, read Goddard, A. (2011) *Doing English Language: A guide for students*. London: Routledge.

REVIEW YOUR LEARNING

- What are the main sections needed in your report?
- Give three examples of things you can do to prepare for your investigation.
- Give three examples of areas you are interested in investigating.
- Define the following terms: research question, focus, scope.
- Give as many examples of research methods as you can.
- How should an analysis be approached?

References

Graddol, D. (1996) 'The semiotics of a wine label', in S. Goodman and D. Graddol (eds) *Redesigning English: New Texts, New Identities*, London: Routledge, in association with the Open University.

Lemke, J. (1998). 'Metamedia Literacy: Transforming Meanings and Media', in Reinking, D., McKenna, M., and Labbo, L., (eds.), *Handbook of Literacy and Technology: Transformations in a Post-typographic World*. London: Routledge.

Further reading

The Routledge *Intertext* series includes individual books on many language topics, including the language of children, language and region, language change, language and gender, language and the media, and language and technology. To see the full series go to http://www.routledge.com/books/series/SE0313/

There is also a wide range of topic coverage in Clayton, D. (ed.) (2012) *Language: A student handbook of key topics and theories*. London: English and Media Centre. This is a concise and accessible collection of articles by different academics explaining approaches to their fields of study and suggesting useful directions.

Support for text analysis can be found in: Carter, R. and Goddard, A. (2015) *How to Analyse Texts: A Toolkit for Students of English*. London: Routledge.

What do we mean by 'original writing'?

In A Level English Language, the term **original writing** refers to writing other than that of text analysis, essays, or reports. This is where you show how well you can use language creatively, which is one of the practical skills developed and tested as part of the course.

The term is also used to distinguish the task from 'creative writing' (although this work is certainly creative, as suggested above) because that phrase tends to make people think of stories and poems, and A level original writing includes articles and other non-fiction forms, as well as texts intended to be spoken.

The original writing task

As mentioned in the previous chapter, the original writing and commentary in your coursework will total 1,500 words and be worth 10% of your A level (making 20% in total for the non-exam assessment). The original writing and the commentary are equally weighted and each has a maximum word count of 750 words.

This part of the coursework is assessed using the following Assessment Objectives.

Assessment Objective 5 (AO5)

Demonstrate expertise and creativity in the use of English to communicate in different ways.

As you might expect, this is the most heavily weighted Assessment Objective for this part of your coursework folder. The original writing is assessed solely using this objective, which covers how effectively you write. For this subject and level, effective writing is writing that works for its intended reader. It does not necessarily use impressive techniques or aim to sound 'clever', but it does need to use the conventions of the genre you have chosen.

Assessment Objective 4 (AO4)

Explore connections across texts, informed by linguistic concepts and methods.

This objective, along with the other four, is applied to the commentary piece. It considers the extent to which you are able to discuss the way your original writing connects with the **style model** you submit and how it belongs within a genre.

Your original writing needs to demonstrate your ability to manipulate language under one of the following strands:

- The power of persuasion
- The power of storytelling
- The power of information

The word 'power' in these descriptions doesn't imply that you need to write about power. It simply means you are learning about the power that different

---

This chapter will:

- help you to understand what original writing is
- give you ideas for developing your own writing in the three set areas
- explain how your writing will be assessed.

Key terms

Original writing. Writing of all kinds that derives from individual ideas.

Style model. An example of a style of writing that has helped to shape ideas for a piece of original writing.

You can remind yourself about AOs 1, 2 and 3 by looking at Chapter 7, where it was explained that these are also used to assess your investigation.

communication functions have in our society. Writing that persuades, writing that narrates and writing that informs are all powerful forms of writing if done well.

Persuasion, narrative and information don't exist individually in isolation. Texts normally have more than one function. For example, forms of advertising need to give you some information in order to persuade you. Stories can be very persuasive, and information can be conveyed by adopting a narrative technique. So you need to think of these different functions as interrelated. However, you need to assign your writing to one or other of the headings, and this will be on the basis of what you believe to be the primary function of the piece.

What you write can be on any topic, provided that your teacher thinks it is challenging enough for you to embark on. This doesn't mean that you should choose something beyond your reach, but simply that you should think about how you can best demonstrate your creativity and skill. This can be difficult to do if you choose an overly simple format. For example, small ads in newspapers give information, as do train tickets, but it would be hard for either of these types of text to showcase your skills.

Beyond the idea of presenting a reasonable challenge, the text you choose to write needs to be a recognizable genre and one that can be said to be primarily either persuasive, narrative or informative. In terms of mode, you also have a wide range of choice. You are free to choose a traditional form of writing that stays firmly on paper, a **hybrid mode** such as web pages, or something written to be spoken, such as a **script**. Remember, though, that a script is different from a **transcript**. A script is written before something happens, while a transcript is a recording of what happened. If you write a script, it won't have all the 'ums' and 'ers' and other aspects of natural speech that occur in real talk, but those things are part of a transcript.

If what you are planning to write would, in the real world, involve only the briefest of planning notes, then it will not be a feasible option for this assessed work.

Key terms

Script. A plan for what speakers are going to say and do.

Transcript. A record of what speakers said and did.

Activity

All of the examples below, except one, would be likely to involve only brief planning notes. An exception would be a fully written script. Which is the exception?

- A story told as part of a stand-up comedy performance.
- A TV chat show interview with an actor promoting a new film.
- A voiceover narration to a television documentary.
- A radio phone-in collecting audience opinion on a topical issue.

The answer is at the back of the book.

Your submission must also include an annotated style model, which will help you to demonstrate that your writing does fit into a specific genre. It will also support your commentary writing. Style models are explored in more detail below.

Deciding what to write

As in all coursework and extended tasks, it is crucial that you choose something of interest to you. You will need to spend a reasonable amount of time on this task – working on the style model, planning and drafting your writing, and producing a commentary. Given how much control you have over its content, it would be sensible to make it something that you are really interested in. Also, it is likely to be of better quality if you are able to feel enthusiasm for it.

Choosing to write about a topic that you already know something about, or to write in a form that is familiar to you, is also likely to enable you to produce better-quality work.

 Activity

To start generating ideas, write down as many answers as you can to the following questions. At this stage, do not attempt to refine your ideas. Just for now, aim for quantity – you can focus on quality later in the process.

1. Which publications (magazines, newspapers, websites, blogs, forums) do you regularly read?

2. Which media sources (radio stations, TV programmes) do you regularly listen to or watch?

3. Which topics and issues always attract your interest? For example, if someone sends you a link to an article that you would click on and read, what would it be likely to be about?

4. What do you spend your spare time doing?

5. What interesting experiences have you had? Think about unusual hobbies, holidays, work experience, family stories.

6. Look back through this textbook. Which texts did you find most interesting?

7. Which language topics in this book and in class have you found most interesting so far?

If you are working in a group situation, share your thoughts with others. Other students' ideas will help to move your own thinking forwards.

 REMEMBER

Language itself can be a topic for you to write about.

Some students seem to feel that they ought to write something more 'intellectual' or more 'mature' than their own tastes, but there are two problems with this approach:

- Loss of motivation – it is very difficult to keep yourself working at your best on something that you are not interested in.

- Lack of familiarity – it is very difficult to adopt the correct register and style for a topic that you do not know well.

The writing that you produce will not be assessed on how impressive the genre is, but on how well you adopt it. It is true that the mark scheme talks about 'challenging' audiences and using genres in 'original and innovative ways', but this can be achieved within contexts that are familiar to you. To have access to the full range of marks, it is important to choose a genre that will help you to stretch yourself, but that doesn't mean choosing from a narrow range of forms that you feel will impress the moderator.

For example, you could challenge an audience and use genre creatively by taking an angle that goes somewhat against your chosen publication's usual stance. In a music magazine piece, this might mean arguing that a popular artist (in that magazine's favoured area) has slipped up in the latest album or song. Your task would then be to create that argument in sufficiently subtle and effective terms so that the audience would not be alienated. You can challenge your audience as well as yourself.

Working with style models

For your assessment, you will need to submit an annotated style model alongside your writing. This model will help you to be certain that you are shaping your writing for a particular audience, purpose and genre, and it will also support your commentary writing. It is vitally important that you take your time choosing a good style model, and that you then use it well.

It is likely that your style model will be the same in all contextual details as your own piece, but on a different topic. This stage of the process helps you to be clear about the context of your writing before you start, and avoids vague plans such as 'I'll write a story' with no real sense of audience, while also avoiding the trap of being so close to the style model that it feels like copying.

Finding a good style model

The first stage of preparing this coursework, then, is deciding on the context for your piece and finding possible style models to guide your work. It would be best to find and study a few possible models, and certainly to discuss them with your teacher, before beginning any detailed annotation.

Think about how much you want – or are able – to adopt the style in the texts you have found. If you find that you are explaining a style model with too many hedges and 'buts' – 'mine will be sort of like this magazine piece but for women, and a bit less mainstream, and not all adults' – you need to find a more appropriate model.

Using your style model

Once you have settled on your style model, you need to annotate it to show its distinctive features. You should then plan the content of your own piece – writing the features you want to use onto your plan. Then, once you have started writing, you can put the style model aside so that you are not relying on it too heavily.

Following the discourse structure of your style model is the right thing to do; slavishly following a matching argument line by line is not. There is more detail on the drafting and writing process at the end of this chapter.

The power of persuasion

This is the first of the three possible headings under which your original writing needs to fit. Many types of text can be persuasive, so this heading offers you plenty of scope. The following are some of the forms that could be chosen for this category:

- Promotional materials for a product or service or organization.
- A leaflet seeking support for a charity or a local cause.

- An opinion or comment article.
- A script for a television or radio advert.
- A political speech.

Most of these forms can be produced on a range of varied topics. As noted above, do not fall into the trap of selecting something based on how impressive or academic you feel it is. This is true of content as well as form: an opinion piece about an issue that is specific to you and that you already have opinions about is likely to be far more effective than a piece about a cause that you have chosen for its perceived intellectual value.

Activity

1. Use the information and ideas below to draft the opening of two of the following:
   - A letter seeking funds to support a cause.
   - An opinion article for the local newspaper to raise awareness and state your support.
   - A script for a radio advert to raise both awareness and funds.
   - Another persuasive text type of your own.

   Base your work on this information:

   A new local charity has been set up to help families who are struggling to make ends meet. It provides basic food items, second-hand school uniforms, and equipment to families facing financial difficulties, as well as running sessions to help people filling in job applications and preparing for interviews. The charity is run entirely by volunteers and operates from a local community centre. It needs: money to buy food items, volunteers to help staff the centre, outgrown but usable school uniforms, unwanted stationery items, schoolbooks, and so on.

2. Having written two different styles of text beginnings, take a close look at the language you chose to do this. What features did you use to focus audience attention and make it likely that they would read on or continue listening? These are the types of features that you would write about in your commentary.

Extension activity

Start a collection of style models for texts that you might write in future. What are the distinctive features of the style models you have collected? Choose a model you are interested in and annotate its features.

Advertising texts

Advertising can operate through various text types, although not all of them would be sensible choices for this task, because of the word count you need to work to.

Billboard advertisements and one-off print adverts that use minimal amounts of language are unlikely to work, as 750 words would usually be far too much writing for that kind of text. Effective choices, if you are interested in the

> **! REMEMBER**
>
> Your original writing piece and commentary have a maximum word count of 750 words each. There is no minimum, but it wouldn't be sensible to choose to write something that involved only a few words, such as a minimalist-style print advert. However, it's fine to choose something that would normally exist as a longer text and to produce a part of it.

language of advertising, would be: advertising in leaflet form, where there are several parts to the text; an advertising campaign involving interrelated texts; advertorials; and media scripts.

As the name suggests, an advertorial is essentially advertising copy masquerading as editorial content, although it does need to be flagged as paid-for advertising somewhere (usually in a small flash or heading indicating that it is an 'advertising feature'). Since this is not usually immediately noticed, advertorials can get away with being a bit less obvious about their persuasive tactics, as the reader is not always responding to the text as an advertising text from the beginning. These texts will often adopt an advisory tone, rather than an explicitly persuasive one, and follow the features of editorial writing. They may also look as though they are offering straightforward information, for example in pieces about travel.

Scripts for television or radio advertisements are more explicit about their status as adverts and will use more obvious methods of persuasion, because they are competing with a lot of other things for the audience's attention. Many advertising scripts will use a problem–solution discourse structure. This means that they present the audience with a problem for which the service or product offers a solution. Sometimes they address the audience directly, to imply that they need this product or service, but they may also present a character suffering with some problem that can be solved. 'Problems' can of course come in many forms, including the idea that the consumer is not sufficiently attractive, wealthy or successful. Advertising is aspirational: advertisers appeal to an ideal version of how they imagine consumers want to be seen. Many professional advertising campaigns involve humour, others use science, and still others present mini-stories that are rather like serial dramas.

Cause or charity texts

Texts seeking support for a cause or charity can come in different forms, including letters, emails, leaflets, print adverts and broadcast advertising. What they have in common is their structure and their tactics.

Charity texts can share with many other forms of advertising the problem–solution discourse structure, but they tend to present this in a particular way. Often, the text offers its audience both a sense of the problem being large in scale, as well as the specifics of an individual case. Using a specific case study helps people to empathize and identify with an individual, while the inclusion of a sense of scale ensures that the audience recognizes it as a sizable issue that will require the help of many people, including themselves. At the same time, the scale of the solution – the audience providing money or, occasionally, something else – is minimized to make it appear to have low impact on the audience, but maximum impact on the problem or issue. Minimizing techniques include hedge words such as 'just' or the use of comparison or analogy: 'less than the price of a cup of coffee'.

Did you know?

The term 'advertisement' comes from a Latin verb 'advertere', meaning 'to turn towards'. Advertisements are attention-seeking texts. They compete for our attention against many other media as well as other advertisements, so they have to be original to work.

Activity

Go back to the charity advertisement that featured in Chapter 1 (pages 17 and 28). It was placed in the folds of a national newspaper in the run-up to Christmas.

What strategies does this text use to persuade its audience? Could you use these strategies in your own writing?

Articles

Newspaper and magazine articles which are written to persuade can appear in a number of different guises. Editorials are statements offering the views of the newspaper or magazine as a whole, and tend to relate to issues that are current at the time of publication. As the name suggests, they are usually written by the editor. But articles also appear in other parts of publications. They can be in a 'comment' or 'opinion' section of a newspaper or magazine, often written by a regular columnist but also occasionally by an invited commentator.

Regular news articles that populate specific parts of a newspaper, such as sports articles, can also be opinion pieces, if they are less concerned with particular facts than with an issue. For example, in the case of sports, an article could be not about a particular game or match, but about bribery, drugs, racism, or funding issues.

 Activity

Look back at the dangerous dogs article in Chapter 2 (page 39) for an example of an opinion piece. What features does the writer use to make her points?

 Extension activity

Survey a range of publications, looking at examples of editorials and opinion articles. You could explore books about journalism, where articles by well-known journalists are collected together in one place. You could also search for the work of a known journalist. If you are interested in finding a style model for presenting more than one side of an argument, you will need to search for where you know there have been different opinions. For example, the journalists Grace Dent and Simon Kelner, both from *The Independent*, took very different views in the 6 January 2014 edition about whether a footballer called Ched Evans, who had been convicted of rape, should being allowed back into professional football. Searching this edition or searching the journalists' names alongside the footballer's name would bring up their articles.

- Whatever sources you identify, make some notes on the topics covered and on the kinds of language features used.
- Could any of these examples provide you with a good style model?

 Link

In carrying out a survey of editorials and opinion articles, you will be developing an awareness of journalism that will help you in other parts of the specification, for example A level Paper 2 Section B.

Speeches

A traditional rhetorical or political speech would, of course, fit the bill for this task perfectly, but it is also possible to think less grandly. Talks given to local groups or at public meetings would also be appropriate here.

 Activity

Go back to the speeches featured in Chapter 1 (page 21) and remind yourself about some of the techniques discussed there. Could you apply these same techniques to a more local issue in your home context?

Extension activity

Do some research on different speeches that you can find online. In Chapter 1, you were given the following web address: http://www.americanrhetoric.com but there are many other sources that you could try, including books of speeches.

Representational aspects of persuasive writing

The concept of representation is an important one, and worth considering in your original writing, whatever text type you choose, but it is particularly important in persuasive texts. Considering how your style model creates, perpetuates or challenges representations will be a useful exercise in helping you to prepare for your own writing.

Chapter 2 had a strong focus on language use and representation in texts; Chapter 3 included discussion of how different groups are represented in the discourses that are all around us; Chapter 5 also focused on representation in discussing language change and language reform. Of course, language and representation can be an interesting topic to write about in itself. But you also need to think about how you are representing aspects of experience and people, both in what you write yourself and in how you analyse your writing in your commentary.

The power of storytelling

Stories are told in many different contexts, both literary and non-literary, and many would make appropriate texts for this assessment. Note that the specification chooses to call this 'the power of storytelling' rather than, for example, 'writing stories', so it is very clear that forms other than prose are welcomed.

Here are a few examples of texts that tell stories. See if you can add to this list and give some examples of publications:

- autobiography and biography
- fiction published in writing magazines or on online sites
- literary monologues
- narrative poetry
- 'real-life' stories in magazines
- television, radio and theatrical drama
- travel memoir
- magazine fiction
- stories in fanzines or other special-interest publications

Power in short-form storytelling

Whichever form you choose, if you are telling a story it is usually more effective to tell an entire story than a part of one. This does not, however, mean that you cannot choose a form that is usually longer than 750 words, such as autobiography or TV drama. In these examples, you can plan an extract or scene to tell the complete story of a single event. A novel extract would be permitted, but it is a much better idea to work on a short story, as this will enable you to demonstrate more plotting skill in resolving your story within the word count.

For short fiction to work, whatever its format, its scope needs to be fairly narrow in terms of plot, characters and setting. Anything overly complex – such as a twisty spy thriller plot, or a fantasy world – is unlikely to be successfully developed in the space available, but this doesn't mean these genres are not available to you. Such stories need to be focused closely on a single event, but clearly placed within the genre.

It is crucial that you find an appropriate style model, so if you want, for example, to write a spy story, a short story in the spy genre will be much more useful to you than an extract taken from a novel.

Story as conflict

Plot is probably the first consideration for most storytellers. What will happen in the story? Often, especially with shorter-form fiction, plot arises out of character – or more specifically, out of the central character's key conflict. There is a reason 'happily ever after' is an ending and not a beginning! There are various basic conflicts to choose from: characters may want something they can't have; characters may need to do something they don't want to do; characters may be forced into some new situation. There are also internal conflicts, where characters are essentially battling against their own nature.

In a piece of short fiction, it is a good idea to focus on just two or three characters, with your main character facing some kind of conflict or opposition. This can come from another character, or from a situation, or be an internal conflict. Whether you are thinking of writing a script, a literary short story or a 'real-life' story, these factors will still apply. The factors that will vary are more about how you tell the story.

Narrative decisions

For prose fiction, issues to be decided include point of view and tense. There may be particular conventions in your chosen genre, and you should certainly make sure that your style model exemplifies the way to write. In short fiction, it is usual to select a single point of view. A novel may offer multiple viewpoints, but that is far harder to manage within a low word count. Some of your options are shown in the table below.

> ### Did you know?
>
> Some theorists suggest that there are only seven basic plotlines, with all fiction and myth adapting one of these key stories: overcoming the monster, voyage and return, rags to riches, the quest, comedy, tragedy, rebirth. This is why the centre for children's books in Newcastle is called 'Seven Stories'.

> ### Key terms
>
> **Heterodiegetic narrator.** A narrator who is not an active participant in the story.
>
> **Homodiegetic narrator.** A narrator who is an active participant in the story.
>
> **Omniscient narrator.** An 'all-knowing' figure who can report everything, including the thoughts inside all of the characters' heads.

Homodiegetic narrator (sometimes called 'first-person narrative')	The narrator is part of the story, so refers to himself/herself within it. Narrators of this type can only describe what they themselves feel and experience.
Omniscient narrator	A single narrator is able to reveal what is inside all the characters' heads, as well as tell the reader things that the characters themselves don't know.
Heterodiegetic narrator (sometimes called 'third-person narrative')	The narrator is not part of the story, so narrates what happens to other people in the story. This isn't necessarily presented at a distance – this type of narrator can stick with one of the characters quite closely.
Multiple narrators	This would be a context where different viewpoints are presented one after another. This is rather complex for a short space, but recent examples are *Gone Girl* by Gillian Flynn, and *The Slap*, by Christos Tsiolkas.

The structure you follow in a prose story will also need consideration: Where is the beginning of your story? Will you tell it from the beginning? Could you start near the end of the action and fill in the rest using flashback or the characters' memories? Are you 'showing' all the action, or will some be related by a character to another character?

Other prose forms, including travel writing, autobiography, and biography, involve a similar decision process. Obviously, if you want to write in the third person, biography would be appropriate while autobiography would not, but there are still choices to make in terms of structure and tense. Real-life stories in magazines, however, have quite a fixed style and are generally presented chronologically in the first person, using the past tense. With these less straightforward forms of storytelling, the text may have another purpose besides narration, for example to create a thematic point or to allow the reader to share in an interesting or unusual experience. If you identify such a secondary purpose in your style model, you will need to create something comparable in your own writing.

Activity

Examine the extract below, taken from Bill Bryson's memoir, *The Life and Times of the Thunderbolt Kid*. In this passage, he is remembering his work as a paperboy, aged around 11.

1. What narrative viewpoint does he adopt?
2. How would you describe the 'voice' of his narrator?
3. How does he construct a sense of the character of Mrs Vandermeister?

Mrs Vandermeister was 700 years old, possibly 800, and permanently attached to an aluminium walker. She was stooped, very small, forgetful, glacially slow, interestingly malodorous, practically deaf. She emerged from her house once a day to drive to the supermarket, in a car about the size of an aircraft carrier. It took her two hours to get out of her house and into the car and then another two hours to get the car out of the driveway and up the alley. Partly this was because Mrs Vandermeister could never find a gear she liked and partly because when shunting she never moved forward or backward more than a quarter of an inch at a time, and seemed only barely in touch with the necessity of occasionally turning the wheel.

Getting money from Mrs Vandermeister was a perennial nightmare. Her front door had a small window in it that provided a clear view down her hallway to her living room. If you rang the doorbell at 15-second intervals for an hour and 10 minutes, you knew that eventually she would realise someone was at the door – 'Now who the heck is that?' she would shout to herself – and begin the evening-long process of getting from her chair to the front door, 25 feet away, bumping and shoving her walker before her. After about 20 minutes, she would reach the hallway and start coming towards the door at about the speed that ice melts. When eventually she came to the door, you would have an extra half-hour of convincing her that you were not a murderer.

The Life and Times of the Thunderbolt Kid, by Bill Bryson

Narrative poetry and spoken genres

If you choose to write narrative poetry, you will need to make many of the same decisions as for prose fiction, as well as thinking about poetic form. You may wish to use a specific form, such as the ballad, to tell a story, or you may want to write in different forms for different stages of the story. Again, selecting a helpful style model is important – it is no good using a style model written as a sonnet if you want to write in free verse, or something using a single narrator when you want multiple perspectives.

With spoken genres, structure is still an issue. If you wish to produce a script, it is important to examine scripts in the form you want to use, and to watch or listen to performances as well – you will need a clear understanding of how the script translates into performance, and this can be discussed in your commentary. Performed stories of all kinds have well-established conventions which you should use, whether that is Alan Bennett's use of reported speech and detailed stage directions, or the way soap opera scripts create pace and drama using interruption and gesture.

Thinking of writing a children's story?

The average picture book is 500–1000 words long, so this is a possibility in terms of word count, but do make sure you use a full story text aimed at young children as your style model, and do actually count the words to make sure that it is appropriate for length. You should scan the text or retype it into a single document so that you can annotate it, with brief notes on the pictures where they add something to the story that is not present in the words alone. Your own text can be presented in a similar way. There is no need for you to produce illustrations, although there is nothing to stop you describing the pictures you would like to have.

In writing for children, many people assume that you need to write simply in short sentences. This is just not true. Even early graded reading books are not written solely in simple sentences, because they would be so boring to read. It's also not true that the lexis in children's books is always simple – many complex words are used even in picture books, especially if they contribute to a phonological effect. In a sense, children are accustomed to not understanding every word spoken, so they are better at letting language wash over them than adults. If you would like to write for children, remember that you can be more adventurous and playful with language, especially with phonology, in these texts.

Stories and representation

Many fiction texts tackle representational issues consciously by using an element of surprise or by describing things and people in an unexpected way. The *Noughts and Crosses* trilogy by Malorie Blackman achieves this very effectively with its race-reversal theme. Similarly, Jeanette Winterson, in *Written on the Body*, never reveals the sex of the first-person narrator, and it is an interesting exercise to try reading it both ways. Karen Joy Fowler, in *We Are All Completely Beside Ourselves*, suddenly reveals that a representation built up by the book in its early pages is something else entirely.

At the same time, stereotypes abound in fiction, and in a short piece it is very difficult to produce effective characterization without using any form of stereotype, particularly if you want to make clear that you are working in a specific genre. This is especially true of secondary characters. One way of

Link

Some good starting points for potential style models are books by Julia Donaldson, Oliver Jeffers, Debi Gliori, Emily Gravett, or any books long-listed for the Carnegie Medal or UKLA awards, 3–6 category.

Link

Go back to the activity you completed in Chapter 4 on children's early reading books (page 134). Remind yourself of the features you observed in your survey, and import the work you did there into this aspect of the specification.

tackling this is to directly challenge a stereotype with a single unusual detail, to make your character an individual rather than a 'type'. Again, as with persuasive writing, representational issues in your work and your chosen style model are worthy of discussion in the commentary.

The power of information

Writing informatively offers you the chance to exploit your hobby, interest or pet topic for assessment. If you have expertise about a particular topic, this can easily be put to good use as an informative text for original writing. Extracurricular interests, family hobbies and topics from your other A level subjects could all be used for this type of work. A key consideration for writing under this heading is (as always) audience. If you have in-depth knowledge of something, it is not always easy to write for a beginner, so it may be a good idea to find a specialist source to use as your style model. On the other hand, introducing a broad audience to your pet topic or interest may very much appeal to you, in which case you will need a style model doing just that on a different topic.

Activity

Think carefully and list the range of text types that aim to inform as their primary purpose. Where do you go when you need information? You should consider:

- texts using different modalities
- texts for different audiences.

How many different genres of writing can you list?

Key features for informative writing

Whichever text type is used, the most important thing for informative writing is its clarity. This must be evident in both its structure and its language. How this plays out specifically will depend on the audience: for example, an article for a specialist water-sports magazine will be able to use much more field-specific lexis than a text for a broader audience. A piece for such a magazine would also need to focus in on much more specific content. This requirement for clarity does not, however, mean that less skill is needed.

Information above all else

Texts in the real world rarely have a single purpose. In selecting a genre for your text (and your style model), you need to be certain that your text is primarily informative. You would be surprised at how often students describe texts as informative when they are intended more to argue, persuade, instruct, entertain or advise. Clearly, your text may well have a secondary purpose which is one of these – or it may, for example, use entertaining features to help it make its points – but it would be a bad idea to produce a text under this heading where informing is not its primary, most obvious purpose.

Activity

The following are initial ideas submitted by some students as potential 'power of information' submissions. Discuss the suitability of these ideas, and make suggestions about how to adapt any ideas that are not appropriate for this category – either by making them more informative, or by adjusting them to fit another of the categories:

- A review of a film for a broadsheet newspaper.
- An article for an equestrian magazine, explaining how to choose a riding school for a child.
- A blog explaining my views on feminism.
- A script for a how-to video on replacing a smartphone screen.
- An article for a fashion magazine, describing this season's key trends.

Preparing your original writing submission

Your first task is to decide exactly what you are going to write, and then you will need to find an appropriate style model to annotate and work with. You may find it easier to combine these tasks, making some broad decisions about your writing and then fine-tuning this as you research potential style models. There are four initial choices to be made.

- Which heading are you working under: persuasion, storytelling or information?
- What is the genre of your writing?
- Who is the audience for your writing?
- What is the subject of your writing?

You may find one or two of these decisions easier than the others. It is usually a good idea to at least consider a range of possibilities before deciding firmly: our first choices are not always automatically the best ones. It is possible that you are brilliant at writing voiceover narration, but have never tried before. Ideally, you will have time to experiment with writing a few different kinds of text before deciding what your coursework will be. It is your own work, so don't make an instant, rushed decision about what and how to write. You have more chance of producing something good if you consider it carefully.

You should be prepared to consider a few ideas for your original writing, rather than picking something early in the process and rejecting everything else. Writing is above all a creative process. It is worth having a place to record any ideas you have about this task, so that when you really need to decide, you have some options to consider. Sometimes ideas that you aren't serious about when you first jot them down turn out to be enjoyable and interesting to work on. If you don't record ideas as and when they come to you, you will lose them. Most professional writers carry notebooks to jot down their ideas, and lots of these remain undeveloped. Nonetheless, many a tale is told about the idea that was nearly dismissed but that in fact became the basis of a successful piece.

One source of potential stories could be the 'thumbnails' that appear in popular or free newspapers or online news feeds, where a whole narrative is given in a couple of lines. You could use one of these starting points and expand it, shaping it in your own way. But if you don't collect and keep sources as you go, you will forget what you have read.

Activity

Refer back to your answers to the activity on page 219 at the beginning of this chapter, in which you produced a list of publications and media sources that are familiar to you, of hobbies and interests you have, and of topics that concern or interest you. Use these lists to help you generate a set of possible texts that you could produce for the original writing task, creating something like the outline below, or a mind map if that feels more natural to you. Consider all the subjects covered in your original lists, and think about potential text types that you are familiar with. Make any notes you need to in order to help you with the next stages.

<u>Interest: Reading vampire-based teen/young adult novels</u>

Persuasion	Podcast script arguing there's nothing wrong with reading fantasy novels
	Opinion article arguing against the idea that only 'classic' literature is worthwhile
Storytelling	Short vampire-based story (need a style model that isn't vampire??)
	(Not comfortable with radio story/TV script)
Information	Webpage content on L J Smith for Vampire Diaries series mini-site (biography, ways books differ from series etc)
	Voiceover narration for section of a documentary on vampires in fiction

Working with a style model

The reason why this task requires a style model is so that you can demonstrate that you can write in a particular form – adapting appropriate features to create the right style. Attempting this without closely analysing existing texts is very difficult.

Also, looking for style models involves you in wider reading and in considering how texts of different kinds work. This, in turn, will pay off in the examined parts of the specification, where you are expected both to analyse texts and to write them.

Ideally, you will explore several possibilities before selecting your style model; you will then annotate it closely and refer to it in your commentary. It is important to remember that your writing will be assessed at least partially in terms of how well you have appropriated the style of your model text, so you must choose a text you like that is as similar to the way you want to write as possible. For this reason, it is expected that you will find your own model, although you should seek and listen to advice from your teacher about possible sources. You will also want your teacher's approval before working in detail on your style model.

Your style model will need to be annotated in detail to enable you to engage closely with its features. Consider the following:

- discourse structure
- point of view and audience construction
- register and style
- connotations
- graphological features
- grammar
- any other features of the text's context (audience, purpose, genre, mode).

Planning your work

The mark of good planning is that you should know precisely what you're going to express before you start writing. A useful plan will take time, but the payoff is improved writing. If you are sitting down to write without knowing what it is that you want to say, then you haven't planned enough. It may help to think of planning as the thinking stage – once you've planned, you should not need to do any more thinking about what to say. Thinking in the writing stage should only be about exactly how to convey the ideas you've had.

- Planning = what to say
- Writing = how to say it

Planning for the commentary

For the original writing task, you need to produce a commentary as well as the text itself. If you plan the text carefully, you can make sure that it helps you to produce a good commentary. Your commentary needs to contextualize your piece by explaining briefly where it would be published and who your audience would be. It should also explain in a detailed linguistic way how you have achieved what you set out to do, with reference to your style model.

To help you with this, a plan for this task should include a reminder of the key features of your style model. A plan for your original writing work, in other words, needs to help you with the *how* of writing as well as the *what*.

Producing a commentary

Your commentary needs to be roughly the same length as your piece. Its purpose is to help you demonstrate that:

- you wrote your piece carefully, consciously selecting appropriate and effective linguistic features
- you wrote your piece with a clear sense of how it fits into a genre, informed by your style model.

In the A level specification, commentaries that are awarded the top range of marks must do the following, with reference *both to your own writing and the style model*.

- Apply language levels in an integrated way (AO1). This means that you shouldn't go through the language levels doggedly one by one, but join up your ideas about the features you refer to.

> **! REMEMBER**
>
> Annotate your style model closely, list the key features on your plan for writing, then put your style model aside to help you write freely while using the most important features you have identified.

Looking ahead

The planning and drafting skills outlined here will also stand you in good stead for degree-level work. You may not have done much planning work in your earlier school career, but as the writing you need to do increases and gets more demanding, it will become more and more important that you separate out the thinking phase from the writing phase, in order both to save time and to produce better work. Planning is also important in all your exam assessments.

- Demonstrate understanding of genre as a dynamic process (AO2). In other words, you should approach the idea of genre not just as a formula for writing but something that can change and be creatively adapted.
- Evaluate use of language and representations according to the two contexts (AO3). This means that you show awareness of how both your writing and the style model give messages about the world they represent, and are shaped to suit audience, genre, purpose and mode.
- Evaluate the significance of connections found across texts (AO4). You need to make explicit connections between your writing and the style model.
- Write accurately and guide the reader with a coherent structure (AO5). This refers to the necessity for clarity and good organization in your commentary writing.

Checking and editing

Many students fail to check their work. This costs marks, because it results in a far less polished result. When you check your writing, you are assessing a number of things at once, but primarily you are checking for both accuracy of expression and for sense and style (does your text match the form you are intending to create?).

It helps to read aloud. This is not something you can do in an exam situation, but for non-exam assessment it's well worth getting into the habit of reading your work aloud, especially if you have any thoughts about writing being part of your career later. Reading aloud helps to catch overlong sentences, or those sentences that you never quite finished, especially if you make sure that you pause after each sentence and consider each as a single unit.

If spelling is an issue, it can help to check backwards, one word at a time from the end to the start. This works because when reading sentences, we tend to read for meaning and so do not always notice our own spellings. If you pay attention to each word individually, however, it is easier to see those errors. A further strategy is to check line-by-line with a ruler, so that you concentrate on one line at a time. A longer-term idea is to create your own small study group in order to exchange work in progress with each other, so that you can both comment on and check each other's writing.

Checking and editing go together – there is no point in spotting changes that need to be made, if you are not going to make them. Some people like to correct anything they spot straight away, while others just note that something is wrong and come back to it another time.

It can be a good idea to separate the critical, fault-spotting work from the creative rewriting work. You should carry out several edits of a text, especially if it is long or needs more than one kind of check. Novelists sometimes run through separate edits to look at aspects such as each character's development, the setting and plot development. For your original writing, you will probably need to edit for accuracy and sense, and separately for the effects you hope to have created. You should be matching the style of your chosen style model, and it's worth doing a read-through and edit specifically asking yourself whether you've achieved that aim to the best of your ability.

The commentary needs checking for accuracy and sense as well, of course, and also to make sure that you have included the best possible features and sufficient analytical detail.

Looking ahead

Use this information about the Assessment Objectives as a checklist when you are working on any commentary writing.

REVIEW YOUR LEARNING

- What are the three possible categories you can use for your writing?
- What are the purposes of a style model?
- What are the word-count requirements for this part of the non-exam assessment?
- Give some examples of text types that you are considering writing.
- What is the function of the commentary?

References

Bryson, B. (2006) *The Life and Times of the Thunderbolt Kid*. New York: Doubleday

 Further reading

Cusick, E., La Tourette, A., and Newman, J. (2004). *The Writer's Workbook*. Bloomsbury Academic.

Stein, S. (1999). *Solutions for Writers: Practical Craft Techniques for Fiction and Non-fiction*. Souvenir Press.

Each of the chapters in this book has begun with details about how the learning in that chapter relates to specific assessments and their associated Assessment Objectives (AOs). Below is some further practical advice to help you maximize your effectiveness and achievement in the different types of assessment that you will face for English Language.

Non-exam assessment

Chapters 7 and 8 have already provided a great deal of advice about how to approach this area of study. The following key points provide a summary:

- Make a work schedule for yourself and factor in some realistic deadlines.
- Have a 'Plan B' in case your initial ideas don't work out.
- Get into good study habits – keep accurate records, back up your data and writing drafts, take advantage of electronic tools and resources.
- Prepare for the regular meetings that you will have with your supervisor/teacher and make the most of the time you are given.
- Try something new – don't go over old ground.

Exam assessments

Make sense of the exam paper

English Language exams often come with extra sheets, such as data booklets and inserts. Make sure that you've located all of the different parts of the paper before you start; check through it to ensure that you haven't ignored any pages, or not realized that a text continues onto a following page.

Make a plan before you write

Sometimes candidates feel that they should start to write as soon as possible – because they need to use every second for writing rather than thinking. This is a mistake. You need time to make sense of the question, and time to think about how to produce a relevant and well-organized answer. You should aim to produce an answer that groups your points together in a coherent way, and that has been written concisely – in legible handwriting. Don't let students who write fast and furiously make you feel panicked. Quantity is not the same thing as quality.

Do some annotation

When you are given data or texts to analyse, annotate any relevant aspects of language that you notice during your several readings of the material. Grouping points together is much easier if you can do some visual labeling, rather than trying to organize your points in your head. However, don't annotate so much that you obscure the original text or data.

Answer the question

Answer the question set, not the question that you would have liked to see. Examiners cannot give you marks unless you do this – even if the points you make are good ones. Only relevant points count. Also, make sure that you indicate which question you are answering.

Remember that questions come in different types:

- An instruction to analyse a passage requires a text analysis as an answer.
- A question that asks you to discuss an idea requires a discussion essay as an answer.
- If a question asks you to refer to two examples, you need two – if you give one example, you've only done half the job.

Take particular note of the trigger words in the questions, because they hold the key to what the examiners expect you to do:

- If you are being asked to 'evaluate' something, that task is different from being asked to 'discuss' something.
- If you are being asked to 'analyse' a text, that is different from being asked to 'compare and contrast' two texts.
- If a question offers you a set of steps to go through – take them.
- If you have been given data to comment on before producing a discussion, make sure that you do both.

In short, do what the question asks – in the most appropriate way. Whatever the exam question is asking you to do, will form the basis of any mark scheme that rewards you for your response.

Use all of the details that you have been given

Examiners go to great lengths to explain the contexts from which they take data, texts, quotes and passages. Read these sources of information carefully, because they are there for a reason. They are there to help you understand how to link the language features that you find with the factors that shaped their occurrence.

If texts are in colour, think about why they may have been reproduced in that way. Examiners have choices about how much material to include as part of the exam paper. Therefore, if features are present on the paper which are not central to the text – for example, advertising around a webpage – think about why those items may have been included. The only wastage on exam papers is the blank pages – everything else that has been included on the paper is there to be commented on.

Transcripts require extra attention for a number of reasons:

- They often involve sets of participants, and you need to get a sense of who the people were in the original interaction. It's a bit like understanding a playscript – you need to get a sense of the different characters and the roles they are playing.

- Look carefully at transcription keys and the features that have been marked.

- Use the line references given, so that you can refer economically to speakers and to sections of interactions.

- Remember that, although you are looking at a flat representation, it was once a dynamic event that unfolded in real time. As a reader, you can see how the interaction ended, but the participants couldn't foresee that at the time.

Terminology

Only use terms that you understand. It is better to show understanding of language without terminology, than to use terminology with no understanding.

If you are going to quote academic names – for example, of researchers and their work – try to represent them accurately. There's nothing wrong with counting yourself as a researcher: if you have completed your coursework folder, then you are one, so include some details about what you have learned – but only if it's relevant to the question you're answering.

Chapter 1

Page 13

through	/θru:/
thorough	/θʌrə/
cough	/kɒf/
thought	/θɔːt/
bough	/baʊ/
dough	/dəʊ/

Pages 14–15

- The stressed words have been given emphasis because their meanings are being questioned.
- Pauses in B's speech suggest that the speaker is trying to recall items from memory.
- There is reciprocal laughter about the odd nature of those items.

Speech between strangers often involves routine topics, such as the weather, which is the case here. The topics that are considered routine vary from culture to culture. The talk here is also, typically, context related – the speakers share a view of their surroundings, so this easily becomes a topic which everyone can contribute to. The same context-related nature of much talk can make it hard to understand just from a transcript.

Seven of the turns involve speakers not talking in sentences (i.e. utterances without a main verb). Even where an utterance has a main verb, there are sometimes other elements ellipted – for example, the final line has no subject. This is all entirely normal in speech. To speak in full sentences the whole time, would make a speaker sound unnatural (even robotic).

The non-verbal aspects of this conversation, as with many others, would have been very important – for example, where people were sitting, their facial expressions and their physical gestures would have both shaped their opportunity to talk and also demonstrated their level of engagement in it.

Page 16. Capital letters indicate increased volume. Repetitions of letters suggest elongation of sounds, which can represent the idea of slowing down the pace of the communication. Repeated dots indicate time passing and a person thinking something through.

The students were interviewed about their representations of laughter and they said that 'ha ha ha' and 'he he he' were more straightforward laughter than 'heh heh', which was a chuckle. 'Tee hee' was seen as sniggering, 'oh har har' and 'a-hah-hah-hah' as false or sarcastic laughter, and 'hee hee hee ha ha ha hooooo hoo' as prolonged laughter.

Page 19

- bungalow: Hindi (17th century), meaning 'belonging to Bengal'
- chocolate: Nahuatl (Mexico), via Spanish conquest of much of South America
- banana: Portuguese
- nosh: Yiddish
- arsenal: Arabic
- skipper: Dutch (related to the word 'ship')
- cafeteria: Spanish
- jockey: possibly Romany (Gypsy) or Gaelic
- bureau: French
- boss: Dutch
- rap: in original sense of 'tap', Danish or Swedish, then in context of music, Caribbean English
- ouch: German
- ravioli: Italian
- teenager: American English
- bangle: Hindi
- berserk: Old Norse (Scandinavia)
- tea: Mandarin Chinese
- coffee: Turkish

Page 20. Some Greek and Latin elements occur more than once in the table. Greek – 'tele' (far); 'phone' (voice or sound); 'logy' (discourse or body of knowledge); 'graph' (to write). Latin – 'videre' (to see), 'sub' (under).

- post mortem: Latin for 'after death'
- video: from the Latin 'videre'
- television: Greek 'tele' (as above) and 'vision' from the Latin videre (as above)
- telegraph: as above
- automobile: 'auto' from the Greek 'self' and 'mobile' from the Latin 'mobilis', moveable
- telephone: as above
- periscope: Greek 'peri' (around) and 'skopein' (to examine)

- psychology: Greek 'psyche' (the mind) and 'logy' (as above)
- subterranean: Latin 'sub' (as above) and 'terra' (earth)
- sub-aqua: Latin 'sub' (as above) and 'aqua' (water)
- submarine: 'sub' (as above) and 'marine' from the Latin 'mare' (the sea)
- photography: Greek 'photo' (light) and 'graph' (as above)
- megaphone: Greek 'mega' (great) and 'phone' (as above)
- phobia: Greek 'phobia' (meaning panic or fear of)
- graph: as above
- biology: Greek 'bios' (life) and 'logy' (as above)

Pages 20–21. The two political speeches contrast noticeably in their formality – particularly as a result of the lexis being used. Reagan uses many abstract nouns of Greek and Latin origin, such as 'totalitarianism', 'optimism', 'democracy', 'repression', 'regimes', 'legitimacy'. By contrast, King's lexis is familiar – with many simple words of Anglo-Saxon origin, such as 'dream', 'hills', 'son', and 'children'.

The effect of Reagan's formality is distancing. His use of 'we' at the start is very general in its reference, compared with the personal effect of King's 'I have', strengthened by its repetitions. However, King's speech rises above the strictly personal and intimate details of his own life, when he uses the metaphor of 'the table of brotherhood' – an image of harmony based on a domestic scene, but referring outwards to different nations and races.

Page 22. There are many plausible variants of the definitions below, so if you had an alternative explanation, you are not necessarily wrong.

'Top dog' and 'underdog' may have referred to sawing wood using a two-handled saw, called a dog. In a sawpit, the person at the bottom end would have been the 'underdog'. Older trades could have given us 'hitting the nail on the head' (carpentry), 'getting the sack' (workmen carried their tools in a sack), and having a 'chip' on your shoulder. One explanation of the latter is that the 'chip' was a wooden block and part of a sport where loggers would try to shoot it from a fellow worker's shoulder.

Other expressions come from sport, too: 'square one' goes back to a time when radio football commentators indicated where the ball was by referring to an agreed 'map' of the pitch, drawn out in squares. 'Kicking into touch' comes from rugby,' 'stepping up to the plate' from baseball.

Some expressions are from military contexts. 'Lock, stock and barrel' refers to shooting, and a 'deadline' was part of a military manoeuvre where armed troops stood in a

defensive line. 'Hitting the ground running' could also refer to warfare in the sense of making a parachute jump.

'Boiling over' and getting the 'cold shoulder' are terms from domestic contexts. The cold shoulder represented a chilly reception where guests were given cold cuts instead of a hot meal.

'Putting a sock in it' is from music, referring to muffling the sound of a brass instrument by putting a sock into the end of it.

Page 22. The basis of each metaphor is as follows: the postal service; building work; gardening; sport; photography; medicine; law; eating; travel; religion.

These metaphors could affect behaviour, because they suggest that teachers should exert different levels of influence and behave in different ways. For example, a builder intervenes actively to construct a building, while a gardener might consider it best just to water plants occasionally and leave them to their own devices. Someone from a postal service delivers items, so this sees learning as a 'thing' to be simply handed over.

Page 24. Aspects of cohesion across the text include the following:

- Pronoun use – 'we' becomes 'you' and the final lines equate the two.
- Adjectives – 'smart' (we) becomes the comparative adjective 'smarter' (you)
- Modality – use of modal 'could' and clauses of condition (all starting with 'if') suggest options for the reader. But note that the hotel's preferred option (leaving the towels on the rail) occurs first.
- The colours, shapes and images are cohesive. There is a recurring house-like shape in the hotel logo, the white shape at the bottom (also resembling a bed with pillows) and the towels. The hotel chain uses a characteristic purple colour; white suggests cleanliness and purity; green reflects environmentalism. The green of the 'smart' paragraph becomes the white of 'smarter', tying together both the change of colour as we read down the text and also the different aspects of the theme of conservation – the hotel's efforts and the behaviour being asked of their customers.

Pages 24–25. John Simon's use of 'we' doesn't refer to anyone specifically, but he suggests by default that it does not include people who are 'poorly educated' or part of a 'subculture'. 'We' are therefore in his view a mainstream educated group who, he claims, want to identify with the literary figures and orators in history.

His metaphors revolve around inheritance (niceties handed down to us) and architecture (beautiful old building). The metaphors represent language as a valuable cultural commodity that is part of 'our' heritage, with 'us' as civilized protectors against 'barbarians'. The metaphor of language as architecture is frequently used by conservative prescriptive commentators – perhaps because buildings fit the idea of connections with a cultural past, often symbolize cultural distinctiveness and can give a tangible image of the idea of destruction.

Of course, what Simon is really claiming is that people like him own the language and that other speakers are not allowed to use it in the way they want. Countering his argument first involves laying bare the metaphors that he uses, by showing them to be part of a particular view. Languages and buildings are nothing like each other in reality, and language does not 'belong' to anyone. The idea of English as the preserve of one elite group can be challenged by showing how many varieties of English there are, how English varies across social groups within the UK as well as across the world, and how varieties of English are both logically structured and expressively rich.

A further argument is that even prescriptive grammarians would see that there are two possible views of the correctness of the grammatical structure that he points to. The subject of the verb 'to be' in that part of the text could be argued to be 'one' (in which case, 'was' is correct) or 'writers and speakers' (in which case, 'were' is correct). Grammar is not a cut and dried issue, even for analysts who are not particularly focusing on regional or ethnic varieties.

Pages 28–29. All three texts take creative approaches towards communication and language use:

- The first text uses a humorous cartoon style 'zzzz' to represent both the snoring of a sleeper and the sound /z/ in the word 'please'. The unconventional spelling is coupled with a graphic design that suggests the snoring noise travelling upwards – a style familiar from comics. If someone wasn't familiar with comics, the onomatopoeic language play would be much harder to understand.

- The second text offer a fresh twist on the idea of what a guarantee promises the purchaser – in this case, a compliment on wearing the article. The text is written in an informal style – for example, 'if you find something wrong with it', which in a more formal text might read 'in case of any fault'. The text is also interactive – 'Easy, huh?' addresses the reader directly, in a simulation of casual speech. (The customer is addressed in French as well as in English, because the article was bought in Canada, where there are many speakers of French as a first language).

- The third text uses symbols to replace words in the expectation that the symbols will be easy to comprehend. (On the back of the card there was an explanation, just in case). Some of the symbols are easier to understand than others, because they have a tradition of representation – but only within certain cultures. Below is the back of the card with the official explanations of the symbols:

Chapter 2

Page 34. The voice created is humorous, informal and light-hearted, partly because of the language play – picking up the poop, clean up their act, scooping the poop, drop them in it – and also because of the comical image on the 'stamp'. This works because the notice constructs the narratee as a sympathetic concerned citizen – and not as the offender. The narrator can share a joke with the narratee, but the red bar at the bottom makes it clear that the offence is a serious one and those responsible will be dealt with. The narrator gives three different ways in which the reader can report an offence, which strengthens further the idea that dog fouling is being taken seriously.

Chapter 3

Page 70

BUS	/bʊs/ /bʌs/ /bʊz/	Northern / RP / Northern
CAR	/kɑː/ /kɑr/	RP / West Country and other areas
BATH	/bæθ/ /bɑːθ/	Northern / RP
COT	/kɒt/ /kɔːt/	RP / Scottish
FUR	/fɜː/ /fɜːr/	RP / West Country and other areas
FAIR	/fɜː/ /feə/	Liverpool / RP
PUT	/pʊt/	RP and many regional accents
PUTT	/pʊt/ /pʌt/	Northern / RP
PAW	/pɔː/	RP and many regional accents
POOR	/pʊər/	Scottish
SINGING	/sɪŋɪn/ /sɪŋɪŋ/ /sɪŋgɪŋg/	many regional accents / RP / Liverpool
THREE	/θriː/ /friː/ /triː/	RP / Cockney / Irish (or Caribbean English)
BOTTLE	/bɒʔəl/ /bɒtəl/	Cockney (or Estuary) / RP
ABOUT	/əbɑːt/ /əbaʊt/	Cockney / RP
THEM	/ðem/ /vem/ /dem/	RP / Cockney / Caribbean English

Page 78. There are many representations of certain workplace settings – for example, police stations, law courts, and hospitals. These are all workplaces which provide settings for dramatic action (with human stories about crime and punishment, life and death). These particular workplace settings also provide the opportunity to include a large and varied cast of characters; and can form the basis for a series of episodes, as well as one-off dramas.

There are no workplaces that are obviously undramatic, apart perhaps from the garden shed of a novelist. It is more the case that the action involved needs to be dramatic. Many hours are spent in police stations, courtrooms and hospitals doing routine paperwork or staring at a computer screen, but those are not the parts that are shown. Having said that, some very successful TV programmes have in fact been created from very little action – for example, *The Royle Family, The Office, Early Doors,* and *Gogglebox.* In these examples, it is the characters who are interesting rather than the settings.

Page 79

- voir dire: French 'voir' (true), 'dire' (say). An examination of a witness in court.
- estoppel: French 'estopper' (originally meaning a bung or stopper). The principle of stopping someone from saying something that contradicts what they said earlier.

- laches: French, based on Latin 'laxus' (meaning lax or loose). An unreasonable delay, which could result in the dismissal of a case.
- prima facie: Latin 'primus' (first), 'facies' (face). Based on the first impression, which will stand until proved otherwise.
- novation: Latin 'novare' (make new). The replacement of an old contract with a new one.
- waiver: French 'weyver' (abandon). Deliberate giving up of a right.
- sub judice: Latin 'sub' (under), 'judice' (judge). Subject to a court case and therefore not able to be discussed publicly.
- habeas corpus: A Latin phrase that means literally 'you shall have the body'. The idea that lawful grounds for a person's detention need to be put forward.
- tort: Latin 'tortum' (injury). A wrongful act that leads to legal liability.
- subpoena: Latin 'sub' (under), 'poena' (penalty). A writ requiring someone to attend court.
- covenant: French 'covenir' (to agree). An agreement.
- fee simple: French 'fie' (fee). The word order of this phrase is French, with the adjective coming after the noun rather than before it. A charge or payment.

Page 80

1. Farming, accountancy, men's barber, spinning and weaving.

2. Boxing, thought to be from horse racing (jockeys not needing to spur their horses on because they are already winning can relax their grip), tennis, wrestling, cricket, chess, baseball.

Page 80. Subject, lessons, tasks, steady, progress, lively, class, discussion, improve, concerted effort, sociable, considerable, sufficient, hindered, attendance, conscientious, capable, pupil, listens, effort, pleased.

Chapter 4

Page 110

● Tiger: Categorical overextension. Tiger appears to be the term used to refer to all similar animals within this category.

● Socks: Analogical or categorical overextension. There are two alternatives here. One is that the child is making an analogical overextension and likening some property of the glove to that of their concept of 'sock' (perhaps because they are both covers for parts of the body, or because similar material is used for each). The other alternative is a categorical overextension, in which the word 'socks' is being used as a term for all types of clothing.

● Duck: Categorical overextension or mismatch. Again, there are two possibilities here. The child may be using the term 'duck' to refer to all birds, or might be using the holophrase 'duck' to refer to the whole process of feeding birds in the park, or even to the whole activity of walking to the park and then feeding the birds.

● Cat: A mismatch. The cat is often there, so the word is conveying some abstract information about its absence.

● Shoes: Underextension. The child is using the word 'shoes' in a very narrow sense – relating its meaning only to her own shoes and not to those belonging to others.

Page 112

a   Deletion of final phoneme /s/

b   Deletion of unstressed syllable /kəm/

c   Substitution of /w/ for /r/ (also overgeneralizing of verb ending 'ed', showing that a grammatical rule has been learned)

d   Deletion of first consonant and addition of final consonant sound.

e   Consonant cluster reduction of /bl/ to /b/

f   Substitution of final consonant sound /t/ for /k/

g   Substitution of /b/ for /r/ and assimilation (b–b).

Page 113

a   'What you doing?' = 4
    What + *you* = 2
    do + *ing* = 2

b   'Not eat that daddy.' = 4
    1 morpheme in each word

c   'Where's man going?' = 5
    Where + *'s* (contracted form of 'is') = 2
    man = 1
    go + *ing* = 2

d   'The mans are laughing.' = 6
    man + *s* = 2
    The and *are* = 2
    laugh + *ing* = 2

e   'The soldiers falled over when they got hitted.' = 11
    The, over, when, they, got = 5
    soldier + *s* = 2
    fall + *ed* = 2
    hit + *ed* = 2

Page 115

● Example 1 shows how the child's increased sophistication in grammatical structure can now lead to more precise meanings. The main content, or lexical words, are there, but grammatical words are missing. The auxiliary verb 'is going' is missing, as is the preposition 'to work', along with the determiner 'the train', and on the level of morphology the -ing inflection on 'going' is lacking. This type of running commentary is also fairly typical of children at this age and above.

● In Example 2, a slightly different grammatical structure is used by the child. A subject + verb + direct object + indirect object is clear from this utterance: the direct object is the thing being given ('blanket') and the indirect object is the recipient of the blanket ('monkey'). The auxiliary verb 'am' is omitted, leaving just the main verb 'giving'.

● In Example 3, the child has constructed a question but has omitted the non-essential grammatical items: in this case the auxiliary verb 'has' and the determiner 'the'. Syntactically, this is more advanced than Example 2, because the child has created a question structure.

● In Example 4, a similar question structure has been used to that in Example 3, but again the auxiliary verb 'What *is* her doing?' is missing. On this occasion, the correct person pronoun has been used ('her' is a third-person pronoun), but the wrong form (object *her* rather than subject *she*).

Page 116. In Example 1, the child is using a compound sentence containing three clauses linked by coordinating conjunctions (*and* and *but*). Within a few months, however, he and his brother are regularly using complex sentence structures with subordinating conjunctions, such as *because* ('cos') and *when*, as seen in Examples 2 and 3. This added complexity allows the children to express a more developed sense of the world around them, with issues such as cause and effect emerging, as seen in Example 4 ('*because* you'll hit the men and they'll fall over'). Clauses of condition also appear, as seen in Example 5 ('if the baddies attacked'), while a relative clause ('which Liam was playing') is added in Example 6, to offer more information about the subject of the whole sentence.

Pages 117–118

- In Example 1, two verbs in the past tense (*could* and *found*) are used when only one is required to be in the past tense.

- In Example 2, he is closer to the adult target, but uses the auxiliary verb 'has' with the past tense form 'did', rather than its participle form 'done'.

Page 118

The following comments are suggestions for what the child might have been trying to say. When you analyse your own child language data, be open-minded in your approach and offer a range of possible interpretations.

a   'I runned.'

The child has used an overgeneralized past tense -*ed* ending on an irregular verb.

b   'There was three mans.'

The child has used an overgeneralized plural -*s* ending on an irregular noun and formed a version of the past tense without creating grammatical agreement between the verb and the nouns (i.e. the verb is a singular form and the noun plural).

c   'I eating.'

The child has successfully used a progressive -*ing* ending on the main verb, but has omitted the auxiliary verb (*am* or *was*).

d   'This goody is more braver than that one.'

The child has successfully used a comparative -*er* ending on the adjective brave, and has also realised that some comparatives take 'more' rather than an 'er' ending. But only one of these two strategies is ever needed.

e   'He's hitting him with a hitter.'

The child has created a noun *hitter* from the verb *to hit* plus an -*er* ending that turns it into 'a thing that hits'.

f   'They shotted their arrows at the baddies.'

The child has used an overgeneralized past tense -*ed* ending on an irregular verb, but has applied the ending to the correct past tense form (*shotted* rather than *shooted*).

g   'Daddy go work.'

The child may have omitted two words and a morpheme: the auxiliary *is*, the -*ing* morpheme and the preposition *to*.

Page 122. This appears to be a good example of child-directed speech and parental scaffolding at work. For example, the mum immediately involves Tom in a shared account of events that they have both experienced, by using the inclusive first person 'we', tag questions such as 'didn't we?' and 'didn't you?' to facilitate responses and avoids correction of virtuous errors such as 'I stroke one chicken', preferring to model standard English past tense by saying 'you did (.) didn't you? you stroked it'. The child is also given a chance to go beyond a simple recount of events and to offer his own perspective on what happened.

Pages 128–129. 'Alfi' and 'Story opener' are both narratives that show, in their different ways, characterization, scene setting and a problem emerging in the narrative to create interest. There is a third person narrative in 'Alfi', compared to the first person of 'Story opener'. The first person narration allows more detail, with the character-narrator able to introduce herself to the reader and describe her feelings and her context, as well as to set up the 'complication' in the narrative. The Alfi story is third person narrative and more sparing in its detail, although the idea of the dark 'talking back' is spooky and imaginative.

'Alfi' is organized as a multimodal text, building perhaps on Imogen's knowledge of the layout of young children's books. She tells the story in pictures, showing cohesion with the written text presented above. The written text shows the use of a compound sentence and of declarative functions.

'My blue eyes' is a list but seems in the style of a nursery rhyme, based on developing numeracy and literacy skills. Her list is organized for her in a template provided for her with prompts and blank lines for her to complete with her personal selection of phrases. Imogen's list shows knowledge developing of noun phrases using a variety of different adjectives as modifiers, plurals and sound symbolism in the form of alliteration.

Imogen's more advanced writing in 'Story opener' is given a date of completion and underlined, as is the title of the literacy activity that she is undertaking. She has advanced in her use of materials, too – using an exercise book rather than plain paper and a template – and she can clearly organize her writing into paragraphs. Imogen constructs her text using compound and complex sentences. She mainly uses declaratives but the interrogative suggests an awareness of creating a character's thoughts. She moves between the present and past tense and is grammatically accurate with these. Her lexical choices show her understanding of descriptive storytelling, such as the adverbials 'suddenly' and 'one day' and the adjectives 'big, gleaming'.

Page 135. There are many children's books featuring pirates but recent films also could have influenced the game. The play is set in Joel's parents' room. The bed becomes the boat and his mum's jewellery box is the treasure chest.

Joel and his aunt share a familiar semantic field to create and sustain their pirate world via lexical items (such as treasure, necklace, boat, and waves); and via 'pirate' phonology (oh ar oh ar) and onomatopoeic scene setting. Both participants are drawing on sociocultural knowledge and representations of what 'convincing' pirates are like. The drama has been encouraged by his aunt, who has established this play as a ritual and she starts the game by involving Joel as a pirate character, using repeated interrogatives and teasing about the idea of being too small to be a 'proper' pirate.

Page 138. These examples replicate genres that we would see elsewhere: an evaluation of that day's experiences, and a group science report.

The children are learning that different genres need different language choices, registers and structures. The account of the communication with the French penfriend includes French terms as part of representing the conversation between the writers. The report into bugs requires a more objective style, using descriptive terms for the qualities of the insects.

All of the examples show an awareness of mode. The children are learning how to use new technologies as part of their formal education. The Year 6 text refers to Skype as well as to email, so different modes are being experienced, and valuable authentic language will be available to the participants without having to travel to another country.

The bug reports are all timed very closely together, so the children were experiencing writing almost in a real-time context. They were seeing each other's writing and this encouraged everyone to participate.

There is a strong sense of audience in the Year 6 report, with the French terms translated for the reader and a careful use of an accent on 'méchant'.

Page 142

Child's spelling	Actual spelling	Type of spelling error (s)
suddnly	suddenly	omission or salient sounds
peculier / perculiar	peculiar	phonetic
cloke	cloak	phonetic
kitchin	kitchen	phonetic
discusting	disgusting	phonetic
(golf) corse	course	omission / phonetic
shale	shall	over-generalizing / phonetic
exspensis	expensive	phonetic / salient sounds
twincling	twinkling	substitution / phonetic
butifull	beautiful	omission / over-generalizing
kitins	kittens	phonetic
fraindly	friendly	phonetic / transposition
becuase	because	transposition
correg	courage	phonetic / over-generalizing
bissnis	business	phonetic / over- and under-generalizing
cheerfull	cheerful	over-generalizing
intelgent	intelligent	salient sounds

Page 146. Both children show the pragmatic understanding that politeness is needed in invitations and certain types of letters, notably those in which you make a request. In the letter to Santa, Luke repeats words ('please'), foregrounding this at the beginning of each sentence, as well as using modal auxiliary verbs ('can', 'may') to reinforce the polite tone. This repetition of sentence structure also makes the text cohesive. Although careful to put his own wish first, Luke also refers to his parents and identifies items that they may (or may not in the mother's case) be grateful to receive. You might perceive some gender stereotyping here! His use of the possessive pronoun ('my') could be an acknowledgement that Santa needs to know the recipients of the presents.

Within the letter to Santa, Imogen understands letter conventions, choosing 'Dear' to address Santa formally. In the tea invitation she also demonstrates strong awareness of generic conventions with the address ('To Tedey') and the sign-off ('love Imogen'). Imogen is also aware of certain conventions associated with invitations in her request for 'Tedey' to join her at an event (a picnic), offering a time, but not a venue, which shows that she has still to learn all of the information that Teddy logically would need to know in order to attend. Not only does she show an awareness of genre conventions, but she also demonstrates an understanding of the persuasive nature of an invitation – tempting teddy with promises of jelly and buns. Both texts display an understanding of the correct register, and both have a formal tone.

Page 148. The recount of a weekend's activity is chronological, as evidenced by the action verbs 'helped, 'went', and 'had'. The temporal connective 'then' has a sequencing effect. By contrast, the report about leaves is more factual and contains a non-chronological list of declaratives outlining some of its key features.

After surveying all of the texts in this section, you will have found different ways of classifying them using Perera, Christie, Martin and Rothery. A helpful thing to do is to find linguistic evidence for your decisions about which genre they fit into and think about how children advance in their understanding and use of the associated conventions.

Chapter 5

Page 151. Depending on your sources, you will have found some possible explanations for how and why these words came into existence.

- YOLO is an acronym meaning 'You Only Live Once', which has been popularized by the singer Drake and also through its use as a hashtag on Twitter (perhaps seriously but also ironically).

- Hashtag is a term used to describe the Octothorpe symbol (#), which has gained popularity as a means of tagging topics and attitudes in Twitter. It has crossed over, to some degree, into spoken language.

- Jeggings is a recent blend of *jeans* and *leggings* to describe a new form of legwear.

- Credit crunch is a compound word (some would say phrase) that has become popular in the aftermath of the global financial crisis of the late 2000s. Many new words catch on for their sounds, as well as their novelty or meanings, and the alliteration of /kr/ sounds in both words probably helps.

- Gas guzzler is a term used to describe fuel-inefficient vehicles, which compounds the American term for petrol (*gas*) with the colloquial term for someone who drinks rapidly (*guzzler*).

- Bae is a term from Black American slang that has become popular in the last year or two – usually referring to a girlfriend or boyfriend. Perhaps derived from a shortened version of *baby* or *babe*.

Page 155

IMHO	In my humble opinion	Initialism
SIM	Subscriber Identity Module	Acronym
Mansplain	An ironic way of describing how some men explain things to women	Either affixation of a new prefix (man-) or blending of man with explain
Chick noir	A violent and dark genre of literature aimed at women	Compounding (and borrowing from French in the original sense of noir, meaning black)
App	Short version of application	Abbreviation and/or clipping
Malware	Malicious software	Affixation of 'mal-' and/or blending of *malicious + software*
Springador, Labradoodle and Puggle	Breeds of dog	Blending
Cyberbullying	Online bullying and abuse	Affixation of the prefix 'cyber-' (generally meaning online or influenced by technology) to the word *bullying*.

Page 160

- 'I tell thee, churlish priest, / A ministering angel shall my sister be / When thou liest howling.' (William Shakespeare, *Hamlet*, c.1602). 'Thee' is being used as a second person object pronoun (rather than 'you'). 'Thee' was a form of address that could denote intimacy between people (like an endearment today), but when used by a powerful figure, it could be a mark of disrespect – positioning the addressee as powerless and inferior. The word order is different to that used today: modern English would probably begin with the subject (my sister) and combine the two verbs (shall be) into a single verb phrase, with the grammatical complement coming last (a ministering angel). The suffix -st has now disappeared from modern English. 'Shall' and 'churlish' are not exactly archaic, but they are used less frequently in modern English.

- 'I like it not' (William Shakespeare, *Romeo and Juliet*, c.1597). Negative formation in modern English tends to involve the use of 'do' as an auxiliary verb ('I do not like it').

- The curse is come upon me (Lord Alfred Tennyson, 'The Lady of Shalott', 1832). In past times, the verb 'to be' could be used with verbs indicating motion or transition, to create a past tense meaning (as here, with the verb 'come'). Modern English uses the verb 'has' instead. Sometimes, people still use the archaic 'is' if they want a statement to sound momentous. For example, Robert Oppenheimer (viewed as the main creator of the atomic bomb), said 'I am become death, the destroyer of worlds' to lament what his discovery had led to.

Page 173

- Extract 2 uses a discourse of conflict and warfare and some extreme vocabulary to describe the parallel between invasion by a hostile and uncivilized force and text messagers. The use of the present progressive verbs (e.g. 'are destroying') suggests an ongoing and present threat.

- Extract 3 draws on an ecological and environmental discourse, using the semantics of animals and a parallel between the indigenous red squirrel being forced out by foreign invasion and UK words being supplanted by foreign imports.

- Extract 4 uses an unpleasant discourse of xenophobia and thinly veiled racism with the references to poverty and 'pointless' countries when referring to a variety of English. A clear link is being made between language use and social values.

- Extract 5 represents the English language in very definite terms, using declarative sentences that express certainty ('The English language is…'). The language is represented as a fixed and unchanging object passed down from one generation to the next. The semantics of wealth and value are highlighted through several linguistic choices.

- Extract 7 uses a discourse of disease ('plagued') and equates language use with intelligence and social class.

Chapter 8

Page 222. A voiceover narration to a television documentary.

Glossary

Accent. The way that people pronounce sounds.

Accent variation. The way that pronunciations vary between different speakers, or the variations a single speaker might produce in different contexts.

Acrolect. A term used to refer to a standard or official language variety in contexts where creole is spoken.

Acronym. Initials that can be pronounced as words (e.g. SIM).

Active voice. This is when the person or thing doing the action specified by the verb is the subject of the sentence. For example, in the sentence 'I ate a good dinner', 'I' is the subject, doing the eating. 'A good dinner' is the object (person or thing affected by the action of the verb).

Adjacency. The positioning of elements in an interaction, so that one follows on from another, although they don't have to occur immediately afterwards. Elements in an **adjacency relationship** often occur in **adjacency pairs**. For example, greetings are usually reciprocal, questions are followed by answers, etc.

Adjective / Adjectival. Adjectives give more information about nouns, describing the qualities of people and things.

Adverb / Adverbial. Adverbs give more information about verbs – typically, where, when and in what manner the action of the verb takes place. Adverbial elements can be phrases, so aren't necessarily single words.

Affordances. Things that are made possible. For example, a website can be read by many people simultaneously.

Agent. An alternative word for the **subject** in a sentence.

Amelioration. A process whereby a word or phrase develops more positive connotations. For example, 'nice' used to mean ignorant (from the Latin 'nescire' meaning 'to not know').

Analogical overextension. Extending a label from one item to another by connecting their functions or how they are perceived. Although the connections may

have some logic to them, they differ from existing categories.

Anthropomorphism. Imposing human qualities on the animals and objects around us.

Arbitrary. Having no real connection beyond that of social convention.

Aspect. This refers to the way in which certain grammatical markings on verb forms indicate whether an action or state is ongoing. For example, the 'ing' form in 'looking' suggests continuous action: the 'ing' ending is called a 'progressive'.

Asymmetrical. Unequal.

Audience construction. In language study, texts are seen as constructing audiences, not just addressing them. This means that texts create an idea of who the audience is, by 'speaking' to them in a certain way.

Auxiliary verb. These are verbs that help other verbs and include the verbs 'be', 'do' and 'have'.

Basilect. A term used to refer to an informal language variety in contexts where creole is spoken.

Behaviourism / Behaviourist. Within studies of language acquisition, a notion of learned behaviour as a set of responses to stimuli.

Blending. Using parts of existing words to form a new word.

Borrowing. Incorporating words and phrases from another language.

Bound morpheme. A morpheme that does not exist as an independent word but adds meaning to a free morpheme, For example, the free morpheme 'help' can have the bound morphemes 'un', 'ful' and 'ly' added to it to create the 4-morpheme word 'unhelpfully'.

British Black English. A wide-ranging label, but often referring to a variety used by some speakers within the Caribbean community in the UK.

Broadening. A process by which words acquire a broader reference. For example, 'hoover' can be used as a general label for

vacuum cleaners, but it was formerly the name of a particular brand.

Case study. An in-depth study of a single context that can be used to offer insights for further studies or other cases.

Categorical overextension. Inappropriately extending the meaning of a label to other members in the same category. For example, a child calling all leafy green vegetables 'cabbage'.

Child directed speech (CDS). The speech that parents and caregivers use to children.

Chronological. Structured with reference to time.

Citation. A reference to an example of language use or research.

Clause. Clauses are grammatical units and can be main clauses, which stand on their own, or subordinate clauses, which cannot stand alone but have to accompany main clauses. A main clause gives information about people or things (nouns and pronouns) and their states or actions (verbs).

Clause of condition. A clause introduced by conjunctions such as 'if' or 'unless', suggesting that something will happen only if certain conditions are met.

Code mixing. The inclusion of words and phrases from one language in another.

Code switching. Switching between different languages in a sustained way.

Cognitive. This refers to thinking processes in the brain.

Cohesion. The way sentences or utterances join together to form a whole text.

Collocation. The regular occurrence of a word or phrase alongside others.

Colloquial. Colloquial expressions are items of everyday language used in informal contexts.

Community of practice. A group of people who share understandings, perspectives and forms of language use as a result of meeting regularly over time.

Complaint tradition. A tradition of complaining about the state of the language.

Complex sentence. A sentence involving at least one main or independent clause (one that can stand alone and make sense) and a subordinate clause (one that cannot stand alone and make sense). For example, in the sentence 'When I came into the house, I saw the flood damage', the first clause is subordinate and the second is a main clause.

Compounding. Adding two existing words together to create a new word.

Compound sentence. Two main clauses joined by a connective. For example 'I came into the house and I saw the flood damage'.

Comprehension. The ability to understand language, which might differ from how much an individual can produce.

Computer-mediated communication (CMC). Human communication that takes place via the medium of computers.

Concordance line. A line of text from a corpus, showing where the searched item occurred within a sentence or utterance.

Connective. A word that joins elements together, such as 'and' and 'or'. These are also called **conjunctions.**

Connotation. The associations that we have for a word or phrase.

Constructed dialogue. Dialogue that is artificially created rather than occurring naturally. For example, in novels or playscripts.

Construction. In language acquisition, constructions are ready-made chunks of language that can be used productively to express many ideas. This model is also called a **usage-based approach**.

Convergence. In language study, changing one's language in order to move towards that of another individual.

Conversation Analysis. A field of analysis devised by the sociologist Harvey Sacks focusing on the routines that occur in spoken language.

Co-operative principle. An idea from the philosopher H. P. Grice that in conversations, speakers expect others to share certain basic rules of co-operation, such as telling the truth.

Co-ordination. Joining elements together by using a co-ordinating conjunction, such as 'and' or 'or'.

Corpus (plural corpora). A collection of searchable language data stored on a computer.

Covert prestige. Status gained from peer group recognition, rather than public acknowledgement.

Creole. A variety that has developed from a 'pidgin' or trade language to become a stable language used by speakers as their mother tongue.

Critical discourse analysis. A type of text analysis that tries to reveal the power structures that are maintained in society through the discourses used.

Critique. A critical analysis that pays attention to all aspects of a text or topic, seeing different perspectives.

Cyborg. A blend of 'cybernetic' and 'organism' describing a part machine, part human individual.

Declarative. A clause or sentence that has a statement function.

Declinism. The idea that language is in constant decline.

Deficit model. An assumption that something is lacking or deficient.

Deixis. The act of pointing to something by using certain language items. Deictic expressions refer to aspects of space (spatial deixis, for example 'over there'), time (temporal deixis, for example 'yesterday') and person deixis (who is being referred to, for example 'they').

Density. In studies of social networks, density refers to the number of connections that people have.

Descriptivism / Descriptivist. The belief that correctness is dependent on context and should be defined by what is appropriate in any context. Descriptivists take their norms from observing what the majority of people do, not what any particular authority says they should do.

Determiner. Determiners, as the name suggests, help to determine what a noun refers to. Determiners can be wide ranging in their reference, including quantity ('some', 'many'), definiteness ('the' or 'a'), possession ('my', 'our') and demonstrativeness ('these', 'those'). Demonstratives are also called **deictics**, or pointing words.

Determinism. The idea that language determines the way we think and behave.

Diachronic variation. Variation through time.

Dialect. A style of language used within a particular geographical region.

Dialect levelling. The way in which dialect terms have been dropping out of use.

Diaspora. The dispersal of people (and their languages) to different parts of the world.

Directed writing. A writing activity where you are asked to write to a specific brief, rather than inventing your own.

Discourse. A stretch of language (spoken, written or multimodal) considered in its context of use. The plural use of the term – **discourses** – refers to repeated ways of talking or writing about a topic.

Discourse community. An alternative term for a **community of practice**.

Discourse structure. The internal structure of a text.

Disjunct. An adverb that expresses a writer's or speaker's attitude, such as 'frankly', 'fortunately'.

Distribution. Where a feature is used, within the language inventory of an individual or group.

Divergence. In language study, changing one's language in order to move away from that of another individual.

Dysphemistic / Dysphemism. A direct form of language that doesn't attempt to disguise sensitive or difficult topics.

Elaborated code. An idea advanced by Bernstein (and much disputed) that middle-class speakers use context-free, complex forms of language.

Emoticon. A blend word, consisting of 'emotion' and 'icon', which refers to symbols that express the attitude of a writer in digital contexts where non-verbal elements are missing.

Endearment. A term used to address someone without using the person's name.

Endonormative. Looking within the immediate community for the norms of language use.

English as a lingua franca. The role of English as a bridging language in interactions where it is not everyone's first language.

English as an additional language. The use of English where it is not the person's first language learned.

Estuary English. A recent accent variety used in south east England which combines RP with some aspects of regional southern accents. 'Estuary' refers to the Thames Estuary area.

Ethnic identity / ethnicity. Feeling connected with people who have similar cultural backgrounds, heritage, or family ties.

Ethnography / Ethnographic. The study of how a group of people communicate. Ethnographers are often part of the community they study.

Ethnolect. A style of language thought to be characteristic of a particular ethnic group.

Etymology / Etymological. The study of word origins.

Euphemistic / Euphemism. An indirect form of language that enables speakers to avoid mentioning something unpleasant or offensive.

Exonormative. Looking beyond the immediate community for the norms of language use.

External factor. A factor to do with external forces. For example, many French terms came into English after the Norman conquest of 1066.

Eye dialect. Using the regular alphabet to represent sounds, rather than a phonetic or phonemic alphabet.

Face Theory. The idea that we all have a public self-image that we need to project and protect.

Face-threatening act. In Face Theory, something that threatens a person's self-image.

Facework. The effort that we put in to manage our public image.

Familect. A style of language used within a family.

First language (L1). The first language learned by an individual, usually in childhood.

Focus. The area where most attention is concentrated.

Formal / Formality. Designed for use on serious or public occasions where people pay attention to behaviour and appearance.

Framing. The idea that speakers mark their understanding of the context they are in. For example, by smiling or laughing to show that they are being playful.

Free morpheme. A morpheme that can exist as an independent word.

Functional. Emphasizing what something is for, its purposes.

Functional theory. The idea that language changes because society does.

Gender. The social expectations that arise as a result of being one sex or another.

Genderlect. A style of language thought to be distinctive of either men or women.

Generic. For general use or general reference.

Genre. In language study, a type of text in any mode which is defined by its purpose, its features, or both. In literary fields, genre tends to refer primarily to the literary genres of prose, poetry and drama, but it can also refer to types of content (for example, crime or romance).

Genre theory/theorists. How different genres of writing are structured and how people learn to produce them.

Gestalt expression. The term gestalt is German for 'shape' or 'form' and refers to the way in which children at a certain

stage can compress a string of words into a single utterance. For example, while an adult would say 'what is that?' a child might say 'wassat?'

Global English. The idea of English as a worldwide language.

Glottal stop. A closure of the vocal cords. This can be used to replace /t/ in some regional accents.

Grammar. The structural aspects of language that tie items together. Grammar includes **syntax**, or word order; and **morphology**, or the elements added to words to show their grammatical role (such as 'ed' to indicate the past tense of a verb).

Grapheme. Graphemes are visual symbols, for example alphabetic letters.

Graphology. All the visual aspects of textual design, including colour, typeface, layout, images and logos.

Grapho-phonemic. The relationship between symbols and sounds.

Hegemonic. Culturally dominant.

Heterodiegetic narrator. A narrator who is not an active participant in the story.

Heteronormativity. A set of norms or expectations based on heterosexuality. For example, the idea that in a gay couple, one partner should be 'masculine' and the other 'feminine'.

Holophrase / Holophrastic stage. Holophrase means 'whole phrase' and, as it suggests, refers to the stage of language acquisition where whole phrases can be expressed via a single word. Also called the **one-word stage**.

Homodiegetic narrator. A narrator who is an active participant in the story.

Hybrid. Hybrids are blends of two or more elements. For example, new forms of communication are often seen as having some of the characteristics of both spoken and written language.

Hypernym. The name of a category. For example, 'vegetable' is a hypernym, and 'carrot', 'cabbage' and 'onion' are all hyponyms.

Hyponym. The name of a category member. For example, 'carrot' is a hyponym of the category 'vegetable'.

Hypothesis. A proposed explanation for how something will work.

Idiom / Idiomatic. An expression whose meaning is not dependent on the meanings of the words it contains. For example, saying that someone 'has a chip on their shoulder' or that something costs 'an arm and a leg'.

Illiteracy. Failure to become literate.

Inference. Using assumed knowledge in order to determine meaning.

Inferential framework. Knowledge built up over time and used in order to understand meanings that are implicit.

Infix. A particle added to the middle of a word.

Inflection. A morpheme on the end of a word to indicate a grammatical relationship or category. For example, many nouns in English add an 's' to indicate plurality.

Informant. Someone who offers information to a researcher.

Initialism. Initials that cannot be pronounced as words (e.g. DVD).

Innate. Something in-built, already in place.

Interlocutors. People engaged in a spoken interaction.

Internal factor. A factor to do with the internal structure of the language system. For example, English used to have different singular and plural forms of 'you': 'thee' and 'thou' to address an individual or to express closeness, and 'ye' and 'you' to address groups or to express respect to a powerful individual.

International English. The idea of English as a language that is used in international contexts of all kinds.

Intertextuality. The way in which one text echoes or refers to another.

Intonation. Tunes, created from variations in pitch, that convey meaning in the speech of a particular language.

Inventory. A list of items. For example, in phonology, a list of the sounds used in a person's accent.

Isogloss. A geographic boundary indicating where certain items of language are used.

Language acquisition. The development of language within an individual.

Language acquisition device (LAD). Chomsky's idea of an innate capacity for language learning in humans.

Language reform. A term used, usually by liberal commentators, to support the idea of consciously changing language because it is considered unfair to different groups.

Lexical priming. The way in which some words appear to be ready-made for certain meanings, as a result of their habitual use in the same contexts.

Lexis. The vocabulary of a language.

Libfix. A 'liberated' suffix, or one which has been taken from its original context and applied to new situations. Libfixes are creations of their time. For example, after the launch of the Russian spacecraft 'Sputnik' in 1957, there was a growth in the West of terms ending in 'nik' – beatnik, peacenik, refusenik – to label people associated with dubious causes.

Limitations. Things that are prevented or restricted. For example, an SMS has no way to convey the subtleties of non-verbal communication (hence the need for emoticons).

Lingua franca. Where speakers don't share the same first language, a lingua franca acts as a kind of bridging language enabling them to communicate. In modern times, English acts as a lingua franca in many parts of the world.

Linguistic appropriacy. The way in which language choices reflect ideas about what is appropriate for any given context.

Linguistic relativity. The idea that language shapes our thinking but does not completely control it.

Linguistic variable. An item of language that is likely to vary and is therefore of interest to sociolinguists.

Literacy. Literacy refers primarily to reading and writing, including the new types of reading and writing that occur in digital contexts.

Macro-level. Operating on a large scale.

Marking. In language study, identifying an item as different from the norm.

Matched guise technique. An experimental technique where a single actor puts on a different accent for different audiences, but keeps the content of the speech the same.

Matronyms. Names that reflect female lines of inheritance.

Meanings. Messages that are communicated. Meanings are never fixed, but are negotiated between speakers (or writers) and listeners (or readers), and vary considerably according to context.

Mesolect. In contexts where creole is used, a middle style of language between standard and colloquial varieties.

Metaphor. A language strategy for bringing two unrelated ideas together in order to suggest a new way of looking at something. Metaphors are common where something is difficult to understand because it is complex or abstract, so it is compared with something simpler or more concrete.

Methodology. The study of different ways to research ideas.

Micro-level. Operating on a small scale.

Mismatch statement. In child language studies, when a child makes a connection based on what is normally the case, but isn't the case on this particular occasion.

Modal verbs. Modal verbs accompany main verbs and are often used to express degrees of certainty, desirability or obligation.

Mode. Speech and writing are called different modes. Digital communication can draw on both of these modes, so is often called a hybrid form of communication.

Modifier / Modification. Modifiers add information. For example, adverbs add information to verbs (run *quickly*), and adjectives add information to nouns (a *lovely* day).

Monostylistic. Having only one style of communication.

Morpheme. A morpheme is an element of meaning smaller than a word. Morphemes often mark grammatical features. For example, 'talked' has two morphemes – 'talk' and 'ed', which indicates that the talk occurred in the past. Morphemes can also occur as bigger elements, such as the suffixes 'ship' and 'hood' in the nouns 'partnership' and 'neighbourhood'.

Morphology. The aspect of grammar that refers to grammatical markings. For example, the 's' ending on nouns can indicate a plural form (one book, two books).

Multicultural London English. A recent variety combining elements of the language of different ethnic groups, particularly Afro-Caribbean English. The variety arose in London but has spread to different parts of the UK.

Multicultural Urban British English. A label that refers to the way in which Multicultural London English has spread to other large conurbations in the UK.

Multimodal. A multimodal text employs more than one mode of communication – for example, by using images as well as words, or by drawing on an aspect of speech as well as writing.

Multiplexity. In studies of social networks, multiplexity refers to the number of ways in which two individuals might relate to each other, for example, as friends, workmates and family members.

Multiplicative meaning. The process by which one part of a text does more than just add to the meaning of another part. For example, readers understand images in the context of the words that surround them, and vice versa.

Narratee. A fictional receiver; the person that the text appears to be aimed at.

Narrator. A fictional 'teller'; the apparent voice behind the text as created by the author.

Narrowing. A process by which words acquire a narrower reference. For example, 'deer' used to refer to animals in general, not to a specific animal.

Nationality. An aspect of identity that refers to the country of a person's birth or citizenship.

Nativist / Nativism. A belief that language acquisition relies on an in-built capacity for language in humans.

Negative face need. In face theory, the need not to be imposed on by another person.

Nexus. A cluster of connections.

Nominalization. The process of turning different grammatical elements into nouns or noun phrases. For example, in the title of the TV comedy show *Feed My Funny*, the adjective 'funny' has been nominalized, or turned into a noun.

Non-chronological. Not structured with reference to time but shaped by other factors.

Non-linear. In studies of literacy, non-linearity refers to new forms of literacy such as webpages, where we don't read line by line but often click through to further pages.

Non-literacy. An oral society is non-literate, i.e. it has no system of literacy.

Non-regional. An alternative name for the **RP** accent.

Non-standard. Different from normal or majority usage.

Non-verbal behaviour. Communication that takes place via the body (such as gesture and facial expression).

Noun phrase. A phrase that has a noun or pronoun as its main word (called the head word).

Nurture. The idea that language development results from being socialized by people around the learner.

Object. The thing or person on the receiving end of the action of the verb.

Object permanence. The idea that objects exist even when they cannot be seen.

Observer's paradox. The paradox that the only way to collect natural speech is to observe it – but the very act of observation is likely to destroy its naturalness.

Omniscient narrator. An 'all-knowing' figure who can report everything, including the thoughts inside all of the characters' heads.

One-word stage. Also called the **holophrastic** stage, this refers to the stage of language acquisition where a single word can stand for a whole expression.

Onomatopoeia. The way in which some words appear to echo the sounds they describe, such as 'crash' and 'thud'.

Oracy. Speaking and listening, the skills required to communicate in spoken language.

Original writing. Writing of all kinds that derives from individual ideas.

Orthography. The spelling system.

Overextended / Overextension. Applying a label to more referents than it should have. For example, a child saying 'sea' to label any body of water.

Overgeneralization. Applying a rule and assuming that every example follows the same system, without realizing that there are exceptions.

Overt prestige. Status that is publicly acknowledged.

Paralanguage. Aspects of an individual's vocal expression, such as whispering, laughter, breathiness.

Passive voice. Use of the passive voice turns elements around, so that the thing or person being acted upon goes at the front. So, when changing the active sentence 'I ate a good dinner' to a passive, it becomes 'A good dinner was eaten (by me)'. The last part is in brackets because it can be left out and the sentence still makes sense.

Patient. An alternative word for the **object** in a sentence.

Patois. An alternative term for creole, sometimes spelt 'patwa' to distance the language from apparent connections with Europe, and to suggest how it should be pronounced.

Patronyms. Names that reflect male lines of inheritance.

Pejoration. A process whereby a word or phrase develops more negative connotations. For example, 'cunning' used to mean knowledgeable.

Phatic. Language that is devoid of content but that supports social relationships.

Phonemic alphabet. An alphabet for transcribing general sounds, suitable for a specific language. An individual sound is called a **phoneme.**

Phonetic alphabet. An alphabet designed for transcribing the sounds of all of the world's languages.

Phonetics / Phonology. The study of the sound system. Phonetics refers to the physical production and reception of sound, while phonology is a more abstract idea about all the sounds of a particular language.

Phonological system. The system of sounds within any language variety.

Pidgin. A trade language, usually not the language of either of the speakers.

Pilot study. A study done in advance of a main study in order to test out different approaches.

Pivot schema. The use by children of certain key words as a 'pivot' to generate many utterances.

Politeness. An aspect of pragmatics that refers to the cultural rules of a community and regulates how social relationships are negotiated. Everyday use of the term 'polite' tends to be associated with surface aspects such as table manners and saying 'please' and 'thank you'. These aspects are connected with the academic concept but it goes much deeper than this, including all aspects of cultural rules about appropriate language use in social engagements.

Political correctness. A term used, usually by conservative commentators, to object to the idea of consciously changing language because it is considered unfair to different groups.

Positive face need. In face theory, the need for positive reinforcement, a feeling that we are appreciated and liked by others.

Possessive determiners. Determiners, as the name suggests, help to determine what a noun refers to – in this case, ownership ('my', 'our').

Post-colonial. The time since former colonies gained their independence.

Post-telegraphic stage. A developmental stage that goes beyond children's use of abbreviated speech.

Post-vocalic /r/. Pronouncing an /r/ after a vowel where there is an r in the spelling. For example, 'farm', 'sir', 'horse'.

Pragmatic rules. The unspoken rules that operate in interactions between people who share a common understanding.

Pragmatics. Assumptions made about what is meant, or the inferences drawn from what is said or written.

Predicate statement. An alternative term for **mismatch statement**.

Prefix. A particle added to the front of a word.

Preposition. A word that typically indicates direction, position, or relationship, such as 'into', 'on', or 'of'.

Prescriptivism / Prescriptivist. The belief that there is an absolute authority determining what is correct usage; that correctness is something absolute and unchangeable, based on rules established in the past.

Production. The language that people can produce, which might be different from how much they can understand.

Productive vocabulary. Vocabulary that can be put to use.

Progressive form. The 'ing' ending in words such as 'walking' and 'running', indicating ongoing activity.

Pronoun. Pronouns can stand in place of nouns, hence the term 'pro-noun'. Standard English personal pronouns are: I, you, he, she, it, and one (singular); we, you and they (plural).

Prosodics / Prosody. Prosody is the melody that our voices create via prosodic aspects such as rhythm and intonation.

Random fluctuation theory. The idea that language change is not a logical and ordered process.

Received pronunciation (RP). An accent traditionally associated with high social status. 'Received' refers to the idea of social acceptance in official circles.

Reference. Reference within a text is a general term for the various ways items are related to others.

Referent. The thing or person being referred to.

Reflectionism. The idea that language reflects the society that produces it.

Register. A form of specialist language. For example, the language of sport or science.

Relativizer. Another word for a relative pronoun, for example, 'which', 'who' 'that', often used at the front of a subordinate clause.

Repertoire. The range of language forms or styles used by a speaker.

Representation. Something that stands in place of something else. Representation is how something *appears* to be, not how it really *is*.

Resistance identity. An identity that goes against mainstream culture.

Restricted. Used only within a specific context.

Restricted code. An idea advanced by Bernstein (and much disputed) that working-class speakers use context-based, limited forms of language.

Retroflex. A particular way of producing the sounds /t/ and /d/ with the tip of the tongue curled back and touching the roof of the mouth.

Rhetoric / Rhetorical. Rhetoric is the study of persuasive language, an area of study dating back to ancient Greece.

Rhetorical question. A question that is posed for its persuasive effect and not because the speaker really expects an answer.

Rhotic. Accents where speakers produce the post-vocalic /r/, such as in many rural accents in the south-west region of the UK.

Salient. Most important, prominent, or noteworthy.

Sapir-Whorf hypothesis. The idea, derived from the work of Edward Sapir and Benjamin Lee Whorf, that our language constructs our view of the world and that it is difficult or even impossible to think beyond it.

Scaffolding. An idea from Vygotsky's theory of learning that structures need to be in place to help learners on to the next stage.

Schwa. The sound /ə/, sometimes called the middle or central vowel in English because of where it is produced in the mouth.

Scope. How far a study extends, how much is covered.

Script. A plan for what speakers are going to say and do.

Secondary sources. Books and articles where researchers and commentators put forward different theories and ideas about language.

Second language (L2). The second language learned by an individual.

Segment. To be able to segment something is to perceive the boundaries or breaks between the units. This is a skill that is gradually acquired. Adults may not be aware of how they run words together in speech. For example, a child once asked a teacher how to spell 'sponner': he'd heard 'Once upon a time' as 'One sponner time'.

Self-reported usage. People describing their own language use (as opposed to being recorded using language).

Semantic field. A group of terms from the same domain. For example, names for food or aspects of computer communication.

Semantic reclamation. Taking language that has had negative connotations and trying to overturn them by using the language in new ways.

Semantics. Semantics refers to the meanings of words and expressions. Semantics can also refer to meaning in a broader sense, i.e. the overall meaning of something.

Semiotics. The study of how signs and symbols work within human communication.

Seriation. The idea of objects being in a series.

Sex. A classification of people into 'man' or 'woman' based on biological characteristics.

Shibboleth. A language item used as a marker or test of group membership.

Slang. Language that is used in informal contexts and widely recognized (unlike dialect usage, which occurs only in particular regions).

Social constructivism. The idea that reality is socially constructed and that groups construct knowledge for each other.

Social group. Individuals who share interests and connections with others, or who are classified as having something in common.

Social network. A network of relations between people in their membership of different groups.

Social practices. The ways in which people in groups habitually behave.

Social variation. The variation that occurs as a result of the social groups that people connect with. For example, groups based on common interests such as sport or cookery.

Sociocultural. Related to social and cultural factors.

Sociolect. A style of language used within a particular social group.

Sociolinguistics. The study of the relationship between language use and social factors.

Solidarity. A feeling of connection with others, mutual support.

Sound symbolism. The way in which sounds are used to represent ideas – for example, in onomatopoeia, where sounds represent noises. There is no logical connection between the sounds and the ideas they represent.

Speech event. A spoken interaction of a recognizable type. For example, a lecture or a phone call.

Standard. Used or accepted as normal or average. In language study, socially agreed usage that is familiar to most language users.

Standard English (SE). A language system that acts as an agreed common language, especially for formal uses. This primarily refers to the writing system of English.

Standardization. The process by which a form of language is developed and used as a common code.

Stereotype. A stereotype is based on the idea that whole groups of people conform to the same, limited, range of characteristics.

Sticklerism. An intrusive concern with correcting others' language use.

Storyboard. A set of images to represent the action within a moving text such as a TV programme or advertisement.

Stress-timed. Intonation that is based on applying stress at regular intervals.

Style. In language study, a distinctive way of speaking or writing for different contexts (akin to styles of dress in studies of fashion).

Style model. An example of a style of writing that has helped to shape ideas for a piece of original writing.

Subject. The thing or person carrying out the action of the verb.

Subject position. The perspective taken on a topic, where some aspects are foregrounded and emphasized while others are downplayed.

Subordination. A subordinate clause is one that depends on another to make complete sense.

Suffix. A particle added to the end of a word.

Super-standard forms. Language use that deliberately intensifies the standard forms of mainstream culture.

Syllable-based. Intonation that is spread across syllables evenly.

Synchronic variation. Variation across society at a single point in time.

Synonym. Synonyms are words that have a similar meaning, such as 'help' and 'assist'

Syntax. Syntax is about how words are arranged, or the word order that is typical of a language.

Taboo. Something that is off limits or forbidden.

Tautology. Producing redundancy in meaning by saying the same thing twice.

Telegraphic stage. A stage where children produce abbreviated speech that, like SMS messages in the modern world, misses out the grammatical structures and markings that are not essential for understanding.

Tense. This refers to the way in which verbs can indicate time, for example the 'ed' ending on a verb such as 'look' indicates past time.

Theolinguistics. The study of the relationship between language use and religious faith.

Thesaurus. A type of dictionary that groups words together on the basis of similar meaning.

Transcript. A record of what speakers said and did.

Turntaking. The way in which participants take turns at talk in interactions.

Two-word stage. This involves children using two words to create mini-sentences, with the word order often resembling adult speech.

Underextended / Underextension. Applying a label to fewer referents than it should have. For example, a child saying 'milk' to refer to milk in their own cup, but not a picture of some milk in a book.

Usage-based approach. In language acquisition studies, the idea that children use ready-made chunks of language to create many different meanings. These chunks of language are termed **constructions.**

Virtuous error. A mistake that has an underlying logic, showing that learning has taken place.

Vocal fry. A vocal effect where the speaker produces a rasping, creaky sound by blowing air through the vocal cords.

Wave model. A model of language change that likens it to throwing a stone into a pond, with the ripples representing change spreading from a central point.

World Englishes. Varieties of English that are used in different countries around the world, mainly in areas that were formerly colonised, such as India and Singapore. These countries have their own version of Standard English.

Zone of proximal development. In Vygotsky's theory of learning, the difference between what a learner can do without help and what they can do with help.

Index